BASIC PROCESSES IN READING

BASIC PROCESSES IN READING
VISUAL WORD RECOGNITION

EDITED BY

DEREK BESNER
University of Waterloo

GLYN W. HUMPHREYS
University of Birmingham

Routledge
Taylor & Francis Group
NEW YORK AND LONDON

First Published by
Lawrence Erlbaum Associates, Inc., Publishers
365 Broadway
Hillsdale, New Jersey 07642

Transferred to Digital Printing 2009 by Routledge
270 Madison Ave, New York NY 10016
2 Park Square, Milton Park, Abingdon, Oxon, OX14 4RN

Library of Congress Cataloging-in-Publication Data

Basic processes in reading : visual word recognition / edited by Derek
Besner, Glyn Humphreys.
p. cm.
Includes bibliographical references.
Includes index.
ISBN 0-8058-0219-3/ISBN 0-8058-0994-5(pbk.)
1. Reading, Psychology of. 2. Word recognition. I. Besner, D.
(Derek) II. Humphreys, Glyn W.
[DNLM: 1. Cognition. 2. Neurophysiology. 3. Reading. 4. Visual
Perception--physiology. WW 105 B311]
BF456.R2B218 1990
418'.4'019--dc20
DNLM/DLC
for Library of Congress 90-13987
CIP

Publisher's Note

The publisher has gone to great lengths to ensure the quality of this reprint but points out that some imperfections in the original may be apparent.

CONTENTS

Preface

Edited books, even more than those of single authored texts, depend on the help and goodwill of a number of people. The authors of the chapters, of course, in their attempts to meet the deadlines set along the way (Jim Neely deserves special mention in this regard - he was last by a year but it was well worth waiting for!). The secretarial and computing staff of our institutions, who have helped us cope with the intricacies and vagaries of electronic mail, virused discs and crashes of the system! Our colleagues, who have borne with our obstinacy in producing an edited book, despite going against the current academic zeitgeist. Finally, our significant others, who may even regret no longer having this text to blame for our irritability.

Special mention is due to Philip Quinlan, who was a particular help with file editing and transfers. Very special thanks to Lucy LeMare, who edited all the manuscripts, helped with the proofreading, and generally made sure the book was produced at all. We are also grateful to Keith McGowan for making figures and to both Keith and Richard Crispin for trouble shooting.

Derek Besner
Glyn W. Humphreys

BASIC PROCESSES IN WORD RECOGNITION AND IDENTIFICATION: AN OVERVIEW

DEREK BESNER

Department of Psychology
University of Waterloo
Waterloo, Ontario, Canada

GLYN W. HUMPHREYS

Department of Psychology
University of Birmingham
Birmingham, England

I. Word recognition and identification as a growth industry.
II. Some hitches.
III. The book.
IV. Conclusions.

I. WORD RECOGNITION AND IDENTIFICATION AS A GROWTH INDUSTRY

Over the past two decades, more cognitive psychologists have paid more attention to the processes involved in visual word recognition than to almost any other subject in their field. The annals of cognitive psychology have thus burgeoned with papers on word recognition while work on other topics, many relating to other aspects of reading such as syntactic parsing or discourse memory, have been substantially less popular. Why has this been so? Has the work had any theoretical or practical success? And, why another book devoted to the topic now ?

There are many reasons why work in one research area can take off and flourish; reasons which are sociological and pragmatic rather than just scientific. As far as visual word recognition is concerned, there are several sociological/pragmatic factors. One relates to the advent of new technology. The development of the microcomputer provided ready access to procedures for on-line control of reaction time (RT) and tachistoscopic experiments, and there are few simpler stimuli to present on-line than single printed words. With simplicity comes some degree of popularity. The advent of the microcomputer stimulated research into visual word recognition in a less trivial way too, because microcomputers allowed more sophisticated experimental procedures to develop than were hitherto possible . In particular, by linking computer controlled displays to eye movement recording apparatus, experimenters began for the first time to gain direct evidence of the relations between eye movements and reading (e.g., Balota & Rayner, this volume; Rayner & Pollatsek, 1987).

A second reason for the popularity of visual word recognition is that simple tasks are at hand, for which accurate and sensitive measures can be derived, such as lexical decision, naming, and semantic classification. Further, and perhaps most importantly, these tasks can be related to models of word recognition, in which task performance is decomposed into a series of processing stages characterized by access to different knowledge representations. An example of this is the logogen model in its revised form (e.g., Morton & Patterson, 1980). This model hypothesizes the existence of separate stored representations for orthographic, semantic and phonological representations of words. Different tasks may tap into different levels of representation. For example, lexical decisions may be accomplished by monitoring activation in the orthographic lexicon (e.g., Coltheart, Davelaar, Jonasson & Besner, 1977); word naming will require access to the phonological lexicon (at least for words with irregular spelling-sound correspondences); semantic classification requires access to stored semantic knowledge. By using such tasks, investigators could attempt to tap and test the characteristics of the different stages in the processing system (see Besner & McCann, 1987, for one application of this approach). Thus, visual word recognition has proved attractive because it has a broadly specified multi-stage architecture, with the stages apparently open to testing via the judicious use of different tasks. Consequently it can serve as a test-bed for experiments concerned with such general issues as how stored knowledge influences perception.

A third reason for the large body of research on word recognition is that it is a basic process in reading upon which all other reading processes are predicated. Moreover, other processes in reading, such as syntactic parsing, sentence comprehension and so on, may exert only relatively weak influences on the recognition of fixated words, at least in skilled readers (see Humphreys, 1985). In essence, skilled word identification may operate as a relatively free-standing module, and so can be studied in isolation from factors affecting other reading processes.

A fourth reason is that word identification is the interface between higher-order cognitive processes (such as those concerned with text comprehension) and eye movements. The effect of such higher-order cognitive processes on eye movements can be assessed by testing whether saccadic and fixation patterns on particular words vary according to the syntactic ambiguity of the sentence or according to whether the sentence contains a "garden path." Studies of the relations between eye movements and word processing therefore speaks to the general issue of how the eye movement system is controlled (Balota & Rayner, this volume).

II. SOME HITCHES

Nonetheless, word recognition research is not without its problems. Though inferences concerning how a particular task may be performed seem clear, given the assumed "functional architecture" of a system, the evidence is often more muddy. For example, lexical decisions may be affected by the imageability of words (James, 1975), word frequency effects can be larger in lexical decision than in tasks such as naming and semantic classification (Balota & Chumbley, 1984; though see Monsell, this volume), and particular forms of priming are more pronounced in lexical decision than in naming and vice versa (Neely, this volume). All this suggests the general point that we cannot take it for granted that all subjects perform a particular task in a given way that maps directly onto an assumed functional architecture. For example, when performing lexical decisions, subjects may check whether the letter string is meaningful or whether it is visually familiar, in addition to checking activation levels in the orthographic lexicon (cf. Besner & McCann, 1987). Although a task, may, in theory, tap a particular processing stage, in reality performance may be based on a number of processing stages whose precise contribution may alter on a trial-by-trial basis.

A second problem is that there are many functional architectures and many models of visual word recognition. The problem with this is that, as the models tend to be broadly defined, it becomes increasingly difficult to generate predictions that are uniquely tied to one account. Given the multi-stage nature of most models, and that performance at any given time could be derived from a number of processing stages (see above), there are sufficient degrees of freedom to fit data to any number of apparently competing accounts of performance (see Humphreys & Evett, 1985, and the associated commentaries, for an example of this problem relating to the existence of an independent "nonlexical" processing route in word naming).

One way to address the latter problem is to assess performance when the reading system has been lesioned (e.g., in cases of acquired dyslexia). Providing we assume that a lesioned system behaves essentially as a reduced normal system (see Patterson, 1981), we gain insight into the working of the model operating with fewer degrees of freedom. Indeed, it can be argued that predictions concerning acquired dyslexia provide some of the clearest tests of current reading models (with some patterns of dyslexia being distinctly uncomfortable for some models; see Patterson, Seidenberg & McClelland, 1989). This is not to say that tests of the models using neuropsychological data do not have problems of their own (e.g., concerning the vexing question of whether any individual brain damaged patient uses a reduced but otherwise normal reading system; see Seidenberg, 1988); it is simply that such evidence can be used to help constrain accounts of normal performance. For instance, models of normal reading that assume that the pronunciation of a word can only be accessed after the word's meaning has been retrieved have severe difficulties explaining how patients may read aloud irregular words (requiring lexical access to phonology) and yet show no comprehension (e.g., Schwartz, Saffran, & Marin, 1979).

It can also be argued that the research into normal word recognition has had practical benefits in fostering a better understanding of both acquired and developmental reading problems (see Coltheart, 1985). The benefits are of two kinds.

The first is in assessing different reading disorders. The various tasks and variables (such as word frequency, imageability, spelling to sound regularity, etc.) used to tap different stages of normal reading provide clear diagnoses of different reading disorders. Most accounts agree that there are differences between surface dyslexics whose reading is phonologically based (so they have problems reading irregular words) and phonological dyslexics who are impaired at assembling phonological representations (contrast Coltheart et al., 1983, with Funnell, 1983). Patients with these different reading problems can be teased apart by contrasting the reading of regular words, irregular words and nonwords, using a logic similar to that used to assess the components of the "normal" reading system.

The second benefit concerns the guidance for rehabilitation programs given by the processing models. Here therapy may be directed at reconstituting or by-passing the supposed deficit within one component of the reading system (e.g., see de Partz, 1986).

A second way around the problem of increased degrees of explanatory freedom in complex processing accounts is to construct detailed working simulations of performance. In this respect, recent "connectionist" models have been influential. In such models, knowledge is represented in terms of the pattern of weights on the connections between processing units at different levels within the system. Such models can be "trained" to associate input and output patterns, so that a given output will be established more easily for patterns presented more frequently. They can "learn" regular mappings between input spellings and output pronunciations, and, following training, they can perform such transformations more easily for words than for nonwords, even though the model is not explicitly given a spelling-to-sound rule system (e.g., Seidenberg & McClelland, 1989). Such models give us some indications of the patterns of performance that emerge from systems adopting the simplest possible representational assumptions (see also Masson, this volume). To the extent that the models are consistent with or are contradicted by data drawn from both skilled readers and patients with acquired reading disorders, they are open to future amendment and development. Thus, computer simulations should not be thought of as a one-way development, based around the simulation of already acquired data, but as a valuable part of an interactive research exercise, in which the models evolve as more specific empirical tests are produced. The trend toward simulation also indicates a second practical benefit of research on visual word recognition, in that in the long term it may be possible to develop machines capable of fast and accurate automatic reading. Further, such machines could also learn, so that they operate as "experts" with their own specialized vocabularies and domain-specific knowledge.

We have thus argued that there has been considerable research into visual word recognition for both theoretical and sociological/pragmatic reasons, and that in spite of the difficulties involved, the work has had some practical successes (e.g., concerning the understanding and retraining of reading disorders).

III. THE BOOK

In the present book, we bring together chapters relevant to recent debates and what we think are likely to be future developments in the field. It is thus no coincidence that the chapters pick up on many of the themes that we believe are relevant to the growth in research on the topic. In particular, these themes include (a) the development of processing accounts of performance that have either been implemented as computer simulations or are sufficiently well specified to enable them to be so, (b) further examination of the contrasting patterns of performance that emerge under different task conditions, and (c) the application of processing models to patients with acquired reading disorders.

The chapters are organized in an order roughly reflecting a sequence of processes from the early visual analysis of words to semantic influences on word identification.

The chapter by Manso de Zuniga, Humphreys and Evett is concerned with the effects of handwriting on visual word identification. These authors relate attempts to build computational models capable of reading handwriting to empirical studies examining how handwriting affects word identification in humans. They propose that handwriting requires a specific process not required in the reading of printed words, which they term *cursive normalization*, that acts to segment letters in cursive script. The empirical work reported in the chapter shows that cursive normalization operates subsequent to the effects of contrast reduction, and that it interacts with lexical processes (as indicated by the effects of word frequency and long-lasting word repetition). The reading of handwriting can also be guided by the use of stored episodic representations, which may be matched against incoming script in order to bypass the cursive normalization process. The evidence for lexical interactions and episodic matching in humans fits with some of the ideas developed from computational modelling, and illustrate how computational and empirical studies can converge to provide a common solution concerning practical information processing problems. The chapter also shows how our knowledge of early visual processing in word identification can be increased by more detailed studies examining the effects of visual factors, such as handwriting, that are commonly encountered outside the laboratory.

Handwriting is particularly difficult to read for patients who, following brain damage, suffer the reading disorder described as "letter-by-letter" reading (see Warrington & Shallice, 1980; see also Dejerine, 1892, for the original description of the syndrome). Because such patients often read words by first naming their constituent letters aloud, it is commonly assumed that the patients are using a serial letter identification process in order to read words (e.g., Patterson & Kay, 1982; Warrington & Shallice, 1980). In Chapter 3, Howard presents a reevaluation of this disorder, in which he concludes that such patients, like normal subjects, read using a parallel letter identification process. Howard argues convincingly that, for the patients, parallel letter identification is an abnormally noisy and error prone process, thereby producing large effects of word length upon single word reading time. This chapter illustrates the usefulness of the interplay between theory, data and methodology from both the experimental and neuropsychological literature.

Most current accounts of visual word identification assume that, in normal subjects, letter processing takes place in parallel across the word. A much more controversial issue concerns the nature of the representation that mediates lexical access. This controversy has a long history in both experimental psychology and education. In recent years, the traditional view that reading is parasitic upon some form of speech code has given way to the view that orthographic codes (at least in skilled readers) dominate lexical access. In Chapters 4 and 5, Van Orden and Brown reassert the traditional view that phonological coding is a necessary preliminary to word recognition.

Van Orden extends his original line of work (see Van Orden, 1987; Van Orden, Johnston & Hale, 1988) to proofreading. The experiments reported here demonstrate that misspelled words which preserve phonology (e.g., SLEAT for SLEET) are particularly difficult to detect in proofreading. These results are interpreted as strong evidence that phonology is dominant not only in single word identification but also in text processing.

In his chapter, Brown outlines a connectionist account of visual word recognition which also assumes phonology to be a necessary preliminary to semantic access and oral reading. He then argues that a wide range of findings in both the experimental and neuropsycholgical literature are consistent with this account. Brown's general approach is buttressed by some clever experiments that develop Yantis and Meyer's (1985) priming technique to demonstrate rapid and automatic access to phonology. The chapters by Van Orden and Brown provide strong challenges to the view that orthographic codes are of primary importance in lexical access.

In Chapter 6, Monsell reviews a large body of work on the word frequency effect. The more efficient identification of high relative to low frequency words is one of the most robust findings in the word recognition literature. Monsell points out that the effect is fundamental to connectionist accounts of word processing. Within a connectionist word recognition system, the weights on the connections between different levels of representation are affected by the frequency with which words occur in the language. Connectionist models therefore predict that word frequency **must** affect word identification. Monsell reevaluates recent evidence suggesting that identification is not affected by word frequency, and argues that, providing the tasks adopted are sensitive to lexical access processes, word identification can reliably be shown to affect word identification. The chapter constitutes an important state-of-the-art evaluation of work on this topic.

One of the pieces of evidence that Monsell uses to support his argument that word frequency affects lexical access is that fixation durations in text reading are influenced by word frequency (e.g., Rayner & Duffy, 1986). Since the mid-1970s, measures of eye movements during reading have provided a major line of evidence for the processes operating on-line during reading. In Chapter 7, Balota and Rayner consider the evidence for the extraction and use of various kinds of information from words falling on parafoveal regions of the retina whilst reading - an issue central to understanding the kinds of visual information used to control eye movements. They conclude that there is good evidence to suggest that information concerning the identities of parafoveal letters is utilized, but there is virtually no evidence that higher order semantic information is utilized from parafoveal words. They further point out the importance of attentional processes in determining the use of parafoveal information whilst reading, a topic which has hitherto been neglected in eye movement research.

One important aspect of the work on eye movements is that it stresses text reading, and the fact that word identification does not take place isolated from context. The final two chapters by Masson and by Neely are concerned with how prior semantic context affects word identification.

In Chapter 8, Masson presents a new model of semantic context effects based on a connectionist architecture (in this case, a Hopfield net). The model is able to account for many of the vageries of semantic context effects, including those context effects that occur even when other words are interposed between a target word and the related context. It seems likely that Masson's approach will stimulate work on the relationship between semantic representation and word identification in the context of a connectionist framework. It will be interesting to see if Hopfield nets provide a more congenial architecture than other nets such as those using back propogation learning algorithms.

In the final chapter, Neely presents a major review of the extensive semantic context literature following the seminal experiments by Meyer and Schvaneveldt (1971). Neely considers 18 phenomena in the context of both lexical decision and pronunciation tasks, and discusses how well current theories fare in accounting for these effects. Neely argues convincingly that no single process theory can provide a complete account of all these findings. He goes on to argue that the findings can be best explained by means of a hybrid theory which incorporates three mechanisms: automatic spreading activation, top-down expectancies, and a post-lexical semantic matching process. As well as accounting for the large body of data on semantic priming, Neely also points to several areas where further research is needed.

IV. CONCLUSIONS

It is often said that a failure to appreciate history dooms one to repeat the mistakes of the past. The chapters in the present volume look back to the literature on word recognition and identification in order to better shape future directions. Taken together, these chapters cover many of the major topics in current research on word recognition and identification, and highlight some of the important questions that future research must face if long term theoretical and practical developments are to accrue.

ACKNOWLEDGMENTS

This work was supported by a grant from the Natural Sciences and Engineering Research Council of Canada to D. Besner and by a grant from the Economic and Social Research Council of Great Britain to G.W. Humphreys.

REFERENCES

Balota, D.A., & Chumbley, J.I. (1984). Are lexical decisions a good measure of lexical access? The role of word frequency in the neglected decision stage. *Journal of Experimental Psychology: Human Perception & Performance*, **10**, 340-357.

Besner, D., & McCann, R.S. (1987). Word frequency and pattern distortion in visual word identification and production: An examination of four classes of models. In M. Coltheart (Ed.), *Attention and performance XII*. Hove, East Sussex: Lawrence Erlbaum.

Coltheart, M. (1985). The cognitive neuropsychology of reading. In M.I. Posner & O.S.M. Marin (Eds.), *Attention & performance XI*. Hillsdale, N.J.: Lawrence Erlbaum.

Coltheart, M., Davelaar, E., Jonasson, J.T., & Besner, D. (1977). Access to the internal lexicon. In S. Dornic (Ed.), *Attention & performance VI*. London: Academic Press.

Coltheart, M., Masterson, J., Byng, S., Prior, M., & Riddoch, J. (1983). Surface dyslexia. *Quarterly Journal of Psychology*, **35A**, 469-497.

Dejerine, J. (1892). Contribution a l'etude anatomoclinique et cliniques des differentes varietes de ceciteverbale. *Memoires de la Societe de Biologie*, **4**, 61-90.

de Partz, M. (1986). Re-education of a deep dyslexic patient: Rationale of the method and results. *Cognitive Neuropsychology*, **3**, 149-177.

Funnell, E. (1983). Phonological processes in reading: New evidence from acquired dyslexia. *British Journal of Psychology*, **74**, 159-180.

Humphreys, G.W. (1985). Attention, automaticity and autonomy in visual word processing. In D. Besner, T.G. Waller and G. E. MacKinnon (Eds.), *Reading research: Advances in theory and in practice. V.5*. New York: Academic Press.

Humphreys, G.W., & Evett, L.J. (1985). Are there independent lexical and nonlexical routes in word processing? An evaluation of the dual-route theory of reading. *The Behavioral and Brain Sciences*, **8**, 689-740.

James, C.T. (1975). The role of semantic information in lexical decisions. *Journal of experimental psychology: Human perception & performance*, **1**, 130-136.

Meyer, D., & Schvaneveldt, R.W. (1971). Facilitation in recognizing pairs of words: Evidence of a dependence between retrieval operations. *Journal of Experimental Psychology*, **90**, 227-234.

Morton, J., & Patterson, K.E. (1980). In M.Coltehart, J.C. Marshall & K.E. Patterson (Eds.), *Deep dyslexia*. London: Routledge and Kegan Paul.

Patterson, K.E. (1981). Neuropsychological approaches to the study of reading. *British Journal of Psychology*, **72**, 151-174.
Patterson, K.E., & Kay, J. (1982). Letter-by-letter reading: Psychological descriptions of a neurological syndrome. *Quarterly Journal of Experimental Psychology*, **34A**, 411-441.
Patterson, K.E., Seidenberg, M.S., & McClelland, J.L. (1989). In R.G.M. Morris (Ed.), *Parallel distributed processing: Implications for psychology and neurobiology*. Oxford: Oxford University Press.
Rayner, K., & Duffy, S.A. (1986). Lexical complexity and fixation times in reading: Effects of word frequency, verb complexity and lexical ambiguity. *Memory & Cognition*, **14**, 191-201.
Rayner, K., & Pollatsek, A. (1987). Eye movements in reading: A tutorial review. In M. Coltheart (Ed.), *Attention and performance XII*. Hove, East Sussex: Lawrence Erlbaum.
Schwartz, M., Saffran, E., & Marin, O.S.M. (1979). Language dissociations in dementia. *Brain and Language*, **7**, 277-306.
Seidenberg, M.S. (1988). Cognitive neuropsychology and language: The state of the art. *Cognitive Neuropsychology*, **5**, 403-426.
Seidenberg, M.S., & McClelland, J.L. (1989). A distributed developmental model of word recognition and naming. *Psychological Review*, **96**, 523-568.
Van Orden, G. (1987). A ROWS is a ROSE: Spelling, sound and reading. *Memory and Cognition*, **15**, 181-198.
Van Orden, G., Johnston, J.C., & Hale, B.L. (1988). Word identification in reading proceeds from spelling to sound to meaning. *Journal of Experimental Psychology: Learning, Memory, and Cognition*, **14**, 371-386.
Warrington, E.K., & Shallice, T. (1980). Word form dyslexia. *Brain*, **103**, 99-112.
Yantis, S., & Meyer, D. (1985). *Dynamics of spreading activation in information processing*. Paper presented at the annual meeting of the Psychonomic Society, Boston.

2

ADDITIVE AND INTERACTIVE EFFECTS OF REPETITION, DEGRADATION, AND WORD FREQUENCY IN THE READING OF HANDWRITING

CHAS MANSO DE ZUNIGA

Department of Psychology
Birkbeck College
London, England

GLYN W. HUMPHREYS

School of Psychology
University of Birmingham
Birmingham, England

LINDSAY J. EVETT

Department of Computing
Trent Polytechnic
Cambridge, England

I. INTRODUCTION

A well-worn criticism directed at cognitive psychologists is that their experimental methodologies are too contrived to capture human processing in its natural environment in any realistic sense. As far as reading is concerned, this criticism can be applied in various ways. For instance, as is reflected in this volume, a good deal of experimental research on reading has stressed word recognition. Now, while word recognition may comprise an essential part of the reading process (Besner & Humphreys, this volume), it can be argued with some justification that reading involves much more than word recognition alone, and that word recognition itself may be strongly affected by higher-order contextual factors. Such factors may mislead attempts to extrapolate from word recognition in isolation to word recognition in context (see, for instance, Humphreys, 1985; McClelland, 1987, for alternative views on this). However, even if such extrapolations are valid, it remains the case that the very stimuli habitually used in these studies are to some extent artificial. This is because in very nearly all instances the stimuli are presented in a type-written format. Typescript has existed only since William Caxton. Although it appears widely in everyday life, in newspapers and books etc., typescript is by no means the sole or even the predominant means of presenting words visually. Our understanding of word recognition, and, by extension of reading, will at best be incomplete if it is confined to typescript.

Further, most work on word recognition in the past twenty or so years has focused on what we may term "high level" processes - concerned with (for instance) the nature of the internal lexicon and the transcoding of identified letters and supra-letter units when the pronunciation and/or the meaning of words is retrieved (see the chapters by Monsell and by Van Orden, this volume). These studies by and large by-pass the "visual end" of visual word recognition. This negligence of visual processing is reflected in current popular models, where the input into the word recognition system is often assumed to be a normalized set of "clean," position-coded letter features (e.g., McClelland, 1986; McClelland & Rumelhart, 1981). Our understanding of the "front end" of visual word recognition, and particularly the visual processing of words at fixation, remains limited (though see Balota and Rayner, this volume, for a discussion of the processing of words not at fixation). One way to increase our knowledge is to manipulate the visual properties of words and to explore how these manipulations affect various tasks. One ecologically valid manipulation, whose effects are little understood, is to use handwritten words.

There are two clear ways in which handwritten words differ from typed words. First, within any one font and case, typed letters are identical: every time the key for an upper case A is pressed, the same visual pattern appears on the page or the monitor screen. Second, typed letters are typically noncursive; they are not joined up to their neighbouring letters but enjoy a certain "personal space." These characteristics contrast with handwritten words. Handscript is usually written in a continuous manner, without letters being physically separated within each word. In addition, handwriting is inherently variable. Even signatures, our most practiced form of handwriting, are never twice identical. At least two forms of variation can be identified: accommodation and ambiguity. Accommodation refers to the adaptation in shape that letters undergo so that the end of one letter continues smoothly into the beginning of the next (see Henderson, 1982). Ambiguity is present because the diversity and ill-formedness of handwriting reduces the chances of deterministic identification. A number of perceptual interpretations may be possible to a given cursive script pattern (see

Nash-Weber, 1975). Surrounding context may be necessary to resolve conflicting interpretations.

The demands that handwriting places on the word recognition system may thus affect both visual and higher-order processes. Higher-order processes may be required to overcome inherent ambiguity (see above). Visual processing demands are increased because of the extra problems involved in segmenting the letters of handwritten words. To be sure, segmentation problems may arise even with typed stimuli - characters may sometimes touch due to errors in the printing process or due tomistyping (*sic*), also, segmentation demands will increase when image resolution is low (as when words appear in the visual periphery) - nevertheless, the consequent demands are generally less than those presented by cursive handwriting. Indeed, given the variability of handwriting, and the effects on letter formation from the other letters within a word (see below), segmentation demands are formidible. Studies investigating how handwriting affects reading can usefully inform us about the interaction between visual and higher-order processes in reading, and about the operation of the visual processes themselves.

II. MACHINE READING OF HANDWRITING

In recent years our understanding of vision, and in particular the visual processes involved in object recognition, has increased considerably. It can be argued that many conceptual developments have come about because of the development of computational models of object recognition (see Humphreys & Bruce, 1989; Watt, 1988). Such models enable us to gain new and richer perspectives on the constraints imposed by particular stimuli and particular tasks (see Marr, 1982). They also provide detailed accounts of how processing may proceed, which can serve as a framework for guiding empirical studies. Marr's account of the processing stages and representations mediating object recognition has been influential in shaping much subsequent empirical work (see Humphreys, 1983; Palmer, 1985), even if the empirical work shows the original account to be flawed (see Biederman & Ju, 1988; Humphreys & Quinlan, 1987; Tarr & Pinker, in press). Accordingly it may be profitable to look to computer models of the reading of handwriting to gain insights into the kind of processes that may operate with humans too.

It turns out that various attempts have been made to implement the reading of handwriting in computers. However, a word of caution is necessary in interpreting this work. Many of the computer models depend on the movements made in the course of handwriting, in that they take dynamic movement patterns as their inputs. Such models cannot recognize a word that is already written, and so they are of little relevance here. We are interested only in how models code form information (letter and word shapes).

1. The Segmentation Problem in Handwriting

In order for a computer to recognize a wide sample of handwritten words, it must extract features that remain invariant across many styles and instances of handwriting. Such features could correspond to aspects of the patterns of whole words or to characteristics of individual letters. As we shall see, both types of features have been used in different models. However, if individual letter features are to be used, there needs to be some form of segmentation procedure to parse a continuous string into discrete letters.

One of the earliest programs for reading handwriting was described by Frishkopf and Harmon (1961). They reported two separate yet complementary approaches: one which calculated individual letter identities and another which operated at the whole word level ignoring letter structure. We consider letter mediated recognition first.

Three conditions were imposed upon the writer: (a) all writing had to be in lower case; (b) all small letters (i.e., those without ascenders or descenders) had to fit between two parallel lines; and (c) the writer was asked to write carefully. Within these constraints Frishkopf and Harmon classified the alphabet into subgroups depending upon certain topological features such as vertical extremes in relation to the baseline, whether or not there was a retrograde stroke in the letter, where cusps occurred (i.e., sharp peaks or pointed ends), the presence or absence of line closure in letters, and special marks such as the dots in i's and j's. To code these features the letters of each word first had to be segmented. This involved marking the location of rough letter landmarks given by (for example) points of vertical extensions and retrograde strokes. The number of letters in a string was also coded by counting the number of centerline crossings and dividing this by the average number of crossings per letter (approximately 3). By coding the word length, an average letter width was computed and centred on the landmarks to segment the letters. Having done this, a decision tree was applied, based on the letter characteristics described above, until the characters were uniquely identified.

This approach confronted the segmentation problem but placed constraints on relative letter size, and it could not classify the letters without the aid of externally fixed guidelines. If a small letter was written outside its assigned zone the system failed to recognize it. In addition, decision errors proliferated: when working down the decision tree one wrong turn ensured an incorrect response. Nevertheless, the system achieved correct segmentation on about 87% of the sample words and correct letter identification on about 60% of the items. In subsequent work, the hit rate for the letter mediated system was increased by using orthographic knowledge (digram and trigram transition probabilities) to aid segmentation (Harmon, 1962; Sayre, 1973).

The whole word coding technique employed by Frishkopf and Harmon employed fewer constraints (e.g., words were not obliged to occur within specified writing zones). Stimuli were compared to a dictionary of stored words on the basis of certain extracted features. The system transformed examples of handwriting into points coded in terms of local extreme horizontal and vertical displacements (local maxima and minima). The sequence of maxima and minima was noted and compared to the stored entries for dictionary items. A stimulus was identified as the dictionary item whose code bore the closest resemblance to its own. Note that this process codes characteristics of whole words, and no attempt is made to segment words into their component letters. The operation generally achieved less success than the letter mediated system, and correct word recognition occurred on about 30% of the trials when the same writer produced both the dictionary and stimulus items (see also Earnest, 1962, for a somewhat similar whole-word coding approach).

There are at least three morals that we can draw from this work. One is that wholistic coding of handwritten words does not always result in better word identification than a letter mediated approach. A second is that whole-word coding may be of little use for the *identification* of nonwords (e.g., in order to assign a nonword a particular phonological representation), as the input descriptions are matched against stored word-level representations. Nonword identification may be optimized if input descriptions are coded across subword components (see Patterson, Marshall & Coltheart, 1985). A third is that, if whole-string descriptions of handwritten words are very imprecise, they may not even enable us to judge the familiarity of the string (note that precise identification may not be necessary for familiarity judgments; see Besner & McCann, 1987).

2. A Clever Correction Algorithm

Due to the ambiguities inherent in cursive script, letter-based approaches to reading may go astray for various reasons. For instance, letters may be segmented correctly but then misclassified. In other cases though, the segmentation itself may be incorrect. "Splitting" errors occur when one character is mistakenly interpreted as two; "merging" errors occur when two characters are identified as one (see Bozinovic & Srihari, 1982).

The deleterious impact of such errors can be reduced with the help of context. One of the most popular correction mechanisms has been the "edit distance" method of dictionary look-up (Kashyap & Oomen, 1981; Levenshtein, 1966; Okuda, Tanaka & Kasai, 1976). When a cursive string has been segmented, the resultant units are checked against stored representations. If a match is found the word is "recognized." However, due to inaccuracies in segmentation, the matching process may be fruitless. In such cases the edit distance algorithm calculates the minimum number of transformations necessary to convert the incorrectly segmented stimulus into one of the strings it considers to be legal (i.e., in its lexicon).

Bozinovic and Srihari (1982) have pointed out that the edit distance approach classifies splitting and merging errors unnaturally. Both error types are considered to involve two separate mistakes each. Splitting is viewed as an insertion of a letter plus a substitution. Merging is viewed as a deletion of a letter plus a substitution. Thus if a handwritten stimulus CHAR is parsed as CLICRR, the edit distance method would choose CLICHE as its response. Only two transformations are necessary to change CLICRR into CLICHE, whilst four steps are required to change CLICRR to CHAR. Bozinovic and Srihari put forward a model that treats splitting and merging as singular parsing mistakes. They also incorporated into their correction algorithm a sensitivity to error probabilities. By knowing that the splitting errors H-LI and A-CR are more likely than the substitutions H-R and E-R, this model would recognize CHICRR as CHAR.

Doubtless this is an improvement. Even so, both forms of correction mechanism are prone to the same criticism: they forget about the original cursive stimulus. Given the parsed string CLICRR, one method would always output CLICHE, the other CHAR. A better solution might be to check which of the selected alternatives best fits the input. Such a feedback loop would create an important measure of flexibility, allowing the visual characteristics of the input to bias the choice of output.

3. Summary

The attempts at computer-based recognition of handwriting that we have described have not been concerned with mimicing human performance. Nevertheless, the models provide an indication of the sorts of problems that the human reader can encounter with handwriting, and they suggest possible solutions. By and large whole-word approaches have not proved successful. Other programs adopt a letter-mediated approach, where letter recognition is preceded by segmentation of the letters in the string. Various segmentation techniques exist, but a common factor is the incorporation of orthographic and other forms of contextual knowledge to facilitate processing. Typed stimuli, that come with their letters already segmented, may make the first segmentation process redundant. Accordingly, the differences between the reading of handwriting and of print may reside solely at the initial parsing stage; subsequent processes may be common to both scripts.

III. HUMAN PERCEPTION OF HANDWRITING

Corcoran and Rouse (1970) published one of the few articles to investigate the processing of handwritten words. They studied the perceptual identification of handwritten and typed words presented under rapid exposure conditions (median duration 30 msec). The scripts were either randomly presented or blocked. There was an advantage for typed words in the blocked conditions (relative to the handwritten words). In the mixed condition, performance on both scripts fell to approximately half that of their respective levels in the blocked conditions. Mixing either two styles of handwriting or upper and lower case typescript did not reduce performance relative to the blocked conditions.

Corcoran and Rouse concluded that each script was processed via separate "subroutines." The decrement in mixed set identification was attributed to an early time consuming binary decision that categorized the script. This decision was only required when the scripts were mixed, and it consequently reduced performance in that condition.

However, this account does not explain the data satisfactorily. If a binary decision occurs prior to a recognition stage, then the time taken to make the decision should influence subsequent identification equally for handwritten and typed words. For instance, if the handscript system takes on average X msec to identify a word, and the typescript system takes Y msec, then the time taken by a primary decision process should not reduce the performance of both systems by half (X/2 and Y/2), but by an equal amount (e.g., X- 20 msec and Y - 20 msec). To maintain Corcoran and Rouse's suggestion of separate processing pathways for the two scripts, it appears necessary to posit that under tachistoscopic presentation conditions, the decision about script identity is made at about chance level. When the decision mechanism fails, stimuli are entered into the wrong processing system, and consequently misidentified.

At this point, it is fruitful to ask why the dual route model was proposed in the first place. Just how far into the language processing system does one go before the two scripts share procedures? The strong position is that the routes remain independent even at the output stage, never converging. However, it is hard to believe that there is one phonological lexicon required for the naming of handwritten words and another for the naming of typescript; and a similar argument can be proposed concerning the stored orthographic representations mediating visual word recognition. Indeed, we believe there are good grounds for arguing that stored orthographic representations are not just script independent but even case independent (Besner, Coltheart & Davelaar, 1984; Evett & Humphreys, 1981; Rayner, McConkie & Zola, 1980).

An alternative account to that proposed by Corcoran and Rouse (1970) is that the processes involved in reading typescript are *identical* to those involved in reading handwriting; it is simply that handwriting requires extra processes, to deal with segmentation and item variability. We term these extra processes *cursive normalization.*

Perhaps typewritten words do not escape cursive normalization. It is possible that normalization processes are always invoked by words and letter strings, but that the reading of typescript is little delayed by such processes because there are few segmentation demands and no item variability. This would do away with the need for an initial binary decision mechanism that categorizes scripts. However, if this were so, typewritten words should not suffer when mixed with handwritten words. As we know, Corcoran and Rouse (1970) reported just this result. An implication of this is that cursive normalization is an optional procedure, initiated when cursitivity is detected. Corcoran and Rouse's finding with mixed scripts can then be attributed to this detection process operating at chance level under brief exposure conditions. Without cursive normalization, handwritten words are likely to be misidentified; with cursive normalization, typed words suffer because of the extra time taken up by the preprocessing stage.

The idea that the reading of hand- and of typescript differ mainly in early normalization processes fits with the attempts to implement the reading of handwriting in computers. Psychological evidence for this account comes from Ford and Banks (1977). They employed Sternberg's (1969) memory search paradigm, where subjects are asked to remember a set of items and subsequently have to decide whether a probe item is a member of the stimulus set. Typically, as the memory set size increases, decision times get longer. Stimulus encoding and serial memory comparison processes are suggested to be reflected respectively in the intercept and slope values of the RT-set size function. Ford and Banks performed this task using both hand- and typewritten stimuli. They found that the two scripts produced comparable slopes but that the intercept was significantly greater for handwritten stimuli. The implication is that the scripts only differ in their encoding requirements, and that the two scripts are transformed into the same form for memory comparison processes.

From the above analysis of the work on machine reading and the few studies on human reading of handwriting, we can suggest that unique procedures exist for the normalization of handwriting, after which processing proceeds in the same way for hand- and typewritten stimuli. We now consider some new experiments where this suggestion is put to further empirical test.

IV. SOME EXPERIMENTS

Our initial questions concerned: (a) the extent to which handwriting demands different rather than simply additional processes to those involved in the reading of print; and (b) the role of higher-order, lexical processes in the reading of handwriting. To assess these questions, we looked at the effects on the reading of handwriting of several variables known to affect the recognition of print: repetition, contrast reduction and word frequency.

1. Experiment 1: The Effects of Repetition

Word repetition is known to facilitate identification under conditions where the initial and repeat presentations of the word are clearly perceptable as separate perceptual events (e.g., where both are presented for unlimited exposures and RTs are measured), and where the first stimulus is masked so that subjects fail to classify it as perceptually separate from the target (see Humphreys, Besner & Quinlan, 1988). The mechanisms by which repetition facilitates word identification are potentially numerous, and are not the main concern of this chapter (see Monsell, this volume). Our aim is solely to use repetition as a well-studied device for assessing contextual influence on perception.

Experiment 1 examines the effects of repetition on lexical decisions to words presented in handwriting and in print. The scripts of the initial and the repeat presentations of the words were varied orthogonally, so that we could assess the effects on performance of changing the script. Repetition effects were also examined across two time intervals (immediate and after a lag of 15 intervening items).

The word repetition effect with typed stimuli manifests two components as a function of the lag between repetitions. When words are repeated immediately after one another there is a substantial repetition effect. This substantial effect decreases rapidly as the lag between repetitions increases, leaving a smaller but longer-lasting benefit (Humphreys et al., 1988; Ratcliff, Hockley & McKoon, 1985). The sharp change in the size of the repetition effect as the repetition interval increases has led to the suggestion that immediate and "lagged" repetition effects differ qualitatively as well as quantitatively. Monsell (1985) suggested that immediate repetition effects can be caused by episodic factors (a temporary memory of the last event). As such episodic factors dissipate with time, then some other factor is implicated in the residual repetition effect - such as persistent activation of a word's lexical representation (e.g., Morton, 1979). Consistent with this, there are often only negligible effects of repeating nonwords across long time intervals, presumably because nonwords lack lexical representations (Monsell, 1985, 1987; though see Salasoo, Shiffrin & Feustel, 1985).

Other accounts of lagged repetition effects are also possible. For instance, these repetition effects may occur because identical processing procedures are invoked by words on their initial and repeat presentations, which save the procedures from being recomputed *ab initio* when the word is re-presented (e.g., Kolers, 1979). Such procedures may include not only lexical access but also specific encoding processes (such as those required to read spatially transformed text, or, as in the present case, handwriting). According to these different accounts, we can expect different repetition effects as a function of the interval between repetitions and of the script of the words on their initial (prime) and repeat (target) presentations. For instance, let us propose that the reading of handwriting and print differs only in that handwriting requires cursive normalization to operate (see above). If lagged repetition effects reflect persistent lexical activation, and if lexical representations are abstract and do not code script, then equivalent effects should emerge irrespective of whether primes and targets maintain or change their script. In contrast, if these repetition effects are sensitive to specific encoding procedures, repetition effects should be maximized between handwritten primes and targets which require the same normalization procedure (note that in the other script combinations of prime and target, on only one presentation (at most) will a word be handwritten, so the normalization procedure will not be repeated). Finally, if handwriting and print are read using completely independent procedures (cf. Corcoran & Rouse, 1970), then any repetition effects across-script should at least be smaller than those within-script.

Method

The same general method was used in all the experiments reported in this chapter. The experimental paradigm was a " name and then decide " task. Two letter strings were presented on each trial. The first was always a word, the second was either a word or a nonword. Subjects named the first item and then made a lexical decision to the second. There are several important aspects of this procedure. One is that, as the first item on each trial was always a word, nonword repetition effects were not examined. The second is that other targets, rather than primes, acted as controls in a no-repeat baseline condition. The third is that repetition is examined across different tasks (words on their initial presentation were named, whilst lexical decisions were made on all repeat presentations). This eliminates any task-specific components of the repetition effect (see Monsell, 1985).

Sixty-four subjects performed lexical decisions on 160 words and pronounceable nonwords. In the naming component of the procedure, 40 of the words acted as primes to lexical decision targets, while the remaining 120 words were fillers. Equal numbers of hand- and typewritten items were displayed in both the naming and the lexical decision components of the task, and all possible pairings of script were used equally often. Consequently, it was impossible to predict the lexical status or script of the target from the identity or script of the prime. Lexical decision latencies formed our main measure of performance, allowing us to relate the results to the large body of data on lexical decision with typed words.

All items were between 5 and 7 letters long. Handwritten stimuli were constructed to be of equal length to their typed partners. All the words were of medium frequency. Other words from the same frequency range were used to generate the nonwords by a one letter substitution method. Items were rotated across subjects but within the target script conditions. The stimuli were presented on a three-field tachistoscope controlled by an Apple II Europlus microcomputer.

On each trial the naming stimulus was presented for 1000 msec, during which time subjects read it out aloud as quickly as possible. There was then an inter-stimulus interval of 800 msec, followed by a letter string for 2500 msec. Subjects made a lexical decision to this second string. "Word" responses were always generated with the dominant hand.

Half the subjects served in the *Immediate repeat* condition, where repeated items appeared on the same name-then-decide trial. The other subjects served in a *Lagged repeat* condition, where items were repeated only after 15 intervening items.

Results

Mean correct latencies (in msec) and percentage errors in the different conditions are shown in Table 1.

Table 1.
Word Lexical Decision RTs (in msec) and Percentage Errors in Experiment 1.

Prime script	Target script	Control RT (%Error)	Repeat RT (%Error)	Repetition effect **
Immediate repetition:				
Handwritten	Handwritten	744 (8.4)	582 (1.3)	+162 (+7.1)
Printed	Handwritten	739 (6.3)	619 (1.6)	+120 (+4.7)
Handwritten	Printed	697 (3.8)	569 (0.0)	+128 (+3.8)
Printed	Printed	684 (3.1)	575 (0.3)	+109 (+2.8)
Lagged repetition:				
Handwritten	Handwritten	737 (10.9)	678 (1.6)	+59 (+9.3)
Printed	Handwritten	728 (8.1)	686 (0.9)	+42 (+7.2)
Handwritten	Printed	657 (5.0)	624 (0.9)	+33 (+4.1)
Printed	Printed	658 (2.2)	635 (0.6)	+23 (+1.6)

** The difference in RTs and %Errors between the repeat and control conditions. + signifies facilitation in the repeat condition.

Because items were rotated within but not across target script conditions, target script was treated as a between-subjects factor in the analyses. Also, subject group was included as a factor in order to generalize any results across the different stimuli (see Wike & Church, 1976).

In the immediate repeat condition there was a three-way interaction between script correspondence, repetition and target script ($F(1, 56) = 6.92, p < 0.02$), indicating that there were differences between the immediate repetition effects produced by the two target scripts (handwritten and printed), depending on whether or not there was a positive script correspondence. For handwritten targets, there was a reliable interaction between immediate repetition and prime-target script correspondence ($F(1, 28) = 5.96, p < 0.05$). This confirms that repetition effects on handwritten targets were larger when the prime and target were in the same script than when they were in different scripts: the repetition effect from handwritten primes onto handwritten targets was 162 msec; from printed primes onto handwritten targets it was 120 msec. For printed targets, this interaction was not reliable ($F(1, 28) = 1.44, p > 0.05$): the repetition effect from printed primes onto printed targets was 109 msec, while for handwritten primes onto printed targets it was 128 msec. For printed targets there was no influence of the prime-target script correspondence on the size of the repetition effect.

In the lagged repetition condition the three way interaction between script correspondence, target script and repetition was not significant ($F(1, 56) = 1.43$, $p > 0.05$). Instead, the only reliable effects were of repetition ($F(1, 56) = 37.88$,

$p < 0.001$) and target script ($F(1, 56) = 6.46$, $p < 0.02$). RTs were faster to repeated than to nonrepeated words, and they were faster to printed relative to handwritten stimuli. However, the size of the repetition effect did not differ as a function of whether the target was handwritten or printed, nor as a function of whether primes and targets were in the same or different scripts. In both the immediate and the lagged repetition conditions the error data followed the RT data, and there were no speed-error trade-offs (see Table 1).

Discussion

Consistent with many previous findings, repetition priming effects were larger for words repeated immediately than for words repeated after 15 intervening events (e.g., Humphreys et al., 1988; Ratcliff et al., 1985). More interestingly, only the immediate repetition effect was sensitive to the script of the target and the relative scripts of the prime and target. At the long lag there was no effect on priming of the relative typescripts of primes and targets.

The long-lasting repetition effect from handwritten primes onto printed targets confirms a previous finding by Clarke and Morton (1983) using tachistoscopic identification.

A new result is that, at the long-lag, repetition effects tended to be stronger on handwritten than on printed targets (the repetition effect on handwritten targets was 50.5 msec, whilst the effect on printed targets was 28 msec, averaging over the prime script conditions). Manso de Zuniga (1988) has reported a similar result in a number of experiments, and it probably reflects a small but genuine increase in the lagged repetition effect for handwritten targets. Even so, the script of the prime then makes little difference. It would appear that, by the time that 15 intervening events have taken place, the specific processes demanded by handwritten as opposed to printed primes no longer have any effect on processing. This does not fit with the idea that lagged repetition effects reflect the processing procedures invoked by primes and targets, since we would then expect particularly strong repetition effects between handwritten primes and targets (since the same extra procedures are then demanded by both stimuli). It also provides strong evidence against the idea that handwritten and printed words are analyzed by completely separate processes, since within-script priming should then be stronger than across-script priming. We will not consider this "separate processes" account further. However, the data are consistent with the suggestion that lagged repetition effects reflect persistent activation in a lexical system that is abstracted from script. Consequently, irrespective of the script of the prime, the target's representation remains in the same state of activation, producing equal benefits from handwritten and printed primes. The tendency for this benefit to be larger on handwritten relative to printed words may then be attributed to feedback from the lexicon to the specific cursive normalization processes demanded by handwritten words (see Section 3 below).

When the words were repeated immediately there was one main change in the results. Now, repetition effects between handwritten primes and targets were substantially larger than those in any of the other repetition conditions. The most obvious account of this finding is that the processing of handwritten targets benefits greatly from an episodic representation of an identical prime. Perhaps the episodic representation of the prime can be matched directly against a visual representation of the target. If the two representations match, subjects can identify the target without having to undertake cursive normalisation. In this respect it is interesting that RTs in the immediate repetition condition with handwritten primes and targets were as fast as those to repeated printed targets (the largest difference was a nonsignificant 13 msec, relative to the handwritten prime - printed target repeat condition). In all other cases responses to handwritten targets were reliably slower than those to printed targets (see Table 1). This is consistent with the cursive normalization process being omitted when handwritten targets immediately follow an identical prime. This kind of visual matching process may benefit typed targets relatively little since they require minimal normalization. Hence there is no extra repetition effect in the printed prime - printed target condition relative to when the scripts of the repeated stimuli differ. Over time the episodic representation of the prime decays or is overwritten, so that the benefit for repeated handwritten words is lost at the longer repetition interval.

2. Experiment 2: The Effects of Contrast Reduction

The results of Experiment 1 support the existence of a cursive normalization process that operates on handwritten words. However, once normalization has been undertaken, we suggest that subsequent processes (such as lexical access) proceed in much the same way irrespective of whether a word is handwritten or printed. The primary evidence for this is that long-term repetition priming effects are equivalent for words repeated in the same and in different scripts.

In Experiment 2 we examine the relations between the putative cursive normalization process and a variable thought to influence the early visual processing of words: contrast reduction. Visual processing of form information is slowed under dim illumination conditions (Julesz & White, 1969; Wilson & Anstis, 1969). Accordingly it is assumed that variables that interact with contrast reduction also influence early aspects of word processing, at least if we apply additive factors logic (see Miller, 1988; Sternberg, 1969). Both repetition and associative priming have been found to interact with contrast reduction: essentially, the deleterious effects of contrast reduction are lessened when words are repeated or preceded by an associate (see Becker & Killion, 1977; Besner & Swan, 1982; Norris, 1984). This suggests that lexical and/or semantic information can feedback to influence the visual processing of words (see Neely, this volume). If handwriting also affects the early visual processing of words, we may also expect it to interact with contrast reduction. For instance, the effects of contrast reduction may be more severe on hand- than on typewritten words because contrast reduction exacerbates segmentation and ambiguity problems with handscript.

Method

Subjects made lexical decisions to handwritten or printed words that were either presented under clear illumination conditions or under conditions that reduced the contrast of the displays. Under clear illumination conditions words were presented at a brightness of 5 footlamberts; under the dim conditions, words were viewed through a low band-pass perspex mask that reduced the brightness to 2 footlamberts and probably also eliminated some of the higher spatial frequency components from the words. The experiment was originally run to include an immediate repetition condition. Subjects named the first (prime) stimulus and made a lexical decsion to the second (target). However, our main interest here concerns the combined effects of handwriting and contrast reduction, and so we report only the relevant data from the no repeat baseline condition here (see Manso de Zuniga, 1988, for a full report of the experiment). Words were of medium frequency of occurrence. There were 256 trials, half with words and half with nonwords created by substituting one letter from the words. Target words were rotated across the script conditions across subject groups. Sixteen subjects took part.

Results

The mean correct RTs (msec) and percentage errors are given in Table 2. There were reliable main effects of both script and contrast reduction ($F(1, 8) = 42.74$, $p < 0.001$, and $F(1, 8) = 16.10$, $p < 0.01$, respectively). There was no trace of an interaction between script and contrast reduction ($F < 1.0$). There were also no speed-accuracy trade-offs. The finding of additive relations between handwriting and contrast reduction is replicated in Manso de Zuniga (1988).

Table 2.
Word Lexical Decision Times (in msec) and Percentage Errors in Experiment 2.

Target display	Target script	RT (%Error)	Effect of contrast reduction
Degraded	Handwritten	848 (7.8)	94 (2.7)
Clear	Handwritten	754 (5.1)	
Degraded	Printed	785 (7.8)	106 (5.8)
Clear	Printed	679 (2.0)	

Discussion

Contrast reduction slowed RTs and increased the errors made to both handwritten and printed words, but it did so equally for the two scripts. The results do not support the idea that contrast reduction magnifies the problems of segmentation and ambiguity presented by handwritten words - indeed the effects of contrast reduction was 12 msec larger for printed words (see Table 2). This result shows that handwritten words are not simply "harder" to recognize than printed words (since the more difficult stimuli ought to suffer most when degradation is added); it is more that handwriting and contrast reduction affect selective aspects of the word recognition process. The simplest interpretation of the additivity between the two variables is that handwriting and contrast reduction influence separate, sequential stages in word recognition. We now outline two accounts that are consistent with this idea.

Early cursive normalization

One proposal is that cursive normalization processes are set into operation early on, irrespective of stimulus contrast, with contrast reduction affecting a subsequent stage. If cursive normalization is completed before contrast reduction affects performance, the effects of handwriting and of contrast reduction will combine additively. Figure 1 illustrates this account.

Early contrast clean-up

An alternative account holds that the effects of contrast reduction occur early on during word recognition, for instance by affecting the rate of feature extraction. Cursive normalization is undertaken only after feature analysis has been completed. Consequently, there are additive effects of contrast reduction and handwriting on performance. This account is illustrated in Figure 2.

The early contrast clean-up account has more degrees of freedom than the early cursive normalization account in explaining the relations between cursive normalization and lexical access. More specifically, according to the early contrast clean-up account, handwriting could be normalized in a discrete stage prior to lexical access taking place, or it could directly affect the rate of lexical access (as shown in Figure 2). The early cursive normalization account is tied to the notion that handwriting is normalized in a discrete processing stage. The possibility that handwriting directly affects the rate of lexical access is attractive, given the tendency for lagged repetition effects to be larger on handwritten than on printed targets (Experiment 1). Lagged repetition effects can be thought to reflect a raise in the base level of activation in the lexicon (see Monsell, this volume). Raising the base level of activation in this way will have greater effects the slower the rate of lexical access.

One further way to separate the early cursive normalization and the early contrast clean-up accounts is to examine how handwriting combines with a variable typically taken as a marker of lexical access, word frequency (see Monsell, this volume). For instance, if we hold that word frequency affects the activation thresholds for lexical representations, then the effects of word

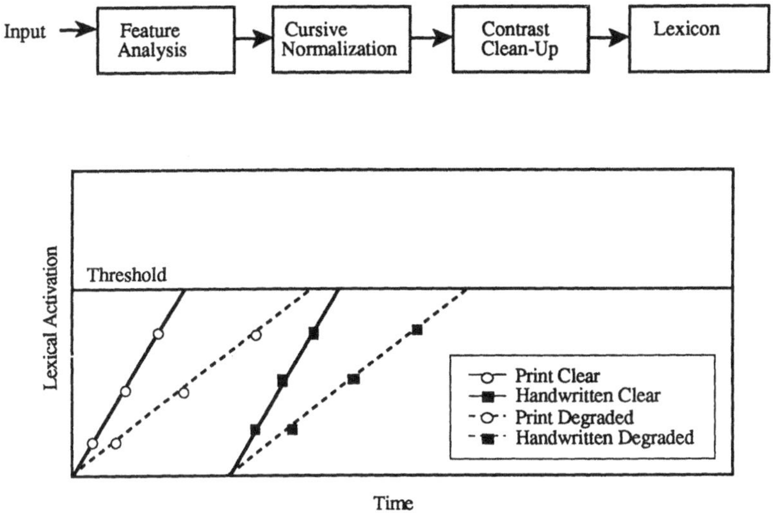

Figure 1. Early cursive normalization. In this account, handwriting is first normalized before information is passed on to the lexicon, so that handwriting adds a constant time increment to lexical access. Contrast reduction affects the rate of lexical activation. Cursive normalization and contrast reduction combine additively.

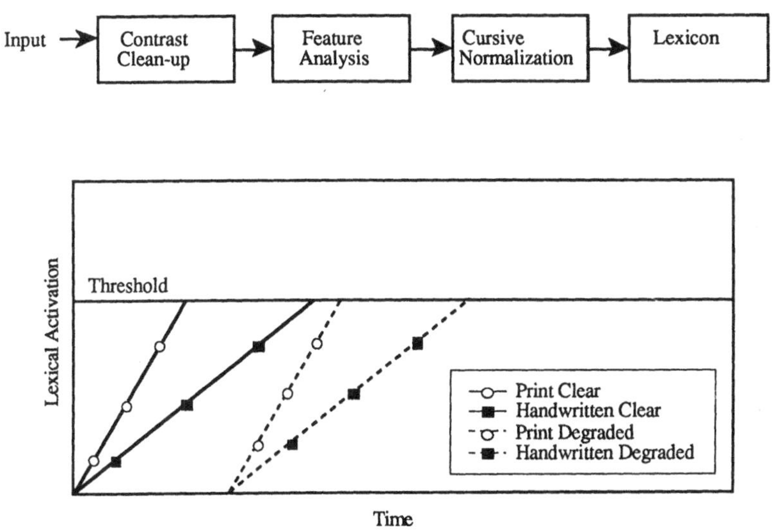

Figure 2. Early contrast clean-up. In this account, contrast reduction affects early processes in word recognition, such as feature analysis. The effects of contrast reduction are cleaned-up before either cursive normalization or lexical activation takes place. Cursive normalization affects the rate of lexical activation. The effects of contrast reduction and of handwriting combine additively.

frequency should interact with variables affecting the rate of lexical access, in much the same way as repetition does. This is illustrated in Figure 3. An interaction between handwriting and word frequency would be consistent with the early contrast clean-up account, and inconsistent with the early cursive normalization account.

3. Experiments 3 and 4: The effects of word frequency

Method

Similarly to Experiment 2, this experiment was originally designed to examine repetition effects in combination with the effects of script and word frequency. However, this overcomplicates matters as far as our present interests are concerned, and so we report only the relevant data on the combined effects of script and word frequency in the no repeat baseline condition (see Manso de Zuniga, 1988, for a full report of the experiment).

Subjects took part in a "name-and-then-decide" task. The targets were 40 high (above 80 per million) and 40 low frequency words (below 10 per million), between 5 and 7 letters long. These words were combined with 80 pronounceable nonwords, which differed by one letter from a set of medium frequency words. Target words and nonwords appeared equally often in handwriting and in print. Subjects named the first word on a trial and then made a lexical decision to the second letter string.

The experiment was run twice. In Experiment 3, different groups of subjects received the handwritten and the printed stimuli. In Experiment 4 the same subjects saw both scripts, with the words in each script rotated across two subject sub-groups. There were 16 subjects in each subexperiment.

Results

Table 3 gives the mean correct RTs (msec) and percentage errors to high and low frequency words in the two scripts in Experiments 3 and 4.

In Experiment 3 there were reliable main effects of frequency and script ($F(1, 28) = 51.94$, and $F(1, 28) = 6.04$, $p < 0.001$ and $p < 0.05$ respectively)[1]. The frequency x script interaction failed to reach statistical significance ($F(1, 28) = 2.05$, $p > 0.10$). Despite the interaction failing to reach significance, the trend was for frequency effects to be enhanced for handwritten words.

Experiment 4 replicated Experiment 3. There were reliable main effects of frequency and script (F(1, 12 = 122.51 and $F(1, 12) = 24.96$, both $p < 0.001$). The frequency x script interaction was marginally significant ($F(1, 12) = 4.16$, $p = 0.06$).

In both experiments the frequency effect for handwritten words was 45 msec larger than the frequency effect for printed words.

There were no speed-accuracy trade-offs in either experiment.

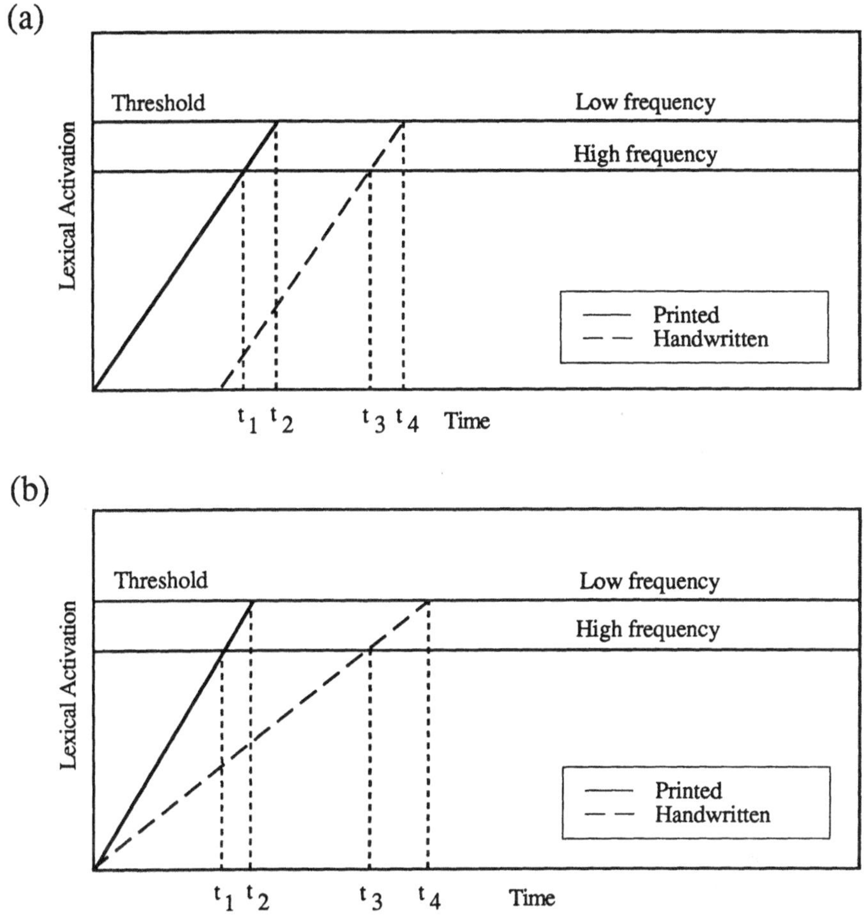

Figure 3. The relations between word frequency and handwriting, according to whether (1) handwriting affects an early, discrete processing stage (a), or (2) handwriting affects the rate of lexical activation (b). In (a), handwriting and word frequency combine additively ($t2 - t1 = t4 - t3$); in (b) the two variables interact ($t4 - t3 > t2 - t1$).

Discussion

In both Experiments 3 and 4 the effects of word frequency tended to be larger on handwritten than on printed words. This result is consistent with the early contrast clean-up account, which allows handwriting to affect the rate of lexical access. The result is inconsistent with the early cursive normalization account.

Table 3.
Word Lexical Decision RTs (in msecs) and % Errors in Experiments 3 and 4.

Word frequency	Word script	RT (%Error)	Frequency effect
Experiment 3:			
High	Handwritten	786 (10.6)	134 (13.7)
Low	Handwritten	920 (24.3)	
High	Printed	671 (1.9)	89 (8.7)
Low	Printed	760 (10.6)	
Experiment 4:			
High	Handwritten	691 (2.7)	144 (9.0)
Low	Handwritten	835 (11.7)	
High	Printed	636 (0.4)	99 (7.0)
Low	Printed	735 (7.4)	

The above conclusion rests on the assumption that word frequency is a lexical variable. This assumption has recently been questioned (see Monsell, this volume). For instance, visual encoding procedures may vary as a function of the amount of practice we have reading words, so that high frequency words are encoded more efficiently than low frequency words (cf. Kolers, 1985). High frequency words may also be more visually familiar, biasing a word response in lexical decision (see Besner & McCann, 1987). Both of these arguments stress that word frequency does not necessarily affect lexical access time.

Encoding procedures and visual familiarity judgments may be sensitive to the familiarity of the script that words are presented in. In an unfamiliar handwritten script, high frequency words may suffer because they require novel visual encoding procedures and because they lose their visual familiarity. The frequency effect may then be reduced for handwritten words. Clearly this did not occur. The data instead suggest that some other factor is determining the word frequency effect, so that a larger effect is produced when the words are handwritten. The data argue against nonlexical processes, such as enhanced encoding or familiarity discrimination, being the sole cause of the word frequency effect. However, they are consistent with the word frequency effect being lexically based.

V. GENERAL DISCUSSION

We have argued that the reading of handwritten words differs from that of printed words primarily because handwriting requires the operation of specialized cursive normalization processes. These normalization processes seem to be separate from, and occur subsequent to, other processes affected by contrast reduction (Experiment 2). However, once cursive normalization has taken place, handwritten and printed words seem subject to similar processes. Consequently, the persistant effects of having read a prime word are much the same irrespective of whether the prime was handwritten or printed (Experiment 1). The data fit nicely with what we have termed the early contrast clean-up account (Figure 2).

The model shown in Figure 2 presents a very simple account of word identification, in which lexical access occurs following a series of discrete processing stages for contrast clean-up and then for cursive normalization. However, cursive normalization itself seems to interact with lexical access processes, given the enhanced long-term repetition effect for handwritten targets (Experiment 1), and the enhanced word frequency effect (Experiments 3 and 4). In particular, these enhanced effects are consistent with handwriting affecting the *rate* of access (see Figure 3). The *rate* of lexical access would be affected if, for instance, lexical activation fed-back to influence cursive normalization.

The proposal that contrast reduction affects an early discrete processing stage in word identification fits with the finding that the effects of contrast reduction and word frequency combine additively in lexical decision with printed words (Becker, & Killion, 1977)[2]. However, contrast reduction does interact with both repetition and single word associative priming (e.g., for data on repetition see Besner & Swan, 1982; Norris, 1984; for data on associative priming, see Becker & Killion, 1977; Meyer, Schvaneveldt & Ruddy, 1975). Such interactions would occur if repetition and associative priming are at least in part due to top-down expectancies. Such expectancies may be matched against input representations and so minimize the effects of contrast reduction on performance (see Neely, this volume). The opertion of such expectancies is also suggested by the data from Experiment 1 here, where the effects of handwriting were eliminated when handwritten prime words were immediately repeated as targets.

The interaction between word frequency and handwriting that we have observed in lexical decision stands in contrast to the additive effects of frequency and another manipulation of word script, CaSe AlTeRnAtIoN (see Besner & McCann, 1987). Besner and McCann have argued that case alternation and frequency combine additively in lexical decision because of a trade-off between two factors. There is an interaction between frequency-sensitive lexical processes and the processes that normalize case alternated print, that tends to increase the word frequency effect (much as seems to be the case for handwriting). Against this, case alternated words appear visually unfamiliar and so lessen the effects of word frequency on visual familiarity judgments that contribute to lexical decision. The net effect is that the word frequency effect remains about the same size for single case and for case alternated words. The present result with handwriting would be consistent with Besner and McCann's account provided that high frequency words still appear familiar when they are handwritten. This could be tested by combining the effects of handwriting with those of case alternation. The familiarity judgment account would hold that the interaction between frequency and handwriting would then be weakened since the handwritten high frequency words would then lose their familiarity advantage.

The account we have proposed is not the only one possible, but it does have some success in explaining the pattern of additive and interactive effects of particular variables on word identification. Other models can account for some aspects of the data but have problems when the whole pattern is considered. For instance, the verification model (Becker, 1976, 1985) holds that word identification always depends on a top-down verification process that matches visually derived lexical candidates with the input. The verification process is frequency ordered, so that matching occurs for high frequency words prior to low frequency words. According to this account, frequency and contrast reduction combine additively because the set of lexical candidates is not derived until after the effects of contrast reduction have occurred. The frequency x handwriting interaction could be explained if verification could be set into operation before cursive normalization is completed.

The verification model must explain the additive relations between case alternation and frequency in much the same way as it explains the data on the effects of contrast reduction; that is, that verification operates after case alternation has been normalized. The difference between the effects of handwriting and case alternation can then be attributed to the relative difficulty of the normalization processes. Case alternation can be normalized relatively quickly, and is completed before lexical candidates are derived and verified. Cursive normalization is slower and so is not completed before verification gets underway.

A problem for the verification model is that case alternation and word frequency do interact when naming latencies are measured, yet the model holds that verification processes are the same for both tasks (see Neely, this volume). The familiarity judgment account is more comfortable with this result, since the familiarity judgments that are detrimentally affected by case alternation only affect lexical decision.

Irrespective of the precise details of the account that best fits the data, the point we wish to stress here is that cursive normalization is open to lexical influence. In this respect, our conclusion meshes with the suggestion made in our discussion of the literature on computer models for reading handwriting; namely, that a flexible lexically based segmentation-correction procedure is useful for parsing cursive script and for resolving the ambiguity of individual letters.

The main point of the chapter has been to sketch out a general framework for modelling the reading of handwriting, in which handwritten and printed words share many of the same processes. Additional work is now needed to flesh out the details of the account, and, in particular, to specify the procedures involved in what we have termed cursive normalization. For instance, we have suggested that an important aspect of this process is the segmentation of a letter string into its component letters. We believe this is important because wholistic perceptual descriptions of handwritten words may be too inaccurate for the words to be uniquely identified. It is even possible that such descriptions are too inaccurate to allow familiarity discrimination to occur. In this respect, our account differs from others in the literature, where it is assumed that handwritten words depend on wholistic coding procedures (e.g., Howard, 1987). Experiments examining the effects of factors such as case alternation and word length on the reading of both scripts would help resolve this.

FOOTNOTES

1 These analyses are taken from the analysis of the larger experiment, in which repetition and subjects groups were included as additional factors.

2 Norris (1984) and Wilding (1988) have reported interactions between word frequency and contrast reduction in lexical decision with printed words. However, there were relatively severe effects of contrast reduction in Norris's study. Under such circumstances, contrast clean-up may not be sufficient to minimize the effects of degradation on lexical access. Wilding (1988) replicated Norris's finding using a long (3 sec) interval between stimuli and responses. The response-stimulus interval used both here and in other studies (e.g., Becker & Killion, 1977) was about half that used by Wilding, and so his results are not applicable.

ACKNOWLEDGMENTS

This work was supported by a research studentship and a grant from the Economic and Social Research Council of Great Britain to CMdZ and GWH, and from a grant from the Science and Engineering Research Council of Great Britain to LJE. We thank Derek Besner for his comments on an earlier version of the paper.

REFERENCES

Becker, C.A. (1976). Allocation of attention during visual word recognition. *Journal of Experimental Psychology: Human Perception and Performance*, **2**, 556-566.

Becker, C.A. (1985). What do we really know about semantic context effects during reading? In D. Besner, T.G. Waller & G.E. MacKinnon (Eds.), *Reading Research: Advances in Theory and in Practice*. V.5. New York: Academic Press.

Becker, C.A., & Killion, T.H. (1977). Interaction of visual and cognitive effects in word recognition. *Journal of Experimental Psychology: Human Perception and Performance*, **3**, 389-401.

Besner, D., Coltheart, M., & Davelaar, E. (1984). Basic processes in reading: Computation of abstract letter identities. *Canadian Journal of Psychology*, **38**, 126-134.

Besner, D. & McCann, R.S. (1987). Word frequency and pattern distortion in visual word identification and production: An examination of four classes of models. In M. Coltheart (Ed.), *Attention and Performnce XI*. London: Lawrence Erlbaum Associates.
Besner, D. & Swan, M. (1982). Models of lexical access in visual word recognition. *Quarterly Journal of Experimental Psychology*, **34A**, 313-325.
Biederman, I. & Ju, G. (1988). Surface versus edge-based determinants of visual recognition. *Cognitive Psychology*, **20**, 38-64.
Bozinovic, R. & Shrihari, S.N. (1982). A string correction algorithm or cursive script recognition. *IEEE Transactions for Pattern Analysis and Machine Intelligence*, **4**, 655-663.
Clarke, R.J. & Morton, J. (1983). Cross modality facilitation in tachistoscopic word recognition. *Quarterly Journal of Experimental Psychology*, **35A**, 79-96.
Corcoran, D.W.J. & Rouse, R.O. (1970). An aspect of perceptual organisation involved in reading types and handwritten words. *Quarterly Journal of Experimental Psychology*, **22**, 526-530.
Earnest, L.D. (1962). Machine recognition of cursive reading. In C.M. Popplewell (Ed.), *Information Processing: Proceedings of the IFIP Congress*. Amsterdam: North Holland.
Evett, L.J. & Humphreys, G.W. (1981). The use of abstract graphemic information in lexical access. *Quarterly Journal of Experimental Psychology*, **33A**, 325-350.
Ford, B. & Banks, W.P. (1977). Perceptual differences between reading handwritten and typed words. *Memory and Cognition*, **5**, 630-635.
Frishkopf, L.S. & Harmon, L.D. (1961). Machine reading of cursive script. In C. Cherry (Ed.), *Information Theory*. London: Butterworth.
Harmon, L.D. (1962). Handwriting reader recognizes whole words. *Electronics*, August 24.
Henderson, L. (1982). *Orthography and Word Recognition in Reading*. London: Academic Press.
Howard, D. (1987). Reading without letters? In M. Coltheart, G. Sartori & R. Job (Eds.), *The Cognitive Neuropsychology of Language*. London: Lawrence Erlbaum Associates.
Humphreys, G.W. (1983). Reference frames and shape perception. *Cognitive Psychology*, **15**, 151-196.
Humphreys, G.W. (1985). Attention, automaticity and autonomy in visual word processing. In D. Besner, T.G. Waller & G.E. MacKinnon (Eds.), *Reading Research: Advances in Theory and in Practice. V.5*. New York: Academic Press.
Humphreys, G.W., Besner, D., & Quinlan, P.T. (1988). Event perception and the word repetition effect. *Journal of Experimental Psychology: General*, **117**, 51-67.
Humphreys, G.W., & Bruce, V. (1989). *Visual Cognition: Computational, Experimental and Neuropsychological Approaches*. London: Lawrence Erlbaum Associates.
Humphreys, G.W., & Quinlan, P.T. (1987). Normal and pathological processes in visual object constancy. In G.W. Humphreys & M.J. Riddoch (Eds.), *Visual Object Processing: A Cognitive Neuropsychological Approach*. London: Lawrence Erlbaum Associates.
Julesz, B. & White, B. (1969). Short-term visual memory and the Pulfrich phenomenon. *Nature*, **222**, 639-641.
Kashyap, R.L. & Oomen, B.J. (1981). An effective algorithm for string correction using generalised edit distances - I. Description of the algorithm and its optimality. *Information Sciences*, **23**, 123-142.
Kolers, P.A. (1979). Reading and knowing. *Canadian Journal of Experimental Psychology*, **33**, 106-117.
Kolers, P.A. (1985). Skill in reading and memory. *Canadian Journal of Psychology*, **39**, 232-239.
Levenshtein, A. (1966). Binary codes capable of correcting deletions, insertions and reversals. *Soviet Phys-Dokla*, **10**, 707-710.
Manso de Zuniga, C.M. (1988). *The effects of handwriting and repetition on visual word identification*. Unpublished Ph.D. thesis, University of London.
Marr, D. (1982). *Vision*. San Fransisco: W.H. Freeman.
McClelland, J.L. (1986). The programmable blackboard model of reading. In McClelland, J.L. & D.E. Rumelhart (Eds.), *Parallel Distributed Processing: Explorations in the Microstructure of Cognition. V.2*. Cambridge, Mass.: MIT Press.

McClelland, J.L. (1987). The case for interactionism in language processing. In M. Coltheart (Ed.), *Attention and Performance XII*. London: Lawrence Erlbaum Associates.

McClelland, J.L. & Rumelhart, D.E. (1981). An interactive activation model of context effects in letter perception: Part 1. An account of basic findings. *Psychological Review*, **88**, 375-407.

Meyer, D.E., Schvaneveldt, R.W. & Ruddy, M.G. (1975). Loci of contextual effects on visual word recognition. In P.M.A. Rabbitt & S. Dornic (Eds.), *Attention and performance V*. London: Academic Press.

Miller, J. (1988). Discrete and continuous models of human information processing: Theoretical distinctions and empirical results. *Acta Psychologia*, **67**, 191-257.

Monsell, S. (1985). Repetition and the lexicon. In A.W. Ellis (Ed.), *Progress in the Psychology of Language. V.2*. London: Lawrence Erlbaum Associates.

Monsell, S. (1987). Nonvisual orthographic processing and the orthographic input lexicon. In M. Coltheart (Ed.), *Attention and Performance XII*. London: Lawrence Erlbaum Associates.

Morton, J. (1979). Some experiments on facilitation in word and picture recognition and their relevance for the evolution of a theoretical position. In P.A. Kolers, M.E. Wrolstad & H. Bouma (Eds.), *Processing of Visible Language. V.1*. New York: Plenum Press.

Nash-Weber, B. (1975). The role of semantics in automatic speech understanding. In D.G. Bobrow & A. Collins (Eds.), *Representation and Understanding*. New York: Academic Press.

Norris, D. (1984). The effects of frequency, repetition and stimulus quality in visual word recognition. *Quarterly Journal of Experimental Psychology*, **36A**, 507-518.

Okuda, T., Tanaka, E. & Kasai, T. (1976). A method of correcting garbled words based on the Levenshtein method. *IEEE Transactions in Computing*, **25**, 172-177.

Palmer, S.E. (1985). The role of symmetry in shape perception. *Acta Psychologia*, **59**, 67-90.

Patterson, K.E., Marshall, J.C. & Coltheart, M. (1985). *Surface Dyslexia: Neuropsychological and Cognitive Studies of Phonological Reading*. London: Lawrence Erlbaum Associates.

Ratcliff, R., Hockley, W. & McKoon, G. (1985). Components of activation: Repetition and priming effects in lexical decision and recognition. *Journal of Experimental Psychology: General*, **114**, 435-450.

Rayner, K., McConkie, G.W. & Zola, D. (1980). Integrating information across eye movements. *Cognitive Psychology*, **12**, 206-226.

Salasoo, A., Shiffrin, R.M. & Feustel, T.C. (1985). Building pemanent memory codes: Codification and repetition effects in word identification. *Journal of Experimental Psychology: General*, **114**, 50-77.

Sayre, K.M. (1973). Machine recognition of handwritten words. *Pattern Recognition*, **5**, 213-228.

Sternberg, S. (1969). The discovery of processing stages: Extensions of Donder's method. In W.G. Koster (Ed), *Attention and Performance II*. Amsterdam: North Holland.

Tarr, M.J. & Pinker, S. (in press). Mental rotation and orientation-dependence in shape recognition. *Cognitive Psychology*.

Watt, R.J. (1988). *Visual Processing: Computational, Psychophysical and Cognitive Research*. London: Lawrence Erlbaum Associates.

Wike, E.L. & Church, J.D. (1976). Comments on Clark's "The language-as-fixed-effect fallacy." *Journal of Verbal Learning and Verbal Behaviour*, **15**, 249-255.

Wilding, J. (1988). The interaction of word frequency and stimulus quality in the lexical decision task: Now you see it now you don't. *Quarterly Journal of Experimental Psychology*, **40A**, 757-770.

Wilson, J.A. & Anstis, S. (1969). Visual latency as a function of luminance. *American Journal of Psychology*, **82**, 350-358.

3

LETTER-BY-LETTER READERS: EVIDENCE FOR PARALLEL PROCESSING

DAVID HOWARD

Psychology Department
Birkbeck College
London, England

I. INTRODUCTION

1. Letter-by-Letter Reading: Why?

Recognition of written words by normal subjects is massively parallel, at least when they are presented undistorted with the letters in their normal order in free fields. Recent models of the processes of word recognition (e.g., McClelland & Rumelhart, 1981) have therefore assumed that all the visual elements making up a word are processed simultaneously and in parallel (see Fig. 1). This assumption is based on a series of results showing that the effects of word length on oral reading time or accuracy are small: a range of studies reviewed by Henderson (1982) show effects of between 6 and 63 ms per letter, but as Schiepers (1980) demonstrates, such effects can be eliminated entirely when words are presented at the fovea.

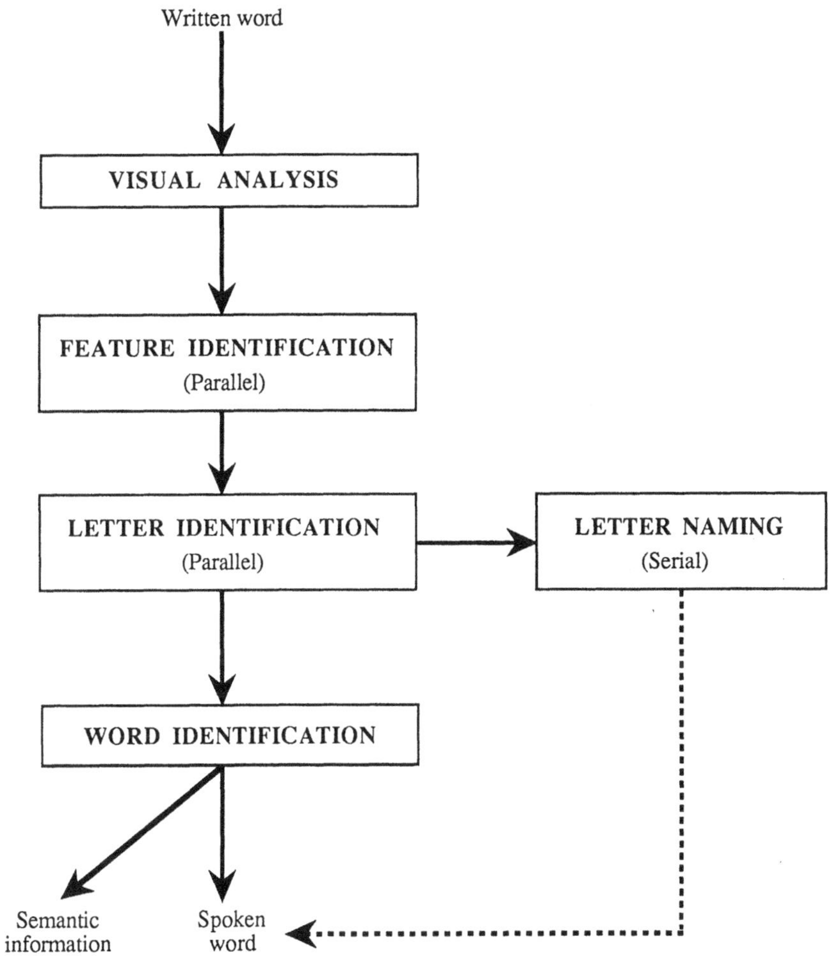

Figure 1. An outline model of normal word recognition: letters are processed in parallel.

Yet, under certain circumstances, this parallel processing can break down. In normal subjects with words presented centrally latencies for word reading or lexical decision can show marked effects of word length when, for instance, words are written vertically, when they are reflected left-to-right in a vertical plane (e.g., Navon, 1978), when they are rotated through more than 60 degrees (e.g., Koriat & Norman, 1985; Terry, Samuels & LaBerge, 1976), and where the letters of a word are displaced vertically above or below their normal position in a horizontal row (e.g., Seymour & May, 1981). Not all distortions result in length effects in reading; thus Terry et al. (1976) showed that there was no interaction of word letter length with either degradation of visual letter information, or spacing letters irregularly.

Studies which have presented stimuli to normal subjects in the left and right visual fields show that in both lexical decision and naming there are substantial effects of word length with left visual field presentation even where words are presented in a normal undistorted left to right order (Bub, 1982; Young & Ellis, 1985; Ellis, Young & Anderson, 1988). It is only with right visual field presentation that effects of word length disappear, and then only when words are presented in a single horizontal line.

These experiments on the effects of word length appear to show that in normal subjects the letters in a word are only processed in parallel when the letters of a word are presented with their letters correctly oriented, in the correct left-to-right order, either centrally or to the right visual field. What happens when these conditions are violated? There seems to be general agreement that the length effects indicate that some kind of sequential letter-by-letter processing strategy is involved, and parallel processing of the letters in the word is no longer possible. Koriat and Norman (1985) note that there is a striking similarity between this letter-by-letter strategy in normal subjects, and the letter-by-letter reading shown by brain damaged patients; is it possible, then, that an analysis of the processes involved in letter-by-letter readers will shed some light on the sequential processing strategies used in word recognition by normal subjects?

Letter-by-letter reading in acquired dyslexia is a striking symptom. Confronted with a written word these patients will often say the names of the letters one after the other before producing the whole word. Often one or more of the letters will be misidentified and, having produced an unpronounceable string of letters, the patient will start again, naming each letter in turn, until a word is identified. Clearly, reading of this kind is a considerable handicap, and most patients will avoid reading text of any length because of the unconscionable time that the process can take.

Many letter-by-letter readers are comparatively good at writing, and, to their distress, may be unable to read back a sentence that they have written just a few minutes before. In the the classical neuropsychological literature this problem was called "pure alexia" or "alexia without agraphia" and the available accounts concentrated on explaining how a disorder of reading could occur in the absence of aphasia or agraphia (e.g., Dejerine, 1892; Greenblatt, 1973). Most (but not all) letter-by-letter readers have a right hemianopia (loss of the right visual field). The classical account of "pure alexia" is based on a disconnection of the visual areas in the right hemisphere from the areas involved in word recognition in the left cerebral hemisphere. There is an obvious parallel here between the letter-by-letter reading of "pure alexics" (in whom visual stimuli are first processed by the right hemisphere) and the length effects shown by normal subjects when words are presented to the left visual field (e.g., Young and Ellis, 1985).

The process of letter-by-letter reading in dyslexic patients is very distinctive, and more recently cognitive neuropsychologists have offered explanations of the way in which these patients do read. Two recent and influential accounts from Patterson and Kay (1982) and Warrington and Shallice (1980) agree that there is persuasive evidence that these patients are unable to use letter recognition processes that operate in parallel to drive word recognition. Instead, the subjects are forced to use a process of serial letter processing as a compensatory strategy, so there is a monotonic linear relationship between the length of a word and the mean time taken to read it aloud. The data from Patterson and Kay's patient TP, for example, suggest that each letter increases the mean reaction time by about 2 seconds, which is strikingly different from normal subjects with undistorted stimuli presented in free fields.

The reading latencies of letter-by-letter readers demonstrate that parallel letter processing routine is disrupted at some point. Investigators of letter-by-letter reading disagree about the level at which the impairment arises. Patterson and Kay (1982) suggest that the difficulty may lie in using the output of a letter identification system which (normally) operates in parallel; instead patients are forced to rely on a serial letter identification process, which then feeds its information into the normal lexicon used for visual word identification. Warrington and Shallice (1980) suggest that the breakdown may occur at the level of the visual word form system (or visual input lexicon); patients cannot recognize whole words at this level, but instead rely on using spelling processes in reverse to access the semantic system. Shallice and Saffran (1986) describe a letter-by-letter reader, MIL, who can perform lexical decision with some accuracy when written words are presented for two seconds, even though he needs much longer exposures to read the word aloud. They suggest, therefore, that for MIL, word recognition processes are intact up to the level of the visual input lexicon; his problem lies in the post-lexical process of access to the semantic system, which is a rather more central level of impairment than Warrington and Shallice (1980) had claimed.

Some authors have argued for more peripheral sources of difficulty in their letter-by-letter readers. Friedman and Alexander (1984), for example, show that their subject was slowed both in word and in picture recognition when items were presented tachistoscopically although performance with pictures was clinically normal when the patient was not put under any time pressure. They suggest that their patient's difficulty is not specific to word reading, but reflects "slow and inefficient identification of visual input" (p. 22). To compensate for this problem the patient is obliged to focus attention deliberately on each element of the visual array in turn. The reading disorder is the most salient feature of this strategy; because of the patient's need to focus attention successively on each letter in order to identify it , it causes conspicuously slow processing. With pictures, on the other hand, attention only needs to be focused once, and so the effects of slowed processing are not so readily apparent. Letter-by-letter reading, in Friedman and Alexander's account, represents a strategy of "focused sequential scan of the features and/or letters," which is used when more automatic parallel identification of letters fails.

A very similar kind of account was developed by Kinsbourne and Warrington (1962, 1963) for letter-by-letter reading, in their patients who they describe as "simultanagnosic." Apart from letter-by-letter reading, these patients fail to interpret the meaning of the whole of complex pictures; in describing them they will name individual objects accurately but fail to appreciate the significance of the picture of the whole. Wolpert (1924), who first described this disorder, felt that it could be attributed to a general difficulty in apprehending objects as a whole, although the parts were accurately perceived. In tachistoscopic presentation of items to five patients of this kind, Kinsbourne and Warrington (1962, 1963) showed that single letters could be recognized accurately at exposures of 10-25 ms, but well over a second was needed before both of a pair of letters could be reported correctly; at shorter exposures the subjects could report only one letter in the array. Similar results were found with pictures and geometric shapes, showing that the problem was not confined to letter recognition. Normal controls, by comparison, needed only a few extra milliseconds to identify the second item in an array. Kinsbourne and Warrington (1962) went on to show that the difficulty could also be observed with successive presentation of letters; errors were still observed when 500 ms intervened between presentation of the letters. Kinsbourne and Warrington (1962) interpreted this as showing that "a certain time, longer than is normal, must elapse after the first, before a second act of form perception may occur" (p. 478). This, they argued, is responsible for the letter-by-letter reading: "only one letter can be read at a time, and the interval before the visual system is ready for perception of the next is so long that reading must be a laborious hardship" (p. 481).

Studying a set of similar patients, Levine and Calvanio (1978) reject Kinsbourne and Warrington's (1962) account. They point out that this predicts that the number of letters correctly reported should slowly increase with exposure duration, until after enough time had elapsed all letters would be correct; their patients were, however, unable to report all the letters in a trigram even with 5 seconds exposure although a single letter was accurately named at only 20 ms. Levine and Calvanio's subjects misrecognized letters as other visually similar letters; they suggest that the underlying problem is one of "insufficient capacity for feature discrimination." With a single item there is sufficient capacity for correct identification, but "if they attempt to divide their perceptual capacity among a larger number of letters while maintaining the depth of discrimination required to identify these letters, they make errors because the perceptual capacity per letter is less than required for the task"(p. 77). Although Levine and Calvanio never explain how this theory accounts for letter-by-letter reading, it might result from a strategic decision to concentrate all the (limited) perceptual capacity on each letter in turn; these patients "retain considerable flexibility in deciding which of the letters of an array to analyze with their limited capacity" (p. 77).

Both Kinsbourne and Warrington (1962), and Levine and Calvanio (1978) argue for a simultanagnosia which is demonstrated by a difficulty in identifying items when more than one item is presented. But it is not at all clear what constitutes an "item"; they demonstrate that patients perform normally with single letters, numbers and object pictures. Each of these could be interpreted either as a single object or as an array of simultaneously presented features all of which need to be processed in parallel to recognize the item; why then do these subjects not treat whole familiar words as single items? There does not seem to be a principled reason for assuming that picture recognition consists, in Kinsbourne and Warrington's term, of a single "act of perception" while word recognition does not. Indeed, in another paper, Shallice and Warrington (1977) report two patients who can correctly name single letters, pictures and words, but who make frequent errors when more than one item from the same category is in the display. This results in a pattern of reading disability which Shallice (1988) calls "attentional dyslexia" where the patient can read single words accurately but cannot report the letters of which they are composed. In one sense, then, these patients are "simultanagnosic" in that they can attend to only a single "item" in an array, and where a word counts as a single "item." In contrast, Kinsbourne and Warrington's account of letter-by-letter reading as a form of "simultanagnosia" suggests that the patients can only attend to a single letter in a word. Thus in "attentional dyslexia" a variety of "simultanagnosia" which is defined over a different set of "items," results in a reading disorder which is apparently the polar opposite of letter-by-letter reading.

It is clear that not all letter-by-letter readers are "simultanagnosic," at least in the sense adopted by Kinsbourne and Warrington (1962) and Levine and Calvanio (1978). Warrington and Shallice (1980) presented both of their subjects, RAV and JDC, with letters either as single items or as a letter in red flanked on each side by two black letters; this manipulation, which had caused a significant decrement in performance with Shallice and Warrington's (1977) "attentional dyslexics," had no effect on either of Warrington and Shallice's "word form dyslexics." Another task was used both by Warrington and Shallice with RAV, and by Patterson and Kay with one of their patients, TP. A word whose length varied from 4 to 8 letters was presented for 150 ms flanked by two numbers; the patient's task was to report the numbers. Both patients managed impressive levels of accuracy at an exposure duration which would preclude report of more than one letter for any classical "simultanagnosic," and accuracy was independent of the length of the intervening word. It is clear from these results that these letter-by-letter readers do not have a primary difficulty in processing several items presented simultaneously in arrays.

While these accounts of letter-by-letter reading differ on the level at which parallel reading processes are breaking down, they agree that, in these patients, word recognition can only be achieved using a strategy of serial letter identification. Under Warrington and Shallice's (1980) account where the problem is caused by defective representations in a visual word form system, it is possible that lexical entries for some words will remain intact; for these items, normal, fast, parallel word recognition should still be possible.

2. Do Letter-by-Letter Readers Always Read Letter-by-Letter?

In normal subjects when reading speed or accuracy declines with increasing length, and when similar results are found with letter-by-letter readers, researchers have assumed that the processes involved in parallel processing of the letters in a word are unavailable and the subjects are resorting instead to some serial strategy. In this chapter I shall argue that latencies which increase monotonically with word length do not necessarily indicate that the primary method of processing is serial. Instead it will be argued that the latency data from two letter-by-letter readers can be better accounted for by a primary process of parallel identification of the letters in a word where this process is subject to a significant rate of error; a serial letter-by-letter identification strategy is only resorted to when word recognition on the basis of parallel processing fails.

The patients who are reported in this chapter are both letter-by-letter readers in that (a) mean word-reading latency is a monotonically increasing function of the number of letters in the word, and (b) they sometimes say each of the letters in turn before producing a response. The mean reading latencies, however, conceal considerable variation; although PM takes on average more than 15 secs to read a nine letter word, his fastest correct reading response for a word of this length took less than 2.5 secs. These "fast" reading responses are not easily explicable on any account that asserts that word recognition depends exclusively on serial letter recognition. The available data on reading of tachistoscopically presented words by letter-by-letter readers tends to support the conclusion that not all reading responses are necessarily generated letter-by-letter. Both of Prior and McCorriston's (1983) patients could read virtually all words presented for 400 ms, and Warrington and Shallice's (1980) patient RAV read 58/72 (81%) of words presented for 100 ms, and 83/100 when presented for 500ms. With a stimulus presentation of 250 ms, Coslett and Saffran's (1988) patient JG read 88% of high imageability words and 63% of low imageability words, and JC read 98% and 65% from the same lists. However, not all letter-by-letter readers seem to be able to extract information from briefly-presented stimuli. Patterson and Kay (1982) found no evidence that their subjects could perform lexical decision when words were presented for less than a second; one of them (CH) denied being able to see any stimulus presented for any shorter duration.

Evidence from another task also suggests that letter-by-letter readers may not always read letter-by-letter. Warrington and Shallice (1980) compared their patients' reading of words written in lower case with words where alternate letters were in uPpEr and lOwEr case. With mixed case stimuli the patients read more slowly and made more errors. If patients were focusing attention sequentially on each letter, there is no reason to predict a disadvantage for mixed case words, because this manipulation leaves the sequence of individual letters unaffected - only more global features such as word shape and transitional features between letters are disrupted and these are features which, under the sequential letter recognition hypothesis, letter-by-letter readers are unable to use.[1]

3. A Letter Recognition Problem For Letter-by-Letter Readers?

Reviewing the available evidence on letter-by-letter readers, Friedman and Albert (1985) claim that "letter identification is usually good but rarely perfect." A variety of observations support the idea that processes of letter recognition are, to some extent, disrupted in these patients. All four subjects reported by Patterson and Kay (1982) made errors in naming single letters, and three of them made a substantial number of mistakes in matching letters across case. Where case descriptions report on patients' reading errors, it is clear that letter misidentification is often the cause; Patterson and Kay cite examples such as SORT ---> "soft" (patient TP), MADE ---> "wade" (CH) and SPADE ---> "shade" (KC). When letters are misidentified the error responses are very often visually similar to the target letters; typical confusions with upper case letters are between Q/O, V/W/N, C/G (Levine & Calvanio, 1978), and with lower case letters between b/d/p, t/l, m/w, a/o (Patterson & Kay, 1982)). Many case reports of letter-by-letter readers mention that patients showed some degree of visual agnosia in object or picture recognition at least in the early stages of their illness. Conversely, many reports of visual agnosic patients mention that when these subjects attempt to read, they do so letter-by-letter (e.g., Humphreys & Riddoch, 1987; Rubens & Benson, 1971). Under these circumstances it is tempting to speculate that the difficulty in letter recognition may represent a residual sign of object agnosia, possibly because letter recognition involves finer and less redundant discrimination than most other visual tasks.

Not all accounts of letter-by-letter readers, however, concede that the patients made errors in letter recognition. Of RAV Warrington and Shallice write that he "had no difficulty in reading the constituent letters of the word" (p. 101); although they report that in word reading "very occasional errors were made" (p. 100), they volunteer no further information on the nature of these mistakes. And Kinsbourne and Warrington (1962) report that the errors made by their simultanagnosic subjects in letter recognition were not visually related, although they do not present the evidence that supports their result.

4. Predictions About "Fast" Reading Responses

This evidence suggests that some letter-by-letter readers may have a problem in letter identification. Let us assume that some patients process letters in parallel but on the basis of visual information that is noisy or in some other way defective. As a result letters might be misrecognized, and processing might, as Friedman and Alexander (1984) suggest, be slowed. On this basis alone a simple mathematical model can be erected. Suppose that the probability of a letter being correctly recognized is p. In an n letter word, the probability that all the letters are correctly reported, C, is p^n. Thus $\log(C) = n \log(p)$. On the $(1-p)^n$ trials where one or more letters is misidentified, the sequence will either constitute a word (an error) or it will not. Where it does not make a word, I assume that the patient will initiate a compensatory strategy which involves deliberate serial identification of the letters in the word, which often involves saying them aloud. This proposal, therefore, makes precise predictions about the form of the relationship between word length and the proportion of (relatively) fast reading responses which result from parallel letter identification processes. When the log probability of a correct response is plotted against word length, there should be a linear relationship passing through the origin, whose gradient represents p - the probability that an individual letter is misidentified.

Warrington and Shallice (1980) suggest that the letter-by-letter readers' deficit lies in the visual word form system. If some words' representations at this level remain intact then, for these items, fast parallel reading responses will be possible. Whether items remain intact at this level will be independent of word length, being instead a result of other lexical factors - perhaps word frequency. In this case then $C = k$, where k is a constant. Shallice and Saffran's (1986) argument that their subject, ML, has difficulty in accessing semantic representations from the visual word form system makes a similar prediction: the probability that semantic access is achieved will be a function of the variables affecting this defective procedure (e.g., word concreteness) and presumably independent of word length.

A different prediction is made by those accounts where word recognition depends on an obligatory sequential letter identification procedure; this prediction will, of course, be the same irrespective of the reasons why this serial strategy has to be adopted. Suppose that identifying each letter takes time t (standard deviation s). Then identifying all the letters of an n letter word, will take nt seconds (with a standard deviation $s\,n$). This linear relationship between mean reading latency and word length is what has classically been observed. We, however, are concerned only with the "fast" reading responses - those that occur in less than a criterion time. The precise form of this curve will depend on the values of the different parameters, but the general form of the relationship is that the probability of a correct response within a criterion time drops off very rapidly with word length. There are a number of ways in which a model of this kind might be made more sophisticated. The time needed to identify each letter (t) can be made a declining function of n to take account of the increasing redundancy of letters toward the end of longer words; the distribution of identification times for individual letters might be more accurately described by a Poisson rather than a normal distribution. The overall effects of such manipulations are not great; essentially all variants of this model predict that, at a latency where any nine letter word is read correctly, all three letter words will be easily and reliably correct.

The predictions of these three models for the relationship between C (the proportion of fast correct reading responses) and n (word length) are shown in Fig 2, where C is plotted on a logarithmic scale. It is clear that the predictions are radically different in form. It is less clear what criterion one should take to define a "fast" reading response. As a first approximation, in this chapter I shall consider all reading responses that occur in less than twice the shortest recorded latency in that experiment to be "fast," on the grounds that the operation of any compensatory strategy should take at least as long as processing the letters of a word in parallel. This procedure is obviously somewhat arbitrary; in the course of the chapter I will present a number of independent lines of evidence that suggest that this criterion is reasonable, although perhaps somewhat conservative.

5. Word Comprehension In Letter-by-Letter Reading

A number of reports have suggested that, on occasions, letter-by-letter readers may have access to some aspects of the meaning of words that they cannot report. Landis, Regard and Serrat (1980) claim that, on the sixth day after the onset of his illness, their letter-by-letter reader was able to demonstrate comprehension of written words, by selecting the appropriate item from an array of objects when the name was presented for only 30 ms. One name was read correctly, even with this exposure, but with the other seven items although the patient claimed to see nothing of the stimulus, he was able to select the correct object on five occasions. When Landis et al. tried to replicate this result in a repeat experiment twenty four days later, their subject no longer showed evidence of ability to understand words that he could not report.

Other investigators have also tested their subjects for evidence of comprehension of words presented at an exposure too brief to allow oral reading. Warrington and Shallice (1980) presented two sets of 50 object names to RAV at 500ms exposure; the patient was asked to report the word, if possible, and if not to select the corresponding picture from a choice of four. Interestingly RAV reported most of the words correctly (42/50 and 41/50), but he was at chance in selecting the picture when he failed to report the word (3/8 and 1/9, where chance is .25). Patterson and Kay (1982) conducted a more extensive series of tests of word comprehension in their letter-by-letter readers, asking their subjects to categorize items, and with one patient using a version of the Stroop (1938) test

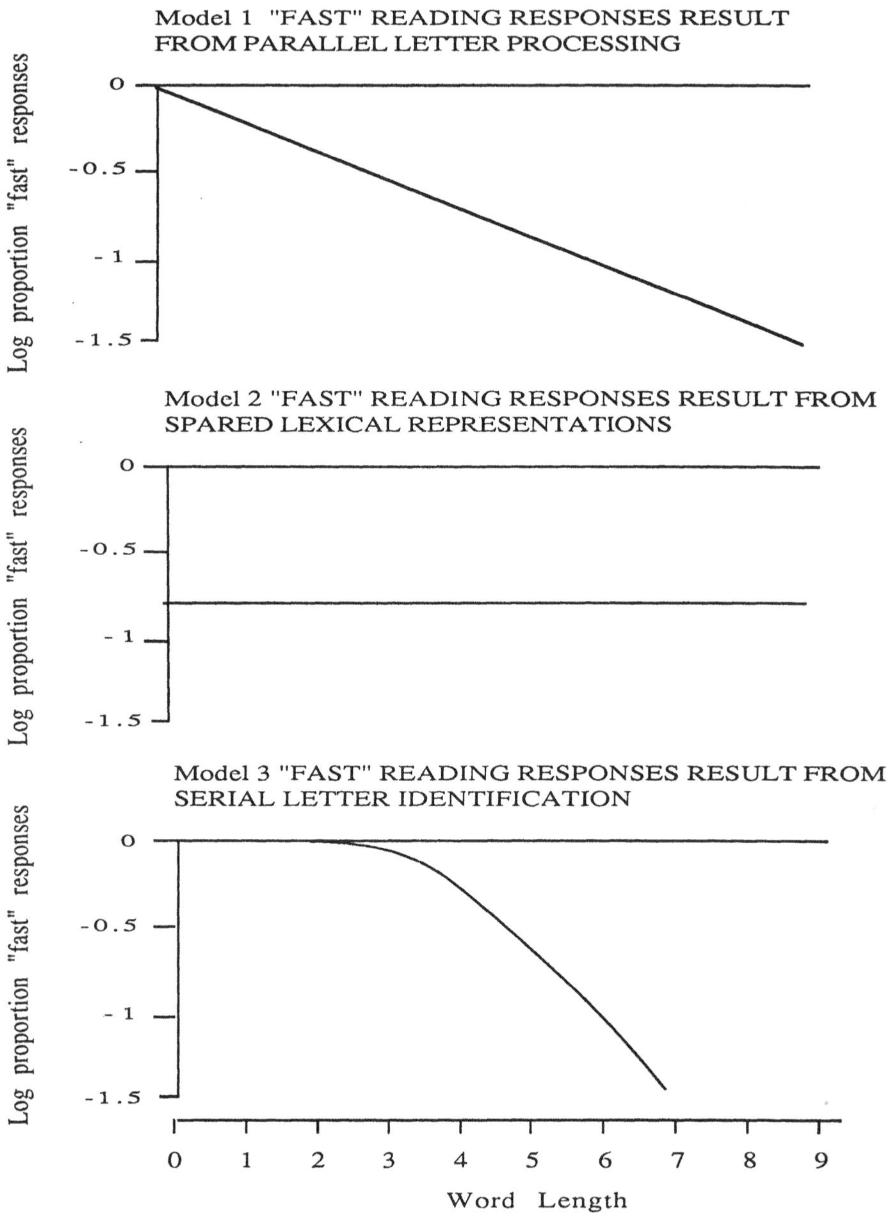

Figure 2. Predictions of three models for the distribution of "fast" reading responses in relation to word length.

to investigate whether written colour names could influence her speed of colour naming. Their results were uniformly negative. In no case was there any evidence that subjects had any knowledge of the meaning of words that they could not report. They could only find evidence of word comprehension when their patients were able to read the words aloud.

Shallice and Saffran (1986) used a binary classification task to study comprehension in their patient, ML. With lists of items he had to decide whether they were living or nonliving, whether they were the names of authors or politicians, whether they were names of places inside or outside Europe etc. When items were exposed for 2 seconds, ML was able to report only a small proportion of the words (varying from 0-28% across lists); he was however significantly better than chance in five of the seven lists in categorizing the items whose names he could not read. Shallice and Saffran interpret these results as evidence that, while ML relies on a (slow) letter-by-letter strategy for reading words aloud, he has some ability to understand the words using a different strategy in which the letters of the word are identified in parallel. As Shallice and Saffran acknowledge, their results do not provide unequivocal evidence for separate strategies for oral reading and comprehension. One potential problem is that the two second exposure was long enough for ML to read at least some words correctly; he may on other occasions have had enough information about the component letters in the word to constrain a forced choice classification response, without giving him confidence in the actual identity of the word. Patterson and Kay (1982) showed that their subject, TP, could sometimes categorize words correctly on the basis of knowledge of only one or two initial letters in the word. To exclude this possibility, Shallice and Saffran contrasted categorization with a procedure where ML was forced to guess the identity of the word. Although this forced guessing procedure raised his identification performance to 38% correct this was still substantially worse than his categorization (94%); Shallice and Saffran therefore argue that artifacts of this kind cannot explain ML's ability to categorize words that he could not identify.

Coslett and Saffran (1988) describe four further patients with a pattern of performance very similar to that shown by ML. In lexical decision with stimuli presented for only 250 ms, performance was better than chance. With similar exposure times the patients were able to categorize words as animals/non-animals, foods/non-foods or men's/women's names with levels of accuracy significantly better than chance. At this exposure duration the subjects could name very few of the words correctly (9% or less across experiments and subjects), and their categorization performance was just as good when these responses were excluded.

These results establish clearly that some (but not all) letter-by-letter readers know something of the meaning of words that they cannot identify. However it remains unclear whether access to word meaning in letter-by-letter readers depends on the same processes that are used to generate oral reading responses, or on a routine with different processing characteristics.

6. The Present Study

The experimental sections that follow describe a number of experiments with two letter-by-letter readers. In the first section, the relationship between word letter length and the incidence of "fast" responses in oral reading and lexical decision is examined to evaluate the hypothesis of parallel but inaccurate processing of the letters of the word. The next section explores the patients' ability to comprehend briefly presented words that cannot be explicitly identified. To establish whether the processing routines used in word identification are specific to tasks involving real words, the final section reports on the patients' ability to report the letters from briefly presented displays of strings of unrelated letters of different length.

II. CASE REPORTS

Patient PM. PM was a railway line maintenance worker aged 57 who, on September 22, 1982, developed double vision, slurred speech and unsteadiness. The next day he was unable to walk and was admitted to the hospital. On examination he was found to be drowsy, and dysarthric, with a left IIIrd nerve lesion. He had right facial weakness and a right cerebellar ataxia. He was hypertensive (BP 160/100). He was diagnosed as having suffered a mid-brain vascular lesion.

On January 4, 1983 he was transferred to a rehabilitation unit. On admission he was noted to have a moderate degree of hypertension. He still had a severe left oculomotor weakness, for which he wore a patch over the left eye. There was a marked right upper motor neurone facial weakness, and severe bilateral cerebellar ataxia. His muscle tone was flaccid, but power was normal. Both plantar responses were extensor. A CT scan on February 16, 1983 showed some generalized atrophy with enlarged ventricles and sulci and small focal lesions in both occipital lobes.

His improvement was limited and PM was discharged home in April 1983 still markedly ataxic and unable to walk unaided.

Tested in March 1983, on the WAIS, PM achieved a verbal IQ of 99; meaningful assessment of performance IQ was precluded by severe cerebellar ataxia and a mild visual agnosia. Assessment on the Boston Diagnostic Aphasia Examination (BDAE; Goodglass & Kaplan, 1972) showed no signs of aphasia, aside from a problem in visual word recognition, severe motor agraphia (which was probably attributable to his ataxia), and cerebellar dysarthria. On the Peabody Picture Vocabulary Test (Dunn, 1965) he scored 97/150 with spoken word presentation and 94/150 with written words. His digit span was normal (7 forward, 6 backward), but on Warrington's tests (Forced choice memory for faces (29/50), and Forced choice memory for words (30/50)), long term memory was severely impaired.

Cross case matching of letters was slow, but PM made no errors. In naming letters he achieved 49/52 (mean correct RT 1.6 secs) with upper case stimuli and 40/52 (mean correct RT 1.7 secs) with lower case. Word reading was not affected by word imageability (high imageability 19/28, mean correct RT 7.3 secs, low imageability 18/28, mean correct RT 7.7 secs), or spelling-to-sound regularity (regular words 30/39, mean correct RT 5.1 secs, irregular words 29/39; mean correct RT 4.7 secs; stimulus sets from Coltheart, 1980a).

The "Pyramids and Palm Trees" Test (Howard & Patterson, unpublished) involves conceptual matching of pictures; thus a picture of a "pyramid" has to be matched to a picture of a "palm tree" or a picture of a "pine tree," or a picture of a "kennel" is matched to a "cat" or a "dog." Normal subjects score 49/52 or better; PM scored 39/52, which is consistent with some degree of visual agnosia. On the Southern California Visual-Ground Discrimination Test, which involves identification of superimposed pictures, he scored 16 which is a normal score for an 8 year old; to the extent that identifying superimposed pictures involves simultaneous object identification, this suggests that PM cannot be severely simultanagnosic.

PM sometimes said the letters of a word aloud while reading it; his reading responses were generally accurate. On a set of 100 words he read 91 aloud correctly. Of these words he spelled 86 aloud. By comparison, his ability to recognize words spelled aloud by the examiner was poor; he managed only 65 correct.

The experiments reported here were performed between February 7 and March 10, 1983.

Patient KW. KW is a 61 year old consultant engineer with a history of diabetes and hypertension, who suffered a CVA in the distribution of the left posterior cerebral artery on December 24, 1986. During the night he felt that "there was an explosion" in his head, and the following day he noticed right sided visual problems, and some clumsiness and numbness in the left arm and leg. The problems with the arm and leg resolved rapidly.

Neurological examination four months later showed that KW was hypertensive (blood pressure 150/90). There was a "rather incomplete" right homonymous hemianopia, slight clumsiness in fine finger movements in both hands with brisk normal reflexes and equivocal plantar responses. He read letter-by-letter, but had no dysgraphia or problems in language comprehension. A CT scan showed "moderate atrophic changes" and an infarct in the left occipital region, with "small lacuna infarcts in the lentiform nuclei bilaterally."

Language evaluation showed that KW had some degree of word retrieval problem; he scored 37/60 on the Boston Naming Test (Kaplan, Goodglass & Weintraub, 1976) and 66/100 on the Hundred picture naming test (see Howard & Franklin, 1988); both scores are below the normal range. His errors were mostly semantic (e.g., DUCK ---> "a hen or the chicken or the goose or the crow"), or visual (e.g., ROPE ---> "oh this is like the snake"), although some responses had a confabulatory air (e.g., FOUNTAIN ---> "a water display unit in a decorative garden of some description"). Naming showed a significant effect of word frequency. A difficulty in picture recognition was confirmed by poor performance in picture matching in the Pyramids and Palm Trees Test (45/52; Howard & Patterson, unpublished). On the PVT he scored 131/150 with auditory presentation, corresponding to the 91st percentile in the American norms. On Coltheart's (1980a) synonym judgment test, KW made no errors with pairs of concrete and abstract words with auditory presentation. Sentence comprehension was slightly impaired; on Bishop's Test for the Reception of Grammar he scored 74/80 with spoken and 72/80 with written sentences. His digit span was unimpaired (8 digits forward). Spelling was generally accurate although there were some letter substitutions and omissions with longer words (e.g., "expense" ---> EXPANSE; "physician" ---> PHYSIAN). He scored 29/36 on Raven's Coloured Progressive Matrices.

Letter naming was fairly accurate although slow: upper case 25/26 mean RT 1.2 secs, lower case 25/26 mean RT 1.3 secs. Oral reading as letter-by-letter, with a strong relationship between word length and oral reading latency (analyzed in detail below). Single syllable nonword reading was good (13/15). On Coltheart's (1980a) word sets there was no effect of spelling-to-sound regularity (regular words 36/39, mean correct RT 8.0 secs, irregular words 35/39, RT 8.6 secs), but there was a trend toward better performance on high imageability words (27/28, mean correct RT 3.59 secs) than low imageability words (24/28, mean correct RT 5.64 secs). Testing with a larger word set (matched for frequency and length) confirmed a significant difference (high imageability words 77/80, 2.8 secs; low imageability 70/80, 6.1 secs; rts differ significantly $t(145) = 5.06$, $p < .001$). There was also a significant effect of word frequency: with sets matched for imageability and length, words with frequencies 50-150 wpm 43/45, mean correct RT 4.5 secs, words with frequencies 10-25 wpm 68/75, mean correct RT 7.3 secs (rts differ significantly, $t(110) = 2.14$, $p < .02$).

III. THE ORIGINS OF "FAST" READING RESPONSES

1. Experiment 1: Reading Latencies and Word Length

Method

In each experiment 100 words were presented for oral reading. There were 25 words of 3, 5, 7 and 9 letters in length; the lists were matched for word frequency (from the Kucera & Francis, 1967, word count) and rated imageability (from the MRC Psycholinguistic Database, Coltheart, 1981). The items were presented in lower case on a VDU screen in random order, preceded by an auditory bleep and two crosses at either end of where the word was to appear. Reaction times were recorded by the experimenter pressing a key when the patient produced a reading response. Attempts to use a voice key to record reaction times were abandoned because the subjects would frequently trigger the key prematurely when reading the words letter-by-letter. This method of manual recording of reaction times was validated in a control experiment. Synthetic speech reading responses were produced by the computer with random latencies whose distribution approximated to the distribution of the patients' reading responses. The correlation between true reaction times and manually recorded reaction times was very high ($r(99) = 0.998$); there was a delay of 370 ms in the manual reaction times. All manually recorded reaction times presented in this chapter have been corrected for this delay.

Results

Patient PM undertook this experiment on two separate occasions with different lists, and KW once only. The proportion of correct reading responses for words of each length are shown in Table 1. For both patients reading accuracy is independent of word length. However, as the data in Figure 3 show there is a striking relationship between word length and mean correct reading latency. In each case the correlation is significant (PM list 1, $r(77) = 0.450$, $p <.01$; list 2, $r(87) = 0.407$, $p < .001$; KW, $r(89) = 0.212$, $p < .05$). By comparison with normal subjects these latencies are extraordinarily large. These means, however, conceal even greater variability; on occasions these subjects can take more than one minute to produce a correct reading response for a word.

However, as I argued in the Introduction, these very long latencies are not particularly informative about these patients' reading processes. Figure 4 presents data on "fast" reading responses. Responses here were calculated by taking a cut off equal to twice the shortest reaction time and computing the porportion of correct responses made within this cut off for each word length. The data are plotted on a logarithmic scale.

Inspection of the results in Fig 4 and comparison with the predictions in Fig 2 supports three conclusions: (a) The hypothesis that "fast" reading responses represent the fastest of the responses produced by a serial letter identification procedure predicts that the graph should start relatively flat and then fall off very steeply as in the bottom of Fig 2. The data in Fig 4 clearly do not conform to this pattern, so this hypothesis can be rejected. (b) The hypothesis that "fast" correct reading responses are due to some representations that remain intact within a disrupted visual word form system (assuming that the probability that a representation is intact is independent of word length) predicts that the proportion of "fast" responses will be independent of stimulus word length (see the middle of Fig 2). Again the data in Fig 4 show that the proportion of "fast" responses declines with stimulus length. These responses cannot then be easily accounted for by the hypothesis that some representations in a visual word form system remain intact. (c) When plotted on a logarithmic scale, the proportion of "fast" correct reading responses is captured accurately by a straight line through the origin. This is the pattern predicted by the hypothesis that a deficit in the

Table 1
Effects of Word Length on Oral Reading (25 words of each length: matched for word frequency and imageability).

Word length	PM 7.2.1983		PM 10.3.1983		KW 30.4.1987	
	pcorr	RT	pcorr	RT	pcorr	RT
3	80	3.72	1.0	2.33	.84	4.15
5	.80	7.62	.80	2.93	.92	4.80
7	.76	14.13	.80	3.32	.96	6.24
9	.76	16.13	.92	5.89	.92	6.35

(pcorr = proportion of correct responses; RT= mean correct reaction time in seconds)

processes of letter recognition is responsible for the reading disorder in these patients, and "fast" reading responses result from parallel processing of the constituent letters in the word (see the top of Fig 2). In these linear plots the gradient of the fitted line corresponds to the logarithm of the probability p that any individual letter is correctly identified. This gives estimated values of p for PM of 0.68 in experiment 1 and 0.75 in experiment 2, and 0.74 for KW.

2. Validating the Criterion

The predictions tested in this experiment depend on identifying "fast" reading responses. By the standards of normal skilled readers even the fastest responses recorded in these experiments are inordinately slow.

Figure 5 shows the results from the first experiment with PM and from the experiment with KW of varying the criterion for "fast" responses. As can be seen, the general shape of the graph is very similar for a wide range of criterion times. The pattern of results in this experiment are robust and therefore not an artifact of the choice of a particular criterion. Similar results can be found varying the criterion with other data sets. I argued that responses in which words are read letter-by-letter are the result of a compensatory strategy, which takes longer than letter identification in parallel. One of the subjects, KW,

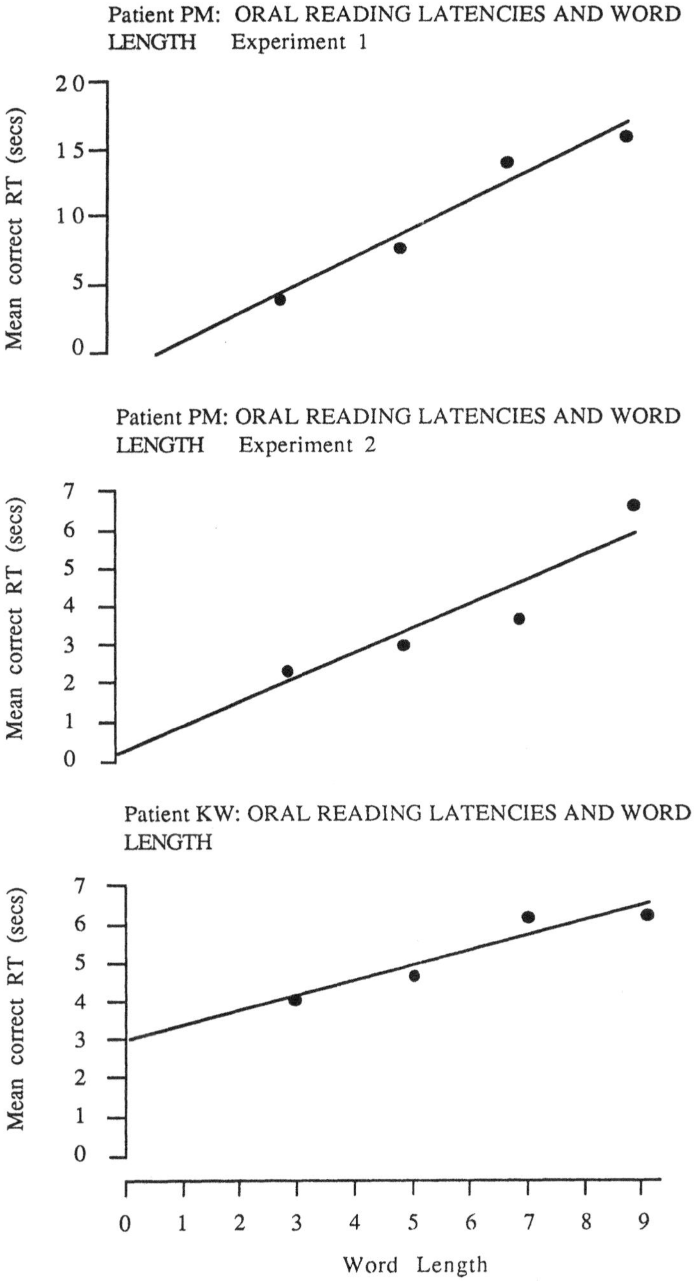

Figure 3. Mean reading times and word length.

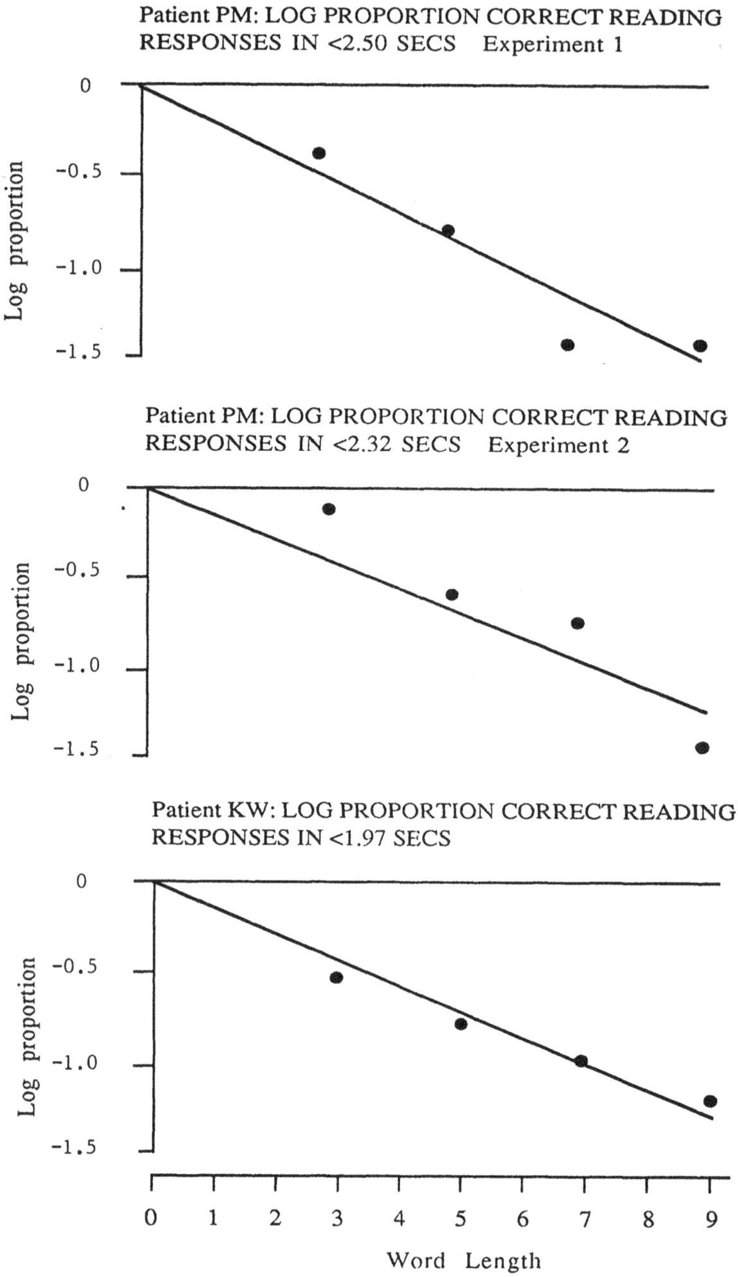

Figure 4. "Fast" reading responses and word length.

frequently named letters aloud before producing a reading response. Figure 6 shows the distribution of reading times for correct responses where one or more letters were said aloud, compared to responses where no letters were named overtly. Letter-by-letter responses are clearly slower than those where no letters were said aloud. The fastest letter-by-letter response took 2.00 secs, and this was the only response that fell within the criterion. It is, therefore, clear that, by adopting this criterion, responses that result from a serial letter identification strategy were successfully excluded.

3. Experiment 2: Lexical Decision Latencies and Word Length.

On the basis of the results in the previous experiment, I argued that "fast" correct reading responses depended on a parallel letter identification process. Where this process yields a sequence of letters that make a nonword, a compensatory strategy of serial letter identification has to be adopted. In visual lexical decision, where parallel processes identify a real word, the patient can produce a "yes" response. Where the letter sequence specifies a nonword, the patient will not know whether this is because the stimulus is a real word in which one or more letters have been misidentified, or because the stimulus really is a nonword. To resolve this uncertainty the subject will be obliged to adopt the serial compensatory strategy. On this basis, one can make three predictions:

1. As in oral word reading, the logarithm of the proportion of fast correct "yes" responses will be a linear function of word length.
2. There will be very few "fast" correct "no" responses to nonwords, but there may be fast false positives.
3. Correct "no" responses will be slower than correct "yes" responses. And, because, under this hypothesis letter identification processes are disrupted, lexical decision performance will be poor.

Method

The patients were presented in random order with the 100 real words of list 1 in the previous experiment, and 100 pronounceable nonwords derived from them by substitution of a single letter. KW responded by pressing a key with either hand to indicate his responses. PM, whose ataxia precluded accurate key presses, responded verbally and the experimenter pressed a key; his reaction times have been adjusted to allow for this.

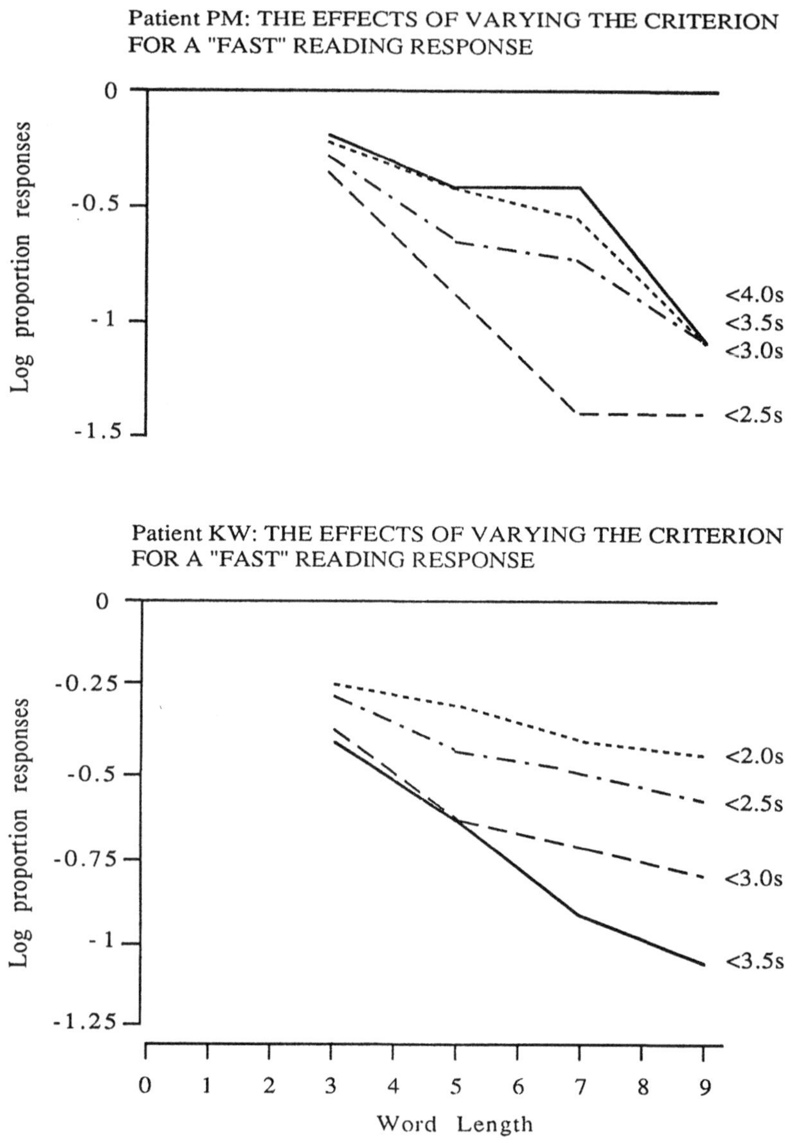

Figure 5. The distribution of "fast" reading responses; the effect of changing the criterion for selection of "fast" responses.

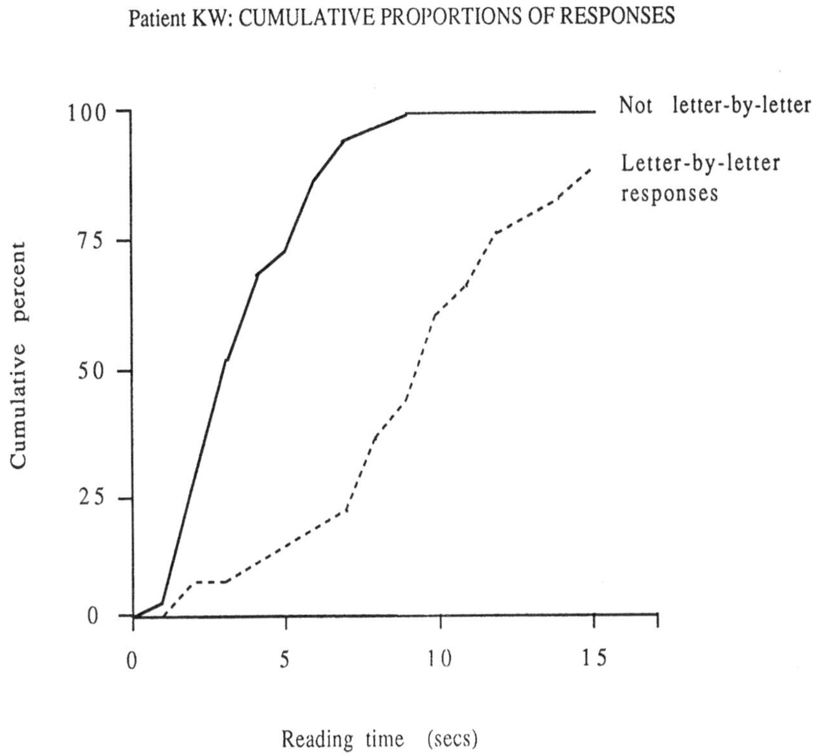

Figure 6. The distribution of reading times for letter-by-letter responses and those where no letters were overtly named.

Results

The relationship between correct responses and letter length is shown in Table 2. For both patients accuracy is poor; in particular there is a very high rate of false positives with nonwords. This supports the proposal that there is a real letter identification problem for these patients.

The relationship between mean reaction times for correct responses and stimulus length is shown in Figure 7. Analysis of these reaction times in a multiple regression model shows that there is an overall effect of stimulus length on RTs (patient PM, $F(1, 146) = 13.17$, $p < .001$; patient KW, $F(1, 176) = 8.05$, $p < .01$), and rejection of nonwords takes longer than acceptance of real words (PM: $F(1, 145) = 83.71$, $p < .001$; KW: $F(1, 175) = 25.50$, $p < .001$), but for neither patient is there a significant interaction between stimulus length and response type (PM: $F(1, 144) = 1.65$, ns; KW: $F(1, 174) = 0.92$, ns). This supports the prediction that "no" responses, which have to result from a serial letter identification strategy, will be slower than "yes" responses.

Table 2
Lexical Decision and Word Length (25 words and nonwords of each length).

	PM				KW			
Word	Real words		Nonwords		Real words		Nonwords	
length	pcorr	RT	pcorr	RT	pcorr	RT	pcorr	RT
3	.92	3.02	.64	8.05	1.0	3.29	.80	6.61
5	.98	4.12	.60	9.30	.96	4.41	.92	9.53
7	.76	3.82	.52	8.44	1.0	5.11	.76	10.21
9	.84	5.90	.68	13.21	.84	7.38	.84	8.63

(pcorr = proportion of correct responses; RT = mean correct RT (secs))

The critical prediction concerned the relationship between the proportions of "fast" correct responses and word length. As is shown in Figure 8, these are accurately described by the equation $\log(C) = n\log p$, where p corresponds to the probability of identifying each letter correctly. The fitted lines give estimated values of $p = 0.78$ for PM and 0.81 for KW.

The final prediction was that there should be very few correct "no" responses which fell within the criterion. For PM only 2 of his correct "no" responses took less than 2.54 seconds, both with three letter nonwords. Of his 39 false positives, 10 were within the criterion (2 with seven letter stimuli, 3 with five letters, and five with three letters). For KW 4/83 correct rejections took less than the criterion of 1.72 secs (1 with 7 letter stimuli, 2 with 5, and 1 with 3 letter nonwords). Of his 17 false positives, 4 were less than the criterion (1 with 9 letters, 2 with 7, and 1 with 5 letters). For both subjects, then, a much higher proportion of false positives fall within the criterion, than correct rejections; fast correct "no" responses are infrequent.

Conclusion

The pattern of performance in lexical decision supports the conclusion from the first experiment; the results are consistent with a parallel letter identification procedure where there is a finite probability that letters will be misidentified. Serial letter identification represents only a compensatory strategy.

IV. WORD COMPREHENSION

1. Experiment 3: Cued Word Definition

This experiment investigates whether brief presentation of a cue word can bias the definition of a polysemous word. Thus, for example, the patients were presented with the written word PALM to define, preceded, briefly, by either the word TREE or the word HAND. Evidence that the cue biased definition of the word would show that the patient had access to the meaning of the cue. This is a technique first used with normal subjects by Bradshaw (1974) in an investigation of biasing of word comprehension by peripherally presented cues

Fifty ambiguous words were presented in the same order in two separate sessions. In each session the word was preceded by a cue word intended to give a bias toward one meaning of the word. Thus CROSS was cued with ANGRY in session 1 and with CHURCH in session 2; MATCH by FLAME and GAME; and BULB by FLOWER or LIGHT. After an auditory and visual warning, the cue word appeared in the center of the screen for a brief period, and it was then overwritten by the target word, which remained in full view until the patient responded. The patient's task was to read the target word and say what it meant; when more than one definition was produced, the first definition was scored. With PM the cue was presented for 150 ms, and with KW 250ms.

The first definition response was classified into whether it corresponded to the cue given in session A, to the cue given in session B, or to some other meaning, whether correct or incorrect. The patients were encouraged to report any words they saw. At no point did either report any of the cue words. At the end of the second session they were asked whether they had noticed anything odd about the way the words in the experiment had been presented; even when pressed, they both said that they had noticed nothing. The presence of the cue word was then explained to them, and they were shown some of the stimuli again. Again the patients both denied that they could see the cue words at all. The stimuli were then presented with the cues presented for longer and longer durations; neither patient said that they had any idea of the existence of the cue until it was presented for over one second. It seems, therefore, that the cue words were stimuli which the patients were genuinely unaware of, and were unable to report.

The two subjects' definition responses are given in Table 3. Over the two sessions PM gave 38 responses that corresponded to the cue which had been presented, and 34 which corresponded to the other cue. There is no evidence

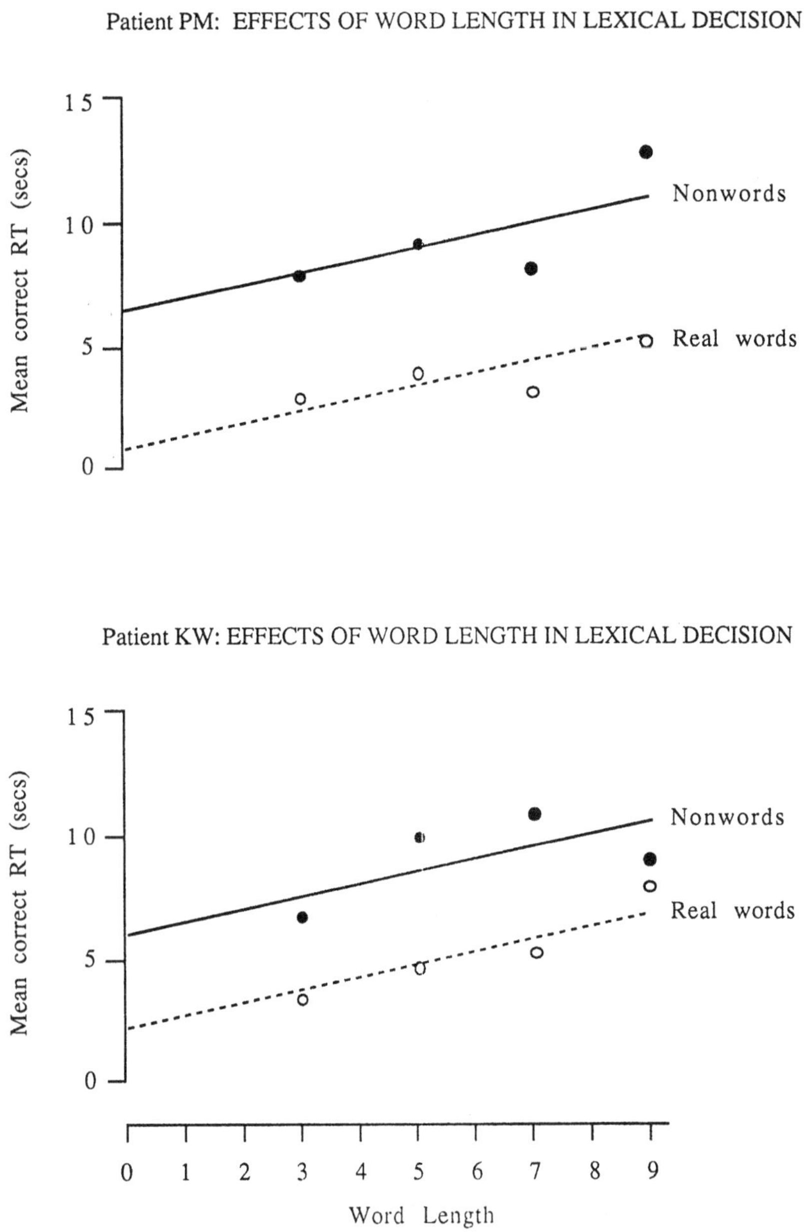

Figure 7. Mean reaction times for correct lexical decisions and stimulus length.

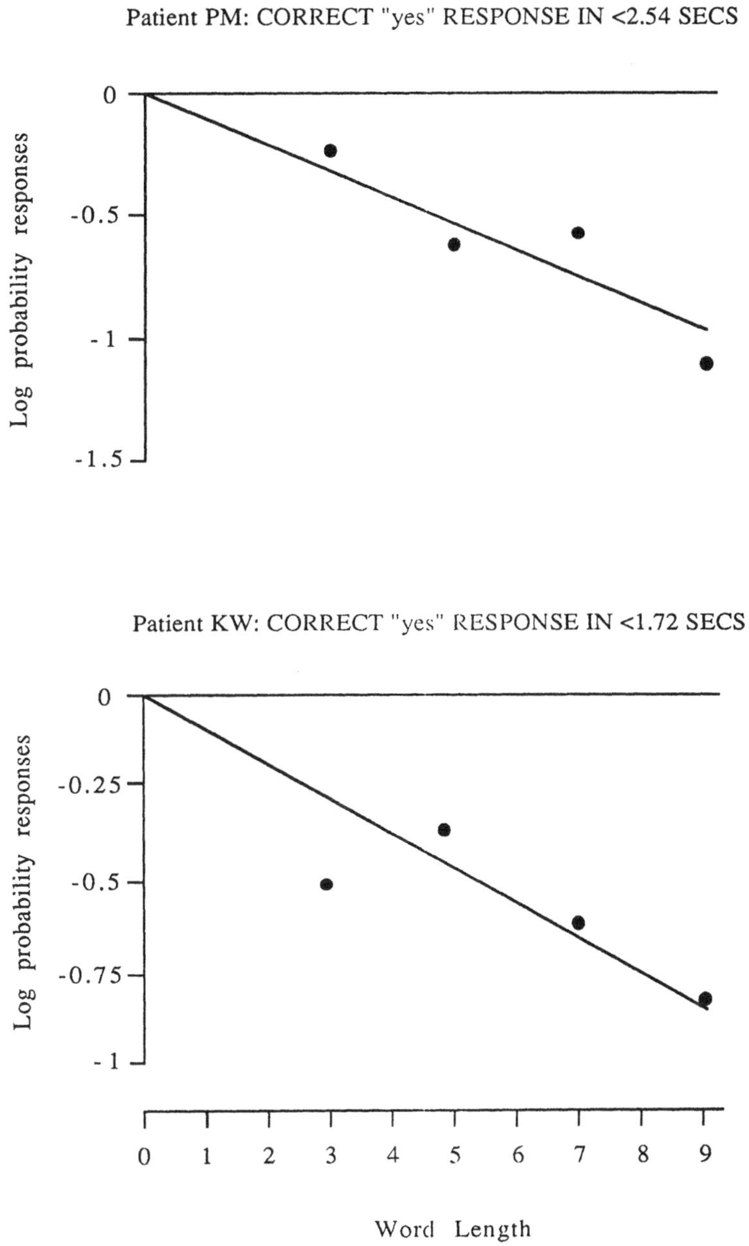

Figure 8. The distribution of "fast" correct "yes" lexical decisions and word length.

that, for PM, brief presentation of the cue word masked by subsequent presentation of the target word, could bias his definition response.

The results for KW are very different. Of his responses, over the two sessions, 56 were in accordance with the cued meaning, and only 6 corresponded to the other cue word. Over the set of items there is a significant tendency for the cue words to bias his definition responses (sign test, 15:3, p = .004, one tailed).

Table 3
Cued Word Definition . (Definition A means the word was defined according to the meaning primed by the cue in session A; numbers of responses).

	Read Correctly			Read Incorrectly
	Defn. A	Defn. B	Other defn.	
PM				
Session A	13	18	6	13
Session B	16	25	3	6
KW				
Session A	25	19	3	3
Session B	17	31	1	1

2. Experiment 4: Word Recognition

2.1. Experiment 4A: patient PM

Experiment 3 suggests that PM does not have access to the meaning of words that he cannot report. In that experiment he was asked to define words, where the cues were effectively masked by subsequent presentation of the target word. In this experiment, he was asked to categorize a set of words presented for 200 ms, as living (e.g., DOCTOR, TROUT, WILLOW) or non-living (e.g., WINDOW, STAIR, BOTTLE); the stimuli were those used by Patterson and Kay (1982) with their patient MW. In order to assess whether there were differences between presentation to the left and right visual fields, the tests were presented in two separate sessions. On each occasion half the items were presented to the LVF and PM had to make a pointing response with the left hand and the other half were presented to the RVF and PM responded with the right hand. Pointing responses were to a small group of toys representing living things (a model man, cow and flower) and nonliving things (a model train, gun and house).

The results were straightforward. PM never reported a word at all, and said that sometimes he was completely unaware of the stimulus (which had been preceded by both a visual and auditory warning). He said that he was guessing; the results show that this was indeed so. With left visual field visual presentation,

PM categorized 30/60 items correctly, and with right visual field presentation 31/60 (chance is 30/60). With 200 ms presentation, there is no evidence that PM has any access to a word's meaning.

2.2. Experiment 4B: Patient KW

Experiment 3 suggested that KW was unaware of a cue word presented for 250ms, when masked by the subsequent target word, but its meaning influenced his definition responses. If KW's comprehension of the cue word in that experiment is mediated by the same mechanisms that are responsible for "fast" responses in word reading, we should predict that their incidence will be a function of word length. If, on the other hand, as Shallice and Saffran (1986) and Coslett and Saffran (1988) speculate, they reflect a different routine for word comprehension, we would not expect to find the same relationship with word length.

KW was, therefore, presented with 92 words varying from 3 to 11 letters in length, half were the names of animals (e.g., rattlesnake, haddock, fox) and half the names of objects (e.g., thermometer, racquet, map). The names were, as far as possible, matched for imageability and word frequency across the lengths, but the set sizes at different lengths were limited by the items with imageability values in the MRC Psycholinguistic Database (Coltheart, 1981). The words were presented in random order for 250 ms following an auditory and visual cue followed by a ######## mask. KW's task was to report the word, if possible, and then to say whether it was an animal or object.

The results are shown in Table 4. KW was able to read a surprisingly large proportion of the words: 69/92 were reported correctly, and all of these were correctly categorized. The proportion of items correctly named declines with increasing length (Jonckheere trend test, $z = 3.27, p < .001$), and, as Figure 9 shows, the log proportion of words of each length read correctly is directly related to their length. Estimating the probability that each letter is correctly identified (p) from the gradient of the best fitted straight line gives $p = 0.87$. KW's reading responses in this task, with brief, masked stimulus presentation, is therefore probably mediated by the same mechanisms responsible for his "fast" reading responses, with unlimited stimulus exposure. When KW did not report the word, he categorized 17/23 words correctly; this is significantly better than chance (Binomial test, $p < .05$). This confirms the result of experiment 4; KW has access to (some aspects of) the meaning of words which he cannot report. Four of his six errors in categorization occur with words of eight letters or more; this suggests that comprehension errors may, like reading errors, be more likely to occur with longer words. Unfortunately KW makes so many correct

Table 4
Patient KW; Reading of Names of Animals and Objects Presented for 250 ms Followed By a ##### Mask. Categorization Performance for Words Not Read Correctly.

Length	Read correctly	Categorized
11	2/6	2/4
9	5/8	2/3
8	6/10	3/4
7	9/12	3/3
5	21/28	5/7
3	26/28	2/2

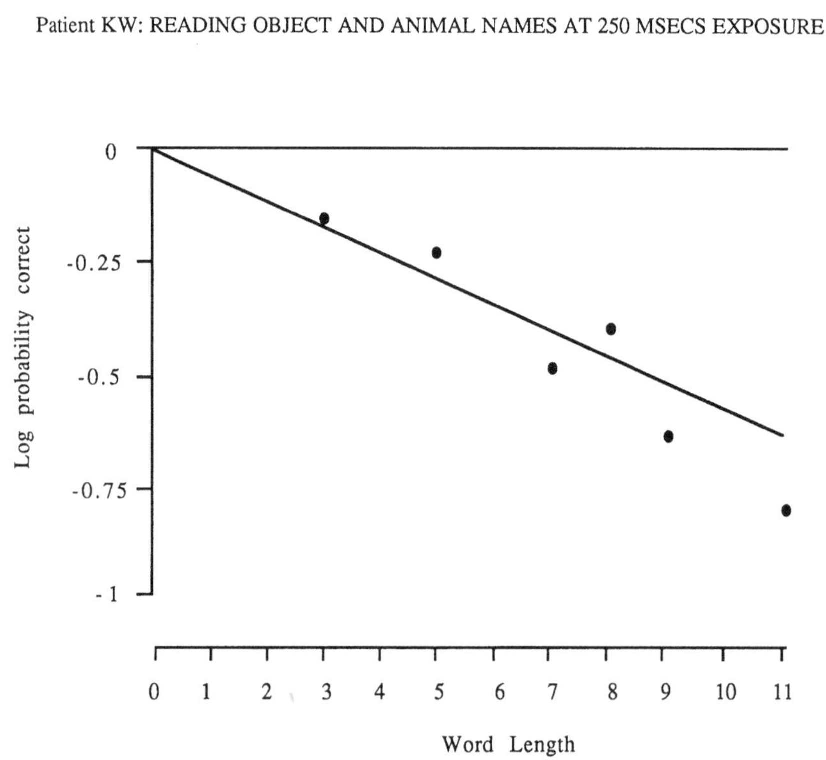

Figure 9. Reading animal and object names with 250 ms masked exposure.

reading responses, and so few categorization errors that it is not possible to be sure whether there is or is not a relationship between categorization and word length.

3. Comment on Experiments 3 and 4

The two patients were similar to each other in oral word reading; both read letter-by-letter on some occasions, both show increasing mean latencies as a function of word length, and both show "fast" reading responses whose incidence is related to stimulus length.

In terms of the comprehension experiments they are very different. PM often says that he does not see a stimulus presented for 200 ms, and shows no evidence of any knowledge of the meaning of briefly presented words.

KW, on the other hand, was biased in word definition by cue words presented for 250 ms, even though he was apparently unaware of their existence. He is even able to report a substantial proportion of words presented for only 250 ms followed by a mask, and even when he does not read the word correctly he is better than chance at categorizing it. There is no evidence, however, against the hypothesis that the same mechanism, in which letters are recognized in parallel with a finite probability of error, is responsible for his fast responses in all tasks, including categorization.

I argued that, underlying both patients' letter-by-letter reading, there was a difficulty in letter identification, without being, in any way explicit about the nature of this difficulty. In the next section, therefore, I describe some experiments which explore the patients' ability to report not words but random strings of letters.

V. REPORT OF LETTERS

1. Experiment 5: Report of Random Letter Strings

In order to explore further whether these patients have difficulties in letter recognition, and to distinguish between some possible causes of difficulty, they were presented with strings of 1, 2 or 4 random letters for 120, 250, 500 or 1000 ms. To establish whether they could detect briefly presented letter stimuli, on 25% of trials no letters were presented. The patients were asked to report as many letters as possible when there was a stimulus, and to say whether or not a stimulus had been presented.

Kinsbourne and Warrington's (1962) simultanagnosic patients were able to report a single letter reliably with unmasked presentation of as little as 10 ms, but could not report both of a pair of letters even with presentation times as long as

1000 ms. If PM and KW show simultanagnosia of this kind, they should be able to report a single letter without difficulty, but show poor performance with the longer strings.

If letter recognition is simply slowed, performance should improve with longer presentation times but be independent of the length of the strings.

Both these subjects show some mild degree of right visual inattention. If this is a limiting factor in their performance with random letter strings they should have difficulty with the letters in the second half. Thus, performance will be poor with the second letter of a two item string, and the third and fourth letters in a four item string. Report of the first letter of these longer strings should be comparable to the accuracy of report of a single letter.

A further possibility is that these patients' ability to recognize letters is limited by an abnormal sensitivity to lateral masking (cf. Bouma, 1978). If this is the case, both letters in two item strings should be reported somewhat worse than a single letter since the two letters will mask each other. With four letter strings, the first and last item (which are masked by only a single neighbouring letter) should be reported with comparable accuracy to the letters in a two item string. The second and third letters (which each have two masking neighbours) should be relatively poorly reported.

The patients were presented with 10 strings of each of the three lengths at each of the four durations. On an additional 40 otherwise identical trials no letters were presented. The letters were drawn at random from a set of 22 (omitting M, W, Q, D which PM was particularly likely to misname), and presented in upper case. To minimize effects of lateral masking the letters were presented with a single space between each one. Stimuli were presented in random order, preceded by an auditory warning, and a pair of Xs on the screen indicating the stimulus location. PM was tested once, and KW twice. KW's results are the mean across the two sessions.

Results

(a) Detection of the stimulus. Neither patient ever reported the presence of a stimulus on the catch trials where no stimulus was presented. KW always correctly reported the presence of a stimulus. PM, on the other hand, missed 13/120 stimuli. Their distribution is shown in the upper part of Table 5. Misses are most likely to occur with stimuli of short duration (Jonckheere trend test, z = 2.98, $p < .01$), but are unrelated to the length of the string.

(b) Letter report accuracy. The patients' ability to report the letters is shown in the middle part of Table 5. For PM the number of letters correctly reported increases gradually with presentation duration (Jonckheere trend test, z = 5.23, $p < .001$). With increasing string length he reports more letters, although the overall proportion which are reported correctly declines. Interestingly, with the shortest exposure duration of 120 ms, PM reports less letters from the longer strings. This suggests that his ability to recognize letters may be affected by the presence of other letters. He is not obviously simultanagnosic; even at 120 ms he reports both letters from a two letter string on two trials. The gradual

improvement in performance with increasing exposure time suggests that the primary limitation in this task is slowed letter recognition.

KW also shows improving performance with increasing presentation time (Jonckheere trend test, $z = 2.77, p < .005$); however this is entirely due to better performance with 1000 ms presentation. Even with the longest exposure duration he never reports all the items from a four letter string, unlike PM who manages 3/10 at 1000 ms. This is a striking contrast to his performance in experiment 4b where he was reading words as long as 11 letters when presented masked for only 250 ms. Over the whole experiment KW reports less letters from strings of four letters than strings of two (72.5/80 vs. 64.5/160); this is primarily due to performance at 120 and 250 ms duration. This suggests that for KW, in a similar way to PM, ability to identify letters is worse in longer strings. Unlike PM, KW is reasonably accurate with two letter strings, even at 120 ms presentation, which shows that he is not in the classical simultanagnosic.

(c) Serial position effects. The accuracy of report over different positions combined across presentation duration is shown for both patients in the bottom part of Table 5. For PM, accuracy with the first letter declines with increasing string length (Jonckheere trend test, $z = 3.64, p < .001$) confirming that letter recognition is affected by the length of the string. With four item strings his accuracy declines gradually across positions which indicates that this difficulty cannot be attributed to lateral masking. His accuracy on the second letter of a two letter string is as good as on the first letter of a four item string indicating that his performance cannot be attributed to inattention to the second half of the stimulus.

Like PM, KW's accuracy with the first letter declines significantly across stimulus length (Jonckheere trend test, $z = 3.54, p < .001$), showing that letter identification is poorer in longer stimuli. That he is worse with the first two items of a four letter string than with the second item of a two letter string rules out an explanation in terms of right visual inattention. With four item strings his accuracy declines very steeply across positions showing that his difficulties cannot be attributed to lateral masking.

2. Comment

Both patients performed poorly in reporting briefly presented strings of letters. Neither subject showed the classical pattern of simultanagnosia, and in neither case were the results consistent with an explanation in terms of inattention to the right visual hemifield, nor with lateral masking by neighboring letters. In both patients recognition accuracy, as indicated by report of the first letter, declined with increasing string length, suggesting that ability to recognize letters is affected by the presence of other letters.

Table 5
Report of Strings of Random Letters, With String Length Varying From 1 to 4 Letters, and Exposure Duration Varying From 120-1000 ms Unmasked.

(i) Stimuli missed: Patient PM (max is 10 in each cell).

	Exposure duration (ms)				
No. of letters	120	250	500	1000	Total
1	2	1	0	0	3
2	4	2	0	1	7
4	2	0	0	1	3
Total	8	3	0	2	13

(ii) Number of letters correctly reported (max = 10 for length 1, 20 length 2, 40 length 4). Strings correct in parentheses.

Patient PM

	Exposure duration (ms)				
# of letters	120	250	500	1000	Total
1	8 (8)	8 (8)	9 (9)	10 (10)	35 (35)
2	6 (2)	10 (4)	15 (6)	13 (5)	44 (17)
4	4 (0)	11 (0)	15 (1)	24 (3)	54 (4)
Total	18 (10)	29 (12)	39 (16)	47 (18)	133 (56)

Patient KW (mean of two sessions)

	Exposure duration (ms)				
# of letters	120	250	500	1000	Total
1	10 (10)	9.5 (9.5)	10 (10)	10 (10)	39.5 (39.5)
2	18.5 (8.5)	18 (8)	16.5 (6.5)	19.5 (9.5)	72.5 (32.5)
4	13 (0)	13 (0)	16 (0)	22.5 (0)	64.5 (0)
Total	41.5 (18.5)	40.5 (17.5)	42.5 (16.5)	52 (19.5)	176.5 (72)

(iii) Serial position effect: probability of correct report of letters (n = 40 in each cell; combined across durations).

	1 letter	2 letters		4 letters			
Position	1	1	2	1	2	3	4
Patient PM	.88	.63	.48	.48	.40	.30	.18
Patient KW	.99	.96	.85	.85	.59	.13	.05

In other ways the patients were rather different. PM's performance improves steadily with increasing exposure time, suggesting that, for him letter recognition processes are very much slowed, but with enough time he can manage to report all four letters in the stimulus. KW's performance was independent of stimulus duration over the range from 120 to 500 ms, and unlike PW he never reports all four letters in a string. This suggests that he is able to establish a reasonably durable perceptual representation even from a brief presentation, but that recognition of the component letters is impaired, primarily by interference from the presence of the other letters in the string.

3. Experiment 6: Report of Letters in Real Words, Pseudowords, and Nonwords

In Experiment 4b, KW was able to read aloud a substantial proportion of words presented for 250 ms with a pattern mask. In Experiment 5 he failed on any occasion to identify all four letters in a random string presented for 1000 ms with no pattern mask. There are two possible kinds of explanation for this remarkable difference: (a) As in normal subjects, letter recognition in real words is very much better than letter recognition in random letter strings, or (b) when asked to report letters KW adopts a slow and impaired strategy of serial letter recognition, unlike the fast parallel letter recognition procedure, which I have already demonstrated KW can use in word reading.

Normal subjects are better at reporting letters in real words than "pseudowords" (i.e., pronounceable nonwords) (the word superiority effect (WSE); cf. Henderson, 1982). They are similarly, and somewhat more reliably better at reporting letters in pseudowords than in unpronounceable strings (henceforth "nonwords") (the pseudoword superiority effect (PSE)). Most of the experimental data on this difference has adopted the Reicher-Wheeler paradigm, where the subject has to make a forced choice between two alternatives for the identity of a letter in a particular position in a briefly presented stimulus (see Henderson, 1982 for a review). However as McClelland (1976) demonstrates, the same PSE and WSE can be found when subjects are asked to report as many letters as they can from a stimulus. This is the approach adopted in this experiment.

There were 56 real words, half of which had three letters and half of which had four. Half of each of these sets were of high imageability words (e.g., GOAT, GYM) and half were low imageability (e.g., PROP, VOW); the sets were matched item-by-item for Kucera and Francis (1967) word frequency. Fifty six pseudowords were generated from these by rearrangement of the letters between words (e.g., GEAD, JOW) and 56 unpronounceable nonwords by a further rearrangement of the letters (e.g., DGAE, WJO). There were no repeated letters in any stimuli.

Better report of letters in real words than pseudowords (i.e., a WSE) will indicate that KW can use lexical information to improve letter recognition. Since he is better at reading high imageability than low imageability words, superior report of letters in high imageability words will suggest that top-down information from a semantic level can aid letter recognition. Better performance on pseudowords than nonwords (i.e., a PSE) will show that KW can use constraints on letter sequences to aid letter recognition.

The stimuli were presented preceded by an auditory and visual warning for 120, 250, 500 or 1000 ms. They were presented in upper case with the letters adjacent to each other. Equal numbers of items of each length and each type occurred at each duration. Equal numbers of high and low imageability words occurred at each duration. The order of presentation was random. KW was warned that a third of the items that he would see were real words, and he might use this to help him to report the letters. His task, though, was to report as many letters as possible from the stimulus.

Results. *(a) Report of the whole string.* KW reported all the letters correctly in 24 strings over the 168 trials. He was more likely to report three letter strings than four letters (21/84 vs 3/84, Fisher exact test, $z = 3.74$, $p < .001$). There were also significant differences in the probability of his reporting real words, pseudowords and nonwords (combined across duration and length, Jonckheere trend test, $z = 2.29$, $p = .011$), but on pairwise comparisons only the difference between real words and nonwords reached significance (Fisher exact test, $z = 2.10$, $p = .018$). KW's ability to report whole strings therefore shows only a small effect of string type. There is no significant effect of exposure duration (combined over string length and type, Jonckheere trend test $z = 1.28$, $p = .10$). On real words there is no effect of imageability (high imageability 8/28, low 4/28, Fisher exact test, $z = 1.00$, $p > .15$).

(b) Report of letters in the string. This shows substantially the same pattern. There is a significant effect of string type (Jonckheere trend test $z = 1.72$, $p < .05$), but the only significant pairwise comparison is between letters in real words and nonwords (Fisher exact test, $z = 1.66$, $p < .05$), and the size of the effect is small. The effects of stimulus duration reach significance (Jonckheere trend test $z = 2.01$, $p = .02$), but, as in the previous experiment, this is entirely due to improved performance at 1000 ms; there is no improvement in accuracy from 120-500 ms. The total number of letters correctly reported is almost identical in stimuli of 3 or 4 letters (3 letters 182/252, 4 letters 185/336). In report of letters in real words there is no effect of word imageability (high imageability 68/98, low imageability 62/98; Fisher exact test $z = 0.70$, $p > .2$).

(c) Serial position effects. These are shown in the bottom part of Table 6. As in the previous experiment, accuracy declines across the string. Again performance on the last letter is worse than the middle letter(s) (supporting the conclusion of the previous experiment that lateral masking is not responsible for KW's difficulty in this task).

4. Comment

In this experiment KW performed with real words at a level which was only marginally better than with nonwords. With normal subjects and (presumably) very much shorter stimulus exposures, McClelland (1976) found very much larger effects, with a comparable overall level of accuracy. When scored by strings correct KW managed .23 for real words and .07 for

Table 6

Patient KW: Report of Letters From 3 and 4 Letter Real Words, Pseudowords and Nonwords. Proportion of Whole Strings Correctly Reported, Proportion of Letters in Parentheses (for strings n = 7 in each cell).

	Exposure Duration (ms)				
	120	250	500	1000	Total
4 letters					
Real words	.00 (.64)	.14 (.57)	.29 (.57)	.00 (.61)	.11 (.60)
Pseudowords	.00 (.46)	.00 (.50)	.00 (.57)	.00 (.68)	.00 (.55)
Nonwords	.00 (.46)	.00 (.50)	.00 (.43)	.00 (.61)	.00 (.50)
Total	.00 (.52)	.05 (.52)	.10 (.52)	.00 (.63)	.04 (.55)
3 letters					
Real words	.29 (.62)	.29 (.76)	.14 (.67)	.71 (.90)	.36 (.73)
Pseudowords	.14 (.71)	.29 (.71)	.14 (.71)	.43 (.81)	.25 (.73)
Nonwords	.14 (.62)	.29 (.71)	.00 (.62)	.14 (.71)	.14 (.69)
Total	.19 (.65)	.29 (.73)	.10 (.67)	.43 (.81)	.25 (.72)
Total					
Real words	.14 (.63)	.21 (.65)	.21 (.61)	.36 (.73)	.23 (.66)
Pseudowords	.07 (.57)	.14 (.59)	.07 (.63)	.21 (.73)	.13 (.63)
Nonwords	.07 (.43)	.14 (.59)	.00 (.51)	.07 (.65)	.07 (.57)
Total	.10 (.58)	.17 (.61)	.10 (.59)	.21 (.71)	.14 (.62)

Serial position effects: probability of correct report of letters (n = 84 in each cell combined over duration and string type)

	4 letters				3 letters		
Position	1	2	3	4	1	2	3
Probability correct	.90	.80	.40	.11	.95	.86	.33

nonwords; McClelland's subjects scored .53 on real words and .03 on nonwords. Scoring by letters correct, KW is .66 on real words and .57 on nonwords, whereas in McClelland's experiment the corresponding scores were .77 and .51. It seems clear, therefore, that KW shows a very much reduced effect of lexical status in this experiment. The contrast between his very poor performance in reporting letters in strings, and his ability to read whole words briefly presented, is maintained even in this experiment where one third of the stimuli were real words. This cannot, therefore, be attributed to any effect of a word context improving his letter recognition; it appears to be a direct effect of the type of task: KW uses very different processing routines for reading a whole word aloud (where he can process the letters in parallel) and in identifying the letters in a word where he uses a much slower serial letter recognition strategy.

Warrington and Shallice (1980) tested one of their patients (JDC) in report of the letters from real words and pseudowords. With three letter stimuli presented for 200 ms, JDC reported 57/72 letters from real words and 52/72 letters from pseudowords. This failure to find a WSE was one motivation for their suggestion that that the visual word form was impaired in their patients. An explanation of this type seems implausible when applied to KW; as argued at length before, the distribution of "fast" responses in reading and lexical decision and of correct responses in reading briefly presented words is incompatible with a primary deficit at the level of the word form. Differences in strategy between tasks of reading words and reporting letters seems a more plausible explanation.

VI. DISCUSSION

1. The Underlying Problem of These Letter-by-Letter Readers

Both patients who are the subject of this chapter read letter-by-letter, and their slow mean-reading latencies which increase with the length of the word reflect the use of a laborious sequential letter identification procedure. The distribution of fast reading responses, however, demonstrates that these patients are processing the letters of a word in parallel; only where these parallel processes fail, do the patients resort to letter-by-letter reading. The original explanation was phrased in terms of a probability of misidentifying a letter, and assumed that only where all letters in a word were identified correctly would a reading response become available. But the data do not justify the conclusion that these subjects have a deficit specifically at the level of letter identification. All that the mathematical predictions require is that there should be an identification problem at a level where the number of elements (visual features, letter forms ...) are directly proportional to the length of the word. Thus any visual difficulty at a level more peripheral than parallel activation of the word form by correctly identified letters should lead to this kind of relationship between the number of letters in the word and "fast" reading responses. Where letter naming remains a possible option, patients will be able to use a serial letter identification strategy to resolve failures in visual analysis of the word form. Formulated in this way, the underlying problem in these letter-by-letter readers is not necessarily associated with words written in an alphabetic script. Readers of logographic scripts such as

Japanese Kanji or Chinese, who have the same kind of problem in identification of visually presented stimuli, should show the same linear relationship between the log probability of fast correct reading responses and the visual complexity of the characters (as measured, say, by the number of strokes in the character). And, where any elements in the character are misidentified, one might anticipate that this (putative) patient will resort to an attempt to resolve this by stroke-by-stroke identification of the elements. The obvious difference is that, because strokes have no names, this strategy will not be open to verbalization.

While these two patients' word reading and lexical decision showed very similar characteristics, when asked to report the letters in strings of unrelated letters they performed somewhat differently. PM's identification was very much slowed, but he showed gradually improving performance with increasing presentation time; this suggested that his primary problem lay in slowed identification of visually presented stimuli. KW, on the other hand, only showed a (small) effect of presentation duration with 1000 ms exposures. More strikingly, both KW and PM consistently reported less letters from a string of four letters, than a string of two, especially with short stimulus exposures. Thus, the presence of more letters in the string reduced the accuracy of letter identification. This same relationship could be found when identification of the first letter is considered; as the length of the string increased the first letter was less likely to be correctly reported. This is evidently not the classical "simultanagnosia" as described by Kinsbourne and Warrington (1962) where a single letter is accurately reported but pairs of letters take very much longer. Nevertheless the patients' performance resembles simultanagnosia in the way that performance is adversely affected by longer arrays. Friedman and Alexander (1984) noticed a rather similar phenomenon with their letter-by-letter reader: The 50% threshold duration for single letters was [...] 45 ms; for two letter items it was double, i.e., 90 ms. However, when the duration was tripled to 135 ms, no three letter items were reported correctly. In fact, even at 300 ms the patient could not report all three letters of a three letter string correctly (p.14).

However the relevance of data from tasks involving the identification of strings of unrelated letters to the processes of word identification is open to doubt. KW could read aloud 75% of five letter words presented masked for 250 msec. When asked to report not the word, but the letters in the word, he was only correct for all the letters for one four letter word presented unmasked for the same time (and none where presentation was for 1000 msec). The most plausible explanation is that KW has some freedom in shifting between a (slow) serial letter identification strategy and (relatively fast) parallel identification of the letters in the word. When asked to report the letters in the word he relies mainly on a serial strategy. There is another striking difference between these patients' performance with single letters and real words. In the plot of log probability of fast correct responses against word length, the gradient corresponds to the probability that each individual letter is correctly identified. Across the experiments this varies from 68% to 78% for PM and from 74% to 87% for KW. In contrast, when asked to report a single letter with limited exposure PM reads 88% correctly, and KW reads 9[illegible]% correctly. Reading single letters with unlimited exposure PM reads 86% and KW 96%. Thus the accuracy of identification of single letters is substantially greater than the (inferred) accuracy of letter identification in word contexts. Furthermore, the straight line log plots with word stimuli are based on the assumption that the probability of each letter being correctly recognized is equal and independent of word length; whereas in reporting letters from random strings accuracy declined with increasing string length. These differences between word reading and letter report tasks cannot be conclusively resolved on the basis of the evidence available from these patients. The most likely explanation however is that the tasks induce very different processing strategies from the patients.

It is clear, though, that a difficulty in identifying the visual elements of the word which are processed in parallel provides a satisfactory account of the behavior of these patients in visual word recognition.

2. Generalizing the Account

The two patients described in this chapter clearly have a problem in word identification more peripheral than identification of the word form (as suggested by Warrington & Shallice, 1980) or parallel processing of letters (as suggested by Patterson & Kay, 1982).

To what extent might the results generalize to other letter-by-letter readers? It is hard to be sure. Reports of other patients have concentrated on mean reading times, which result from the use of the slow serial letter identification strategy. Yet it was the distribution of the fastest reaction times which allowed us to show that these patients were processing the letters of a word in parallel. These patients were fairly prompt and accurate at identifying single letters, and it was only with words that their real difficulty in letter identification emerged. Thus Warrington and Shallice's (1980) demonstration that RAV was accurate in identifying single letters with no time pressure does not demonstrate that letter identification in a word context was preserved.

It is really not possible to assess whether other letter-by-letter readers have a problem with similar characteristics to that shown by KW and PM; the relevant data are not available. Coslett and Saffran (1988) present a post hoc investigation of whether performance in their lexical decision task is related to the length of the words and nonwords. They fail to find any significant differences over a range of lengths from 3 to 5 letters. However there was no attempt to balance the stimuli of different lengths and the numbers of stimuli particularly at length 3 were very small. Reanalysis of their data suggests that they cannot discriminate between the hypotheses that accuracy is independent of word length, or that log proportion correct declines linearly with word length. Assessment of this hypothesis with other patients will depend on using properly matched sets of words with lengths varying over a reasonable range.

In any case, one would not necessarily expect to find the same underlying problem in all patients who read letter-by-letter; any patient for whom letter naming remains possible when word recognition is impaired (at any level) may resort to letter-by-letter reading to try to generate a reading response. It is clear, though, that examination of the distribution of "fast" reading responses can easily distinguish between some possible levels of breakdown in reading, and that mean reaction times may not allow one to draw correct conclusions about the primary method of processing. This conclusion extends beyond studies of disordered reading, to all paradigms where increasing mean reaction times with increasing array size, has been used as evidence for serial processing (e.g., Humphreys, Riddoch & Quinlan, 1985). This pattern of performance may result simply from a compensatory serial strategy, operating where a parallel process has a finite probability of error. Mean reaction times may be less revealing than their distribution.

The classical disconnectionist accounts of letter-by-letter reading concentrated on the fact that most (but not all) of these patients have right homonymous hemianopias (e.g., Greenblatt, 1973); as a result visual stimuli are first processed by the occipital cortex in the right hemisphere. Coslett and Saffran (1988) argue that the (partially) preserved performance of their subjects in visual lexical decision and word categorization may represent the preserved reading abilities of the right hemisphere (cf. Coltheart, 1980b, 1983). The data reported in this chapter suggest a different correspondence between letter-by-letter readers and right hemisphere processing. As mentioned in the Introduction, a number of studies have demonstrated that when stimuli are presented briefly to the left visual field, lexical decision accuracy declines with increasing word length (e.g., Young & Ellis, 1985). When Young and Ellis's data are replotted in the way used in this chapter - that is as log proportion correct against letter length - they fall reasonably close to a straight line through the origin. This suggests that the length effects found in lexical decision with LVF presentation may result from the fact that letter (or letter feature) recognition by the right hemisphere is inherently inaccurate or noisy, rather than, as Young and Ellis suggest, from application of some serial letter processing procedure. Letter-by-letter reading may therefore be simply a compensatory strategy adopted to cope with inaccurate letter identification of stimuli which are presented first to the visual areas of the right hemisphere. This raises the possibility that letter-by-letter reading may not be a particularly exotic variety of dyslexic reading, but instead reflect a basic property of normal visual word recognition.

3. Word Comprehension in Letter-by-Letter Readers

The evidence reviewed in the introduction showed that some letter-by-letter readers were apparently able to gain some idea of the meaning of a word when presented at a duration shorter than they needed to identify the word. In some cases the evidence was flimsy; Landis et al.'s (1980) patient was correct in five of seven trials, but the authors were unable to repeat the observation three weeks later. Shallice and Saffran's (1986) ML was better than chance in categorizing words presented for two seconds, even when he could not report them. With 250 msec exposure, Coslett and Saffran's (1988) patients were considerably better than chance at a range of categorization tasks where the words were not explicitly reported. Shallice and Saffran speculate that different routines may be responsible for comprehension and reading aloud. Comprehension depends on parallel letter identification (which they suggest may be carried out by the right hemisphere), whereas word reading is a result of a serial letter identification procedure.

In terms of comprehension, the two patients described in this chapter behaved very differently. PM, whose primary problem appears to lie in slowed letter identification, showed no evidence of comprehension of stimuli presented for 150-250 msec either in cued definition or in word categorization. KW, on the other hand, showed clear evidence that a cue word of which he was (apparently) unaware could bias his definition of ambiguous words. This is clear evidence of comprehension of words that he could not report. And when presented with names of animals and objects for 250 msec masked, KW was able to categorize correctly 17/23 words that he could not read correctly. However there seems no reason to suppose that KW's comprehension depends on procedures other than those involved in fast word recognition. The reading data in Figure 9 indicate that KW was identifying around 87% of letters correctly at this exposure. Where one or more letters is not correctly identified, there may not be sufficient information to make a response available, but nevertheless there is likely to be more visual information consistent with the correct word than any other. When KW is asked, in the absence of sufficient information to identify the word correctly, to guess its category, the pattern of activation across representations in a lexicon is most likely to be consistent with a correct response. There is, therefore, in these data no evidence to support Shallice and Saffran's suggestion that different routines are responsible for reading and categorization. Both comprehension and "fast" oral reading most plausibly result from a (defective) parallel process - the same process which (working more reliably) is responsible for word identification in normal subjects.

FOOTNOTES

[1]This line of argument may not be conclusive; there may be other reasons why case alternated words are harder. Besner and Johnston (1989) for instance suggest that mixed case words might be harder because "case alternation requires frequent swapping of letter-identification routines, or simply the consideration of more alternative word shapes."

ACKNOWLEDGMENTS

I am grateful to Dr. Marcia Wilkinson and Dr. Elizabeth Gilchrist for permission to report data on PM, and Dr. Richard Greenwood for permission to report data on KW. Mandy LeMay helped with the collection of data on KW. Karalyn Patterson suggested the cued definition experiment, and provided the materials for the categorization experiment with PM. Tim Shallice, Derek Besner and Glyn Humphreys made valuable comments on a draft of the chapter for which I am grateful. This research was supported by the Medical Research Council.

REFERENCES

Besner, D. & Johnston, J.C. (1989). Reading and the mental lexicon: on the uptake of visual information. In W. Marslen-Wilson (Ed.), *Lexical representation and process.* Boston, Massachusetts: MIT Press.

Bouma, H. (1978). Visual search and reading: eye movements and functional visual field: a tutorial review. In J. Requin (Ed.), *Attention and performance VII.* Hillsdale, New Jersey: Lawrence Erlbaum.

Bradshaw. J.L. (1974). Peripherally presented and unreported words may bias the perceived meaning of a centrally fixated homograph. *Journal of Experimental Psychology,* **103**, 1200-1202.

Bub, D.N. (1982). *The nature of half-field asymmetry for word processing as a function of hemispheric specialisation.* Unpublished PhD thesis, Rochester University, New York.

Coltheart, M. (1980a). *Analysing a acquired disorders of reading.* Unpublished manuscript, Birkbeck College.

Coltheart, M. (1980b). Deep dyslexia: a right hemisphere hypothesis. In M. Coltheart, K.E. Patterson and J.C. Marshall (Eds.), *Deep dyslexia.* London: Routledge and Kegan Paul.

Coltheart, M. (1981). The MRC psycholinguistic database. *Quarterly Journal of Experimental Psychology,* **33A**, 497-505.

Coltheart, M. (1983). The right hemisphere and disorders of reading. In A.W. Young (Ed.), *Functions of the right cerebral hemisphere.* London: Academic Press.

Coslett, H.B. & Saffran, E.M. (1988). Evidence for preserved reading in "pure alexia." *Brain,*

Dejerine, J. (1892). Contribution a l'etude anatomoclinique et clinique des differentes varietes de cecite verbale. *Memoires de la Societe de Biologie,* **4**, 61-90.

Dunn, A. (1965). *The Peabody Picture Vocabulary Test.* Minneapolis: American Guidance Service.

Ellis, A.W., Young, A.W. & Anderson, C. (1988). Modes of word recognition in the left and right cerebral hemispheres. *Brain and Language,* **35**, 254-273.

Friedman, R.B. & Albert, M.L. (1985). Alexia. In K.M. Heilman and E. Valenstein (Eds.), *Clinical neuropsychology, 2nd edition.* New York: Oxford University Press.

Friedman, R.B. & Alexander, M.P. (1984). Pictures, images and pure alexia: A case study. *Cognitive Neuropsychology,* **1**, 9-23.

Goodglass, H. & Kaplan, E. (1972). *The assessment of aphasia and related disorders.* Philadelphia: Lea and Febiger.

Greenblatt, S.H. (1973) Alexia without agraphia or hemianopia. *Brain,* **96**, 307-316.

Henderson, L. (1982). *Orthography and word recognition in reading.* London: Academic Press.

Howard, D. & Franklin, S. (1988). *Missing the meaning?* Cambridge, Massachusetts: MIT Press.

Humphreys, G.W. & Riddoch, M.J. (1987). *To see but not to see: A case study of visual agnosia.* London: Lawrence Erlbaum.

Humphreys, G.W., Riddoch, M.J. & Quinlan, P.T. (1985). Interactive processes in perceptual organisation: Evidence from visual agnosia. In M.I. Posner and O.S.M. Marin (Eds.), *Attention and performance XI.* Hillsdale, New Jersey: Lawrence Erlbaum.

Kaplan, E., Goodglass, H. & Weintraub, S. (1976). *The Boston naming test.* Boston: Veteran's Administration.

Kinsbourne, M. & Warrington, E.K. (1962). A disorder of simultaneous form perception.

Brain, **85**, 461-486.
Kinsbourne, M. & Warrington, E.K. (1963). The localizing significance of limited simultaneous visual form perception. *Brain*, **86**, 697-702.
Koriat, A. & Norman, J. (1985). Reading rotated words. *Journal of Experimental Psychology: Human Perception and Performance*, **11**, 490-508.
Kucera, H. & Francis, W.N. (1967). *A computational analysis of present-day American English*. Providence, Rhode Island: Brown University Press.
Landis, T., Regard, M. & Serrat, A. (1980). Iconic reading in a case of alexia without agraphia caused by a brain tumour: A tachistoscopic study. *Brain and Language*, **11**, 45-53.
Levine, D.N. & Calvanio, R. (1978). A study of the visual defect in verbal alexia-simultanagnosia. *Brain*, **101**, 65-81.
McClelland, J. (1976). Preliminary letter identification in the perception of words and nonwords. *Journal of Experimental Psychology: Human Perception and Performance*, **2**, 80-91.
McClelland, J. & Rumelhart, D. (1981). An interaction model of context effects in letter perception: Part 1, an account of basic findings. *Psychological Review*, **88**, 375-407.
Navon, D. (1978). Perception of misoriented words and letter strings. *Canadian Journal of Psychology*, **32**, 129-140.
Patterson, K.E. & Kay, J. (1982). Letter-by-letter reading: Psychological descriptions of a neurological syndrome. *Quarterly Journal of Experimental Psychology*, **34A**, 411-441.
Prior, M. & McCorriston, M. (1983). Acquired and developmental spelling dyslexia. *Brain and Language*, **20**, 263-285.
Rubens, A.B. & Benson, D.F. (1971). Associative visual agnosia. *Archives of Neurology*, **24**, 305-316.
Saffran, E.M. & Marin, O.S.M. (1977). Reading without phonology. *Quarterly Journal of Experimental Psychology*, **29**, 515-525.
Schiepers, C. (1980). Response latency and accuracy in visual word recognition. *Perception and Psychophysics*, **27**, 71-81.
Seymour, P.H.K. & May, G.P. (1981). *Locus of format distortion effects in word recognition*. Paper presented to the Experimental Psychology Society, Oxford.
Shallice, T. (1988). *From neuropsychology to mental structure*. Cambridge: Cambridge University Press.
Shallice, T. & Saffran, E.M. (1986). Lexical processing in the absence of explicit word identification: Evidence from a letter-by-letter reader. *Cognitive Neuropsychology*, **3**, 429-458.
Shallice, T. & Warrington, E.K. (1977). The possible role of selective attention in acquired dyslexia. *Neuropsychologia*, **15**, 31-41.
Stroop J.R. (1938). Factors affecting speed in serial verbal reactions. *Psychological Monographs*, **50**, 38-48.
Terry, P., Samuels, S.J. & LaBerge, D. (1976). The effects of letter degradation and letter spacing on word recognition. *Journal of Verbal Learning and Verbal Behaviour*, **15**, 577-585.
Warrington, E.K. & Shallice, T. (1980). Word form dyslexia. *Brain*, **103**, 99-112.
Wolpert, I. (1924). Die Simultanagnosie-Storung der Gesamtauffassung. *Zeitschrift fur die gesamte Neurologie und Psychiatrie*, **93**, 397-415.
Young, A.W. & Ellis, A.W. (1985). Different methods of lexical access for words presented in the left and right visual hemifields. *Brain and Language*, **24**, 326-358.

4
PHONOLOGIC MEDIATION IS FUNDAMENTAL TO READING

GUY C. VAN ORDEN

Department of Psychology
Arizona State University
Tempe, Arizona

I. INTRODUCTION

The experiments reported in this chapter tested whether phonologic mediation affects proofreading and, by implication, whether phonologic mediation affects reading generally. Printed words activate phonologic codes[1], and these phonologic codes are primary constraints in word identification. This *phonologic mediation hypothesis* is hotly debated, and variants of this hypothesis span the history of the psychology of reading. Recently, my colleagues and I proposed a new phonologic mediation hypothesis which we called the *phonologic coherence hypothesis* (Van Orden, Pennington, & Stone, 1989). This hypothesis was motivated by computational assumptions common to subsymbolic connectionism (e.g., see Smolensky, 1986a; 1986b; 1988).

From our perspective, word identification appears as a subsymbolic, dynamic process which operates via "soft constraint satisfaction." Soft constraints are imposed by activation values passed between representations that affect word identification. Thus, soft constraint satisfaction is the vehicle by which stimulus and contextual representations interact to form lexical representations.

This perspective also leads us to presuppose that phonologic codes are components of, as well as sources of constraint upon, lexical representations (Perfetti, Bell, & Delaney, 1988; Van Orden, 1987; Van Orden et al., 1989). Thus, we do not view phonologic mediation as a way station between orthographic representation and lexical representation (Coltheart, 1978), though we have been instructed by that view. Rather, we imagine that phonologic codes affect other lexical codes via their relative coherence. The initial pattern of lexical activation corresponding to a phonologic code is usually relatively noise[2] free (coherent). This initially coherent phonologic code will thus provide a dynamic frame which will constrain (through interactive-activation or relaxation) the eventual form of other less initially coherent (more noisy) lexical codes (i.e., semantic codes, syntactic codes, etc.) (Van Orden et al., 1989).

Phonologic codes are initially more coherent because, through covariant learning (Van Orden, 1987; Van Orden et al., 1989), orthographic codes have become precisely associated to phonologic codes. Alternatively, other linguistic codes will be less coherent because they covary inconsistently across the contexts in which printed words appear. For example, the meaning and syntactic function of a word can vary widely across contexts. This relative inconsistency of covariance (with orthographic codes) will subsequently be reflected in the relative initial coherence of the corresponding lexical codes. In contrast, because words' names are relatively invariant across contexts, a word's initial pattern of phonologic activation will more closely resemble the final pattern of phonologic activation that emerges from relaxation of the dynamic system that is word identification. Other initial lexical codes will less closely resemble their final forms.

We can also state the foregoing in terms of harmony theory (Smolensky, 1986a; 1986b). Harmony is a measure of the self-consistency of the current state of a dynamic system. Roughly, the self-consistency of, say, an orthographic state is the degree to which a stimulus-driven orthographic pattern matches the orthographic pattern that is reflected back from the phonologic encoding (and other lexical codes). Alternatively, the self-consistency of a phonologic state is the degree to which an orthographic-driven phonologic pattern matches the phonologic pattern that is reflected back again from the orthographic pattern (and other lexical codes). As long as competing representations are present in a lexical encoding, then that encoding will be in a relative state of flux, and will exhibit relatively low harmony. By the phonologic coherence hypothesis, initial phonologic encodings generally exhibit greater harmony than other lexical encodings and will thus more coherently determine other lexical representations than vice versa. In this fashion, phonologic codes fundamentally constrain printed word identification.

Currently, positive evidence supports this and other variants of the phonologic mediation hypothesis. Nonetheless, skilled printed word identification is still widely assumed to occur exclusively via a process of direct access--which works like a direct association between each word's spelling and its lexical entry. Recently, however, Van Orden et al. (1989) argued that this view is maintained by unsupported, unnecessary, and often fallacious *a priori* assumptions concerning the nature of phonologic mediation, coupled with occasional failures to find effects of stimulus phonology. Moreover, they review recent studies that counter the later negative findings with positive results consonant with the phonologic mediation hypothesis (e.g., compare Kleiman, 1975, with Besner, Davies, & Daniels, 1981; or Evett & Humphreys, 1981, with Perfetti et al., 1988; or Shulman, Hornak, & Sanders, 1978, with Hanson & Fowler, 1987).

However, there are yet results which do not support the most general form of the phonologic mediation hypothesis--the version by which phonologic mediation occurs generally in skilled reading. Here, I will re-examine two of those results. The first of these was used to argue that phonologic mediation plays no role in skilled reading of connected text (Banks, Oka, & Shugarman, 1981), and the second was used to argue that phonologic mediation only occurs within a relatively narrow range of stimulus presentation conditions (Pring, 1981). Subsequently, the results of two new proofreading studies will be reported that counter these results and strengthen the case for the general form of the phonologic mediation hypothesis. I will begin, though, with a brief discussion of key evidence that supports the phonologic mediation hypothesis, and then set up the hypotheses tested in Experiment 1.

II. EXPERIMENT 1: PHONOLOGIC MEDIATION IN PROOFREADING

The phonologic mediation hypothesis is best supported by results from semantic categorization tasks in which target foils are sometimes homophones of category exemplars (e.g., BEATS is homophonic to an exemplar of the category VEGETABLE). Meyer and his colleagues demonstrated that extra time is required to respond correctly "no" to homophone foils such as BEATS (indicating BEATS is <u>not</u> a VEGETABLE) than to control foils, and that subjects are more likely to generate false positive "yes" responses to homophone foils than to control foils (Meyer & Ruddy, 1973; Meyer & Gutschera, 1975). These results have been interpreted to indicate that the phonologic code of a foil such as BEATS constrains word identification toward a lexical representation of the category exemplar BEETS; sometimes so much so that BEATS is categorized as a VEGETABLE. Subsequently, Meyer and colleagues' method was improved to include control for spelling similarity, and these improved studies replicated the original findings (Banks et al., 1981; Van Orden, 1987; Van Orden, Johnston, & Hale, 1988). (BEATS is identical in sound, but also similar in spelling to BEETS. This potential confound of sound similarity with spelling similarity was present in the original experiments.)

The phonologic mediation hypothesis is not, however, always supported by experiments that use other tasks. For example, Banks et al. (1981) followed a battery of categorization experiments, which yielded effects that supported the phonologic mediation hypothesis, with two proofreading experiments (and two sentence verification experiments similar to the proofreading experiments) which did not. Experiment 1 examines further the conditions of these null effects toward understanding why the effect of stimulus homophony, that so powerfully affects categorization performance, seems to disappear in the proofreading task.

Experiment 1 uses a proofreading task in which subjects mark misspelled words while reading stories. This proofreading task is similar to the proofreading tasks used by Banks et al. (1981) and others (e.g., see Abramovici, 1983; Haber & Schindler, 1981; Healy, 1981; Healy, Volbrecht & Nye, 1983; Levy, 1983; Levy, Newell, Snyder, & Timmins, 1986).

The experimental hypotheses of Banks et al. (1981) were framed for proofreading using assumptions auxiliary to the phonologic mediation hypothesis, as follows: (a) The orthographic and/or phonologic similarity of a stimulus foil to the orthographic and/or phonologic entries in a subject's mental lexicon was assumed to be the primary cause of false positive word identification. And, (b) false positive word identification was assumed to underlie each proofreading miss error--a proofreading miss error occurs whenever a subject fails to mark a misspelling. Thus, for example, the orthographic-phonologic similarity of the nonword homophone foil SLEAT to the story-word SLEET (that it replaces in a text) is assumed to determine the proofreading miss error rate to SLEAT.

Auxiliary assumptions that are cousins to the above are also used to derive predictions for the categorization task. For that task, it is also usually assumed that the orthographic-phonologic similarity of stimulus foils to actual category exemplars is the primary source of false positive word identification, and that false positive word identification underlies false positive categorization responding (as when the nonword homophone foil SLEAT is falsely categorized as a TYPE OF WEATHER--see Van Orden, 1987; Van Orden et al., 1988).

If the foregoing linked auxiliary assumptions are correct for the proofreading task, then simple, straightforward predictions follow from the phonologic mediation hypothesis. The proofreading *miss* error rate to spelling control foils (SPEET) establishes a baseline for false positive word identification caused by foils that are not homophonic to story-words (SLEET). Thus, evidence of phonologic mediation would be found if the miss error rate to nonword homophone foils (SLEAT) was found to be substantially higher than this baseline.

Banks et al. (1981; Experiment 7a) tested this prediction, but their results only marginally supported the phonologic mediation hypothesis. In their experiment, subjects missed (failed to detect) 46% of homophonic misspellings such as SLEAT, and they missed 33.6% of spelling-control SPEET misspellings. However, although this apparent nonword homophony effect was significant across subjects, it was not significant across items. This marginal result (and several outright null results) eventually lead Banks et al. (1981) to reject the phonologic mediation hypothesis--even though the majority of their experiments yielded results consistent with that hypothesis.

Notice, though, that Banks et al.'s (and others') assumptions concerning effects of orthographic-phonologic similarity do not stand alone. They rely on a further assumption by which other potential sources of error in proofreading and categorization tasks do not discriminate between spelling control and homophone foils. This "all other things are equal" assumption may hold well enough for the categorization task, if only because the baseline false positive categorization error rate to spelling control foils is usually very low (usually much less than ten percent, and as low as three percent in the categorization experiments of Van

Orden, 1987, Experiment 1; and Van Orden et al., 1988). For the proofreading task, however, the baseline error rate to spelling controls is much higher (33.6%, in the proofreading experiment of Banks et al., 1981, Experiment 7a).

This large baseline proofreading miss error rate to spelling control foils may result from sources of error that are unique to proofreading. It is fair to speculate that when proofreaders fail to mark the spelling errors in foils like SPEET, there may be sources of these miss errors other than false positive activation of story-word (SLEET) lexical representations. If this is true, then we may consider the possibility that these other sources of error do not respect the assumption that "all other things are equal between homophone and spelling control foils."

For example, a potential source of proofreading errors to spelling control foils such as SPEET is the possibility that SPEET might be perceived by the proofreader as an unfamiliar word. Thus, when subjects come upon a spelling control foil they may form either (or both) of two hypotheses as to why that foil is unfamiliar: (a) It could be unfamiliar because it is a misspelling of some (presumably) known word or, (b) It could be unfamiliar because it is a word that is not known to the subject. It is not unreasonable to suggest that most readers have previously encountered unfamiliar words whose meanings could only be taken from context. Thus, they are likely to have previously experienced the situation that confronts them when they encounter a spelling control foil in the proofreading task. Consequently, some proofreading miss errors may result from spelling controls being interpreted as unfamiliar words. Note, however, that because nonword homophone foils give precise phonologic cues as to the identity of the word for which they are a misspelling, they are less likely to be interpreted as being altogether novel words.

The above speculation is not necessary in its specifics to motivate the present experiments. Any other possibility wherein some uncontrolled factor inflates the proofreading miss error rate to spelling control foils, and thus masks a genuine effect of stimulus phonology, would do just as well. My purpose here is merely to cast doubt upon the "all other things are equal" assumption as it pertains to the proofreading task. This doubt consequently reflects upon the logic whereby "proofreading errors are caused by orthographic-phonologic similarity." And because this chain of logical dominoes may fall, they may not support an adequate test of the phonologic mediation hypothesis. To remedy this doubt, I will adopt a method that better indicates whether proofreading of a foil such as SPEET truly included false activation of a lexical representation corresponding to its story-word SLEET.

Van Orden (1987) describes a pattern of categorization errors that can be taken as evidence that stimulus foils such as SLEAT or SPEET did indeed activate lexical representations of those words. In his Experiment 3, he found that subjects were much more likely to make false positive categorization responses to foils such as SLEAT (for the category a TYPE OF WEATHER) when SLEAT's corresponding sound-alike category exemplar SLEET is a *low frequency word*--that is, he found an effect of the frequencies of true exemplars (such as SLEET) upon the error rates to stimulus foils that were orthographically-phonologically similar to those true exemplars.[3] But, SLEET was never presented in the experiment. Thus, the effect of SLEET's frequency upon performance to SLEAT must arise in the process of word identification. More specifically, and for my present purpose, I assume that this effect originates in access to a lexical representation of SLEET.

By the foregoing logic, when SLEET's frequency affects performance to a foil such as SLEAT or SPEET, then that foil must have activated a lexical representation of SLEET. Moreover, the relative magnitudes of respective *story-word* (SLEET) *frequency effects* may estimate SLEAT's and SPEET's, respective, relative, capacities for falsely activating a lexical representation of SLEET. Thus, in Experiment 1, I seek effects of story-words' frequencies--story-words that have been replaced by homophone or spelling control foils, and thus never appear in the experiment--upon error rates to stimulus foils. In this way, I may estimate whether the stimulus foils falsely activate story-word lexical representations. If the present logic is correct, it circumvents the potential problem, noted previously, of sources of proofreading error that may discriminate between homophone and spelling control foils. I assume this to be true because I require a signature of lexical access, a (story-word) frequency effect, before I will accept that the proofreading miss errors caused by a class of stimulus foils do indeed involve access to story-word lexical representations.

In summary, Experiment 1 examines proofreading error rates to homophone and spelling control foils to determine whether the frequency of their corresponding story-words affects the error rates to either, or both, of these stimulus types. If the error rate to homophone foils such as SLEAT, constructed to be homophonic to low frequency story-words such as SLEET, is found to be greater than the error rate to homophone foils such as GREAN, constructed to be homophonic to high frequency story-words such as GREEN, then we will have evidence that nonword homophone foils activate lexical representations corresponding to their sound-alike story-words. Likewise if the error rate to spelling control foils such as SPEET, constructed to be similar in spelling to low frequency story-words such as SLEET, is found to be greater than the error rate to spelling control foils such as GRELN, constructed to be similar in spelling to high frequency story-words such as GREEN, then we will have evidence that spelling control foils activate lexical representations corresponding to their story-words.

More importantly, however, a comparison of the relative magnitudes of story-word frequency effects tests the phonologic mediation hypothesis. The phonologic mediation hypothesis predicts that homophonic foils such as SLEAT and GREAN should have a greater capacity than spelling control foils for false activation of lexical representations corresponding to SLEET and GREEN. Thus, the story-word frequency effect to homophone foils should be larger than the story-word frequency effect to spelling control foils. This prediction would be supported by a story-word frequency x type of foil (homophones versus spelling controls) interaction effect.

Method

Subjects. The subjects were 52 undergraduates attending Arizona State University who received course credit for their participation. All were native English speakers.

Procedure. Subjects were randomly assigned to conditions and run in groups of approximately 20. (Experiments 1 and 2 were run concurrently to promote comparisons between these data sets.) Half of the subjects (26) read stories in which nonword homophone foils (SLEAT) had been substituted for story-words (SLEET) and the other half read stories in which nonword spelling control foils (SPEET) had been substituted for story-words.

I chose this blocked method of presentation over one that presented both homophone and spelling control foils within the same stories because I wanted to bias my method against the phonologic mediation hypothesis. It is commonly assumed that when simple reading tasks include many homophone foils, then subjects can strategically alter their mode of reading and abandon phonologic mediation (Andrews, 1982; Davelaar, Coltheart, Besner & Jonasson, 1978; McQuade, 1981; but cf. Perfetti et al., 1988; Van Orden, 1984). Thus, if phonologic mediation is indeed an optional mode of reading, then by presenting exclusively homophone foils (SLEAT) to subjects in the homophone condition, I increase the likelihood that subjects will not read via phonologic mediation, and not produce patterns of proofreading errors that support the phonologic mediation hypothesis.

In a typical session, each subject received a booklet containing an instruction cover-sheet and two short stories. The ordering of the two stories in the booklet was counterbalanced across all other conditions. At the beginning of the session, the experimenter read aloud the instructions while the subjects read them silently. Subjects were instructed to (a) read straight through the stories and not backtrack to look for misspellings, but (b), mark any misspellings that they happened to notice while (c) as much as is possible in a psychology experiment, reading the stories as they might read them for their own pleasure. After the instructions were read, the subjects opened their booklets and proceeded to read through both stories.

Stimuli. I wrote the two short stories that were used in this experiment, *Lucille* and *The Hour of Least Resistance* (see Appendices A and B, respectively), in collaboration with John Graham Holden. These stories were written around 20 story-words from which experimental foils were constructed. The constraints on composition were that each of the 20 story-words could appear only once in its respective story (each story contained 10 story-words) and that they were spaced roughly, evenly across the story. The stories were formatted using Word Star word processing software and printed in upper-case using the near letter quality mode of a Citizen MSP printer.

For each of the story-words (e.g., SLEET) I constructed two yoked stimulus foils: (a) a nonword homophone foil (e.g., SLEAT) that was a constructed to sound like the story-word, and (b) a nonword spelling control foil (e.g., SPEET) that was constructed to be as similar in spelling to its corresponding story-word as its respective yoked homophone foil. The sets of story-words, nonword homophone foils, and spelling controls from both of the stories are listed in Appendix C.

Story-word (SLEET) frequency was manipulated using the Kucera and Francis (1967) word frequency count. Half (10) of the story-words had high frequency counts of at least 55 per million (M = 125, SD = 48.3), and half had low frequency counts no greater than 10 per million (M = 5.2, SD = 3.0). Each nonword homophone foil (SLEAT) that had been formed from a low frequency story-word was yoked to another nonword homophone foil (GREAN) that had been formed from a high frequency story-word. These yoked pairs were always both formed by the same spelling change in their respective story-words. For example, SLEAT is formed from low-frequency SLEET by substituting an A for an E; likewise, SLEAT's yoked foil GREAN was formed from high-frequency GREEN by substituting an A for an E into approximately the same local orthographic-phonologic correspondence. I selected stimuli to include a variety of changeable spelling-sound correspondences. Each story was composed around equal numbers of high and low frequency story-words.

To verify the homophony of the nonword homophone foils, I used the method of Van Orden et al. (1988) in which ten judges (students at University of Colorado at Boulder) read aloud quickly a list of pronounceable, nonhomophonic nonwords into which I had randomly inserted candidate nonword homophone foils (the ratio between nonhomophonic nonwords and candidates was approximately seven to one, respectively). For a foil to appear in the present experiments it must have been pronounced to match its sound-alike story-word by at least nine of the ten judges and any "mispronunciations" must be readily attributable to a misperception of the letters in the nonword homophone (e.g., pronouncing SLEAT as SLEEP).

Degree of spelling similarity between homophone foils and story-words, and spelling controls and story-words, was controlled using an estimate of orthographic similarity (OS) that ranges from 0 to 1, where 1 indicates identical spellings. This estimate, described in Van Orden (1987) and Van Orden et al. (1988), was adapted from an estimate devised by Weber (1970). Essentially, OS is computed from the number of letters and letter pairs that two letter-strings share, giving special emphasis to beginning and end letters. Mean OS computed between low-frequency story-words and corresponding spelling controls was .79, SD = 0.04, and between low-frequency story-words and corresponding homophone foils it was .78, SD = .04; between high frequency story-words and corresponding spelling controls it was .78, SD = 0.04, and between high frequency story-words and corresponding homophone foils it was also .78, SD = .04.

I did not control systematically for visual similarity between the story-word letters that were changed to create foils and the corresponding letters that replaced them. Several of the spelling control foils (but none of the homophone foils) were, however, constructed by exchanging an original letter from the story-word for one that only lacked a few features of that original letter, and did not contain additional features other than those that were in the original letter (e.g., compare story-word FEAR and spelling control FLAR). Healy (1981) and Healy et al. (1983) found that letter substitutions such as these cause higher proofreading error rates than substitutions which include letter features not contained in the original letter. Thus, the spelling controls are probably slightly higher in visual similarity between substituted letters and original letters.

The above method involves: (a) yoking each spelling control (SPEET) to a homophone foil (SLEAT); (b) yoking the homophone foil to another homophone foil (GREAN); and (c) yoking the second homophone foil to its own spelling control (GRELN). This yields a yoked-stimulus-quartet item-sampling-unit. Further control closely matched these foil sets for mean number of syllables and letters (low frequency story words and yoked foils: M = 1.6, SD = 0.5, and M = 5.4, SD = .7, for syllables and letters, respectively; high frequency story words and yoked foils: M = 1.5, SD = .5, and M = 5.3, SD = .7, for syllables and letters, respectively.

Results and Discussion

The results of Experiment 1 are presented in Table 1. The dependent variable was the percentage of proofreading miss errors (i.e., failures to detect misspellings) that occurred to target foil items which had been substituted for true story-words.[4] Target foils were either homophones or spelling controls that were substituted for either high or low frequency story-words. ANOVAs were computed appropriate to the homophony (2) x story-word frequency (2) design, considering both subjects and items as random factors. All descriptive statistics that are reported come from subject analyses; item error rates are presented in Appendix C. The alpha level for both Experiment 1 and 2 was set at .05.

Table 1
Percentage of Proofreading Miss Errors in Experiment 1 to Homophone and Spelling Control Foils that were Substituted for Low Frequency or High Frequency Story-Words

	Low Frequency		High Frequency			
	Mean	SE	Mean	SE	Mean	SE
Homophones	48.8	4.6	21.9	3.7	35.4	3.5
Spelling Controls	35.8	4.2	26.5	3.5	31.2	2.8
	42.3	3.2	24.2	2.5		

Type of foil (homophones versus spelling controls). The mean proofreading miss error rate to nonword homophone foils such as SLEAT and GREAN (35.4%) was only slightly greater than the corresponding miss error rate to yoked spelling control foils (31.2%). Neither subject nor item analyses were significant (both subject and item Fs < 1). Thus, if the present analysis had been rooted in the traditional elaboration of the phonologic mediation hypothesis, then the present result would be a failure to support that hypothesis. By that elaboration, false story-word lexical activation due to orthographic-phonologic similarity of stimulus foils is assumed to be the primary source of proofreading errors (this assumption allows the phonologic mediation hypothesis to predict a greater proofreading miss error rate to homophone foils than to spelling control foils). However, I argued earlier that the relative magnitude of the story-word frequency effect offers a better estimate of false lexical activation due to orthographic-phonologic similarity. Consequently, the focus of this discussion will be the interaction between story-word frequency and type of foil.

Story-word frequency. The mean proofreading miss error rate to foils like SLEAT and SPEET (42.3%), that were substituted for low frequency story-words, was greater than the corresponding miss error rate to GREAN and GRELN (24.2%), that had been substituted for high frequency story-words. This main effect of story-word frequency was significant in both subject and item analyses [$F(1,50) = 37.36$, for subjects; $F(1,9) = 5.74$, for items]. This result is evidence that the stimulus foils do indeed activate the lexical representations of their corresponding story-words. I now examine whether nonword homophones and spelling controls differ in their respective capacities for generating this false lexical activation.

Story-word frequency x type of foil. The magnitude of the story-word (SLEET) frequency effect is larger for homophone foils (SLEAT) than it is for spelling control foils (SPEET) (see Table 1) [$F(1,50) = 8.95$, for subjects; $F(1,9) = 4.78$, $p = .057$, for items]. Planned analyses of simple main effects found a significant effect of story-word frequency upon error rates to nonword homophone foils in both subject and item analyses [$F(1,25) = 46.40$, for subjects; $F(1,9) = 9.30$, for items]. In contrast, the effect of story-word frequency upon spelling control foils is only significant across subjects [$F(1,25) = 4.40$, for subjects; $F(1,9) = 1.24$, $p = .30$, for items].

The effect of story-word frequency on nonword homophone foils suggests that these items activate story-word lexical representations. However, we cannot determine whether spelling control foils ever actually activate story-word lexical representations because the story-word frequency effect failed to generalize across items. Thus, either (a) the apparent effect of story-word frequency to these foils arises from uncontrolled properties of a few items, or (b) there is an uncontrolled interaction between a few items and the contexts in which they are presented.

If the magnitude of the story-word (SLEET) frequency effect estimates the capacity of stimulus foils such as SLEAT and SPEET to activate story-word (SLEET) lexical representations, then the above results support the phonologic mediation hypothesis. Only homophone foils show evidence that they activate specific, phonologically identical, story-word, lexical representations. I interpret this pattern of results as evidence that phonologic codes are primary constraints in word identification for proofreading, just as has been previously shown for categorization (Banks et al., 1981; Meyer & Ruddy, 1973; Meyer & Gutschera, 1975; Van Orden, 1987; Van Orden et al., 1988).

III. EXPERIMENT 2: ORTHOGRAPHIC INPUT TO PHONOLOGICAL CODING

In Experiment 1, I found evidence supporting the possibility that phonologic coding is fundamental to word identification. Experiment 2 tests a hypothesis from Pring (1981) concerning the nature of the orthographic input into the process of phonologic coding. Pring (1981) found evidence consistent with a *functional spelling unit hypothesis*. By this hypothesis, the mechanism of phonologic coding requires that orthographic representations be parsed into component graphemes which will subsequently satisfy grapheme-phoneme-correspondence rules.

Pring (1981) reports results from two lexical decision experiments that, taken together, support the functional spelling unit hypothesis. Her experiments tested whether intact functional spelling units are necessary for the process of phonologic coding (the functional spelling units in CHURCH are CH, UR, and CH). A standard finding in lexical decision performance is that nonword homophone foils such as SLEAT take more time to reject than control foils such as SPEET (Coltheart et. al, 1977; Rubenstein, Lewis, & Rubenstein, 1971). The magnitude of this nonword homophony effect (usually called the pseudohomophone effect) was assumed by Pring (1981) to estimate the degree to which subjects read via phonologic mediation in the lexical decision task. Thus, by the functional spelling unit hypothesis, a manipulation that disrupts parsing into functional spelling units, and, consequently, disrupts the process of phonologic coding, should eliminate the pseudohomophone effect.

Pring (1981) used case manipulation to disrupt functional spelling units. Case alteration either maintained the functional spelling units in the word (e.g., CHurCH), or they violated the units (e.g., ChuRCh). Violations should hinder parsing for phonologic coding. Consistent with this hypothesis, Pring (1981) found that case alternations that preserved the functional spelling units of pseudohomophones (e.g., CHerCH) yielded a pseudohomophone effect; in contrast case alterations that disrupted the spelling units of pseudohomophones (e.g., CheRCh) did not.

Suppose, though, that the pseudohomophone effect is not a reliable indicator of phonologic mediation. Van Orden et al. (1988) examined a categorization analog of the pseudohomophone effect; namely, the slowing in correct "no" response times to nonword homophone foils such as SLEAT relative to spelling control foils such as SPEET, when subjects are asked to verify whether the target is an example of a TYPE OF WEATHER. They found that the effect was due to a relatively few, slow, response times (RTs) that skew "no" RT distributions to nonword homophone foils. In unpublished work, Greg Stone and I observed a similar pattern of RTs underlying our replication of the pseudohomophone effect in lexical decisions. A relatively few, slow, correct, "no" RTs to pseudohomophone foils skewed subjects' corresponding RT distributions. Thus, at least in our experiments, the pseudohomophone effect and its categorization analog do not reflect general differences in RT distributions, which should be apparent if correct "no" RTs to pseudohomophone foils were generally shifted toward slower "no" RTs relative to "no" RTs to spelling control foils.

Accordingly, in Experiment 2, I chose to avoid any logic that assumes the pseudohomophone effect to be a reliable indicator of phonologic coding. I did so by extending Pring's (1981) method of case alternation to the proofreading task, and by using the story-word frequency effect to estimate the capacity of stimulus foils for falsely activating story-word lexical representations.

Consistent with Pring (1981), the logic of Experiment 2 follows from a strong version of the functional spelling unit hypothesis. By that strong version, phonologic coding requires intact functional spelling units. Consequently, disrupting the functional spelling units of words in stories should cause word identification to be unaffected by phonologic coding. It follows that, under case-alternating conditions, the magnitude of the story-word frequency effect for nonword homophone foils should be no greater than the magnitude of the story-word frequency effect to spelling control foils.

A weaker version of the functional spelling unit hypothesis might predict that disrupting functional spelling units will not cause phonologic coding to be abandoned entirely. Rather, this manipulation will merely reduce the capacity of phonologic codes to affect the outcome of word identification; perhaps because phonologic coding takes more time for disrupted, case-alternating stimuli. This weaker version predicts, at least, a reduction in the capacity of homophone foils to produce the story-word frequency effect. That is, it predicts a decrease in the magnitude of the story-word frequency effect to homophone foils in Experiment 2, relative to its magnitude in Experiment 1.

A third hypothesis is that phonologic mediation is fundamental to reading, including proofreading of disrupted, case-alternating text. Thus, phonologic codes constrain printed word identification even under extreme circumstances of stimulus presentation. If this last hypothesis holds, then the case-alternation manipulation should not perturb the pattern of results observed in Experiment 1. That is, we should observe a large, undiminished, story-word frequency effect upon error rates to homophone foils. And, the magnitude of the story-word frequency effect to homophone foils should be much larger than the equivalent effect to spelling control foils.

Method

Subjects. The subjects were again 52 native English speaking undergraduates attending Arizona State University who received course credit for their participation.

Presentation condition. The stories that were used in Experiment 1 were presented in Experiment 2 such that multiletter functional spelling units were broken up by case alternation. The rule used to create the case-alternating versions of the stories was that every other pair of letters should be of opposite case, except for strings in which a brief switch to letter-by-letter case-alternation more effectively broke up spelling structure. An example sentence appeared as "i FEel ThE GArdEn's SoFt eArtH bENeATh My BodY aND I sMelL tHE FRagRAncE ThaT ciRCulATes tHRoUgH tHe ROws oF FloWErs tHaT NOw SurROunD mE." Notice that no more than two adjoining letters within the same word appeared in the same case, and that this method of case alternation often disrupts syllabic units as well as graphemic units. Also, notice that this method of case alternation gives false clues to graphemic and syllabic structure--assuming that case alternation affects word identification in the manner proposed by Pring (1981). Consequently, if Pring's functional spelling unit hypothesis is correct, then this method of case alternation should disrupt phonologic coding and should eliminate (or at least reduce) the effect of story-word frequency for nonword homophone foils.

The case assignment for the letters in the nonword spelling controls was the same, position for position, as that of their yoked nonword homophone foils. Other than the use of new subjects, and the change in presentation conditions, the method of Experiment 2 was identical to that of Experiment 1. (As I noted previously, Experiments 1 and 2 were run concurrently to promote comparisons between resulting data sets.)

Results and Discussion

The results of Experiment 2 are presented in Table 2. As in Experiment 1, the dependent variable was the percentage of proofreading miss errors that occurred to target foil items. Target foils were either nonword homophones or nonword spelling controls that had been substituted for either high or low frequency story-words. Subject and item ANOVAs were computed appropriate to the type of foil (2) x story-word frequency (2) design of Experiment 2, and a planned comparison that included data from Experiment 1. All descriptive statistics that are reported come from subject analyses, and item error rates are presented in Appendix C.

Type of foil (homophones versus spelling controls). The mean error rate to nonword homophone foils such as SLEAT and GREAN (42.5%) was greater than the corresponding miss error rate to yoked spelling control foils (30.8%). This main effect of homophony was significant in both subject and item analyses [$F(1,50) = 8.48$, for subjects; $F(1,9) = 5.95$, for items].

Table 2
Percentage of Proofreading Miss Errors in Experiment 2 to Homophone and Spelling Control Foils that were Substituted for Low Frequency or High Frequency Story-Words

	Low Frequency		High Frequency			
	Mean	SE	Mean	SE	Mean	SE
Homophones	57.7	3.8	27.3	3.5	42.5	3.3
Spelling Controls	35.8	3.8	25.8	2.6	30.8	2.4
	46.7	3.1	26.5	2.1		

As I noted in the introduction to Experiment 1, a traditional elaboration of the phonologic mediation hypothesis is supported when homophone foils yield larger proofreading miss error rates than spelling control foils, as here. I argued earlier, though, that this elaboration of the phonologic mediation hypothesis relies too heavily on a questionable assumption whereby "all things are equal other than the manipulation of orthographic-phonologic similarity." Thus, the present discussion will focus, primarily, upon the relative magnitudes of respective, story-word frequency effects to nonword homophone and nonword spelling control foils.

Story-word frequency. The mean proofreading miss error rate to foils like SLEAT and SPEET that were substituted for low frequency story-words (46.7%) was greater than the corresponding miss error rate to yoked foils (GREAN and GRELN) that had been substituted for high frequency story-words (26.5%). This main effect of story-word frequency was significant in both subject and item analyses [$F(1,50) = 53.28$, for subjects; $F(1,9) = 5.52$, for items]. Thus, just as in Experiment 1, the stimulus foils reliably activate story-word lexical representations. However, as in Experiment 1, we require an analysis of the Story-Word Frequency x Type of Foil interaction to test the phonologic mediation hypothesis, and the strong version of the functional spelling unit hypothesis. To test these hypotheses, we must determine whether the magnitude of the story-word frequency effect is greater for homophone foils than for spelling controls.

Story-word frequency x type of foil. As is apparent in Table 2, the effect of story-word (SLEET) frequency is significantly larger for nonword homophone foils (SLEAT) than it is for spelling control foils [$F(1, 50) = 13.58$, for subjects; $F(1, 9) = 12.27$, for items]. Planned analyses of simple main effects found the effect of story-word frequency to nonword homophone foils to be significant in both subject and item analyses [$F(1,25) = 51.31$, for subjects; $F(1, 9) = 12.40$, for items]. However, the effect of story-word frequency to spelling control foils is only significant across subjects [$F(1, 25) = 7.93$, for subjects; $F(1, 9) = 1.11$, $p = .32$, for items]. Thus, again, as in Experiment 1, the nonword homophone foils can be assumed to activate story-word lexical representations, but we cannot determine whether spelling control foils ever actually activate story-word lexical representations. Rather, as noted for Experiment 1, the apparent effect of story-word frequency to spelling controls may be caused by uncontrolled properties of a few spelling control items, or some uncontrolled interaction between a few items and the contexts in which they appear.

The strong version of the functional spelling unit hypothesis predicted that nonword homophone foils should show no greater capacity for activating story-word lexical representations than spelling control foils. This follows because a case manipulation that disrupts the functional spelling units of stimulus words should cause performance to be unaffected by phonologic mediation. But, that prediction is falsified by the observed superior capacity of homophone foils to activate story-word lexical representations (revealed by the Story-Word Frequency x Type of Foil interaction effect). Rather, the evidence favors the phonologic mediation account.

Case x Story-Word Frequency. A weaker version of the functional spelling unit hypothesis predicts that nonword homophone foils' capacity for activating story-word lexical representations should be reduced, though not necessarily eliminated, by the case manipulation of Experiment 2. I tested this hypothesis in a comparison between the magnitude of the story-word frequency effect upon error rates to nonword homophone foils in Experiment 1 (upper-case presentation condition) and the magnitude of that effect in Experiment 2 (disruptive alternating-case condition). That is, I compared the difference between Experiment 1's error rate to nonword homophones that sound like low frequency story-words and Experiment 1's error rate to nonword homophones that sound like high frequency story-words (26.9%) with the like difference from Experiment 2 (30.4%).

The apparent change in magnitude of the story-word frequency effect (to nonword homophone foils) between Experiments 1 and 2 is opposite in direction to that predicted by the "weak" functional spelling unit hypothesis (although this difference was not significant [both subject and item $Fs < 1$]). Thus, neither the strong nor the weak versions of the functional spelling unit hypothesis are supported by the results of these experiments. However, a strong version of the phonologic mediation hypothesis is supported by the similarity of the results in Experiments 1 and 2. Thus, it is not merely the case that phonologic mediation fundamentally constrains printed word identification under relatively ideal stimulus presentation conditions, it is also the case that phonologic mediation cannot be readily discouraged (at least by a disruptive case manipulation) as is often assumed.

IV. CONCLUSIONS

The case alternation manipulation did not disrupt homophone foils' capacity for falsely activating story-word lexical representations. Thus, the present results run counter to the predictions of the functional spelling unit hypothesis and Pring's (1981) account of how case alternation affects word identification. Because the present results failed to support a phonologic coding locus of case-alternation effects, they are at least consistent with Besner's (1983) suggestion that case-alternation effects are localized within a verification procedure in which readers verify their knowledge of the appearance/spelling of each word against any stimulus visual/orthographic representation that pretends to be that word. Essentially, by this argument, case-alternation can affect processing because it presents the verification procedure with an unusual form of the stimulus. This unusual form will be very different from the stimulus form that is typically experienced by a subject, and thus will require more time to be verified against the subject's expectation for that stimulus.

The present results are also at least consistent with the assertion of Perfetti et al. (1988) that phonologic coding is an obligatory process. Perfetti et al. (1988) conducted backward priming experiments in which word identification of target words (e.g., hear), followed by a phonologically similar masking stimulus (e.g., HEER), was superior than to that of target words which were followed by a masking stimulus that was merely orthographically similar (e.g., HEOR). Moreover, they observed this result under presentation conditions in which subjects could only rarely report even parts (letters) of the masking stimulus. Perfetti et al. (1988) argued that this backward priming effect indicates automatic priming of target phonology by masking stimulus phonology prior to word identification, and thus indicates that phonologic coding is an automatic (nonoptional) component process of word identification.

V. GENERAL DISCUSSION

Evidence for false activation of specific story-word (SLEET) lexical representations is found when story-word frequency affects the proofreading of homophone (SLEAT) or spelling control (SPEET) foils. In the present experiments, the frequency of story-words such as SLEET only affected proofreading miss error rates to homophone foils. I assume that the relative magnitude of this frequency effect estimates the relative capacity of stimulus foils to activate story-word lexical representations. Consequently, the larger relative magnitude of the story-word frequency effect to homophone foils (compared to spelling control foils) indicates that phonologic codes are primary constraints in word identification. Thus, the present results support the phonologic mediation hypothesis, and join a family of recent findings that have resurrected this hypothesis (e.g., see Besner et al., 1981; Perfetti et al., 1988; Van Orden, 1987; Van Orden et al., 1988).

Frequency effects and lexical access. For the present logic to hold, it is essential that the story-word frequency effect be localized within or following the process of word identification. By either of these scenarios, access to story-word representations is implicated. Thus, it is consistent with widely held assumptions concerning lexical access to assume that the story-word frequency effect reflects access to story-word lexical representations. It should be noted, though, that an alternative which localized the story-word frequency effect prior to lexical access would undermine the present logic. However, such an alternative seems highly unlikely.

Verification and proofreading. Van Orden (1987) used a verification hypothesis to predict an effect of category-exemplar (SLEET) frequency upon false positive categorization error rates to homophone foils (SLEAT). By that hypothesis, word identification includes a verification process that verifies whether, for example, knowledge of the category-exemplar SLEET's spelling matches the orthographic representation of a stimulus nonword homophone foil SLEAT (cf. Becker, 1976; 1980; Becker & Killion, 1977; Forster, 1976; Grossberg & Stone, 1986; Paap, McDonald, Schvaneveldt, & Noel, 1987; Paap, Newsome, McDonald, & Schvaneveldt, 1982; Rubenstein et al., 1971; Schvaneveldt & McDonald, 1981; Stone & Van Orden, 1989). When readers are highly familiar with a category-exemplar they are likely to have ready knowledge of its spelling. Consequently, they are least likely to be fooled by a homophone impostor that sounds like a high frequency category-exemplar.

Van Orden's (1987) category-exemplar frequency effect parallels the present story-word frequency effect. Due to this similarity, the verification hypothesis accommodates that latter effect as readily as the former. If we assume (a) that accurate verification requires complete and readily available knowledge of story-word spellings, and (b) that the relative availability and completeness of spelling knowledge is a function of frequency (familiarity), then it follows that verification will be most likely to detect homophone foils that sound like high frequency story-words. However, failure to detect the impostor spelling of a nonword homophone foil will result in false positive word identification. And, false positive word identification underlies proofreading miss errors to nonword homophone foils. In other words, proofreaders are more likely to be fooled by nonword homophone foils that sound like relatively unfamiliar words because they are less likely to retrieve quickly and accurately the correct spellings of unfamiliar words.

Proofreading errors to spelling control foils. The pattern of error rates to homophone foils is consistent with the phonologic mediation hypothesis coupled with a verification hypothesis. However, the present experiments do not reveal the source of proofreading miss errors to spelling control foils. Spelling controls yielded high miss error rates in both experiments. But, the pattern of these errors did not provide reliable evidence that proofreading of spelling control foils included false activation of story-word lexical representations. Earlier, I speculated that some proofreading errors to these foils might result because subjects interpret them as unfamiliar words, whose meanings must be, perhaps, derived from context. Unfortunately, though, the present experiments did not test this hypothesis.

Healy and her colleagues (Healy, 1981; Healy et al., 1983) have conducted a very fine-grained analysis of proofreading errors to foils like the present spelling control foils (in that they are not homophonic to story-words), but much more visually similar to their corresponding story-words. They manipulated the similarity between letter pairs, one of which was an original letter in the correct spelling of a story-word, and the other of which was substituted for the original letter to form a misspelling. They observed strong effects of letter similarity--defined relative to letter envelope (Bouma, 1971) and the deletion and addition of features that "create" the substituted letter from the original letter. They concluded that their results were consistent with subjects using a "hierarchical feature test" that gives priority to letter envelope.

Notice that Healy's analysis shows clearly that visual properties of letter strings affect proofreading performance, not just phonologic properties. Nonetheless, the proposed hierarchical feature test could occur either in a process that identifies letters as a preliminary to phonologic coding, or in the process of spelling verification. Thus, the present discussion is not compromised by these prior findings.

One more point concerning errors to spelling control foils is worth noting. In several unpublished lexical decision experiments, I have found an effect of sound-alike word (SLEET) frequency upon false positive error rates to nonword homophone foils (SLEAT). However, I have yet to find this effect upon false positive error rates to nonword spelling control foils--even in a lexical decision experiment in which the overall false positive error rate to spelling control foils was not significantly different from the corresponding error rate to nonword homophone foils.

Notice that the forementioned pattern of unpublished lexical decision results is a qualitative match for the present patterns of story-word frequency effects upon proofreading. To the extent that effects like the story-word frequency effect indicate the capacity of a class of nonword stimulus foils to activate specific lexical representations, spelling control foils apparently have a nonsignificant capacity for such activation. In all of these experiments, however, nonword homophone foils have produced reliable sound-alike word frequency effects which indicate their relatively large capacity for activating corresponding lexical representations. Thus, processing of spelling control foils in lexical decision experiments may differ substantially from processing of nonword homophone foils, just as processing of spelling control foils in the proofreading task may differ from processing of nonword homophone foils. The general point of this digression is that it may pay to re-examine any result (especially any null result) concerning word identification that originates in a comparison between nonword homophones and spelling controls.

The relative timecourse of phonologic mediation in proofreading. One possibility that I have not discussed to this point is that proofreading miss errors are caused by phonologic codes that have an effect late in the process of word identification. If this were true, then the present results would support a hypothesis by which phonology can affect word identification, but not necessarily a hypothesis by which phonologic codes generally mediate word identification. It would be difficult to rule out this possibility for the present data sets without some sort of on-line analysis.

However, concerning this point, it is worth noting again that the present effects upon proofreading mimic effects upon categorization of word and nonword homophone foils (Van Orden, 1987; Van Orden et al., 1988). Moreover, the categorization experiments of Van Orden et al. (1988) included on-line measures of response time (RT). RT distributions of false positive "yes" responses to foils such as SLEAT (for the category WEATHER) were virtually identical in their fast RT ends to those of yoked exemplar controls such as RAIN (again for the category WEATHER). If phonologic codes are relatively late constraints in word identification, then there should have been a shift to longer false positive "yes" RTs that would reflect this possibility. Thus, unless one wishes to argue that the relative time course of phonologic coding in the categorization task is faster than the relative time course of phonologic coding in the proofreading task--a position for which no positive evidence exists--then we are left with the conclusion that phonologic mediation generally affects printed word identification in both of these tasks.

Final Comments. Several of the foregoing arguments relied upon converging evidence from lexical decision, categorization, and proofreading tasks. Presently, Greta Thies, Karen Garlington, Cindy Simonfy, and I are using these three tasks in a more carefully controlled cross-task test of the phonologic mediation hypothesis. We will apply the present logic in a cross-task comparison of sound-alike (spelled-alike) word frequency effects. We expect from pilot work that those experiments will tie up the few loose ends that remain from the present discussion. Hence, I conclude that the present results repair key holes in the empirical support for phonologic mediation. Additionally, at the beginning of this chapter I described computational motivation for phonologic mediation that follows from the phonologic coherence hypothesis. Thus, from my perspective, both empirical and theoretical arguments appear consistent with the most general form of the phonologic mediation hypothesis; the version by which phonologic mediation is fundamental to reading.

FOOTNOTES

[1]The precise nature of phonologic codes is not known; so, here, by phonologic code, I mean some candidate from the superset of articulatory, phonemic, phonetic, etc., codes, or perhaps some code that is invariant across this set. For those readers more familiar with the graphically cumbersome term

phonological, the typical use of *phonological* in the literature concerning printed word identification could be substituted without a change of meaning for every instance of the more graphically economical term *phonologic* that I have chosen.

[2]By noise I mean colored noise corresponding to meaningful phonologic, semantic, syntactic, etc., alternatives, not white noise which would be statistically independent of stimulus orthography.

[3]Actually, Van Orden (1987), Experiment 3, used a method that included only word homophone foils such as BEATS for the category VEGETABLE. However, Van Orden et al. (1988) report correlational analyses that extend this effect to nonword homophone foils, and I have also found this effect of category exemplar frequency using nonword homophone foils in several unreported categorization experiments.

[4]I chose not to report false alarm rates because the hypotheses in question did not yield obvious *a priori* predictions concerning false alarm rates and I did not observe significant differences in false alarm rates that would motivate *ad hoc* speculation.

ACKNOWLEDGMENTS

I thank Antoinette Gesi for technical assistance in the preparation of stimulus items and her help with pilot experiments. I also thank Bruce Pennington, Derek Besner, Glyn Humphreys, Greg Stone, and Krista Rabe for their helpful comments on successive versions of this chapter. Most of all, though, I am indebted to Alice Healy who generously supported the most crucial phase of these studies. All pilot work and stimulus preparation was done in her laboratory at the University of Colorado at Boulder. Alice Healy also deserves special credit for improvements that came from her comments on a very early draft of this chapter.

REFERENCES

Abramovici, S. (1983). Errors in proofreading: Evidence for syntactic control of letter processing? *Memory & Cognition*, **11**, 258-261.

Andrews, S. (1982). Phonological recoding: Is the regularity effect consistent? *Memory & Cognition*, **10**, 565-575.

Banks, W.P., Oka, E., & Shugarman, S. (1981). Recoding of printed words to internal speech: Does recoding come before lexical access? In O. J. L. Tzeng & H. Singer (Eds.), *Perception of print: Reading research in experimental psychology* (pp. 137-170). Hillsdale, NJ: LEA.

Becker, C.A. (1976). Allocation of attention during visual word recognition. *Journal of Experimental Psychology: Human Perceptions and Performance*, **2**, 556-566.

Becker, C.A. (1980). Semantic context effects in visual word recognition: An analysis of semantic strategies. *Memory & Cognition*, **8**, 493-512.

Becker, C.A., & Killion, T.H. (1977). Interaction of visual and cognitive effects in word recognition. *Journal of Experimental Psychology: Human Perception and Performance*, **3**, 389-401.

Besner, D. (1983). Basic decoding components in reading: Two dissociable feature extraction processes. *Canadian Journal of Psychology*, **37**, 429-438.

Besner, D., Davies, J., & Daniels, S. (1981). Reading for meaning: The effects of concurrent articulation. *The Quarterly Journal of Experimental Psychology*, **33A**, 415-437.

Bouma, H. (1971). Visual recognition of isolated lower-case letters. *Vision Research*, **11**, 459-474.

Coltheart, M. (1978). Lexical access in simple reading tasks. In G. Underwood (Ed.), *Strategies of information processing* (pp. 151-216). London: Academic Press.

Coltheart, M., Davelaar, E., Jonasson, J.T., & Besner, D. (1977). Access to the internal lexicon. In S. Dornic (Ed.), *Attention and performance VI*. New York: Academic Press.

Davelaar, E., Coltheart, M., Besner, D., & Jonasson, J. T. (1978). Phonological recoding and lexical access. *Memory & Cognition*, **6**, 391-402.

Evett, L.J., & Humphreys, G.W. (1981). The use of abstract graphemic information in lexical access. *Quarterly Journal of Experimental Psychology*, **33A**, 325-350.

Forster, K.I. (1976). Accessing the mental lexicon. In R.J. Wales and E.C.T. Walker (Eds.), *New approaches to language mechanisms*. Amsterdam: North Holland.

Grossberg, S., & Stone, G. (1986). Neural dynamics of word recognition and recall: Priming, learning, and resonance. *Psychologal Review*, **93**, 46-74.

Haber, R.N., & Schindler, R. M. (1981). Error in proofreading: Evidence of syntactic control of letter processing? *Journal Experimental Psychology: Human Perception and Performance*, **7**, 573-574.

Hanson, V.L., & Fowler, C.A. (1987). Phonological coding in word reading: Evidence from hearing and deaf readers. *Memory & Cognition*, **15**, 199-207.

Healy, A.F. (1981). The effects of visual similarity on proofreading for misspellings. *Memory & Cognition*, **9**, 453-460.

Healy, A.F., Volbrecht, V.J., & Nye, T.R. (1983). The effects of perceptual condition on proofreading for misspellings. *Memory & Cognition*, **11**, 528-538.

Kleiman, G.M. (1975). Speech recoding in reading. *Journal of Verbal Learning and Verbal Behavior*, **14**, 323-339.

Kucera, H., & Francis, W. (1967). *Computational analysis of present-day American English.* Providence, RI: Brown University Press.

Levy, B.A. (1983). Proofreading familiar text: Constraints on visual processing. *Memory & Cognition*, **11**, 1-12.

Levy, B.A., Newell, S., Snyder, J., & Timmins, K. (1986). Processing changes across reading encounters. *Journal of Experimental Psychology: Learning, Memory and Cognition*, **12**, 467-478.

McQuade, D.V. (1981). Variable reliance on phonological information in visual word recognition. *Language & Speech*, **24**, 99-109.

Meyer, D.E., & Gutschera, K.D. (1975, November). *Orthographic versus phonemic processing of printed words.* Presented at Psychonomic Society Meeting, Denver.

Meyer, D.E., & Ruddy, M.G. (1973, November). *Lexical-memory retrieval based on graphemic and phonemic representation of printed words.* Presented at Psychonomic Society Meeting, St. Louis.

Paap, K. R., McDonald, J. E., Schvaneveldt, R. W., & Noel, R. W. (1987). In M. Coltheart (Ed.), *Attention and performance XII The psychology of reading.* Hillsdale, NJ: LEA.

Paap, K.R., Newsome, S.L., McDonald, J.E., & Schvaneveldt, R.W. (1982). An activation-verification model for letter and word recognition: The word-superiority effect. *Psychological Review*, **89**, 573-594.

Perfetti, C.A., Bell, L.C., & Delaney, S. (1988). Automatic (prelexical) phonetic activation in silent word reading: Evidence from backward masking. *Journal of Memory and Language*, **27**, 59-70.

Pring, L. (1981). Phonological codes and functional spelling units: Reality and implications. *Perception & Psychophysics*, **30**, 573-578.

Rubenstein, H., Lewis, S.S., & Rubenstein, M. A. (1971). Evidence for phonemic recoding in visual word recognition. *Journal of Verbal Learning & Verbal Behavior*, **10**, 645-657.

Schvaneveldt, R.W., & McDonald, J.E. (1981). Semantic context and the encoding of words: Evidence for two modes of stimulus analysis. *Journal of Experimental Psychology: Human Perception and Performance*, **7**, 673-687.

Shulman, H.G., Hornak, R., & Sanders, E. (1978). The effect of graphemic, phonetic, and semantic relationships on access to lexical structures. *Memory & Cognition*, **6**, 115-123.

Smolensky, P. (1986a). Formal modeling of subsymbolic processes: An introduction to harmony theory. In N. E. Sharkey (Ed.), *Advances in Cognitive Science 1*. NY: John Wiley & Sons.

Smolensky, P. (1986b). Foundations of harmony theory: Cognitive dynamical systems and the subsymbolic theory of information processing. In D.E. Rumelhart & J.L. McClelland (Eds.), *Parallel distributed processing: Explorations in the microstructure of cognition. Volume 1: Foundations*. Cambridge, MA: MIT Press/Bradford Books.

Smolensky, P. (1988). On the proper treatment of connectionism. *Behavioral and Brain Sciences*, **11**, 1-23.

Stone, G.O., & Van Orden, G.C. (1989). Are words represented by nodes? *Memory & Cognition.*, **17**, 511-524.

Van Orden, G. C. (1984). *A ROWS is a /ROZ/ is a ROSE: Visual, phonological, developmental and strategic influences upon lexical access*. Unpublished doctoral dissertation, University of California at San Diego.

Van Orden, G.C. (1987). A ROWS is a ROSE: Spelling, sound and reading. *Memory & Cognition*, **15**, 181-198.

Van Orden, G.C., Johnston, J.C., & Hale, B. L. (1988). Word identification in reading proceeds from spelling to sound to meaning. *Journal of Experimental Psychology: Learning, Memory, and Cognition*. **14**, 371-386.

Van Orden, G.C., Pennington, B.F., & Stone, G.O. (1989). *Word identification in reading and the promise of subsymbolic psycholinguistics*. (Submitted for publication).

Weber, R. M. (1970). A linguistic analysis of first-grade reading errors. *Reading Research Quarterly*, **5**, 427-451.

APPENDIX A

One of the two stories used in Experiments 1 and 2. Homophone foils have been highlighted in the text.

LUCILLE

I ROUND THE CORNER FROM 42ND STREET TO 8TH AVENUE AND THE FULL BLAST OF THE WIND MAKES TEARS FORM IN MY EYES. THE SPACES BETWEEN THESE DAMN SKYSCRAPERS BLOW LIKE WIND TUNNELS, NEARLY RIPS YOUR EYEBROWS OFF. THIS IS MY FIRST TIME IN NEW YORK, BUT THEN I'VE SEEN A LOT OF FIRST TIMES IN THE LAST TEN YEARS. MOVING IS WHAT I'M DOING, MOVING AND NEVER STAYING.

TOO MANY PEOPLE--NEW YORK IS TOO MANY PEOPLE. SURE, THE ENERGY IS HERE, BUT THAT ENERGY IS FUELED BY PEOPLE ON PEOPLE'S NERVES AND PEOPLE'S NERVES ON PEOPLE'S NERVES. TENSION FEEDS ANXIETY; ANXIETY COMPLETES THE LOOP BY FEEDING TENSION AND THE MENTAL ILLNESS IS SELF PERPETUATING. IF THE NUTS GET TOO CLOSE HERE, THE ILLNESS ABSORBS YOU. MY BEST DEFENSE IS MY RIGHT ***ELBO***. JABS CREATE SPACE AND SPACE PRESERVES SANITY.

I TRAVEL NOW, BUT I USED TO LIVE SOMEWHERE, WITH LUCILLE. I LOVED HER AND I LOVE HER AND TOMORROW IT WILL BE THE SAME. I IMAGINE THAT SHE LOVED ME WITH THE SAME HEAT, BUT HOW CAN YOU KNOW FEELINGS WHEN ALL YOU GET IS TALK. WE SPENT A LOT OF TIME AT THE ZOO. WHO KNOWS WHY--HELL, WHY ANYTHING. SHE FIRST SAID SHE LOVED ME AS WE WALKED FROM THE PRIMATE HOUSE. SHE ALWAYS STOPPED THERE TO VISIT A FAVORITE ***MUNKEY*** NICKNAMED MR. CALABASH. THE NAME WAS ONE SHE'D HEARD ON TV. THE BEAST WAS MERELY PITIFUL AND LONELY, NEVER ABLE TO FIT IN WITH THE REST OF THE TROOP THAT SHARED THE CAGE. MAYBE THAT WAS WHY IT WAS HER FAVORITE, MISFITS ATTRACT EACH OTHER. ANYWAY, MISFITTING NO LONGER MATTERS.

I SPOT A LIKELY BAR AND HEAD FOR ITS ENTRANCE. AS I DUCK THROUGH THE DOOR, I LOOK BACK OVER MY SHOULDER. STUPID, AS THOUGH SOMEONE WOULD RECOGNIZE ME ENTERING A NEW YORK BAR, OR AS THOUGH IT MATTERS. I DON'T KNOW HOW, BUT THE FEELING STILL HOLDS THAT I SHOULD ***SNEEK*** INTO BARS--THE RESIDUE OF EARLY GUILT, THE LEGACY OF MY PASTOR FATHER.

I SLIP INTO THE KHAKI ***GREAN*** VINYL SEAT OF A BOOTH NEAR THE JUKEBOX. BUT I GET BACK UP TO FEED SILVER INTO THE CIGARETTE MACHINE. I CALL OUT MY ORDER AS I RETURN TO MY

SEAT--SCOTCH NEAT, WATER BACK. MY DRINK IS DELIVERED; SWEET SCOTCH, BOTH MY GOD AND THE ***NEKTAR*** OF MY GOD. WORSHIP IS SHORT, MY DRINK IS GONE, AND I ORDER ANOTHER. AFTER A HALF DOZEN SACRAMENTS I CAN FACE MY WORLD, MY NEW BIGGEST CITY WORLD.

THE BRIGHT LIGHT OF THE AFTERNOON SUN GIVES ME SECOND THOUGHTS AND I RE-ENTER THE BAR. AS I ORDER ANOTHER DRINK, SOMEONE ASKS ME FOR THE TIME. I LOOK FOR A CLOCK, BUT DON'T FIND ONE. (MY KIND OF BAR, THE ETERNAL KIND WITH NO CLUE TO TIME'S PASSING.) I TELL THE GUY I DON'T HAVE THE TIME AND I JOKE WITH THE TRUTH, THAT I DON'T EVEN KNOW WHAT ***MUNTH*** IT IS. ONCE I RECLAIM MY BOOTH, I FEEL AT HOME AGAIN; AND, RELATIVE TO ALL OTHER PLACES IN THIS CITY, I AM AT HOME. TO CELEBRATE THIS INSIGHT I TOSS BACK MY DRINK AND ORDER ANOTHER. THIS SACRED CELEBRATION CONTINUES AS MY FOCUS NARROWS AND MY WORLD CONVERGES: HOME, CHURCH, FAMILY AND GOVERNMENT ARE NOW ONE WITH ME IN MY NEW BOOTH, WITHIN MY NEW BAR. I FEEL THE PEACE OF KNOWING MY PLACE AND HOLDING MY POSITION. ALL IS AS IT SHOULD BE.

I MUST HAVE FALLEN TO THE FLOOR AND NOW A CIRCLE OF STRANGE FACES IS STARING DOWN AT ME, BUT I CAN'T FIGURE OUT WHAT FLOOR I'VE FALLEN TO. SOMEONE ABOVE ME ASKS IF I CAN ***SPEEK*** AND I'M NOT SURE IF I CAN. I TRY TO ANSWER AND "YES" COMES OUT OF MY MOUTH--I GUESS I CAN TALK. THEY HELP ME TO A BOOTH AND I NOTICE THE EMPTY GLASS AND THE WATER BACK. ONCE I'M STEADY IN THE BOOTH, I'M LEFT ALONE. I HEAR ONE MAN ASK ANOTHER IF THEY SHOULD CALL A ***DOKTOR***, AS THEY WALK BACK TO THE BAR. THE OTHER GUY SAYS THAT THEY SHOULDN'T BOTHER BECAUSE I'M "JUST A BUM, ANYWAY."

MY PRESENT EXPERIENCE OF SITTING IN THE BOOTH INCLUDES NO KNOWLEDGE OF MY PAST. THE OBLIVION THAT PRECEDED THE CIRCLE OF FACES HAS GIVEN WAY TO A LACK OF MEMORY. BUT THE MOMENT OF AMNESIA TOO SOON REFORMS INTO REMEMBERING AND I RE-ENTER MY HELL OF SELF LOATHING AND RECRIMINATION. IN MY GUILT-EDGED MEMORIES MY CAR SLIPS OUT OF CONTROL, ACROSS THE DOUBLE ***YELLOE*** LINES, AND HEAD-ON INTO THE TRUCK. THE TRUCK'S FORCE SHEARS OFF THE FRONT HALF OF THE CAR AT AN ANGLE THAT INCLUDES THE PASSENGER SEAT, AN ANGLE THAT INCLUDES LUCILLE.

THE LUXURIOUS, ELABORATE, CONSUMING GUILT PROBABLY COMES FROM MY DESIRE TO CONTROL. THE PSYCHIC FORCE THAT DRIVES MY NEED FOR SELF-DETERMINATION NOW DRIVES MY CLAIM, MY NEED, OF GUILT FOR LUCILLE'S DEATH. MY FRIENDS CONSOLED ME; THEY BLAMED THE ACCIDENT ON THE DARK NIGHT, THE WET, FREEZING ***SLEAT***, AND THE CONSEQUENT GLASSY

ROADS. BUT I KNOW THE TRUTH. I REMEMBER MY LAUGHTER AT LUCILLE'S FEAR THAT WE SHOULDN'T DRIVE THAT NIGHT. I REMEMBER HER WARM, QUIET VOICE ASKING IF WE MIGHT TRAVEL THE NEXT DAY. I REMEMBER MY ANGER AT HER STUPID PREMONITIONS. I ORDER A DOUBLE SCOTCH AND ANOTHER WATER BACK.

APPENDIX B

This is one of the stories used in Experiments 1 and 2. As in Appendix A, homophone foils have been highlighted.

THE HOUR OF LEAST RESISTANCE

IN THE GARDEN, ALL IS QUIET. I MOVE NOT AT ALL, LIKE A HUNTED FAWN, THOUGH I AM THE HUNTER. WHEN I FINALLY ADVANCE, MY MOTION IS CALCULATED AND PRECISE. ADRENALINE STREAMS THROUGH MY VEINS AS I WATCH AND LISTEN FROM MY VANTAGE POINT. I AM PREPARED FOR MY DESTINY, I AM FILLED WITH PURPOSE, I AM POISED, CALMLY ELECTRIC, BEFORE MY ENEMY.

THE NIGHT AIR CARRIES DISTANT STREET SOUNDS AND BITS OF CONVERSATION COMING FROM THE OPEN WINDOWS OF THE HOUSE. A ***CRICKIT*** CHIRPS OFF TO MY LEFT AS I INCH FORWARD TOWARD A SIDE DOOR. MY TARGET IS STILL FAR AWAY WHEN DISTANCE IS MEASURED BY MY CAREFUL PROGRESS. BUT, I DO NOT RUSH MY MOVEMENTS, FOR THE EVENT AT HAND NEED NOT COME QUICKLY. I ENJOY THE WAITING TIME AS I WILL ENJOY THE ACTS TO FOLLOW.

AN UNFAMILIAR MELODY BEGINS AND SOMEONE MOVES PAST THE WINDOW THAT IS BEFORE ME. I TAKE ADVANTAGE OF THE ***MUZIC*** TO COVER THE NOISE OF MY MOVEMENT AND I START ONCE AGAIN TOWARD THE DOOR. INCH BY INCH, NO NEED TO RUSH, I WOULD PREFER THAT THEY BE ASLEEP BEFORE I ENTER. A MAN COMES TO THE DOOR AND LOOKS OUT. I FREEZE; IT IS MARCOLA. FOR YEARS HE RULED MY COUNTRY. HIS DEATH SQUADS ENSURED UNQUESTIONED AUTHORITY. BUT NOW HE LIVES IN NEW JERSEY, IN MORRISTOWN, A SIMPLE ORDINARY ***PURSON*** LIVING ON THE MILLIONS THAT HE STOLE FROM MY PEOPLE. MARCOLA MOVES BACK INSIDE THE HOUSE AND I START TOWARD THE DOOR AGAIN. I AM GOD'S INSTRUMENT; MARCOLA AND HIS FAMILY OF DESPOILING PIGS MUST DIE.

I FEEL THE GARDEN'S SOFT EARTH BENEATH MY BODY AND I SMELL THE FRAGRANCE THAT CIRCULATES THROUGH THE ROWS OF FLOWERS THAT NOW SURROUND ME. I PUT MY HAND FORWARD

AND, INADVERTENTLY, RIP THE BLOSSOM FROM A ***PANZY***--MY FIRST VICTIM. SUDDENLY I AM OVERWHELMED BY DEJA VU. IT IS IMPOSSIBLE, BUT I FEEL AN INTENSE FAMILIARITY, AS THOUGH I COULD HAVE PREVIOUSLY CRAWLED THROUGH THIS AMERICAN GARDEN. NONSENSE, IT MUST BE A CONSEQUENCE OF MY FATIGUE LADEN VIGILANCE, A VIGILANCE THAT I MUST MAINTAIN DESPITE HAVING NEITHER SLEPT NOR EATEN FOR SEVERAL DAYS. THAT MUST BE IT, AND THAT MUST BE THE SOURCE OF THE LIGHT-HEADEDNESS, AND THAT MUST BE WHAT OCCASIONALLY CAUSES MY HAIR TO STAND ON END, AND THE CONSTANT, CHILLING, CREEPING FEELING ACROSS MY ***SKALP***. BUT, I MUST NOT SUCCUMB TO THESE DISTRACTING PERTURBATIONS OF EXPERIENCE, MY MISSION REQUIRES ABSOLUTE CLARITY OF MIND.

I AM NOW VERY CLOSE TO THE DOOR. THE LIGHTS HAVE BEEN EXTINGUISHED THROUGHOUT MOST OF THE HOUSE. THE MARCOLA FAMILY HAS GONE TO BED. I MOVE CAREFULLY UP THE FEW STEPS AND PAUSE ON THIS THRESHOLD OF MURDER TO GATHER ALL MY RESERVES OF BODILY POWER, SPIRITUAL ENERGY, AND MENTAL CALCULATION. I WILL REPAY THE DEBT OF HORROR, SETTLE THE ***SKORE*** FOR AN ENTIRE COUNTRY.

JUST INSIDE THE DOOR, I NOTICE A HAT RACK. MARCOLA'S ENGLISH ***DURBY*** HANGS AMONG AN ASSORTMENT OF CAPS. FUNNY HOW, PRIOR TO THE COUP, THIS SILLY HAT BECAME SUCH A HATED SYMBOL OF MARCOLA'S WESTERN WAYS. AS I SCAN THE ROOM, I NOTICE THE EXTENSIVE COLLECTION OF AFRICAN ARTIFACTS. THE SUBTLE IRONY OF THIS COLLECTION YIELDS A BITTER COMIC IMAGE; THE LEADER OF ONE DESPERATELY POOR COUNTRY PROCURING THE COSTLY HISTORICAL REMAINS OF OTHERS. CARVED IMAGES DECORATE ALL THE WALLS AND ABOVE THE MANTLE HANGS A HUGE SHIELD AND A ***SPEER*** THAT IS AT LEAST TEN FEET LONG.

THE STAIRS THAT LEAD TO THE BEDROOMS ARE TO MY RIGHT. MY CAREFULLY CHOSEN SLIPPERS MAKE NO SOUND AS I ASCEND TO THE SECOND FLOOR.

---SOMETHING CUTS INTO MY THROAT. MY BREATH IS CUT OFF. MY HEAD JERKS BACK. ALL IS TERROR. ALL IS ***FEER***. I NEED AIR. I NEED LIFE. SPONGY BLACK OBLIVION SOAKS UP THOUGHT, BIT BY BIT, FROM THE OUTSIDE IN. I SEE PULSE. I HEAR BLOOD--MY GOD! OH, MY GOD! OH, MY MOTHER! PLEASE HELP ME!---

MARCOLA'S BODYGUARD DISPOSES OF THE ASSASSIN'S CORPSE AND FEELS PLEASED THAT THE STRUGGLE HAS NOT DISTURBED THE HOUSEHOLD; AS ALWAYS, THE PIANO-WIRE GARROTE KILLS DISCREETLY. THE BODYGUARD KNOWS THAT HIS EXCELLENCY MUST RISE EARLY THIS NEXT MORNING; MARCOLA HAS AN APPOINTMENT IN THE CITY WITH HIS BROKER. THEY PLAN TO

REVIEW RECENT TRENDS IN THE STOCK ***MARKIT***, TOWARD UPDATING THEIR INVESTMENT STRATEGIES.

APPENDIX C

High Frequency and Low Frequency Story-Words, Their Yoked Homophone and Spelling Control Foils, and the Respective Percentages of Proofreading Miss Errors to Homophone and Spelling Control Items in Experiments 1 and 2

High Frequency Story-Word	High Frequency Homophone	Exp 1	Exp 2	Low Frequency Story-Word	Low Frequency Homophone	Exp 1	Exp 2
YELLOW	YELLOE	42.3	34.6	ELBOW	ELBOE	26.9	34.6
MONTH	MUNTH	3.8	3.8	MONKEY	MUNKEY	7.7	23.1
SPEAK	SPEEK	30.8	34.6	SNEAK	SNEEK	57.7	57.7
DOCTOR	DOKTOR	3.8	3.8	NECTAR	NEKTAR	26.9	69.2
GREEN	GREAN	53.8	42.3	SLEET	SLEAT	69.2	50.0
MARKET	MARKIT	11.5	50.0	CRICKET	CRICKIT	46.2	73.1
MUSIC	MUZIC	7.7	23.1	PANSY	PANZY	88.5	88.5
SCORE	SKORE	11.5	15.4	SCALP	SKALP	19.2	38.5
PERSON	PURSON	15.4	7.7	DERBY	DURBY	76.9	80.8
FEAR	FEER	38.5	57.7	SPEAR	SPEER	69.2	61.5

Spelling Control

High Frequency Spelling Control	Exp 1	Exp 2	Low Frequency Spelling Control	Exp 1	Exp 2
YELLOT	57.7	38.5	ELBOT	19.2	11.5
MINTH	0.0	11.5	MOFKEY	26.9	23.1
SPELK	3.8	0.0	SNELK	7.7	19.2
DOSTOR	7.7	11.5	NESTAR	46.2	80.8
GRELN	15.4	30.8	SPEET	30.8	11.5
MACKET	53.8	46.2	CRINKET	42.3	26.9
MUDIC	15.4	15.4	PAKSY	46.2	53.8
SCOME	30.8	23.1	SWALP	30.8	42.3
PEKSON	30.8	26.9	DERGY	73.1	46.2
FLAR	50.0	53.8	SPLAR	34.6	42.3

5
DEREK: THE DIRECT ENCODING ROUTINE FOR EVOKING KNOWLEDGE

PATRICK BROWN

Department of Psychology
University of Western Ontario
Ontario, Canada

I. INTRODUCTION

Models of even small parts of the reading process are becoming more and more complicated. At conferences, people have trouble getting their model on a single slide. Clearly, for lovers of parsimony, this is a regrettable situation. While it may turn out that the complexity of the models is only commensurate with that of the subject process, this need not be conceded given our current knowledge. The thesis of this chapter is that a simple mechanism which has hitherto been overlooked can account for at least as much data as any of the extant, complex models.

It is difficult to say exactly what I mean by the term *complex*, but a rough idea can be given by reference to models presented recently by Besner and McCann (1987) and by Coltheart (1987). I mention these authors only because they come quickly to mind; almost any others would serve. Perhaps a useful if arbitrary index would be that any model having more than three boxes and three arrows qualifies as complex. This standard is chosen for what should be an obvious reason (my model has three boxes and three arrows). The point, however, is not to quibble over exactly how many boxes should be tolerated, but to observe that a very few boxes and a very few arrows are preferable to many of either, other things being equal.

It is, of course, axiomatic that "other things" are never equal. Part of my purpose in this chapter is to demonstrate that whatever inequality there may be in the performance of simple and complex models of reading favors the former. The model to be presented below is an evolution of one presented in a recent paper on phonological frame theory (Brown & Besner, 1987). I believe it represents substantial progress, however, in simplifying our conception of word recognition. This is achieved through the simple expedient of eliminating lexicons (considered as stores containing information which identifies a word as a word; this would include, for example, case- and font-independent orthographic information, but not semantic information).

Input lexicons are nasty, brutish things. They make no contribution in the way of explaining data which cannot be explained in any other way. To establish this case, I shall first review the origins of the concept of lexicon; I shall then describe a new streamlined model which I call the Direct Encoding Routine for Evoking Knowledge (DEREK); and then review very briefly some major findings from the normal and patient literatures relating to the lexicon, showing how DEREK deals with them.

II. ORIGIN OF THE CONCEPT OF LEXICON

What is a lexicon? It is a way of organizing information. A lexicon can be understood as a way of organizing the sort of knowledge that researchers suspect language users have. That is, we have a sense of what sort of knowledge language users need to perform their task in normal daily life, and our conception of that knowledge can be expressed in terms of a lexicon. At this level, a lexicon organizes for our pretheoretical ruminations the sort of knowledge we want our theories to be about.

At another level, the concept of lexicon can model the actual memory structures with which real language users mediate their language use. The reader is asked to grant the difference in principle between these two senses of the term. Then, we may refer to the first sense given above as the "outer" lexicon, and the second sense as the "inner lexicon." The obvious question is, to what extent do we want our models of the inner lexicon to be informed or constrained by generally-accepted characteristics of the outer lexicon?

At first sight, this is a rather silly question. The reader may want to claim that the distinction between inner and outer lexicons is real but irrelevant, that any progress made in conceptualizing one is willy-nilly applied to conceptualizing the other. I shall argue, however, that the question is important, and that our theorizing about the inner lexicon is held up by our fixation on the outer lexicon. Different conclusions can be drawn if we ignore the outer lexicon and focus instead on questions about the inner lexicon: How would something which is like a brain, which as Dreyfus (1981, p. 197) has said, is always "already in a situation", store and access large amounts of information? To make this case, I shall begin by turning to the roots of the modern analysis of lexical knowledge.

1. The Model-T Lexicon

The first modern treatment of lexical knowledge is due to Treisman (1960), who coined the term *dictionary units* . In the original Treisman model, dictionary units were evidence collectors with two major characteristics: resting levels of activation, and tuneable thresholds. The dictionary unit was a powerful concept because it related some quantitative aspect of the stimulus to some quantitative aspect of the response: This much stimulus dimension gives you that much response dimension. The primary role of the lexicon was to mediate such quantitative relationships (Broadbent, 1967; Broadbent & Gregory, 1963; Morton, 1964, 1969; Treisman, 1960). On the surface, this seems almost Behaviorist in tone, yielding control of performance to the stimulus. However, deeper consideration of the historical context suggests that the dictionary unit was, in fact, a transitional concept between behaviorist and and cognitive views. That is, the dictionary unit introduced subject variables into the equation.

Though many psychologists were unhappy with Behaviorist theories, they had by no means renounced the idea of quantitative relationships between stimulus and response. It is not surprising, therefore, that they were attracted to signal detection theory (SDT). SDT was respectable, mathematically formalized and empirically successful. It allowed psychologists to maintain their quantitative analyses while also introducing subject variables (e.g., criterion) into their explanations (see e.g., Broadbent & Gregory, 1963). Introduction of such variables into theory was, of course, one of the major consequences of the information-processing revolution then underway.

The influence of SDT on these early lexical theorists resulted in the relationship between stimulus and response being couched in terms of probability, rather than meaning, orthography, or phonology. A highly probable stimulus was more likely to be detected and offered as a response than a low-probability stimulus. Base probability could be modified by the subject's attention, criterion, sensitivity and (potentially) other characteristics. Probability, of course, was a function of occurrence, or co-occurrence, frequency. It could be specified without reference to levels of linguistic analysis: that is, without reference to how the information got into the system or what it signified. This lack of concern with other levels was quite natural, but it could not last.

To summarize, by the end of the sixties, a utilitarian model was available which mediated the effects of stimulus probability through dictionary units which had a variable activation level and a tuneable firing threshold. The model seems to have had a great deal in common with signal detection theory, and gave very little consideration to either meaning or the nature of the input process. Like the calculator, the lexicon was a simple machine which did a simple job. And like the calculator, it was changed beyond recognition in the next decade.

2. Death By Tachistoscope

In retrospect, the transitional nature of the dictionary unit approach is evident in its use of modern, cognitive concepts with the vocabulary of an earlier time. In the seventies, the vocabulary changed to reflect the new concerns. During that decade, research on lexical access was driven by two major issues: what is the effect of semantic context, and what is the role of phonological representations. These issues are noteworthy because the debates were not couched in terms of "probability" of a stimulus and "strength" of a response.

Inspired by a serviceable model of a semantic storage system based on Quillian's (1968) metaphor of spreading activation in a network, and by the new "lexical decision" task (Rubinstein, Lewis & Rubinstein, 1971), the research of the seventies led to a complete overhaul of the lexicon concept (e.g., Becker, 1979; Morton, 1979). During those years, information stores and routes between them were added to the basic framework. The impetus seems always to have been to add rather than to subtract.

One of the first observations which caused revision to an important conception of the lexicon was Winnick and Daniel's (1970) report that different amounts of facilitation in a tachistoscopic recognition task were produced by visual and aural priming. Much has been made of this report; it was important in influencing Morton's (1979) reworking of his Logogen model. But on reflection, it is not clear what the real significance of the paper is.

It is certainly the case that in their Experiment 2, Winnick and Daniel found no influence on perceptual identification performance from either naming a picture or offering the name of a word in response to a definition, where these different naming responses occurred in a session preceding a t-scope recognition phase. Seeing (and saying) a word did facilitate responses. (What maybe less widely known is that in their Experiment 1, Winnick & Daniel showed priming effects on t-scope recognition of both written and spoken primes.)

The standard interpretation of these data (see, i.e., Morton, 1979) is that a visual input can facilitate later visual recognition under tachistoscopic conditions, but such facilitation of visual recognition does not result from an auditorily presented prime. The reverse holds for identification of an auditory word in white noise: facilitation by auditory but not by visual primes. This is taken as evidence against multimodal input lexicons.

While it may be tempting to conclude, on the basis of Winnick and Daniel's paper, that we need separate input lexicons for different modalities, it is not necessary to do so. Indeed, Winnick and Daniel's data do not demand interpretation in terms of input lexicons at all. The same comment applies to Morton's various extensions of the effect (Clark & Morton, 1983; Jackson & Morton, 1984; Morton, 1979).

It is possible that recognition of a stimulus is a more complex process than Winnick and Daniel and Morton assumed. In particular, it may be that subjects responded to an item not when it first became visible, but at a later time when their confidence about stimulus identity reached a criterion (see Cheesman & Merikle, 1984). If so, they may well have had one or more looks at the stimulus during the several exposures preceding identification. Such glimpses might produce enough information to make a comparison with (a) lexical entries and (b) representations of recent stimuli. Then, if the primes were stored episodically rather than lexically, subjects might have had time before stimulus decay to make a successful match between a prime word and a target word, but not to convert a prime picture or definition into a word and then make the comparison.

In this connection, it is worth noting that in a recall test before the t-scope recognition phase, subjects recalled the words corresponding to pictures and definitions better than the words simply read. This suggests that the picture and definition stimuli were stored episodically, rather than abstractly. But though they may have been more reliably available, the process of converting them into their associated words eliminated any advantage that might otherwise have accrued.

This is not the only possible reinterpretation of Morton's and Winnick and Daniel's data. While I have focused on a matching process involving the output of stimulus analysis and an episodic representation of the prime, Besner and Swan (1982) challenged Morton's interpretation on other grounds. They suggested that the facilitation effect may have resulted from reinstatement of actual stimulus analysis procedures, in the manner described by Kolers (1979). Either way, Morton seems to have been too hasty in giving up the early, simple model of 1969 (which was reviewed in the previous section).

3. Invasion From Semantic Space

While Morton was revising his Logogen model, other results were being reported, the consequences of which are still not completely clear. By 1970, psychologists had rediscovered semantics. In part, this was due to Katz and Fodor's (1963) feature-based theory of meaning. Katz and Fodor showed people how to decompose concepts into component "features" in the comfort of their own home. Nobody believes in feature-based theories anymore (Lyons, 1977), but they haven't been surpassed as convenient ways to think about meaning. Also important in the rediscovery of meaning was Quillian's (1968) work on how meanings might actually be represented in memory for maximum efficiency.

These developments encouraged people to think about how knowledge might be coded, and in what sort of structure the bits of code might be stored. This changed the focus away from how response strength is determined by subject criterion and stimulus probability, and to the organization of knowledge about words. Psychologists began to study putative knowledge structures and the putative processes which interrogate them. As they did so, they started to investigate a new set of independent variables whose influence was to be explained in terms of those knowledge structures. These variables included "semantic" context, degradation, repetition, what the primary perceptual units are in word recognition, and how these might be associated with phonological units, as well as an old favorite, frequency of occurrence. The various independent and interactive effects of these variables have been reviewed in detail elsewhere (Carr & Pollatsek, 1985; Henderson, 1982; Monsell, this volume). I shall not repeat those views here.

Thus, though major revisions of the dominant formal models occurred at the end of the seventies, an argument can be made that they were not necessary. In fact, they were harmful. There is one major difference between the models of the sixties and the models which supplanted them. Those of the sixties were about humans. That is, they were intended to account for observations about things real people actually do. There is, in retrospect, a certain charm in Cherry's (1953) well-known report on the "cocktail party" effect, as a starting point for a theory. Similarly, Treisman, Moray, Goldiamond, Broadbent, and their contemporaries were interested in something called "attention." Even if this is not rigorously defined, it is still relatively easy to comprehend. We all know roughly what "attending to" something means. There is little reason to doubt that something called "attending" actually happens.

But by the end of the seventies, this human scale was gone. Theories were no longer about people, they were about models. They didn't just use models, they were about the models. They were about input lexicons and phonological codes and resting activations, but they weren't about what humans do. This is not intended as a lament for an innocent, Aquarian era, but rather as a challenge to information processing analyses. Psychology in the last fifteen years has produced masses of data which were interpreted by expanding a general model of the lexicon. Whenever new data presented difficulty for a current model, some route or store was added to eliminate the problem: Separate lexicons for different modalities. Separate lexicons for input and output. Separate storage for semantics. Prelexical and postlexical phonology. Postlexical and articulatory phonology. Familiarity detectors. Grapheme detectors. Subword level orthographic-to-phonological conversion systems.

Certainly, with enough elements, the models can be made compatible with any piece of data derived from humans. But that is not the same as being about humans, rather than about some sort of Platonic form of a lexicon. I have tried to make a *prima facie* case above that some of the empirical reasons we have accepted for making our conception of the lexicon more complex have alternative interpretations that reduce their relevance. I believe it is now time to do some very serious "zero-base budgeting": to begin again, asking, what is the absolute minimum theoretical baggage we can get away with while accounting for the data.

The absolute minimum seems to be that we need to have a system which produces an orthographic code as a response to a stimulus (on the assumption that before any other code can be generated during reading, an orthographic representation must exist); we need to have a system which produces a phonological code, based on the orthographic code, in order to permit oral reading; and we need to have a system which produces a semantic form corresponding to a stimulus word. It is not obvious that any of these systems needs to be frequency-sensitive (though they may turn out to be so), nor do we have evidence demanding different input and output "lexicons." A modest proposal follows.

III. DEREK

We have not considered a number of other streams of research yet, primarily because their implications are even less clear. For example, the work on whether a phonological code is ever used in lexical access has yet to produce any reasonable consensus. Indeed, most models are compatible with almost all extant data (Brown & Besner, 1987; Coltheart, 1987; but see Van Orden, 1987). Similarly, I have not yet addressed the voluminous data on acquired reading disorders. These data are relevant because if a component of a model corresponds to a real psychological element or process, one might expect to see evidence for it in behaviorally observable impairment as a result of insult to the brain.

Patients with a broad variety of disabilities have been reported: so broad a variety, in fact, that Coltheart (1987) has recently spoken of "syndrome dissolution" after reviewing a series of vexing differences among patients ostensibly with the same disorder. It would be impossible to review all such findings here. My approach, in lieu of a review, will be to outline the new, simple model promised above, then show how it handles the patient data in some classic cases.

The model is illustrated in Figure 1. It is convenient here to think in terms of a parallel distributed processing (PDP) model. On the PDP view, information is represented in the pattern of firings in a set of neurons. Each unit in the set can be involved in the response to a number of different stimuli. That is, many different subsets of the set can be defined, with activation of each subset constituting the response to a different stimulus. The contribution of each unit, when active, is always the same[1].

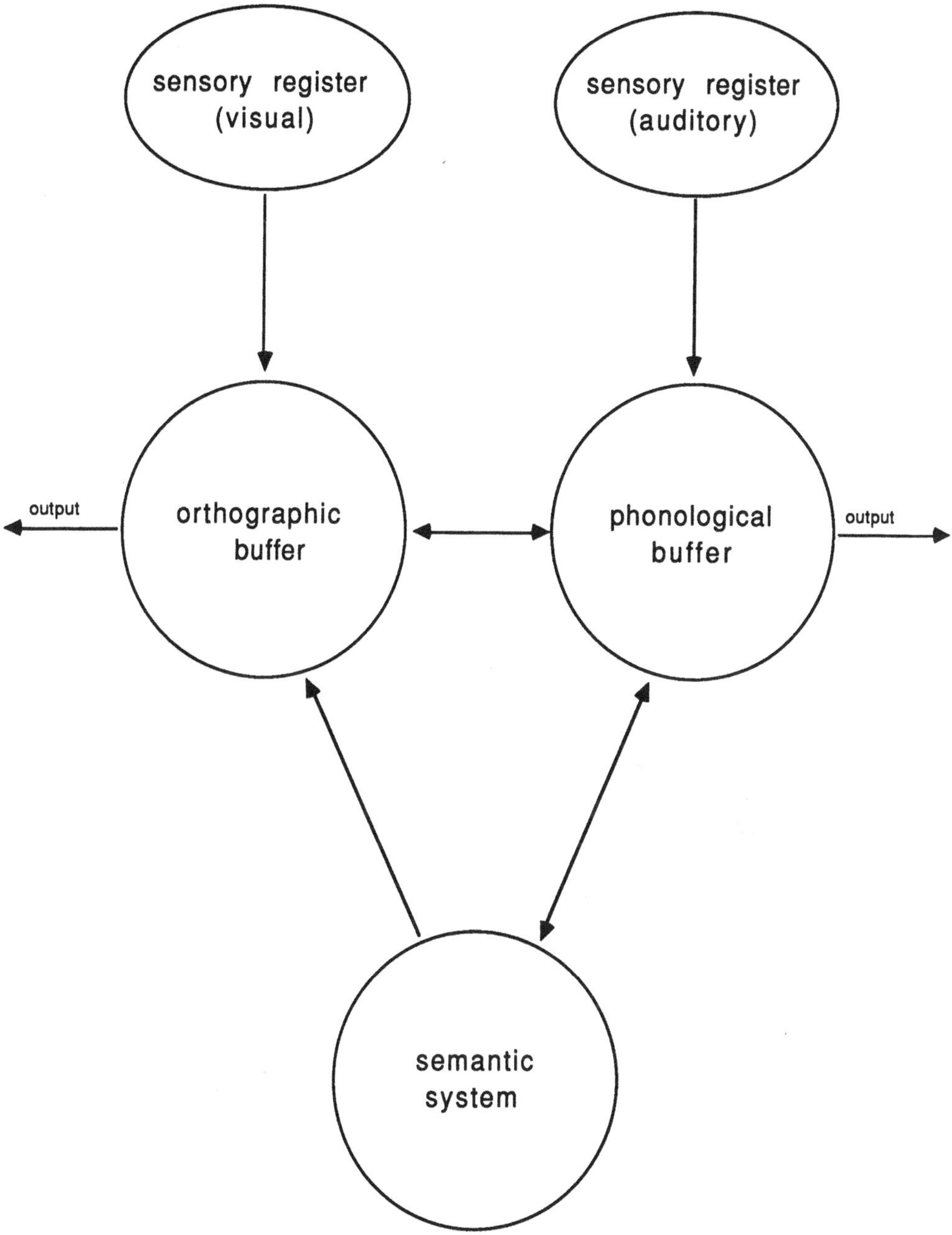

Figure 1 - The Direct Encoding Routine for Evoking Knowledge (DEREK)

In DEREK, a stimulus representation arouses a semantic representation directly (hence the name). It is important to make clear exactly what "directly" means here. DEREK holds that there is no level of representation involving anything like a lexical identity code intervening between the stimulus representation and a semantic representation. All that is necessary to explain the deciphering of print[2] for various purposes is the following: (a) a stimulus representation in the form of a sequence of graphemes (these reside in the orthographic buffer); (b) a set of flexible rules (see below) relating graphemes to phonemes (which rules produce activations in the phonological buffer); (c) a store of semantic knowledge, with characteristics described below. No lexicons, either input or output, either visual or phonological, are necessary. The buffers handle both input and output, but, as is discussed below, are not lexicons.

A stimulus representation in DEREK activates a pattern in the semantic system the way a piano roll activates the keys in a player piano. Notice that, in this metaphor, there is no search or other appeal to a memory store charged with identifying the stimulus. The holes in the piano roll are the stimulus. Their consequence is that levers move and sounds are made, but this consequence does not involve any intermediate representation.

Think of the levers in the player-piano as a "semantic system." When the input arrives (as the piano-roll turns), a pattern is created in that system. Since the system is a semantic one, the pattern is a semantic pattern, the meaning of which is whatever semantic force a musical piece has. Exactly the same pattern is now transferred to the "output system", when the levers strike the strings. Because that is a "phonological" system, the pattern is now a sound. The pattern is always the same, but what it appears to be depends on the system it is in.

Anderson and Mozer made a similar point in 1981:

We are talking about a nervous system where state vectors are things. In the motor system, this is obvious. A pattern of activity causes diverse muscles to contract forming a coordinated pattern of movement. The state vector, which at one place in the nervous system might usefully be interpreted at a cognitive level, now elsewhere in the brain is the actual effective output, executing physical action. The state vector is not representing anything. (1981, p. 216)

I believe this observation is very profound. The system can work with a single pattern moving from level to level. The pattern may well be modified during its journey (see below) but the important thing is that there is no need for anything like explicit "identification" following an appeal to a lexicon. The pattern need only exist, not be identified. Before pursuing the significance of this view, I shall make a formal statement of the model.

1. The Formal DEREK

The model has three sets of units: two buffers and a knowledge store. One buffer is for orthographic codes, the other for phonological codes. The knowledge store contains semantic representations. These elements are united in a cycle of pattern transmission which is the basic operation of the system, and is repeated until a pattern stable enough for current purposes is available. It is important to note that some tasks will require a more stable pattern than others (see below).

Response to an input is not seen as turning appropriate units on, but rather as turning inappropriate units off.[3] That is, at the time input arrives, a pattern of activity is already present in the buffers and the semantic system. The latter is a supraword pattern; it can be thought of as a text-level meaning, or as what is currently being thought about. Identification of a stimulus consists of turning down some of the active units to produce a pattern corresponding to the stimulus: a context-sensitive filtering or pruning of a word out of a supraword pattern. The point of this is to identify a set of units whose weights in the supraword pattern will change at least temporarily as a result of the input word.[4]

Obviously, there must be some mechanism for turning units on again, otherwise units once turned off would remain off permanently. There is no proscription here against turning units on; rather, there is an emphasis on the idea that the new pattern is usually related to the pattern it replaces. This may not hold in the case of reading random words, but it does during reading normal, connected text. In the semantic system, a word once read will be integrated into a text-level meaning. This integration process can be responsible for turning some units back on again, before the next word is read. Thus, the result of a word being read is that the text-level pattern is modified.

A pattern based on sensory input is originally created in the orthographic buffer. That buffer contains n units. A stimulus is ultimately represented by a subset of m units ($m < n$) being active together. In the model, the goal of having the appropriate m units activated in a buffer or system is achieved (if at all) after a number of cycles of the following type: The orthographic pattern in which k units ($m < k < n$) are active is passed to the phonological buffer. There, again, a nonunique pattern (i.e., a pattern which is not yet a response to a particular stimulus because it is consistent with some number of words) is created.[5] That pattern reflects the contingencies relating orthographic to phonological forms, conceptualized, for example as flexible rules[6] (Brown & Besner, 1987). It is important to note, however, that the rules do not operate on a single cycle, but rather across a number of cycles of the pattern being sent from buffer to (semantic) system to buffer (as in Figure 1). The "rules" are expressed as weights on connections from the orthographic buffer to the phonological buffer, and the desired effect on phonological buffer unit activations builds up over time.

The phonological buffer passes its (nonunique) pattern to the semantic system. The semantic system uses semantic knowledge (in the form of distributed representations) about words to clean up the pattern. The actual form of this semantic knowledge is an open question. Whatever the form of the knowledge (propositions, categorical structures, images), it is represented as connections among units within the semantic system. The information contained in these connections eliminates noise in the pattern received from the phonological buffer. Activations of units which are inappropriate are dampened, and those of appropriate units are boosted. One cycle is completed when the semantic system returns the revised pattern to the orthographic buffer, where input from the sensory register continues to arrive. At this point, the pattern is cleaner, and the appropriate activations stronger than originally, due to the interaction of stimulus information with phonological rules and knowledge about words. Semantic information can now interact with sensory information as the cycle begins again. These cycles continue as long as necessary (or, with degraded sensory input, as long as possible).

Thus, according to the model there are three primary sources of variance in an intact system: the quality of the input to the orthographic buffer, the nature of the flexible rules which modify input to the phonological buffer (see below), and semantic context. Each element (buffer or system) acts as a set of "hidden units" for the other two elements. In addition to these sources, the actual sets of units and the links between them can be impaired by brain damage. The three primary sources of variance in an intact system are described in more detail in the next section.

1.1. Sources of Variance in the Model

1. The orthographic buffer: Written input to the system comes to the orthographic buffer. THIS IS NOT A LEXICON: it contains no knowledge about words in the form of weights or in any other form. It has knowledge about letters and can represent sequence information. Its only sources of information are the sensory register, the phonological buffer, and the semantic system. The goal of operations at this level is to achieve a stimulus representation, not to "identify" it. This buffer also acts as the immediate source of orthographic output.

2. The phonological buffer: This element receives a pattern sent by the orthographic buffer (and also receives auditory input). This buffer contains knowledge, in particular, knowledge of the flexible rules central to phonological frame theory (Brown & Besner, 1987), coded as weights on the connections from units in the orthographic buffer. These rules relate graphemic elements to one or more phonemic elements (usually, one output for consonants, more than one for vowels). From the input pattern, the system produces a candidate set of pronunciations - in the form of multiple overlapping subsets of active units - which is then sent to the semantic system. This buffer is also the source of phonological outputs sent to the articulatory mechanism, and mediates phoneme-to-grapheme conversion (as, for example, in spelling to dictation) through connections back to the orthographic buffer.

3. The semantic system: The buffers do not need information about words in order to be able to "relax" into a pattern representing a stimulus word. The orthographic buffer has no knowledge about words at all. Connection strengths between orthographic and phonological buffer units are influenced by rules, but these rules do not refer to words. The semantic system is the only source of knowledge about words in the system, but the knowledge it has is indirect, in the following sense. The semantic system does not contain words (it contains semantic representations), but it can activate patterns in the buffers which are output as words. Words, on this view, are not the currency of the system; they are only vehicles for moving meaning from one location to another. Which output patterns (i.e., words) a given meaning will activate is a nontrivial question.

Transmission of a pattern from the semantic system to the orthographic buffer does not involve a one-to-one correspondence between units. The process involves a mapping rather than a connection.[7] Each semantic pattern can potentially be associated with multiple subsets of orthographic units, that is with different words for roughly the same meaning.[8] Which of those subsets activation is sent to is determined partly by the current state of the orthographic buffer.

Although the orthographic buffer has no internal knowledge about words, it is not a passive recipient of activation from the semantic system. The competition for activation notion (Reggia & Berndt, 1986) provides an elegant way for the model to control "top-down" effects. "Competition for activation" means that when activation from the semantic system arrives at the orthographic buffer to complete a cycle, those buffer units with the strongest current activation will benefit most. That is, units compete for activation, and among units getting similar input, those with the highest current activations will be most successful. Thus, though there is no guarantee that the semantic system will map its activation back on to the orthographic pattern corresponding to the stimulus word, that result is probable in normal operation. Clearly, however, there is room here for other, semantic influences, and for error. Error becomes more likely in an impaired brain, and with low-imageability words, for which the mapping is (for reasons given above) more difficult.

1.2 Son of PDP

It is obvious that, in developing DEREK, I have been very much influenced by the PDP approach to cognition (e.g., McClelland, 1988; Sejnowski & Rosenberg, 1987). However, there are some differences between my conception of how word recognition occurs and the conception offered by PDP theorists (if I understand them correctly). The most obvious of these differences is that for DEREK the challenge presented by a stimulus is to turn off units rather than turning them on. This is not a trivial point: this feature of the model draws out the implication that word recognition is done by a system which is a comprehending system, one that always already has something in it.

One of the most significant aspects of DEREK is the absence of anything like an input lexicon. DEREK can operate without an input lexicon because decoding of the stimulus is done during the process of learning to read, when the correspondences between input and semantic system pattern are originally set up. Once this is done, the weights on connections in the semantic system normally cause the pattern appropriate to a stimulus word to arise. Decoding does not have to be done on every occasion of reading a given word. Recently, PDP theorists have claimed that their models also do away with lexicons (McClelland, 1988; Seidenberg & McClelland, 1989). However, that claim can be disputed. In order to outline my criticism, I shall begin by very briefly reviewing how their PDP model produces a pattern of activation in response to a stimulus.

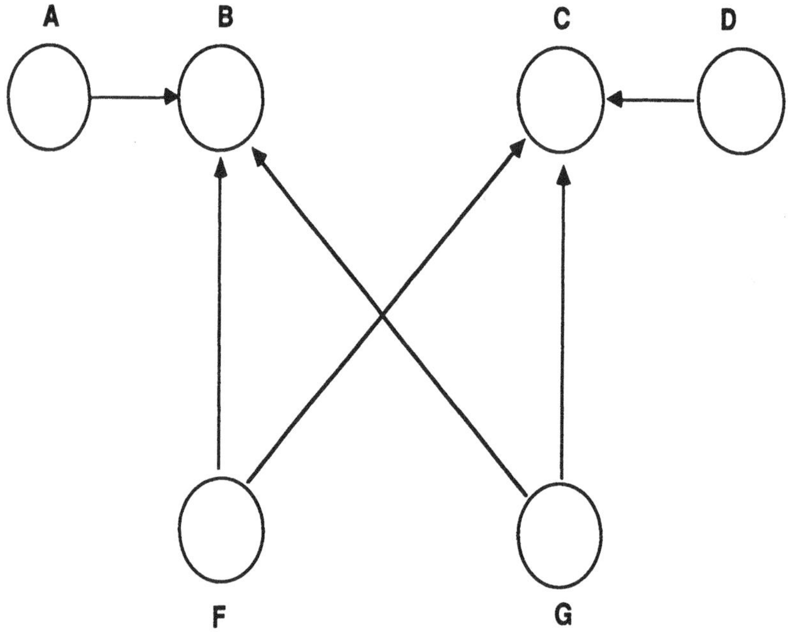

Figure 2 - A Simple Connectionist Model

Figure 2 shows a small set of units in a PDP system. Each unit has connections to other units, and each connection has an associated weight. Let us suppose that the units marked F and G are active as a result of input. The question arises, which of B and C will also be active? Obviously, the answer depends on A and D. If A is active, then B will fire; if D is active, then C will fire. (We assume that because of successful learning A and D will not both be active at the same time.) PDP theorists would point out that F and G are active for both the stimulus that causes A (and B) to fire, and the stimulus that causes D (and C) to fire. The claim that PDP models do without input lexicons is based on this observation. That is, units in the set do not correspond to words. Each unit can be active for many different words that the system can recognize. When a word is not the current stimulus, it is not represented anywhere in the system.

There is, however, an alternative way of looking at this situation. Using the simple model of Figure 2, let us suppose that units A, B, F, and G fire when the input word is "dog" and units C, D, F, and G fire when the input words is "cat." Then, even though no unit corresponds to any particular word, and even though each unit can participate in the response to many different words, the same cannot be said for each subset of units. Subset A, B, F, and G correspond to "dog"; C, D, F, and G to "cat."

Subsets of units must correspond to particular words or the system cannot reliably reproduce a response from one occasion to another. This means that the lexicon in PDP models is hidden in the connections. Arguing that the representations are not there when the pattern is not active is like saying that a car's torque curve does not exist unless the engine is running. The torque curve is information. It is a function of physical parameters of the engine, and so can be said to be stored in the engine. Whether gasoline is exploding in the cylinders is irrelevant.

This point applies also to the semantic system in DEREK, though not to the buffers as they are currently conceptualized. However, in other PDP models, settling on the appropriate pattern achieves only identification of the input string. Any semantic interpretation is the role of some other process. Thus, while both DEREK and the extant PDP models have something like an input lexicon, in the PDP models, it is, in fact, an input lexicon. In DEREK, it is the semantic system. The semantic system contains knowledge about words indirectly. Patterns in the semantic system are associated with strings of graphemes in the orthographic buffer and with strings of phonemes in the phonological buffer. Thus, the system can output words without actually containing words. It contains things which become words when they are outputted.

2. The Functional DEREK

In this section, I shall consider some issues related to the operation of the model. The purpose is twofold: to state explicity, in the absence of an implementation, some features of the model which would constrain implementation, and to draw out some of the implications of the current view for word recognition.

I shall begin with the question, where do patterns of activity come from? This will be divided into two separate questions: what is the nature of the input to the model, and what is the nature of the functional connection between parts of the system (i.e., buffers)? The point will be made that an answer to the first of these questions need not constrain an answer to the second.

Following this, the issue of the different types of response the system can be called upon to support will be addressed. The significance for the processing of a letter string of the response to be made to that letter string will be emphasized. Finally in this section, I shall indicate briefly how DEREK deals with several major results from the literature on word recognition in normals. Patient data will be considered in the subsequent section.

2.1 Input

For the orthographic buffer, the only sources of information which can be impressed upon it are sensory input, the phonological buffer, and the semantic system. The phonological buffer receives input only from a sensory register, the orthographic buffer, and the semantic system (a connection which antedates reading). Given the model of Figure 1, two questions arise: how does external input activate a pattern in the orthographic buffer, and how does this buffer activate a pattern in the phonological buffer?

Consider the first of these questions. Obviously, there must be an analysis of some features of the input which is consistent across exposures to any particular stimulus. These features are what are usually called perceptual units. (Here, we are concerned with analyses which follow generation of a physical description of the stimulus; that is, with purely orthographic analyses.)

A great deal of work has been directed at determining the perceptual units for word recognition (Henderson, 1982; Vellutino, 1982), though without much resolution. The obvious possibilities are letters, words, and parts of words defined on a variety of principles. Originally, people took polar positions, claiming that one type of unit was "the " perceptual unit. More recently, a number of authors have suggested that multiple types of code are normally made available during word recognition, and that different tasks preferentially tap different codes (i.e., Healy, 1980; Healy & Drewnowski, 1986).

Although the idea that multiple levels of code are used has gained currency in the neuropsychological literature (Patterson & Morton, 1985; Shallice & McCarthy, 1985), it has not been the subject of many studies. Greenberg and Vellutino (1988) used a paradigm which they claimed was superior to previously reported paradigms (e.g., Santa, Santa, & Smith, 1977) in not encouraging subjects to adopt a special stimulus analysis strategy which need not be part of word recognition. Their subjects were required to discriminate letters from nonletter stimuli (Experiment 1), and letter bigrams from letter/nonletter pairs as well as letters from nonletters (Experiment 2).

Greenberg and Vellutino found that performance was enhanced when target letters or bigrams were contained in a preceding prime word, relative to performance with targets preceded by unrelated words. Significantly, responses to letters occurring in bigrams were also facilitated when the bigrams were of low frequency of occurrence, but not when the bigrams were of high frequency. Greenberg and Vellutino interpret these data as support for a class of models in which multiple codes can be developed for a word, and higher-level units (here, bigrams) have preference over lower-level units (letters) in being assigned a "cognitive code" (see Johnson, Turner-Lyga & Pettegrew, 1986). They add that the hierarchy of preference is in part functional, meaning that it can vary with task.

Greenberg and Vellutino's report is significant because it demonstrates both effects and a lack of effects. In other words, it shows conditions necessary for a unit to have an effect. In the rush to include all possible units in giant "relaxation" processes, this is salutary. The extrapolation that it is always the highest-level unit appropriate to the task which has preference in being assigned a cogitive code is intriguing but goes well beyond the data (however, see Marcel, 1983 for similar claims).

The latter caveat notwithstanding, Greenberg and Vellutino's (1988) data constitute evidence in favour of a multiple coding levels view. In normal reading for meaning, the semantic system relaxes to a single pattern. This explains why higher-level units, in Greenberg and Vellutino's words, "are assigned cognitive codes before lower level units"[9] (p. 61). The hierarchical preference follows if only the largest unit common to a set of active patterns can be computed. That is, the largest unit can be recovered but is not segmentable to produce information about its constituents.

If a pattern correlated with a word is not segmentable, then, when subword information is necessary (as in Greenberg and Vellutino's task), the information must be obtained before the relaxation process is completed. If 100 patterns, each representing short words with medial A are active, it is in the nature of PDP type models that the fact that the input string contains a medial A can be computed. Once the system has relaxed so that only a few patterns (say, those with final _ANE segments) remain active, the information about medial A is lost, if units are not segmentable.[10] Being actively "assigned a cognitive code" suggests that information about a stimulus is rendered into some form less vulnerable to decay than a sensory register code. On the current view, the same effect is achieved simply by information's survival (in recoverable form) through the various stages of relaxation: instead of an action of assigning a cognitive code to a representation, it is a case of that information not being eliminated by relaxation.

Thus, no special "cognitive code" which is invulnerable to decay is necessary. Availability of a type of information comes from interruption of relaxation before the set of patterns necessary to compute that information is deactivated by relaxation. The logical conclusion is that, in Greenberg and Vellutino's task, responses to letters and bigrams were not primed by the individual words which preceded them, but by sets of words which shared the relevant spelling pattern. If this is the case, then characteristics of the particular set for any given trial should influence the response. Thus, if one were to repeat Greenberg and Vellutino's experiment, one would expect to find that the priming effect would be reduced when the prime word activated more orthographically dissimilar than orthographically similar words (i.e., ache), relative to a primeword-frequency matched condition in which similar words were activated.[11]

Clearly, this interpretion of Greenberg and Vellutino's data is in the spirit of Taraban and McClelland's (1987) "conspiracy effect" on pronunciation latencies. Taraban and McClelland observed that response times to words and pronounceable nonwords were faster when targets were preceded by regular-consistent neighbors than when they were preceded by neighbors with exceptional spelling-sound relations. Their explanation turned on the idea that multiple patterns are activated when a word is read. If word recognition entails elimination of competing readings, until only one is left, anything which helps eliminate incorrect (or, in the case of nonwords, less-favored) pronunciations will speed up the process. A regular-consistent prime will give an advantage to those patterns which share the relevant segment (in Taraban and McClelland's study, either initial or final consonant cluster, with medial vowel). Residual activation from an exception prime will make it harder to eliminate target-generated patterns with the exception pronunciation. I believe it is a similar conspiracy effects which produced the priming observed by Greenberg and Vellutino.

An explanation in the same vein could be provided for another recent report of "neighborhood" type effects on print-to-sound translation. Treiman and Zukowksi (1988) found that the pronunciations preferentially given to medial vowel digraphs were a function of the consonant context in nonwords like *chiend* and *freith*. They found, for example, that the pronunciation of the "ie" digraph, as in friend, was more likely in *chiend* than in *frieth*. In contrast to Taraban and McClelland, Treiman and Zukowski found much stronger effects for word-final contexts than for word-initial contexts. The reason for this difference is not clear. Nonetheless, these results are very easily dealt with by the Frame Theory advanced by Brown and Besner (1987) to account for data from a similar paradigm. DEREK can account for Treiman and Zukowski's results through conspiracy effects. And, if further research supports their claim that word-final segments are more important than word-initial segments in computing phonology, that finding can be built into the relaxation process, though it is obviously not necessary *a priori*.

The conclusion to this section is that "the input unit" is not a useful concept, because information about many levels or sizes of unit can be extracted during the relaxation process. It is more useful to try to determine the conditions under which information about various units can or cannot be extracted, and what influences the efficiency of the system when it is extracting that information. In this enterprise, the set of neighbors of any input string, and the task to be performed upon the input string will be of considerable importance. The idea that the relaxation process must continue longer for some tasks than for others will be elaborated upon below.

2.2 Interbuffer Communication

The next question has to do with how a pattern is translated from one buffer to another. The major debate on the relation of orthographic and phonological codes for words has focused on the issue of whether a phonological code is developed "prelexically," meaning by translation operations on subword units, or only after lexical form has been obtained (Humphreys & Evett, 1985; Patterson & Coltheart, 1987).

In the previous section, the claim was made that the largest unit common to a set of active patterns can be extracted. For example, in a set of patterns which share medial A, and where no other unit appears in all of them, the presence of medial A in the stimulus can be computed. At various times during processing, units of many different sizes thus are participating in the communication between orthographic and phonological buffers. Two consequences of this view are that (a) phonology begins to be available as soon as orthography begins to be available, though clearly neither are in final form at that early stage of analysis; and (b) as with the orthographic "input units," phonology is potentially available (to response selection processes) for multiple types of unit, with the type of unit predominating being functionally determined, within the hierarchy of bigger having preference over smaller.

Evidence in support of the position that phonology becomes available early has come from several recent studies (Perfetti, Bell & Delaney 1988; Van Orden, 1987; Van Orden, Johnston & Hale, 1988). Van Orden and his colleagues have recently shown effects of the phonological code for a stimulus on decision latency even when the stimulus is masked and when there is no measurable effect of the orthographic code. Van Orden's (1987) subjects made category decisions for words homophonic to category exemplars (i.e., ROWS for the category FLOWER). Subjects produced larger false-positive rates to such homophones than to spelling control foils. Van Orden concluded that "Phonological mediation occurs soon enough to exert its influence under the very brief exposure conditions of pattern-masking" (p. 186).

Van Orden pointed out that these results were important because they involved YES response latencies, rather than NO latencies, as was the case with earlier work on phonological mediation of "lexical access" which used pseudohomophones (i.e., Coltheart, Davelaar, Jonasson, & Besner, 1977; Dennis, Besner, & Davelaar, 1985). Van Orden, Johnston and Hale (1988) extended these findings, showing that the false-positive rate was independent of stimulus frequency. In addition, Van Orden et al. found that the reaction time distributions for false-positive and correct YES responses were virtually identical. If a phonological code were NOT available early, one would expect false-positive responses to be delayed with respect to correct YES responses, a prediction clearly not supported by Van Orden et al.'s data.

Perfetti, Bell and Delaney (1988) also used a masking paradigm. Subjects were required to report stimuli from tachistoscopic displays. The stimuli were words. Each was followed by one of three types of mask: control, graphemic, or homophonic nonwords. That is, the masks were nonwords which were graphemically or phonologically related to the targets, or were dissimilar to the targets.

The homophonic masks had a significant facilitatory effect on accuracy of report over and above that of the graphemic masks. Perfetti et al. concluded, on the assumption that the backward mask influences an "identification process," that the phonological activation occurs during word identification, or prelexically. Clearly, these data constitute a further argument for phonology being involved in the earliest stages of word recognition.

IV. NEW EXPERIMENTS

In my own lab, a series of experiments currently underway has produced results which also indicate very early availability of phonological codes.[12] These experiments use a paradigm developed by Yantis and Meyer (1985), in which subjects see either a right- or left-facing arrow, and press either a right- or left-hand button in response. Each arrow stimulus is preceded by a letter string. For reasons of their own, Yantis and Meyer used word and nonword strings, with each class predicting the subsequent arrow's direction with 100% reliability (i.e., if the prime was a word, the arrow would face right). The major change to Yantis and Meyer's procedure we made was to include among the nonword primes a set of pseudohomophones[13] (these are nonword strings which, when pronounced, sound like words - e.g., pruve).

The existence of a priming effect in this paradigm (demonstrated by Yantis and Meyer) suggests that the lexical status of the prime string is used to prepare a response (i.e., left or right hand). If phonological information about a string is available, and the string sounds like, but does not spell a word, the response preparation process will receive conflicting information from stimulus analysis routines. Under such circumstances, performance should be worse than when no conflict arises.

The key prediction here turns on a comparison of when, across SOAs, the basic priming effect begins, and when phonological interference caused by pseudohomophones begins. If phonology is made available early, as predicted by DEREK, then interference from the pseudohomophone prime should occur at the earliest SOA which permits any processing of the letter string.[14] The reason for this is as follows. The orthographic buffer does not produce a representation which can be used to retrieve phonology. Rather, the two buffers and the semantic system work together, continually exchanging information. As soon as the orthographic buffer has any information about the stimulus, it sends that data to the phonological system, which begins its analysis and also sends a signal to the semantic system. As soon as the orthographic buffer gets any information about the stimulus, then the uncertainty about what the next stimulus will be is reduced. The argument based on DEREK is that as soon as the uncertainty about the orthographic form is reduced at all, there is a corresponding reduction in uncertainty about the phonological form. These are, in other words, processes in cascade (McClelland, 1979). Thus, the pseudohomophone effect should occur as early as any other priming effect.

1. Experiment 1

Procedure

In the first experiment, 21 subjects were run. Each subject was given 25 trials for each of the nonword, pseudohomophone and the relevant neutral[15] conditions (collectively, these will be referred to as the "Nonword prime conditions"; henceforth, I shall distinguish within this set between Regular nonword and Pseudohomophone nonword conditions) at each of five SOAs: 50, 100, 150, 250, and 450 msec. Subjects also got 50 Word trials and 25 "right-hand" neutral trials at each SOA. Normal control procedures were used, so that, for example, all prime strings appeared at all SOAs across subjects. Data are shown in Table 1. Both this and the subsequent experiment were run on Commodore 128 microcomputers with Commodore 1802 screens.

Results

Differences from the neutral baseline were computed for both Regular nonword and Pseudohomophone conditions. These data, which are shown in Table 1, were used in the analyses. An analysis of variance on reaction time (difference) data for correct trials in the Nonword Prime conditions used two factors: Nonword class and SOA. Of major interest here is the prime type effect, which was highly significant (MSE = 995.750, F (1,20) = 15.38, p <.001). The most important result is that, by t-test for pairs, responses on Regular nonword trials were faster than responses on Pseudohomophone trials, at all SOAs except 450 msec.

Table 1
Data for Experiment 1

SOA (msec)	Neutral	Nonword	Pseudo-homophone
50	484 (2.3)	470 (2.0)	483 (2.6)
100	515 (3.5)	418 (2.0)	531 (4.3)
150	569 (3.5)	546 (2.6)	569 (5.5)
250	633 (4.5)	603 (3.3)	641 (5.6)
450	774 (5.0)	746 (2.3)	747 (6.8)

Mean reaction times for correct trials, by condition. Error rates (percentages) in parentheses.

Differences between Pseudohomophone and Neutral conditions, and Regular nonword and Neutral conditions are less consistent. It is difficult to account for this. The explanation of the similarity of Pseudohomophone and Neutral conditions may be that, in the Pseudohomophone condition, the benefit due to detection of a nonword (i.e., the Pseudohomophone) is offset by the confusion arising from that nonword's homophony[16] with a real word. Since it is difficult to know exactly what is happening in the Neutral condition, I shall not dwell on comparisons involving that condition.

The RT data are not compromised by any speed-error trade-off, as the faster RTs in the Regular nonword condition were associated with error rates lower than or equal to other conditions. As shown in Table 1, error rates were substantially higher for Pseudohomophone than for Regular nonword trials at the longer SOAs. Error rates were highest of all on Word trials. Since all subjects used their right hand for Word Prime trials, this indicates a strong bias to left-hand (Nonword) responses. Errors for Pseudohomophone trials required right-hand responses -- meaning that the Pseudohomophone effect actually overcame the bias to left-hand responses.

2. Experiment 2

One focus of the second experiment was to vary the probability of pseudohomophone primes. If the interference effect due to the presence of pseudohomophones occurs in a low- rather than a high-probability group, we can conclude that its presence is not dependent upon subjects' strategies. If the effect does not occur in the high-probability group, that would suggest that while the phonological code is normally generated automatically (as in the low-probability condition and in Perfetti et al.'s, 1988 paradigm), its influence on a relevant decision can be countermanded.

Procedure

With the following exceptions, the procedure was the same as in Experiment 1. First, no Neutral trials were used in this experiment. Only Pseudohomophone, Regular (non-pseudohomophonic) nonword, and Word primes were used. Second, two groups of subjects defined by the probability of occurrence of a pseudohomophone were used. For one group, 33% of Nonword Prime trials used Regular nonwords and 67% used Pseudohomophones. For the other group, the reverse was true. Twenty four subjects were run in each of the two groups. Subjects in the Low Probability group received 20 Pseudohomophone and 40 Regular nonword trials at each SOA. Subjects in the High Probability group got the reverse. Thus, for the Low Probability group, Pseudohomophones were 16.6% of all trials, 33% of Nonword trials. For the High Probability group, these numbers were doubled. All subjects also received

60 Word prime trials at each SOA. The SOAs used were 100, 150, 250, and 350 msec.

Results

Mean reaction times and error rates are shown in Table 2. The Pseudohomophone effect was again found, though this time it was manifest in the error data rather than the reaction time data. In the reaction time data, there was no effect of type of Nonword prime. For the Word prime trials, in addition to the expected SOA effect, there was a marginal effect of Probability (MSE = 15087.72, $F(1, 46) = 3.93$, $p < .053$), such that subjects were slower in the high probability group. It would not be surprising if the higher incidence of pseudohomophones made subjects in that group delay acceptance of a prime as a word.

Table 2
Data for Experiment 2

	Low Pseudohomophone Probability				High Pseudohomophone Probability			
SOA	Nonword		Pseudohomophone		Nonword		Pseudohomophone	
(msec)	RT	%E	RT	%E	RT	%E	RT	%E
100	430	10.3	421	15.2	455	14.6	449	11.8
150	414	12.4	418	16.0	438	14.2	432	11.6
250	376	14.7	372	17.7	400	12.9	405	13.1
350	326	15.0	326	15.6	375	15.0	367	10.1

Mean reaction times (msec) and error rates (percentages) by condition.

Low Pseudohomophone = 33% of Nonword trials were Pseudohomophones
High Pseudohomophone = 67% of Nonword trials were

The analysis of variance on the Nonword error data involved one between subjects factor (Probability of Pseudohomophone) and two within subjects factors (SOA and Nonword class). All three of the two-way interactions were significant. Inspection of the means suggested that the SOA by Nonword class interaction was a function of a profound difference between the longest SOA (350 msec) and all other levels. When the analysis was repeated on only the first 3 SOAs (100, 150, 250 msec), this interaction disappeared, but the results were otherwise unchanged. Since the effects at 350 msec are difficult to interpret and not very relevant to the main issue, the SOA x Nonword class interaction will be ignored.

The interaction of Probability and Nonword class was highly significant (MSE = 37.866, F (1,46) = 19.68, p < .001). Separate analyses of variance run on the data for each probability group revealed distinct differences. For the Low Pseudohomophone Probability group,[17] error responses were more likely on trials with pseudohomophone primes than on trials with nonword primes. The main effect of Nonword class was significant (MSE = 43.567, F (1, 23) = 10.23, p < .004), as was the effect of SOA (MSE = 25.478, F (3, 69) = 4.14, p < .009). The interaction of these two factors was not significant. In the High Pseudohomophone group, errors were significantly less likely on Pseudohomophone trials than on Nonword trials. The main effect of Nonword class was the only significant effect in this analysis (MSE = 32.166, F = 9.52, p < .005). It is worth noting that the effect of SOA was not significant for this group.

The SOA x Probability interaction stems from the fact that there were no differences between the groups at the two shortest SOAs. This is because collapsing across Nonword class eliminated differences between the two groups. However, inspection of the data showed that the relation between Regular nonword and Pseudohomophone means was exactly reversed for the two groups at the two shortest SOAs. A post-hoc analysis of variance run over only those two SOAs yielded only one significant effect, the interaction of nonword class with probability (F (1, 46) = 18.93, p < .0001). The importance of this result is that this difference between the the two groups (a) was found at very short SOAs, and (b) was a function of the phonological status of prime strings.

3. Discussion

These two studies provide evidence that phonological information about a stimulus is available very early in the analysis of the stimulus. While subjects can apparently prevent this information from differentially[18] influencing their response time in the high-probability condition, they cannot do so in the low-probability condition. This is of interest because the phonological information about pseudohomophones actually impairs performance. A reasonable explanation of these results is that, in the ordinary way, subjects generate and use phonological information when reading letter-strings. Doing so expedites the analysis of strings in the Word and Regular Nonword conditions, being counterproductive only in the Pseudohomophone condition.

When the Pseudohomophone condition contains only 16.7% of the stimuli, the cost of using phonological codes does not cause subjects to invoke special procedures. However, changes are made when the proportion of pseudohomophones is doubled. It is not clear what the nature of the change is, whether changes to analysis procedures, or to the decision process weighing evidence of lexicality. The important point is that the phonological interference effect occurs when subjects are least likely to be aware of the presence of the psuedohomophones: in the low probability condition and at the shortest SOAs. This argues strongly that phonological codes are normally generated automatically and early. (If activation of phonology is automatic, that would suggest that the strategy change in the high Pseudohomophone probability group involves decision rather than analysis procedures.)

One of the necessary conditions for DEREK to be accepted is that phonological forms be available as soon as orthographic information is available. The data just reported, along with the data reported by Van Orden (1987), suggest that this is the case. In addition, the present data, along with the data reported by Perfetti et al. (1988), suggest that the phonological information is made available automatically.

I shall now consider how the amount of processing of a stimulus required, and the length of time available for that processing, influence performance.

V. TYPES OF RESPONSE

The pattern in any buffer/system approaches stability over time, and a response can be read off at any point. Two variables constrain how long the relaxation process is allowed to continue: the nature of the information required (as discussed in section 2.1 above), and the degree of stability of a pattern demanded by a task. It is important to distinguish between availability and stability of information. Thus, the type of information we hypothesized to support performance in Greenberg and Vellutino's task may be available at some point, but never become stable in the sense of relatively invulnerable to decay. This quality (stability), I suggest, is necessary for overt decision processes such as lexical decision, and it may be that only unique patterns (corresponding to words) can achieve it.

The distinction between availability and stability of information is central to DEREK's accounts of major word recognition findings. We have already suggested that people can alter the level of information they feed into a response selection mechanism, as in Greenberg and Vellutino's task. However, there appear to be limits to this "resolving power", since Greenberg and Vellutino's subjects could not prevent letter-level information from being lost for words with high-frequency bigrams, in a task in which bigrams were the center of attention.

Normally, relaxation continues until a pattern is produced which is appropriate for the current purpose. The time required for this depends on the regularity of the orthography, the consistency of the orthography-to-phonology mapping, (possibly) stimulus frequency, the nature of the response required, and the general "energy-level" of the whole system.[19] This may seem like a lot of variables, though the number is modest by some standards (i.e., McClelland & Rumelhart, 1981). The first three, regularity, consistency, and frequency, are known to be empirically important, so their effects must be explained in the model. The final two variables are more particular. I shall discuss "energy-level" considerations in the subsequent section.

The least demanding "response" is integration of a stimulus into text, that is, into the currently active pattern. This, one presumes, is the goal of most normal reading. If it is the case, as suggested by PDP modellers (Rumelhart & McClelland, 1986) that similar stimuli are represented by similar patterns, then one issue for a word recognition system engaged in integration of a stimulus word into text is how specific a pattern is necessary. Often, the semantic force of a word in text may be available - in the form of category information - while the pattern is still quite general (i.e., with $k > m$ units active).

A second issue is how long a pattern must be maintained for integration, once the pattern has been obtained. The approach taken here is that integration occurs very rapidly - meaning that a pattern does not have to be maintained for very long. This is held to be a consequence of the normal reading process in which a word's meaning is obtained and integrated into text very quickly, following which the word is discarded as the system moves on to the next stimulus.

It is important to note that this view is <u>not</u> equivalent to an abstractionist view (as opposed to an instance-based view) in which actual stimulus characteristics are less important than general, abstract properties such as meaning. All that is being said is that, in the semantic system, a pattern will, by default, decay very rapidly unless it is refreshed. There is no reason why traces of a stimulus which could mediate effects of the type reported by Kolers (1979), Jacoby (1983; Jacoby & Hayman, 1987), and Whittlesea (1987) could not reside in input or output weights of either buffer.

A task which requires a somewhat more stable pattern than integration is naming. For naming, a pattern must be obtained in the phonological buffer and then sent to an articulatory programmer. This task is less forgiving than integration. One obvious reason is that a specific pattern must always be arrived at, to preclude a wrong (but related) response. Presumably, the pattern must also be maintained long enough to permit transmission to the programmer.

Other tasks also require maintenance of a pattern. In particular, these are tasks which require a decision of some sort about a stimulus. Such tasks include semantic categorization, and possibly responding to written commands (i.e., "Point to the door"). Tasks of the latter sort are standard in neuropsychological testing, but are not typical reading tasks, since they require something more than integration of meaning or simple pronunciation. They require, at least, a decision to call a set of muscle movement routines, calling those routines, determination that the correct routines have been called, and a decision to execute the called routines. When, for whatever reason, a semantic pattern cannot be refreshed, any of the first three of these additional operations may be error-prone. Similarly, for the popular categorization tasks such as lexical decision, a stable pattern must be maintained longer than is necessary for integration of meaning, in order to permit an overt decision.

It should be clear that the model can account for context effects quite easily. In particular, semantic and associative priming effects devolve from the integral role of the semantic system in establishing a stable pattern: each of the sets of units (both buffers and the semantic system) are trying to relax to one set of units simultaneously, and are in contact as they do so. Thus, influences on the semantic system facilitate or impede the general process. Both the graphemic priming reported by Evett and Humphreys (1981), if in fact it is graphemic priming (Note 2), and the phonological priming reported by Humphreys, Evett and Taylor (1982) also follow directly, being explained in terms of buffer activations persisting from one input (the prime) to the next (the target). On the current view, in fact, it becomes very difficult, perhaps even impossible, to disentangle graphemic from phonological effects.[20]

1. Frequency and Regularity Effects

It remains to be specified how the model will deal with the effects of some of the other empirically important variables, the two most widely studied being orthographic regularity and word frequency. There is, as yet, little consensus on the source of frequency effects (Balota & Chumbly, 1984; McCann, Besner & Davelaar, 1988; Monsell, Doyle, & Haggard, 1989). Three possibilities worth considering seriously are (a) frequency effects arise inside a store of representations activated by word stimuli (Monsell et al., 1989); (b) frequency effects arise in links between stores (Besner & McCann, 1987); and (c) frequency effects are at least partially due to response output processes (Balota & Chumbly, 1984).

Monsell et al. (1989) have recently presented a very detailed review of the literature on stimulus-frequency effects in word recognition tasks (see also Monsell this volume). They consider recent arguments by Balota and Chumbly (1984, 1985) and McCann and Besner (1987; McCann et al., 1988) against a lexical locus for frequency effects. Balota and Chumbly reported a very small frequency effect in a semantic categorization task (Balota & Chumbly, 1984), and frequency effects in a delayed naming task in which subjects had up to 1400 msec to prepare a response (Balota & Chumbly, 1985). On the basis of these data, they argued against a lexical frequency effect, suggesting (a) that semantic categorization requires lexical access, so should have revealed a lexical frequency effect, and (b) that re-accessing the lexicon is not necessary in delayed naming, so that task should not have been frequency sensitive.

McCann and Besner (1987) found evidence of access to information about word-phonology, which they interpreted as being in a phonological lexicon, when subjects were required to name nonwords. Naming times for pseudohomophones were shorter than those for regular nonwords matched for orthography. Nonetheless, no effect of frequency of basewords (the real words the pseudohomophones sounded like) was observed. However, an effect of baseword frequency was found when subjects were required to judge whether the same stimuli sounded like words. McCann and Besner concluded that frequency effects are not inside lexicons, and therefore must be in the connections between them.

Monsell et al. provide detailed arguments against these conclusions, which I shall not review here, except to point out one curious aspect of their case. Monsell et al. claim, essentially, that frequency effects are always there, but cannot always be seen. They outline "three circumstances in which this frequency sensitivity of the lexical identification process might be imperfectly reflected in RTs, resulting in differential sensitivity to frequency across tasks. . . " (p. 66). The idea that frequency effects may not involve the lexicon, which Monsell et al. are rejecting, is based on the finding that frequency effects do not appear in some tasks. The argument that the effects are there but we can't see them, is, to say the least, very weak.

Of more interest is Monsell et al. 's report of data respecting the size of the frequency effect in several tasks, relative to that found in lexical decision. Their experiments use the same subjects and stimuli across tasks. They suggest that the simplest account of all the data is that stimulus frequency operates on the process of lexical identification. In addition, they discuss how this might be realized in a connectionist framework, suggesting that frequency effects can arise either within or across domains. "Within a domain" means within a set of units (i.e., for DEREK, in a buffer or the semantic system), while "across domains" means in the translation from one set of units to another. Thus, communication between, for example, the phonological buffer and the semantic system occurs across domains.

The current view is entirely compatible with that expressed by Monsell et al. Frequency is, of course, one of two variables whose effects the original dictionary unit model was intended to explain, so any descendant of that first model should be able to deal with frequency. Whether these effects are better conceived as across or within domains, or both, is not yet clear. Given the view of activations proceeding in each of DEREK's distinct sets of units (the buffers and the semantic system) in cascade, it may not be possible to distinguish these alternatives empirically.

Connectionist models in general lend themselves to accounts of phenomena such as the effects of orthographic regularity and of regularity of the orthography-phonology mapping. The standard reference on these effects is the paper by Seidenberg, Waters, Barnes, and Tannenhaus (1984). These authors examined the effects of both variables in two tasks, naming and lexical decision. They found (a) that orthographic regularity influenced performance in both tasks; (b) regularity of spelling-sound correspondences influenced reaction time only in naming, though it also affected error rate in lexical decision; and (c) in all cases, the effects held only with low frequency stimuli. This picture was complicated slightly by Waters and Seidenberg's (1985) finding that regularity of spelling-sound correspondence influenced reaction time as well as error rate in lexical decision when the stimulus list contained "strange" (i.e., orthographically irregular) words, such as *ache* and *yacht*.

That the effects are not found with high frequency words will presumably be accounted for in any model with some variation of the idea that high frequency words are overlearned. Thus, for example, it may well be that orthographic regularity influences lexical access (i.e., relaxation) time for high frequency words, but that all processes run off so quickly for these stimuli that the delay occasioned by irregularity is not detectable with our laboratory tasks. Since, in the absence of variables known to influence the reading of high frequency words, one theory is as good as another, I shall end discussion of such stimuli here.

For low frequency words, the major finding to be explained is the distinction between lexical decision and naming latency tasks in their susceptibility to influence by regularity of spelling-sound correspondence. In lexical decision, such influence appears if the stimulus list contains strange words; in naming, the influence appears regardless of stimulus list composition. An interesting explanation (but one which appears not to have been considered in the literature) is that the distinction between the tasks is, in this respect, a function of accuracy being traded for speed in the case of regular-inconsistent items in lexical decision (Seidenberg et al., 1984, Experiment 4).

It is important to note that Seidenberg et al. , and Waters and Seidenberg, both found higher error rates for exception than for regular words, and both found that the error rates for exception words were comparable to those for strange words. My argument is predicated on the idea that the cost of dealing with exception words is seen in the error rate rather than on RT. For exception words, accuracy was traded for speed. For "strange" words (i.e., *aisle*), the trade-off became so expensive that speed had to be sacrificed, too. On this view, there is very definitely an effect of spelling-sound correspondence in these studies. Should this explanation be correct, the whole set of data can be acounted for in terms of the number of different sets of patterns (each sharing a particular subpattern) activated in response to input. The more patterns are activated, the harder the job of relaxing to a single pattern becomes.

When the spelling-sound correspondence is irregular, other things being equal, more patterns are activated. Or, at least, more patterns remain as credible candidates for a longer time. Thus, with a word like *cave*, a series of *-ave* patterns should get activation, but the activation for *have* should not survive long, since it is not supported by activation for any other word. When *have* is read, however, the activation for *have* should persist, and so should that for the many other *-ave* patterns which share a pronunciation.

The additional finding reported by Waters and Seidenberg, that spelling-sound regularity also affects lexical decision latency when the stimuli include strange words does not compromise this view at all. Nothing in the relevant data suggest any effect of the presence of strange words on results for regular-inconsistent words. One reasonable account of the data is that, when strange words are not present, the lexical decision is driven partly by a familiarity index, partly by lexical analysis using a phonological code. When strange words are included in the list, the familiarity index (particularly if it includes an assessment of the familiarity of word segments) may be less useful, causing subjects to rely more on the lexical analysis, and therefore increasing the effect of the spelling-sound irregularity. Since regular-inconsistent words have regular spelling-sound relations, this change in emphasis should not affect results with such words. However, the change should affect both strange and exception words.

It would be desirable to put these ideas to empirical test. But for now, it is sufficient to point out that they constitute a reasonable alternative interpretation to that advanced by Seidenberg and his colleagues. Thus, at present, there is no reason to take their data as damaging to arguments in favor of "early" phonology.

2. Summary

Clearly, the current view leads to the conclusion that some of the standard laboratory tasks necessitate operations which are more elaborate and difficult than ordinary, unmonitored reading. The implication is that <u>less</u> direct ways of assessing reading ability are <u>more</u> useful. This is not a particularly radical conclusion.

Much was made above about the need to maintain a pattern - to prevent it from decaying very rapidly - in order to permit certain operations to be carried out. Maintenance depends upon a refreshing signal being sent from one buffer/system to another. It is worthwhile considering what sorts of things can prevent such a signal from being sent. We shall do this in the following section, which shows how the model accounts for some patient data.

VI. DEREK DEALS WITH DYSLEXIA

There are some fundamental types of performance breakdown in acquired dyslexia which any theory of reading must address. Before offering accounts of these types of breakdown, I shall make some general comments about how DEREK works. The various accounts focus predominantly, but not exclusively, on the following two issues:

1 Is the response required in testing based on a buffer pattern or a semantic pattern? Normally, we shall assume that a semantic response (i.e., a categorization) depends upon the semantic system. Naming, and other responses about a lexical or sublexical form will, by default, be considered to depend upon a stable pattern residing in either the phonological or the orthographic buffer, as appropriate. (It is an open question how lexical decision is mediated. As suggested above, it appears to involve various kinds of familiarity judgment (Balota & Chumbly 1984; Besner & Johnston, 1989; Besner & McCann, 1987; Seidenberg & McClelland, 1989) which may not draw upon the same resources as the other tasks).

2. Does the task a particular patient can or cannot do require any kind of decision? If a decision is necessary, then a relatively long-lasting representation must be used. The major lab task which does not require a decision of any sort is naming.

These rules of thumb guide the following accounts.

1. Deep Dyslexia and the Distinction Between Concrete and Abstract Words

Three central characteristics of deep dyslexia are the inability to read nonwords, a susceptibility to semantic (as well as visual) errors in reading words (e.g., DAUGHTER for "sister"), and greater difficulty with low imageability than with high imageability nouns (Marshall & Newcombe, 1973). In the discussion of the phonological buffer above, reference was made to the flexible rule model, which produces sets of candidate readings of letter strings. Following that operation, a decision must be made as to which of the candidate readings is the correct phonological form. The lexical status of candidates - where this is understood to mean representation in the semantic system - and contextual information, are two factors influencing that decision, neither of which are helpful with nonwords.

Nonwords can be read by activating multiple patterns for words sharing bits of the target nonword. Synthesis of these patterns ensues to produce a single vector which can output in the normal way. Impaired reading of nonwords could be due to either of two problems. One is that a general damping of activation levels may result from the insult to the brain, making it more difficult to evoke particular patterns in any buffer/system.[21] Signals pass from one unit to another only when an activation threshold within sending units is reached. A reduction in overall activity levels could mean that thresholds are in general harder to attain. This damping would have a larger effect on nonwords, if none of the several patterns evoked for any nonword (each responding to some part of the stimulus) got enough activation. That is, nonwords could be seen as spreading their activation too thinly, so that no one pattern reaches threshold. On this view, if the damage is severe enough, one would also expect to see impaired reading of some types of words.[22] It would be of some interest, in this connection, to see whether deep dyslexics can perform Greenberg and Vellutino's task, and, if so, whether they show the priming effect.

The semantic errors and difficulty with low-imageability words both fall out naturally as well. Hinton, McClelland and Rumelhart (1986) make a useful point:

Almost all types are themselves instances of more general types, and this can be implemented by dividing the pattern that represents the type into two subpatterns, one for the more general type of which this type is an instance, and the other for the features that discriminate this particular type from other instances of the same general type. (p. 84)

In other words, semantically-related items have patterns of activity which share common subpatterns. A failure to make fine distinctions among "microfeatures" (Hinton et al. , 1986) of patterns is a credible explanation of many semantic paralexias. (Semantic paralexias are oral reading errors in which the response offered is semantically related to the stimulus word.)

In the case of low imageability words, we have already discussed the "mapping" process which takes a pattern from semantics to the orthographic buffer. There is a hierarchy of difficulty associated with this mapping. Since the link between a highly imageable concept and the appropriate lexical designation is straightforward, while that between a low imageability concept and a lexical item may be relatively difficult to establish.[23] It may be easier to map high imageability concepts onto an output form than low imageability concepts.

Difficulty reading low imageability words results because the mapping becomes <u>too</u> difficult for those items when activation is damped. That is, low imageability words are more sensitive to the reduced activation levels in the system than are high imageability words. Patterns corresponding to low imageability words, if they have some tendency to diffuse their (damped) activation over more buffer units, may not be able to cause any buffer pattern to reach threshold.

It may even be possible in this way to handle such cases as patient Lisa, reported by Sartori, Masterson, and Job (1986). Lisa could accurately sort words into the categories abstract/concrete, even though she had serious comprehension difficulties. She could also do lexical decision though she could not read nonwords aloud. The logical explanation is that she was able to use information about the difficulty of the semantic system - buffer mapping to support certain decisions: word/nonword or abstract/concrete.[24] Where there is no reason to expect differential difficulty in carrying out a mapping, as for example, in the contrast between animal and non-animal words, one would not expect to find the mapping process supporting a category decision. Lisa, indeed, was not able to sort above chance on that dimension.

The account of Lisa's difficulties just outlined is very much in the spirit of DEREK: an attempt to explain as much as possible using the same mechanism. Here, to review, the mechanism involves two assumptions, each motivated by other evidence: first, that a consequence of brain damage is generally damped activations which make the system work only when patterns are easy to evoke; second, that the semantics - buffer mapping is more challenging for low than for high-imageability words. On the other hand, it is not immediately obvious how DEREK would deal with a patient such as CAV, reported by Warrington (1981). CAV had significantly more difficulty reading aloud concrete words than reading aloud abstract words. He tended to make visual errors on concrete words, suggesting a possible mechanism.

It may be that the problem for this patient was distinguishing among strong candidate pronunciations - i.e., that for certain words it was difficult to relax to one subset of units. This explanation would work if abstract words in general have fewer close neighbors than do concrete words. The more dense neighborhood of concrete words would then offset the advantage normally accruing to concrete words from their more direct links. Ideally, such questions would be answered (a) by tests with CAV taking account of neighborhood densities and (b) by a simulation of this patient's performance. The account rests, too, on the empirical issue of relative neighborhood densities for abstract and concrete words.

2. Phonological Dyslexia

In phonological dyslexia, as in deep dyslexia, the patient has profound difficulty reading nonwords. Some patients read pseudohomophones better than other nonwords. Funnell's (1983) patient WB was unable to read any nonwords, pseudohomophonic or otherwise. In the more usual case, nonword reading is impaired but not completely lost. Phonological dyslexics show visual and derivational errors but, unlike deep dyslexics, they do not make semantic errors.

Keeping in mind that there are differences among phonological dyslexics - recall Coltheart's (1987) comment about syndrome dissolution - it is still possible to point to a major distinction between phonological and deep dyslexics: the absence of semantic errors in oral reading. We explained such errors in deep dyslexics in terms of impaired filtering of a pattern out of the set of all active units, due to the general damping of activation resulting from brain damage. It seems most economical now to claim that this damping is less severe in phonological than in deep dyslexia.

In explaining deep dyslexia, we suggested that the damping of activation was so severe as to make it difficult to distinguish among patterns which differed only in their microfeatures. To account for phonological dyslexia, we need only suggest that word-based patterns can still be evoked, down to the microfeatures, in general. Nonword patterns, on the other hand, cannot be evoked because they spread their activation too thin.[25] Parenthetically, visual errors can be explained by errors in grapheme-phoneme translation (they are very likely to maintain consonant frames and insert incorrect vowel phonology).

Notice, once again, that the simple fact that a pattern is evoked in the semantic system does not imply that a question can be answered regarding the input word: for question answering, feedback from a buffer is necessary to keep the semantic pattern active. This is one way to account for the performance of Funnell's (1983) patient WB, who could orally read words with very little error but was significantly impaired on semantic judgements with written words. An alternative account is presented in section 4 below.

There is a certain elegance in the description of deep and phonological dyslexia as points (or ranges) on a continuum of difficulty in arousing a pattern. To be convincing, of course, the argument must ultimately be backed up by simulations which vary in difficulty and reproduce the syndromes in detail. The model would also gain greater credibility from making predictions about human performance. One obvious prediction is that naming times for words for phonological dyslexics should be shorter than those for deep dyslexics. It should be noted that this prediction need not hold for any particular individual;[26] but it should hold for groups.

3. Surface Dyslexia

Surface dyslexics usually do not have a particular problem in reading nonwords. Rather, their special difficulty is in the reading of exception words (those words whose pronunciation is not easily predicted on the basis of their spelling). Such words appear to be pronounced in surface dyslexia via the Grapheme-Phoneme Conversion (GPC) rules (on the flexible rule view, by the dominant vowel translations). The domain of the rules applied may or may not extend to the target graphemes; in either case, an error results. In general, the incorrect response is visually similar to the target word.

The basic finding is readily accounted for by impairment to the orthography-to-phonology translation mechanism linking the buffers. A compromised flexible rule system produces only candidates containing the most frequent grapheme-phoneme correspondences. In "activation" terms, candidates containing nondominant (i.e., exception) correspondences would not send strong signals to the semantic system. Patterns corresponding to such candidates would stand less chance of stabilizing. Notice, however, that it is in the way of explanations using DEREK to use relative rather than absolute difficulty: the possibility exists for reading exception words correctly, but doing so is unlikely. Notice, too, that this explanation suggests that when such patients misread irregular words their preferred pronunciations should be predictable on the basis of the kind of information flexible rules are based on. Such information has been quantified by Berndt, Reggia and Mitchum (1987).

Patterson et al.'s (1989) observation that misreadings of exception words, in both patient data and a simulation, are likely to differ from the target by one phonemic feature of the vowel, supports this interpretation. Although Patterson et al. claim that that characteristic of misreadings is a unique insight which would not have been obtained without their model, it is, in fact, a prediction which follows very directly from the flexible rule model, with its emphasis on consonant frames and variable vowel readings.

One observation which requires some comment here is that some surface dyslexics can understand words they mispronounce. This might be explained on the grounds that multiple patterns of activity arise in both the phonological buffer and the semantic system, as in Figure 3. In that figure, the stars indicate a "broken connection" between information in the phonological buffer and information at a subsequent stage. The observation suggests that the flaw is in assigning control over the speech musculature to the wrong phonological buffer pattern. This might occur, for example, because there is difficulty in resolving the conflict between two patterns when evidence supporting each is available. Thus, the phonological buffer contains both patterns, but errs when sending a pattern to the speech output buffer (a buffer outside DEREK which deals with articulation).

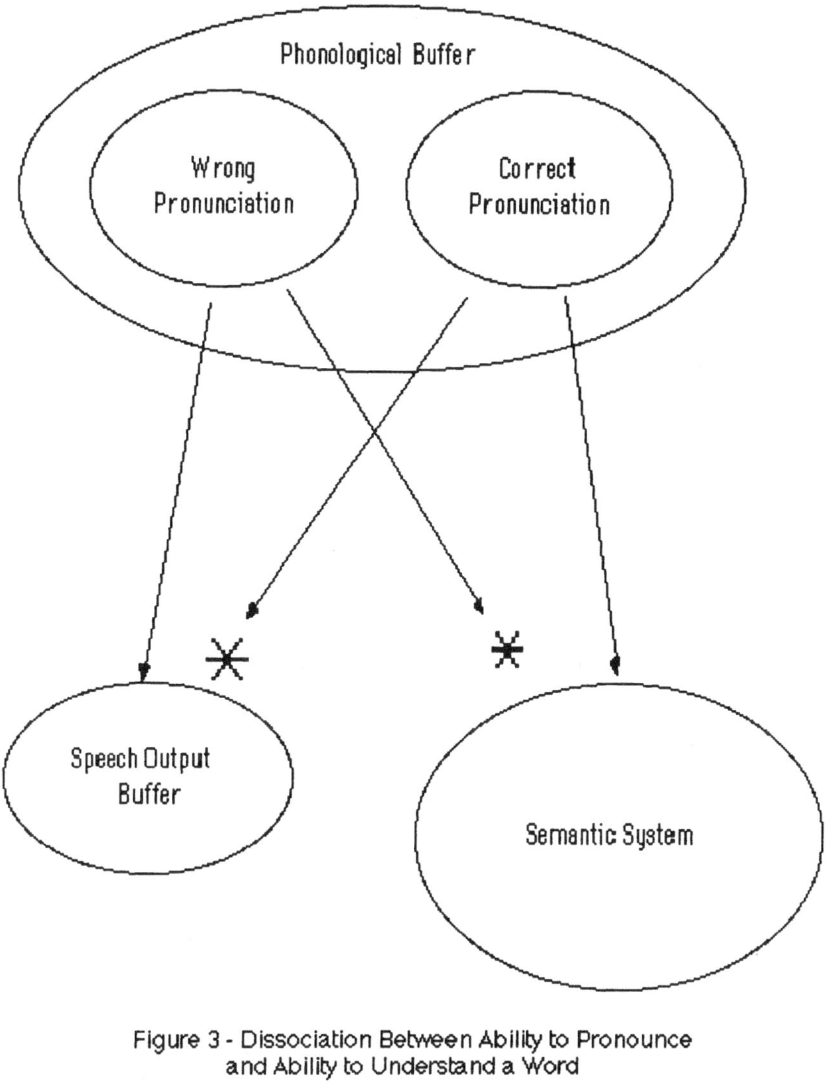

Figure 3 - Dissociation Between Ability to Pronounce and Ability to Understand a Word

Given that it is fundamental to the model that multiple, competing patterns be active simultaneously, this sort of "routing" breakdown can account for some of the data. The reverse deficit to that pictured in Figure 2 - sending the wrong pattern to a processor charged with a meaning decision - would account for a patient being able to pronounce a word like bury correctly, then defining it as a "fruit on a tree." This allows for a certain economy of explanation.

On this view, it is incorrect to say that a patient giving the correct pronunciation and the wrong meaning knows the pronunciation without knowing the meaning (or vice versa). It is possible that they "know" neither, if "know" means having unconditional, voluntary access to information. Consider the following illustration. Suppose a psychologist asks a patient to guess which face of a coin will come up in a coin toss, and the patient does so correctly. Suppose the patient is now asked which of two colored balls, a red or a green one, will be pulled out of a box, and the patient guesses incorrectly. Obviously, we would not want to conclude that the patient is better at predicting coin tosses than at predicting the color of balls. By the same token, if a patient gets the correct pronunciation of a word, but offers a wrong meaning, we should not necessarily conclude that the patient is better at pronunciation than at specifying meaning. If the error involves a stimulus with a homophone, and involves a patient giving the pronunciation for the stimulus and meaning of the homophone, or vice versa, it seems most appropriate to conclude that the subject cannot distinguish between the two words and so selects randomly. Doing so would certainly produce phenomena such as a (chance) correct reading of bury along with a (chance) misinterpretation.

It might also produce a patient like W. B. (Funnell, 1983), who could read orally very well, but had impaired comprehension. The point here is that W. B. made semantic decision errors on some trials of a forced choice between pairs of items. The account above presents an alternative explanation for this performance to that advanced by Funnell.

It would be useful to know whether patients make these errors consistently. That is, when patients mispronounce a particular word which they comprehend, do they do so on every exposure to the word, and always in the same way? Do they show evidence of mispronunciation and correct understanding on words which don't have homophones or very close neighbors? Do they give meanings totally unrelated to pronunciations? Further development of the explanation offered here will require data of that sort.

4. Discussion of the Patient Data

I shall not review any further patient data here. My goal in considering some characteristics of the major syndromes has been to give an idea of how DEREK can be used to reconceptualize the impairments. Several strategies of explanation are worth summarizing. First, in using DEREK, one thinks in terms of patterns of activation. These patterns have the following characteristics (in an intact brain): (a) patterns are evoked first in input buffers which have no lexical knowledge. (b) Similar patterns represent similar concepts. (c) Patterns stabilized in the semantic system in response to words are immediately sent to the phonological buffer for pronunciation. (d) semantic patterns, once activated, decay very quickly unless refreshed. (e) questions about semantic patterns can only be answered if the patterns are kept active. (f) translating a pattern from the semantic system to a buffer is assigning a word to a concept; that function is harder for some concepts than for others.

Of these six points, items c, d, and e are key assumptions of DEREK. They are the only assumptions of the model. Together with the input buffers, the semantic system, and connections between these elements, they constitute the whole model. Accounts of the data using DEREK are intended to replace numberless routes and information stores, with sophisticated claims about the passage of signals among units in a parallel network. All the "magic" in the model is in the claim that patterns evoked by input have semantic force because they are in a semantic system. Why this should be so is a function of the "wet ware"; it is outside the theory. How particular patterns come to have particular semantic force is to be explained by a theory about learning; it, too, is not part of DEREK.

DEREK is presented as a challenge to traditional models. I am taking the strongest position I can defend with any seriousness, because I think that the elaboration of models of word recognition needs to be challenged, that we as theorists need to be much more reluctant to add elements to our models. I have no idea whether I shall be able to sustain such a simple model in the long run, but it will have served its purpose if it draws to the reader's attention some alternative strategies for interpreting well-known data, and encourages the reader to resist the call of the siren lexicon.

VII. SUMMARY

After a brief review of the development of a general approach to modelling word recognition, centered around the lexicon, I concluded that the early versions of such models were abandoned too quickly. Word recognition has been beset of late with a sort of fever which compels victims to elaborate their models for each new piece of data. In an attempt to break the fever, I presented the simplest model of word recognition I could think of, one having only a semantic system, and two buffers which handle input/output but have no lexical knowledge.

Illustrations were made of how the direct encoding model accounts for the major syndromes of acquired dyslexia. The basic strategy was to point out ways that the parallel activation of sets of cells can be interfered with, so that patterns are harder to evoke. Given an (independently motivated) hierarchy of difficulty in either evoking semantic patterns or transferring them to a buffer for output, many of the characteristics of disordered reading follow.

Little was said about comprehension, the claim being that comprehension is orthogonal to naming: A pattern, once stabilized in the semantic system, might be passed to a buffer, then decay almost immediately. It is possible that the semantic pattern could be arousable but not maintainable, if the activations in a damaged brain decay faster than they can be refreshed. If so, patterns could not be maintained long enough for a question to be answered accurately. This is not a particularly new idea. It is in the spirit of the criticism by Cheesman and Merikle (1985) of masked priming studies in which subjects are intended to be unaware of the primes. One supposed "guarantee" of this state is that subjects are asked to tell the experimenter, after the target appears, if they saw the prime. Cheesman and Merikle pointed out that it is possible for a prime to be detected and for the resultant activation to decay so rapidly that it is lost - i.e., forgotten - by the time the opportunity for reporting it occurs. The very same sort of reasoning applies in the case of patients who can read a word without being able to answer questions about it.

I have tried to make the model explicit, to show how straightforward it really is. Although this is the first attempt at formalizing DEREK, the reader may assume that any routes or stores not explicitly mentioned are not part of the model. I shall doggedly resist any attempt to add bits to the model: once little pieces begin to be added, my fear is that simplicity will go the way of virginity. I trust the reader will agree that DEREK is in fact quite simple (though not without a certain rough charm).

FOOTNOTES

[1] This has led some PDP theorists (Rumelhart & McClelland, 1986) to conclude that when a pattern is not active, the corresponding stimulus is not represented anywhere in the system.

[2] I use this phrase as a neutral term intended to cover any kind of translation between codes: in particular, converting written input into phonological or semantic output.

[3] The words "off" and "on" need not be taken literally here: they need only be levels of activity separated by some critical amount. Thus, a pattern of activity may change because some of its units decrease their response rate, while the response rate for some units not in the pattern may increase.

[4] Note that the claim that the word pattern is filtered out of the supraword pattern does not imply that the semantic force of the word was available before the stimulus arrived and initiated the filtering process. The word pattern was present but not active. Isolating and then integrating it has the effect of changing activations on relevant units so that their contribution to the larger pattern is revised.

5 This nonunique pattern is not yet a response to a stimulus because multiple cycles of transmission of information from orthography to phonology to semantics to orthography are necessary.

6 Such rules relate graphemes to one or more phonemes, creating a candidate set of pronunciations of a word. The pronunciations are in the form of an abstract, phonological code, to which phonotactic constraints have not been applied. In general, consonants are translated into single phonemes, vowels into multiple phonemes. From these, candidate readings are created each consisting of a consonant "frame" with various vowel readings.

7 As an analogy, consider the difference between the assignment of offices to professors, and the description of their research interests. The relation of the set of faculty members (F) to the set of office numbers (ON) is 1:1 and easily specified. The relation between the set of faculty members and the set of research interests (RI) is usually more complex. I call the former relation (F - ON) a connection and the latter (F - RI) a mapping. Thus, "mapping" implies that there can be more than one member of set RI associated with each member of set F (and vice versa).

8 Note that these "words" are words only contingently, that is, when they are output. In the orthographic buffer, they are simply sequences of graphemes.

9 Here, "before" is interpreted to mean "rather than," as opposed to "earlier in time."

10 It is important to emphasize the point here: information about subword segments is recoverable from a comparison of multiple patterns which share that segment. It is not recoverable from decomposition of a single pattern into component parts.

11 This is, of course, predicated on an "early" phonological influence on activations. With only orthographic influence, there is no reason for TAKE, BAKE, LAKE, etc. to be activated in response to ACHE.

12 The experiments reported here were designed by the author and run under his supervision by thesis students. Experiment 1 was run by Lloyd Pollard. Experiment 2 was run by Logie Bruce-Lockhart.

13 The pseudohomophones used were taken from McCann and Besner (1987), with some additional stimuli created in our lab.

14 This prediction requires the assumption that at very short SOAs (i.e., 100 msec) there would be no opportunity for subjects to consider and dismiss the

conflicting phonological code, though this might occur at longer SOAs. For this reason, it is of less interest whether interference is found at longer SOAs.

15 Nonword primes preceded left-facing arrows, while word primes preceded right-facing arrows. There was a neutral condition corresponding to each of these types of trial: neutral string followed by left arrow, and neutral string followed by right arrow. Neutral primes consisted of nonletter strings (i.e., %$#[@*).

16 For example, suppose we say that, in the Nonword condition, a decision about the response to expect is available at (T - 20 msec), where T is the average latency for a response decision in the Neutral condition. Then if the presence of a Pseudohomophone produces response competition which takes 20 msec to resolve, no differences in performance between Pseudohomophone and Neutral trials will be found.

17 For this group, Pseudohomophone probability was the same as in the previous experiment.

18 I say "differentially" because the possibility exists that the presence of phonological information about pseudohomophones is not ignored, but rather causes a general slowing down of processing because of greater uncertainty about the correct response. This might account also for the absence of an SOA effect for the High Pseudohomophone Probability group.

19 It seems likely that, in lab tasks, relaxation can also be constrained by the value of a hit relative to the cost of further processing. On this issue, we can summarize by observing that, in principle, the system can support responses at any stage of relaxation if error rates are not of much consequence.

20 Evett and Humphreys (1981) conclude that the facilitation effect in their Experiment II is graphemic rather than phonological because there is no difference between a "graphemic only" prime condition and a "graphemic and phonological" condition. The authors claim that "lexical access can be achieved using a graphemic access route which operates independently of the lexical, as well as the visual, properties of the stimulus" (p. 338). There was no correlation between the size of the priming effect and either of two measure of visual similarity between prime and target, but there was a reliable correlation between effect size and number of letters shared between prime and target. This being the case, one could argue that it was the phonological value of the shared letters that primed a response.

It is hard to imagine a graphemically similar pair of words which do not share some phonology. Good examples of the sort of problem the experimenter runs into are found in the list of words provided by Humphreys, Evett and

Taylor (1982), who reported a related, very similar set of experiments. Their Experiment III used both nonword phonological primes and word graphemic primes in a tachistoscopic recognition task. Inspection of the list of stimuli (Humphreys et al., Appendix C) reveals orthographic target-prime pairs such as CIRCLE - PIRAIL, CLAW - BLET, KALE - DARL, QUEEN - FRENE, and CALM - RAIM. But the list also contains pairs such as DRAW - DREP, DREW - DROF, FALL - FIRL, FORM - FEAM, HAWK - HEEK, and MAUL - MOOL. I would argue that it makes a mockery of the idea of orthographic overlap to suggest that the primes in the first set could facilitate recognition of their targets (it must be noted that words in this condition were selected as orthographic controls for the phonological primes, not for their orthographic overlap with targets. Nonetheless, the point that priming in this condition could be due to phonological similarity between prime and target remains). In the case of the second set, flexible rule theory would be quite comfortable with a priming effect of primes on targets, based on the consonant frames of the stimuli. Thus, Humphreys et al. 's conclusion (and Evett and Humphreys' before them) that there is no phonological priming because there is no advantage of phonological over "graphemic" conditions is suspect.

21 In the report of simulations of acquired dyslexia, Patterson, Seidenberg, and McClelland (1989) have made a similar suggestion for a pathological limitation on activations in units which are otherwise undamaged, as an alternative to damage which eliminates connections or units, as in their implemented model.

22 The other reason for an inability to read nonwords is that, though appropriate patterns for the assembly process are evoked, the assembly process itself is disorderd.

23 For example, there is, for normal purposes, little doubt as to which lexical item applies generally to scaly, finned creatures which live in the sea. But what of the famous feeling one experiences upon seeing one's mother-in-law drive over a cliff in one's new car?

24 Note that even if the mapping succeeds, there is no consequent implication that any of the words read are comprehended, in the sense that a decision about them can be made. Recall the points made above (a) that decisions are held to require longer-lasting representations than naming does, and (b) that semantic patterns decay rapidly unless refreshed. Thus, a pattern could arise, be sent to a buffer, and the difficulty or ease of the mapping noted, while the origninal pattern decays before any decision regarding it can be made. The issue of comprehension, in other words, is orthogonal to the issue of making lexical decisions and abstract/concrete decisions.

25 The other explanation offered for nonword reading difficulty in deep dyslexia was in terms of impaired assembly of phonology. This could also hold for phonological dyslexia. In that case, the distinction between syndromes is still to be accounted for in terms of severity of damping (i.e., whether damping is bad enough to affect word patterns at all).

26 The issue of how severity of deficit is affected by premorbid skill level is, as far as I know, as yet untouched. Differences in performance quality can also arise, obviously, from other considerations, such as age, extent of collateral damage, and the panoply of variables which produce individual differences in unimpaired subjects.

ACKNOWLEDGMENTS

Preparation of this manuscript was supported by Natural Sciences and Engineering Research Council Grant No. 38873.

REFERENCES

Anderson, J.A. & Mozer, M.C. (1981). Categorization and selective neurons. In Hinton, G.E. and Anderson, J.A. (Eds.), *Parallel Models of Associative Memory*. Lawrence Erlbaum associates, Hillsdale: N.J.

Balota, D. & Chumbley, J. (1984). Are lexical decisions a good measure of lexical access? The role of frequency in the neglected decision stage. *Journal of Experimental Psychology: Human Perception and Performance*, **10**, 340-357.

Balota, D. & Chumbley, J. (1985). The locus of word frequency effect in the pronunciation task: Lexical access and/or production? *Journal of Memory and Language*, **24**, 89-106.

Becker, C.A. (1979). Semantic context and word frequency effects in visual word recognition. *Journal of Experimental Psychology: Human Perception and Performance*, **5**, 252-259.

Berndt, R.S., Reggia, J.A., & Mitchum, C. (1987). Empirically derived probabilities for grapheme-to-phoneme correspondences in English. *Behavior Research Methods, Instruments, and Computers*, **19** (1), 1-9.

Besner, D., & Johnston, J. C. (1989). Reading and the mental lexicon: On the uptake of visual information. In W. Marslen-Wilson (Ed.), *Lexical representation and process*. Boston, Mass.: MIT press.

Besner, D. & McCann, R. S. (1987). Word frequency and pattern distortion in visual word identification and production: An examination of four classes of models. In M. Coltheart (Ed.), *Attention and performance XII: The psychology of reading*. Hillsdale, N. J.: Lawrence Erlbaum Associates.

Besner, D., & Swan, M. (1982). Models of lexical access in visual word recognition. *Quarterly Journal of Experimental Psychology*, **34A**, 313-325.

Broadbent, D. E. (1967). Word frequency effect and response bias. *Psychological Review*, **89**,1-47.

Broadbent, D. E., & Gregory, M. (1963). Vigilance considered as a statistical decision. *British Journal of Psychology*, **54**(4), 309-323.

Brown, P., & Besner, D. (1987). The assembly of phonology in oral reading. In M. Coltheart (Ed.), *Attention and performance XII: The psychology of reading*. Hillsdale, N. J.: Lawrence Erlbaum Associates.

Carr, T.H., & Pollatsek, A. (1985). Recognising printed words: A look at current models. In D. Besner, T. G. Waller, and G. E. MacKinnon (Eds.), *Reading research: Advances in theory and practice*, Vol. 5. Orlando:Academic Press.

Cheesman, J., & Merikle, P. (1985). Word recognition and consciousness. In D. Besner, T. G. Waller, and G. E. MacKinnon (Eds.), *Reading research: Advances in theory and practice*, Vol. 5. Orlando: Academic Press.

Cherry, E.C. (1953). Some experiments on the recognition of speech with one and two ears. *Journal of the Acoustical Society of America*, **25**, 975-979.

Clarke, R., & Morton, J. (1983). Cross-modality facilitation in tachistoscopic word recognition. *Quarterly Journal of Experimental Psychology*, **35A**, 79-96.

Collins, A.M., & Quillian, M.R. (1969). Retrieval time from semantic memory. *Journal of Verbal Learning and Verbal Behavior*, **8**, 240-248.

Coltheart, M. (1987). Architecture of a word-recognition system. In M. Coltheart, G. Sartori, & R. Job (Eds.), *The cognitive neuropsychology of language*. Hillsdale, N.J.: Lawrence Erlbaum Associates.

Coltheart, M., Davelaar, E., Jonasson, J.T., & Besner, D. (1977). Access to the internal lexicon. In S. Dornic (Ed.), *Attention and performance VI.*. New York: Academic Press.

Coltheart, M., Besner, D., Jonasson, J.T., & Davelaar, E. (1979). Phonological recoding in the lexical decision task. *Quarterly Journal of Experimental Psychology*, **31**, 489-508.

Dennis, I., Besner, D., & Davelaar, E. (1985). Phonology in visual word recognition: Their is more two this than meats the I. In D. Besner, T.G. Waller, and G.E. MacKinnon (Eds.), *Reading research: Advances in theory and practice, Vol. 5*. Orlando: Academic Press.

Dreyfus, H.L. (1981). From microworlds to knowledge representation: AI at an impasse. In J. Haugeland (Ed.), *Mind Design*, Cambridge, MA.: MIT Press.

Evett, L., & Humphreys, G.W. (1981). The use of abstract graphemic information in lexical access. *Quarterly Journal of Experimental Psychology*, **33A**, 325-350.

Funnell, E. (1983). Phonological processes in reading: New evidence from acquired dyslexia. *British Journal of Psychology*, **74**, 159-180.

Greenberg, S.N., & Vellutino, F. R. (1988). Evidence for processing of constituent single- and multiletter codes: Support for multilevel coding in word perception. *Memory and Cognition*,**16**, 54-63.

Healy, A.F. (1980). Proofreading errors on the word *the*: New evidence on reading units. *Journal of Experimental Psychology: Human Perception and Performance*, **6**, 45-57.

Healy, A.F., & Drewnowski, A. (1986). Investigating the boundaries of reading units: Letter detection in misspelled words. *Journal of Experimental Psychology: Human Perception and Performance*, **9**, 413-426.

Henderson, L. (1982). *Orthography and word recognition in reading*. London: Academic press.

Hinton, G.E., McClelland, J.L., & Rumelhart, D.E. (1986). Distributed representations. In Rumelhart, D.E. & McClelland, J.L. (Eds.), *Parallel Distributed Processing: Explorations in the Microstructure of Cognition*, Vol. 1. Cambridge, MA: Bradford (MIT) Press.

Humphreys, G.W., & Evett, L.J. (1985). Are there independent lexical and nonlexical reoutes in word processing? An evaluation of the dual-route theory of reading. *The Behavioral and Brain Sciences*, **8**, 689-740.

Humphreys, G.W., Evett, L.J., & Taylor, D.E. (1982). Automatic phonological priming in visual word recognition. *Memory and Cognition*, **10**, 576-590.

Jackson, A., & Morton, J. (1984). Facilitation in auditory word recognition. *Memory and Cognition*, **12**, 568-574.

Jacoby, L.L. (1983). Perceptual enhancement: Persistent effects of an experience. *Journal of Experimental Psychology: Learning, memory and Cognition*, **9**, 21-38.

Jacoby, L.L., & Hayman, C.A.G. (1987). Specific visual transfer in word identification. *Journal of Experimental Psychology: Learning, Memory and Cognition*, **13**, 3, 456-463.

Johnson, N.F., Turner-Lyga, M., & Pettigrew, B.S. (1986). Part-whole relationships in the processing of small visual patterns. *Memory and Cognition*, **14**, 5-16.

Katz, J.J., & Fodor, J.A. (1963). The structure of a semantic theory. *Language*, **39**, 170-210.

Kolers, P.A. (1979). A pattern-analysing basis of recognition. In Cermak, L. S. & Craik, F. I. M. (Eds.), *Levels of Processing in Human Memory*. Hillsdale, N. J.: Lawrence Erlbaum Associates.

Lyons, J. (1977). *Semantics*. Cambridge, U. K.: Cambridge University Press.

Marcel, A.J. (1983). Conscious and unconscious perception: Experiments in visual masking and word recognition. *Cognitive Psychology*, **8**, 197-237.
Marshall, J.C., & Newcombe, F. (1973). Patterns of paralexia: A psycholinguistic approach. *Journal of Psycholinguistic Research*, **2**, 1785-199.
McCann, R.S., & Besner, D. (1987). Reading pseudohomophones: Implications for models of pronunciation assembly and the locus of word-frequency effects in naming. *Journal of Experimental Psychology: Human Perception and Performance*, **13**, 1, 14-24.
McCann, R.S., Besner, D., & Davelaar, E. (1988). Word recognition and identification: Do word frequency effects reflect lexical access? *Journal of Experimental Psychology: Human Perception and Performance*, **14**, 693-706.
McClelland, J.L., (1979). On the time relations of mental processes: An examination of systems of processing in cascade. *Psychological Review*, **86**, 287-330.
McClelland, J.L. (1988). Connectionist models and psychological evidence. *Journal of Memory and Language*, **27**, 107-123.
McClelland, J.L., & Rumelhart, D.E. (1981). An interactive activation model of context effects in letter perception: Part I. An account of basic findings. *Psychological Review*, **88**, 375-407.
McNamara, T.P., & Sternberg, R.J. (1983). Mental models of word meaning. *Journal of Verbal Learning and Verbal Behavior*, **22**, 449-474.
Monsell, S., Doyle, M.C., & Haggard, P.N. (1989). Effects of frequency on visual word recognition tasks: where are they? *Journal of Experimental Psychology: General*, **118**, 1, 43-71.
Morton, J. (1964). The effects of context on the visual duration threshold for words. *British Journal of Psychology*, **55**, 165-180.
Morton, J. (1979). Facilitation in word recognition: Experiments causing change in the logogen model. In P. A. Kolers, M. E. Wrolstad, & H. Bouma (Eds.), *Processing of visible language*. New York: Plenum.
Morton, J. (1969). The interaction of information in word recognition. *Psychological Review*, **76**, 165-178.
Patterson, K., & Coltheart, V. (1987). Phonological processes in reading: A tutorial review. In M. Coltheart (Ed.), *Attention and performance XII: The psychology of reading*. Hillsdale, N. J.: Lawrence Erlbaum Associates.
Patterson, K., & Morton, J. (1985). From orthography to phonology: An attempt at an old interpretation. In K. Patterson, J. C. Marshall, and M. Coltheart (Eds.), *Surface dyslexia: Neuropsychological and cognitive studies of phonological reading*. London: Lawrence Erlbaum Associates Ltd.
Patterson, K., Seidenberg, M., & McClelland, J.L. (1989). Connections and disconnections: Acquired dyslexia in a computational model of reading processes. In R. G. M. Morris (Ed.), *Parallel distributed processing: Implications for psychology and neurobiology*, Oxford University Press.
Perfetti, C.A., Bell, L.C., & Delaney, S.M. (1988). Automatic (prelexical) phonetic activation in silent word reading: evidence from backward masking. *Journal of Memory and Language*, **27**, 59-70.
Quillian, M.R. (1968). Semantic memory. In M. Minsky, *Semantic information processing*. Cambridge, MA: M. I. T. Press.
Reggia, J.A., & Berndt, R.S. (1986). Modelling reading aloud and its relevance to acquired dyslexia. *Computer methods and programs in biomedicine*, **22**, 13-19.
Rubenstein, H., Lewis, S. S., & Rubenstein, M. A. (1971). Evidence for phonemic recoding in visual word recognition. *Journal of Verbal Learning and Verbal Behavior*, **10**, 645-657.
Rumelhart, D. E., & McClelland, J. L. (1986). *Parallel distributed processing: Explorations in the microstructure of cognition*. Cambridge, MA: Bradford (MIT) Press.
Santa, J.L., Santa, C., & Smith, E.E. (1977). Units of word recognition: Evidence for the use of multiple units. *Perception and Psychophysics*, **22**, 585-591.
Sartori, G., Masterson, J., & Job, R. (1987). Direct-route reading and the locus of lexical decision. In M. Coltheart, G. Sartori, and R. Job (Eds.), *The cognitive neuropsychology of language*. Hillsdale, N.J: Lawrence Erlbaum Associates.

Seidenberg, M.S., & McClelland, J.L. (1989). The distributed developmental model of word recognition and naming. *Psychological Review*, **96**, 523-568.

Seidenberg, M.S., Waters, G.S., Barnes, M.A., & Tannenhaus, M.K. (1984). When does irregular spelling or pronunciation influence word recognition? *Journal of Verbal Learning and Verbal Behavior*, **23**, 383-404.

Sejnowski, T.J. & Rosenberg, C.R. (1987). Parallel networks that learn to pronounce English text. *Complex Systems*, **1**, 145-168.

Shallice, T., & McCarthy, R. (1985). Phonological reading: From patterns of impairment to possible procedures. In K. Patterson, J.C. Marshall & M. Coltheart (Eds.), *Surface dyslexia: Neuropsychological and cognitive studies of phonological reading*. London: Lawrence Erlbaum.

Taraban, R., & McClelland, J.L. (1987). Conspiracy effects in word pronunciation. *Journal of Memory and Language*, **26**, 608-631.

Treiman, R., & Zukowski, A. (1988). Units in reading and spelling. *Journal of Memory and Language*, **27**, 466-477.

Treisman, A. (1960). Contextual cues in selective listening. *Quarterly Journal of Experimental Psychology*, **12**, 242-248.

Van Orden, G.C. (1987). A ROWS is a Rose: Spelling, sound and reading. *Memory and Cognition*, **15**(3), 181-198.

Van Orden, G.C., Johnston, J.C., & Hale, B.L. (1988). Word identification in reading proceeds from spelling to sound to meaning. *Journal of Experimental Psychology*, **14**(3), 371-386.

Vellutino, F. (1982). Theoretical issues in the study of word recognition: The unit of perception controversy reexamined. In S. Rosenberg (Ed.), *Handbook of applied psycholinguistics*. Hillsdale, N.J: Lawrence Erlbaum Associates.

Warrington, E.K. (1981). Concrete word dyslexia. *British Journal of Psychology*, **72**, 175-196.

Waters, G.S., & Seidenberg, M.S. (1985). Spelling-sound effects in reading: Time course and decision criteria. *Memory and Cognition*, **13**, 557-572.

Whittlesea, B.W.A. (1987). Preservation of specific experiences in the representation of general knowledge. *Journal of Experimental Psychology*, **13**, 1, 3-17.

Winnick, W.A. & Daniel, S.A. (1970). Two kinds of response priming in tachistoscopic recognition. *Journal of Experimental Psychology*, **84**(1), 74-81.

Yantis, S., & Meyer, D.E. (1985). *Dynamics of spreading activation in information processing*. Paper presented at the annual meeting of the Psychonomic Society, Boston.

6
THE NATURE AND LOCUS OF WORD FREQUENCY EFFECTS IN READING

STEPHEN MONSELL

Department of Experimental Psychology
University of Cambridge
Cambridge, England

I. INTRODUCTION

The frequency with which words are used has long been known to influence performance in reading tasks. Such effects are robust, often large, and sufficiently universal that no serious account of the processes underlying reading can fail to incorporate an explanation of frequency effects. However, the task of formulating such an account has been made difficult by controversy about where frequency effects arise in the chain(s) of mental processes connecting printed word to measured performance in reading tasks used in the laboratory. The debate about localization of frequency effects will be one theme of this chapter. Another will be a motive for interest in frequency effects that has tended to be neglected: their relation to learning. Frequencies of occurrence, as listed in the various text-based counts (e.g., Kucera & Francis, 1967), provide a rough estimate of the differential amount of experience an average adult reader of English will have had with particular orthographic patterns (and their interpretation). Experience is the stuff of which all learning is made. My argument will be that if our models of word recognition do not deal with how we learn to recognize *new* words, they are unlikely to deal adequately with effects of frequency upon the recognition of old words.

It is strange but true that, until very recently, information-processing models of word recognition have had no mechanism for learning new words. They have been attempts to represent the "mature" language system, frozen in time. As will be illustrated below, each model has nevertheless been built round assumptions intended to explain frequency effects. Of course there has been a principled, if seldom articulated, motive for ignoring the learning of new words. Theorists cannot solve every outstanding problem in a field at once, and the task of modelling the mature system in any detail has seemed hard enough without worrying about what might appear to be the separate issue of ontogeny. However, this particular placement of the boundary between what is and is not to be explained seems, with hindsight, both unfortunate and paradoxical. The boundary differentiates (arbitrarily, it would seem) two kinds of experience with orthographic patterns: that experience which modifies representations already "in" the lexicon, and that experience which adds new representations "to" the lexicon. Effects of the former kind of experience have been modelled, effects of the latter kind ignored.

It is not obvious that these two kinds of experience can be sensibly distinguished, let alone sharply differentiated. A rare word which we have previously encountered just once or twice, and may only just succeed in identifying, seems less securely "in" our lexicon than a very familiar word. Its status in our lexicon seems a priori more like that of a word that is completely novel to us than that of a very familiar word. Of course, such intuitions are an unreliable guide to theory. More compelling is this simple metatheoretical consideration: an account of frequency effects that was also an account of how new words are learned would surely be preferable to one that accounted for frequency effects alone, and then only by means of assumptions made solely for the purpose of explaining frequency effects.

I believe the shape of the desired account has begun to emerge with the application of "connectionist" or "parallel distributed processing" (PDP) learning algorithms to issues in language processing (see especially McClelland, Rumelhart and the PDP research group, 1986). The computational task of transcoding between lexical domains (orthography, phonology, semantics and syntax) seems like just the kind of pattern association task to which PDP architectures are especially suited. One may view the present headlong rush to connectionist modelling with mixed feelings, and entertain doubts about its ability to cope with certain aspects of language in general (Fodor & Pylyshyn, 1988; Massaro, 1988; Minsky & Papert, 1988; Pinker & Prince, 1988). But transcoding from a word's orthography to its meaning or its phonology is a problem of restricted scope to which many of these problems may not apply. And, as I have already suggested, one consequence of the emphasis on learning algorithms in network modelling is to bring the problem of learning to center stage. The result is to give frequency of occurrence its rightful place as a fundamental shaper of a lexical system always dynamically responsive to experience, rather than treating it as a variable to be dealt with by means of essentially *ad hoc* assumptions applied to a model of the mature system.

An additional consequence emerging from explorations of the PDP framework is a reworking of basic concepts of lexical representation and processing. The standard assumption had hitherto been that one has in one's head a set of lexical "entries" or "units" with associated (orthographic) pattern descriptors, one for each word (or morpheme) known. When reading a word, whether aloud or for comprehension, one is assumed to perform a process I shall refer to as "lexical identification"[1] to find the entry that best matches the input. Deciding upon the best match in turn permits "access to" (or "retrieval of" or "activation of") a representation of the associated meaning and/or pronunciation. "Identification" has thus typically been conceived of as a well-demarcated step in the larger skill of transcoding from print to pronunciation or from print to meaning. This identification process, and the representations of (orthographic) form assumed to support it, have typically been seen as neutral with respect to the transcoding being performed. That is, the same set of (orthographic) lexical entries and the same matching process is typically assumed to support access both from print to meaning and from print to phonology. As I will illustrate in due course, there are emerging PDP accounts which make none of these assumptions. Even if they turn out to be inadequate, the new perspective on an old problem is proving a valuable stimulus to theoretical development.

The other theme of this chapter — the localization of frequency effects — must be approached empirically by comparison of frequency effects across tasks. Most models[2] for visual "word recognition" have been models of the identification process typically assumed (as I have noted) to be common to all tasks. The standard assumption (illustrated below) has been that frequency effects arise within this rather than later processes: more familiar words are more easily *identified.* It would constitute a *prima facie* difficulty for this assumption if different tasks requiring identification of a printed word were to differ radically in their sensitivity to frequency. Until recently, most of the explicit exploration of frequency effects had been within-task, with one important exception: it has long been known that the effect of frequency on naming latency tends to be much weaker than the effect on lexical decision time (Forster & Chambers, 1973; Frederiksen & Kroll, 1976). But this difference has not seemed to challenge the attribution of frequency effects in both tasks to a common identification process, because naming has commonly been thought to depend on two parallel processes. One of these ("assembly" of phonological segments derived by sublexical transcoding between orthography and phonology) is assumed to bypass the frequency sensitive *word* identification process, and thus dilute its influence on average latency. (I elaborate upon this idea in Section VI.)

Recently a number of authors have examined frequency effects in other reading tasks, and discovered discrepancies across tasks which seem to pose problems for the standard assumption that effects of frequency upon performance are to be localized solely, or even primarily, in an identification process common to all tasks. The radical proposal that lexical identification is not a (major) locus of frequency effects conflicts both with conventional (i.e., nonlearning) models of lexical access, to be reviewed in Section II, and, as I shall argue, with expectations derived from the PDP learning models to be discussed in Section III. The empirical basis for this radical proposal needs to be examined with some care; that will be the task of Section IV. Section V summarizes some recent data from my laboratory (Monsell, Doyle & Haggard, 1989) on frequency effects in tasks requiring access from print to meaning; these undermine one component of the "radical proposal." Section VI considers recent data on frequency effects in pronunciation tasks; these data too substantially qualify the radical proposal. Section VII reviews data on effects of frequency on measures made in certain other "reading" tasks, where the measures do not logically depend on lexical identification, but which nevertheless turn out to exhibit "lexical" effects. Finally, Section VIII considers the relation between frequency effects and a related phenomenon with which they ought, a priori, to be linked, namely "repetition priming." At that point I shall also reach some conclusions on a fashionable but often fuzzy idea that will first be elucidated in Section IV, namely that the lexical decision task involves the discrimination of "familiarity."

II. FREQUENCY EFFECTS IN STANDARD WORD RECOGNITION MODELS

There have been three major classes of model: "word-detector" (or "logogen" models), serial search models, and the hybrid of these currently called the "activation-verification" model. Let us consider how frequency effects are dealt with in each of these.

1. Word-detector models. These assume an array of computational units or detectors, one for each of the words we know, to which a lower level of analysis (e.g., letter detectors for each position in the word) broadcasts information about orthographic input in parallel. Detectors have activation levels that vary over time. A detector becomes more activated the more the incoming information agrees with the pattern for which the detector is "looking" and may be inhibited by information that explicitly disagrees with that pattern. There is a long tradition of such models, beginning with the "cognitive demons" in Selfridge's Pandemonium (Selfridge & Neisser, 1960) and Treisman's (1964) "dictionary units" and directly applied to the effects of word frequency (on tachistoscopic report accuracy) in Morton's (1969) "logogen" model. Morton assumed that each logogen had its own recognition threshold[3] which could temporarily be lowered by context (to account for facilitation of recognition by context), and was more permanently lowered by a successful recognition encounter, thus accounting for both frequency and repetition effects. Morton's formulation has been very influential, although it left much unspecified. Coltheart, Davelaar, Jonasson and Besner (1977) extended it to account for lexical decision: the thresholds for high frequency words would be reached earlier than those for low-frequency words given the same amount of sensory evidence; a nonword decision would be triggered if no logogen reached threshold after a deadline set on the basis of the items expected. To deal with the fact that nonword decisions (e.g. for orthographically illegal nonwords) could be faster than some word decisions, they proposed that the deadline was rapidly and automatically adjusted within a recognition episode as a function of the total level of activation being generated in logogens by the orthographic pattern.

The next major advance within this class of models is represented by the "interactive-activation" model of McClelland and Rumelhart (1981), realized in the form of a detailed computer simulation. Its word-detectors were reciprocally interconnected with letter/position units by both excitatory and inhibitory links, and there was mutual inhibition among word units. The focus of the model was on the time course of activation of units at each level, and on accounting for the superiority of report of letters when embedded in words and pseudowords. Word units for high frequency words were simply assumed to have higher baseline levels of activation than low frequency word units. Gordon (1983) applied a similar word-detector model (the "resonance" model) to account for "frequency blocking" effects in the lexical decision task. Glanzer and Ehrenreich (1979) and Gordon (1983) compared lexical decision performance for high, medium and low frequency words for "mixed" blocks in which words of all three frequency bands occurred to "pure" blocks in which words only from one frequency band occurred. For high frequency words, presentation in a pure block yielded an advantage over presentation in a mixed block, and the advantage extended to nonwords in the pure block. Low frequency words showed no such advantage. In Gordon's "resonance" model, word detectors are assumed to be activated to a level and at a rate determined by frequency. In a pure high frequency block, the subject is able to set a less cautious criterion for deciding that no logogen will reach a criterial level. A recent development of the logogen model by Norris (1986) preserves Morton's attribution of frequency effects to word-detector thresholds, but allows these to be adjusted dynamically during identification as the result of a "check" for congruence between a candidate word and its context.

Hence in word detector models, frequency effects have been dealt with by giving word-detectors frequency-dependent thresholds (logogen models), or frequency-dependent baseline activation levels (interactive activation model) or frequency-dependent responsiveness to sensory input (resonance model). While these assumptions work, there is no real rationale for them beyond that of allowing for the existence of frequency effects. Variations in frequency are seen as variations in *predictability* (all other things being equal) of individual words rather than as variations in their *degree of acquisition*. Indeed, these models have no mechanism for acquisition of new words. Those interested in such arcane matters as repetition priming of nonwords (to be discussed briefly in Section VIII; see also Monsell, 1985) have for decades now been uttering the plaintive query: "How long does does it take to *grow* a logogen?" (For a recent example of an author grappling within the conventional framework with the question of how quickly a lexical entry can be created, see Forster, 1985.)

2. *Serial search models.* The simplest serial search models, as proposed by Rubenstein, Garfield and Millikan (1970) and Forster (1976), assumed that the subject compared some encoding of the orthographic input to a lexicon of word forms *one at a time.* To explain effects of frequency (usually on lexical decision time) it was assumed that the search through this store was ordered, at least in part, by frequency. All other things being equal, fewer comparisons would then precede a match for a higher frequency than for a low frequency word.

As is now well known, simple serial search models of this kind face numerous problems. One is computational plausibility. A process that appears to require hundreds or thousands of successive computational steps in well under a second appears unrealizable in a system built of computational elements as slow as neurons (Feldman & Ballard's, 1982, "100-step rule.") Lexical decisions to (orthographically legal) nonwords should be no faster than the slowest correct "word" decisions. Yet some classes of legal nonwords in fact receive more rapid mean RTs than some classes of word (see Monsell, 1985, Exp. 8, for examples). Use of a more sophisticated tree-searching algorithm, or searching for only part of the orthographic pattern (such as Taft's, 1979 "basic orthographic syllable structure") would only mitigate the scale of these problems, not abolish them. Finally, there are problems in accounting for effects related to shifts in decision criterion. For example, models with a frequency ordered serial search process appear incompatible with the results of the frequency blocking experiments already mentioned. If frequency blocking yielded any advantage, it should be for low not high frequency words: knowing that all the words were of low frequency in principle permits one to start the search further down the list, and any change in within-comparison criterion should also have a larger effect for low than for high frequency words. Yet, as already noted, the only advantage observed is in fact for high frequency words. For these and other reasons, the serial search postulate now survives only hybridized with the word-detector idea.

3. *Hybrid (activation-verification) models.* The main contender here is the model which, starting with Becker's (1976, 1979, 1980) "verification" model, has evolved into the "activation-verification" model of Schvaneveldt and McDonald (1981), Paap, Newsome, McDonald and Schvaneveldt (1982) and Paap, McDonald, Schvaneveldt and Noel (1987). The essential features are these. Identification happens in two discrete stages. The first stage ("activation") is a fast parallel activation process like that hypothesized by word-detector models. It terminates not in unique identification, but a (small) set of candidates which meet some fairly crude criterion of compatibility with the stimulus features. In the second stage ("verification") these candidates are examined one at a time: information retrieved

from the lexicon (e.g. about details of their spelling) is compared in a more detailed way to available visual information. As in the pure serial search models, candidates are compared in order of their frequency. (The problem of computational plausibility is now reduced because only a small number of comparisons must be made. Moreover, while the this search process is currently modelled as strictly serial, Paap et al. (1987, p. 223) say that "the serial assumption is not viewed as sacrosanct"). Frequency is held not to influence the activation stage. One rationale for this assumption is the claim that in tasks involving report of masked words, conditions under which it is assumed that the verification stage does not occur, frequency effects are minimal (Paap et al., 1982). We will return to this empirical assertion in Section VII.

Another part of the rationale for the model comes from the effects of context on lexical decision and its relation to frequency effects. Candidates may be entered into the verification set not only by sensory input, but also on the basis of prior context. Subjects may elect to specify a small verification set in this way (a "prediction" strategy) or a large set (an "expectancy" strategy) with corresponding changes in the pattern of context effects (Becker, 1980). In early versions (e.g., Becker, 1980), the verification stage was the only locus for context effects. However, it has turned out that, while context and stimulus degradation are widely agreed to interact in their effects upon lexical decision time, stimulus degradation and frequency tend to have additive effects (see Paap et al., 1987 for review, but Norris, 1984a, for an instance of nonadditive degradation and frequency effects). Paap et al.'s (1982, 1987) conclusion was that semantic context must influence a processing stage sensitive to sensory quality that frequency does not, and they therefore assume that semantic context (but not frequency) directly contributes to the activation process (the mechanism whereby candidates enter the verification set). Note that this is an additive factors argument dependent on the assumption that the hypothesized activation and verification stages are discrete processing stages in the sense of Sternberg (1969).

A third motive for the separate verification stage is the effect of context upon errors. If, as in the word-detector models, context merely reduced the amount of sensory evidence required to raise a detector's activation to a criterial level, we would expect context to increase the rate of false positives in the lexical decision task to nonwords similar to contextually primed words. But, say Paap et al. (1987, p. 225), "we have shown in numerous experiments that primes like DOCTOR do not elevate the error rate to targets like NERSE.........Many of these experiments have also shown that NERSE is classified as a nonword faster when primed by DOCTOR than when primed by an unrelated word like LION." The only published study they cite is that of Schvaneveldt and McDonald (1981). There is at least one published study indicating an opposite conclusion. Glucksberg, Kreuz and Rho (1986) found that presentation of an auditory sentence context increased LDT and error rate to a visual nonword similar to a word likely in that context, and exploited this effect to determine whether multiple meanings of an ambiguous word in the context effect were activated. It may be that the pattern of results obtained by Schvaneveldt and

McDonald (1981) results from a special strategy of checking the spelling against a predicted word, a strategy likely to be adopted only if the subject expects a high frequency of items (or their mutations) predictable by association to the prime. Norris (1984b) reports other evidence for such a checking strategy under similar conditions.

However, our principal task here is to consider the way frequency effects are dealt with in the activation-verification model. Like the pure serial model, it simply translates frequency into search order. Once again the rationale has nothing to do with acquisition, but with predictability: all other things being equal, a token is likely to be of a high frequency type, so if one must verify candidates serially, it will be efficient to check high frequency candidates first. Note that this requires unspecified machinery for determining candidates' frequency and using it to control the search order. The use made of data on frequency effects by activation-verification theorists also depends heavily on additive factors logic. It has been a basic postulate of the model that the activation and verification stages meet Sternberg's (1969) requirements of being discrete stages with independent mean durations. But there seems to be no *a priori* rationale for this postulate. One can without difficulty imagine a version of the model in which verification starts before the activation of candidates is complete (cf. Besner & McCann, 1987). Even if the transmission of a set of candidates from the activation process to the verification process were discrete, it is not obvious why the mean durations of the two stages should be independent: When stimulus quality is changed, would one not expect the number of candidates activated to the criterion required for verification also to change, and should not this not influence the duration of the verification process?

III. CONNECTIONIST LEARNING MODELS AND THE EFFECTS OF FREQUENCY

In none of the models so far mentioned are frequency effects *intrinsic* to the architecture of the model. Word detector models would still detect words even if their thresholds, baseline activation levels, or gain parameters were uninfluenced by frequency. A search process would still find a match if the search were ordered on some basis other than frequency. In contrast, the essence of connectionist learning models is that they learn patterns as a function of their *experience* with them, and their response to a pattern in a given representational domain is a function of the *degree* to which they have learned (a) the relationship between its parts, and/or (b) the mapping of it and its parts onto patterns in another domain. Words of high frequency differ from words of low frequency, all other things being equal, in their *degree of learning or acquisition.*[4] Frequency effects are *intrinsic* to connectionist learning models.

One of the difficulties in illustrating this principle is that connectionist learning algorithms are currently being developed at a rapid rate, and detailed application to specific psychological domains like visual word recognition is still in its infancy. At the time of writing, there exist in the public domain only two PDP *learning* models for word reading: Sejnowski and Rosenberg's (1986) NETtalk system for mapping spelling to sound, and Seidenberg and McClelland's (1989) model (of which abbreviated descriptions are also available in Seidenberg, 1989, and Patterson, Seidenberg & McClelland, 1989). The first is more a "proof-of-concept" demonstration than a psychological model, whereas the latter was developed to simulate phenomena observed in tasks such as lexical decision time and naming, and strong claims are made for its success in doing so. However, both systems model only orthography—>phonology transcoding, though Seidenberg and McClelland see their network as fitting into a larger architecture which includes also as-yet-unspecified networks for transcoding orthography to semantics, semantics to phonology and so on (see below). Allport (1985) has given an attractive qualitative account of the way in which distributed representations of word-form (phonological form in this case) might be accessed and mapped to meaning, and how such an account applies to the dysphasias. Others are even now engaged in the development of detailed simulations of aspects of orthography to semantic transcoding. Perhaps some results will be publicly available by the time this chapter is published. For the moment however, I will try to articulate qualitatively the properties and possibilities of a *generic* connectionist learning model (or family of models) for visual word recognition and transcoding, citing Seidenberg and McClelland's (1989) work for some particular points.

One immediate consequence of the connectionist approach is that word identification, inasmuch as it can be said to occur in these models, is subordinate to the task of transcoding. That is, the system is trained on orthographic patterns always in association with certain semantic patterns[5] and/or with certain phonological patterns. (Is this true of the brain?). Let us, for expository convenience, restrict attention for the moment to semantic patterns. The relationship between orthographic and semantic properties for English and most other modern scripts is relatively arbitrary, at least for morphologically simple words. The brain's task is to learn to generate a representation of the appropriate semantic pattern given an orthographic pattern as input. A connectionist network for reading for meaning will have, minimally, a (large) set of input units, which are activated by elements of orthographic input, and, connected (richly) to them, a (large) set of output units. The pattern of activation which appears over the output units after excitation of the input units is the network's attempt at representing that word's meaning; we may see the output units as corresponding to semantic micro-attributes. Input units might be activated by the presence of certain letters, or their presence in certain positions in the word, or the presence of certain letter sequences (as in the Seidenberg and McClelland model — see below), or all of these. There is no reason in principle why visual attributes less universally approved of by theorists, or harder to define, such as "word shape" , should not also be captured in the pattern of activation of input units. We may be similarly catholic and unspecific, for the present, about which attributes of meaning the activations of output units correspond to. The goal of a connectionist simulation is, when presented with an orthographic pattern, to reproduce an appropriate pattern of activation across the output units, i.e., one corresponding to the "meaning" of the word." It learns to do this by changing the strengths of its connections.

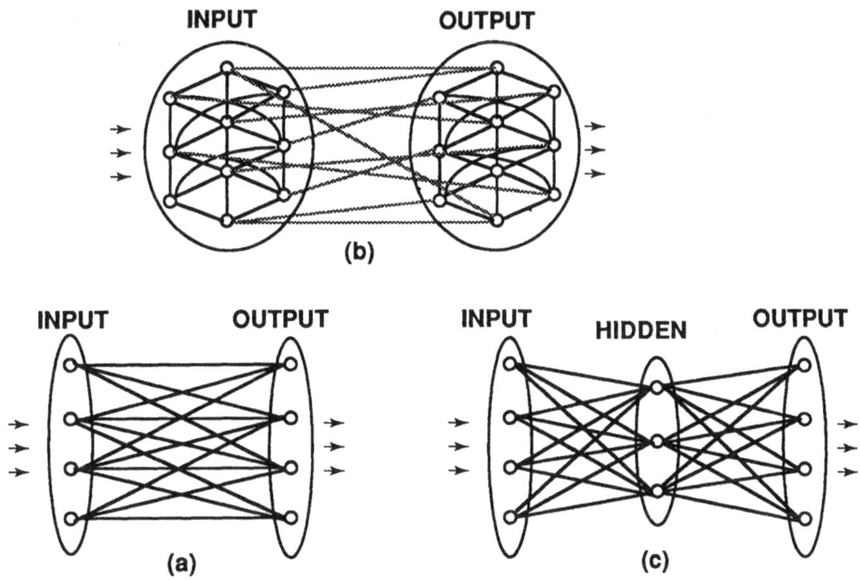

Fig. 1. Three PDP architectures for lexical transcoding. (a) Direct mapping from orthographic input units to (phonological or semantic) output units. (b) The same, plus auto-associative connections among the input (and output) units. (c) Mapping mediated by hidden units.

The simplest kind of network has input units connected directly to the output units, as in Figure 1a. (In a real model, all, or a large fraction of, the possible connections are likely to be realized.) Each connection has a weight associated with it (initially random), let us say between -1 and +1. Activation of an input unit results in either excitation (if the weight is positive) or inhibition (if negative) of output units linked to it, in proportion to the connection weights. The output units integrate (usually by simple summation) their input, and modify their activation level accordingly. Some function, usually a nonlinear "squashing" function, relates the integrated input to the resulting activation level (or probability). The output units can also be fed directly the pattern they should have produced (i.e., a "teacher" may be necessary). The network learns by changing the weights on its connections in a direction that will produce an output pattern closer to this target on the next encounter. This change is, however, completely automatic and local. Each unit "blindly" computes the difference between its actual and target activation levels, and decrements the weights on *all* the connections leading into it if it is overactivated or increments them if it is underactivated. (A common rule for doing this is the so-called "Delta rule.") This simple architecture has a remarkable power to associate arbitrarily related input and output patterns.

Anyone familiar with the connectionist literature will recognize the class of networks I have described so far as including, as a paradigmatic example, Rumelhart and McClelland's (1986) model for the learning of the past tenses of verbs. In their simulation the input pattern is a phonetic representation of the present tense, the output a phonetic representation of the past tense, and the model does a creditable job of learning the mapping between them in spite of the mixture of regular inflexions and various subclasses of irregular forms found for English. But notice that this kind of network in no sense "identifies" whole input patterns; it merely transcodes them, producing an output pattern driven by the net effect of the individual elements of the input pattern. The reason that Rumelhart and McClelland's simulation succeeds is that the built-in coding applied to the input patterns happens to capture most of the structure required to specify the appropriate past tense (see Pinker & Prince, 1988 for detailed discussion of this point). But there is no learning of input *patterns* per se, only learning of which (coarse, overlapping) elements of output pattern are correlated, and to what degree, with which (coarse, overlapping) elements of input pattern.

To learn to "identify" rather than merely to transcode patterns is to learn what elements *co-occur in* input patterns. To learn this, a network needs to be able to form connections among input units. At least two major possibilities for such connections exist. One is direct or "auto-associative" connections among the input units (as in Figure 1b). The basic idea is usefully illustrated by a "toy model" developed for didactic purposes by McClelland and Rumelhart (1985). This has 24 units all mutually interconnected. Sixteen of these units are designated "visual" units, the other 8 are "name" units. Units vary in activation level between -1 and +1. Input to the network consists in a pattern of 1s (feature present) -1s (feature absent) or 0s (don't know) applied to the units. When a pattern is presented, the activation levels of the units are all allowed to influence each other until they settle into a stable state. The model then uses the delta rule to adjust its weights, so that units that were coactivated will tend to turn each other on more strongly in the future, and units that had opposite activation values will tend to inhibit each other more. The model is trained on multiple presentations of (randomly distorted) exemplars of three prototypical combinations of visual pattern plus name, which McClelland and Rumelhart whimsically call the "dog," "cat" and "bagel" patterns (to capture the similarity structure among them). Their simulations show that, when after many learning trials one presents just the visual pattern corresponding to, say, a "cat," the appropriate pattern of activation over the name units is produced. In other words, the system has learned to transcode between input and output patterns. But the system is not just learning to *transcode,* it is also learning to recognize or *identify* inasmuch as it is changing the weights of connections *among* visual pattern units as well as between them and name units. This happens even if the name units are not activated during training; the model nevertheless learns the input patterns, in the sense that connections are strengthened between units representing coactivated elements.

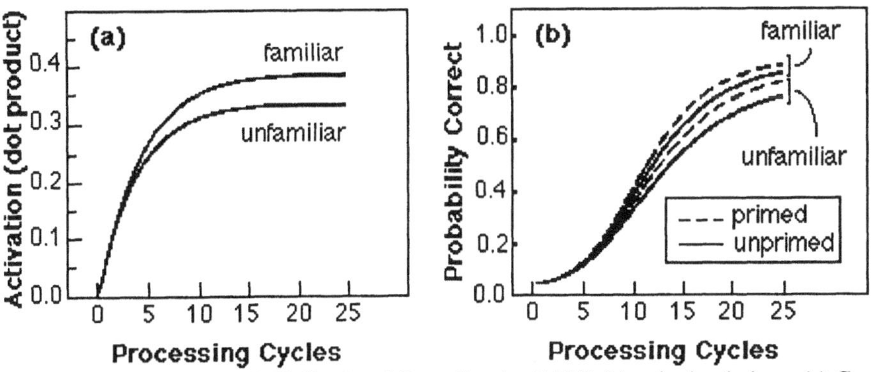

Fig. 2. Two results from McClelland and Rumelhart's (1985) 24-unit simulation. (a) Growth in "pattern activation" (dot product: the pattern of activation over the 24 units times the input pattern, normalized for the number of elements in the pattern) over time following presentation of either a familiar or an unfamiliar pattern. (b) Probability correct as a function of processing time for familiar and unfamiliar pattens. This figure also demonstrates the effect of "priming," i.e., presenting additional learning trials prior to testing. (Redrawn from Figures 6 and 9 of McClelland, J. L. and Rumelhart, D.E. (1985). Distributed memory and the representation of general and specific information, *Journal of Experimental Psychology: General*, **114**, 159-188.)

One way that the learning of input patterns, as such, is manifest in this kind of network is that if one presents *part* of a learned pattern to the model, units corresponding to the missing parts tend to be turned on (or off) appropriately, i.e., activated in the direction they would have been if the missing elements were present. A corollary is that if a whole familiar pattern (or most of one) is presented, the activation initially attributable to one part of the pattern will mutually reinforce the activation pattern initially attributable to another part. The net result is that the system will settle into a more exaggerated stable pattern, and approach that asymptotic state faster, when presented with a familiar than with an unfamiliar pattern. One way to quantify this exaggerated response to previously experienced patterns is to compute the dot-product of the pattern of activation over the units of the module and the input pattern itself (normalized for the number of elements). Figure 2a shows the growth of this global measure over time for a simulated trial using the McClelland and Rumelhart 24-unit model after exposure to 10 random distortions of each of 8 prototypes.

Two important points begin to emerge. First, if we restrict our attention to mutual reinforcement within the "input domain," we are looking at "recognition" or "identification." The concurrent reinstatement of patterns of activation in the "output domain" constitutes transcoding. Clearly, more rapid and more extreme reinstatement of a learned pattern within the input domain (better identification) promotes more rapid and more accurate reinstatement of a learned pattern in the output domain (better transcoding). Thus, although it is possible (as demonstrated by the past tense model) to have transcoding without identification, in auto-associative networks identification will be a component of transcoding.

Secondly, the activation-growth curves in Figure 2a point the way towards linking the behaviour of such a network to the effects of frequency upon *performance*. There must exist a mechanism for translating patterns of activation over output units into responses in any particular transcoding task. To specify this mechanism is a hard problem (see McClelland & Rumelhart, 1985), but we can reasonably assume that the relation between Activation (dot product) and response accuracy is at least monotonic. As an example, the result of McClelland and Rumelhart's (1985) transformation of activation curves like those of Figure 2a into time-accuracy functions is shown in Figure 2b. (Only the "unprimed" functions are relevant here; the effects of priming will be discussed in Section VIII). The point is a simple one. A given level of response accuracy is reached more quickly for a pattern the more familiar (frequent in experience) it is. Hence, under the conditions of limited data (e.g. a tachistoscopic exposure to a printed word) we would expect superior accuracy of transcoding for high frequency words. And, under the conditions of a reaction time (RT) experiment, we would expect subjects to be able to produce an accurate response faster for a high frequency than for a low frequency word. In other words, effects of frequency upon performance would appear to be a basic property of an auto-associative connectionist model, not something that can be added or deleted at whim. Note that frequency will influence the strengths both of auto-associative links among the input units, and of cross-domain links. If, after learning, we disconnected the input from the output units, we would still see an effect of frequency upon the rate at which the former settle into a stable pattern, and the degree to which their pattern of activation is correlated with the input. The processes of "identification of an orthographic pattern" and "activation of meaning/phonology" can be distinguished by virtue of the fact that this disconnected network would do the former without the latter.

Direct linkages among input units (as in Figure 1b) are not the only way that a connectionist network can learn to "identify" recurring subpatterns in the input. An alternative possibility is mediated connection via "hidden" units, i.e., units which are neither input nor output units, but connected to both (as in Figure 1c). Sejnowski and Rosenberg (1986) and Seidenberg and McClelland (1989) both adopt this architecture for transcoding from orthography to phonology. Figure 3 shows the latter's basic framework. There are 400 orthographic input units, and 460 phonological output units. The orthographic units code the spelling pattern in a coarse context-sensitive distributed way. Basically, each possible " Wicklegraph" — a triple of letters (counting space as a letter) turns on a set of about 20 units, and each unit is turned on by any of 1000 Wicklegraphs (many of which, however, like

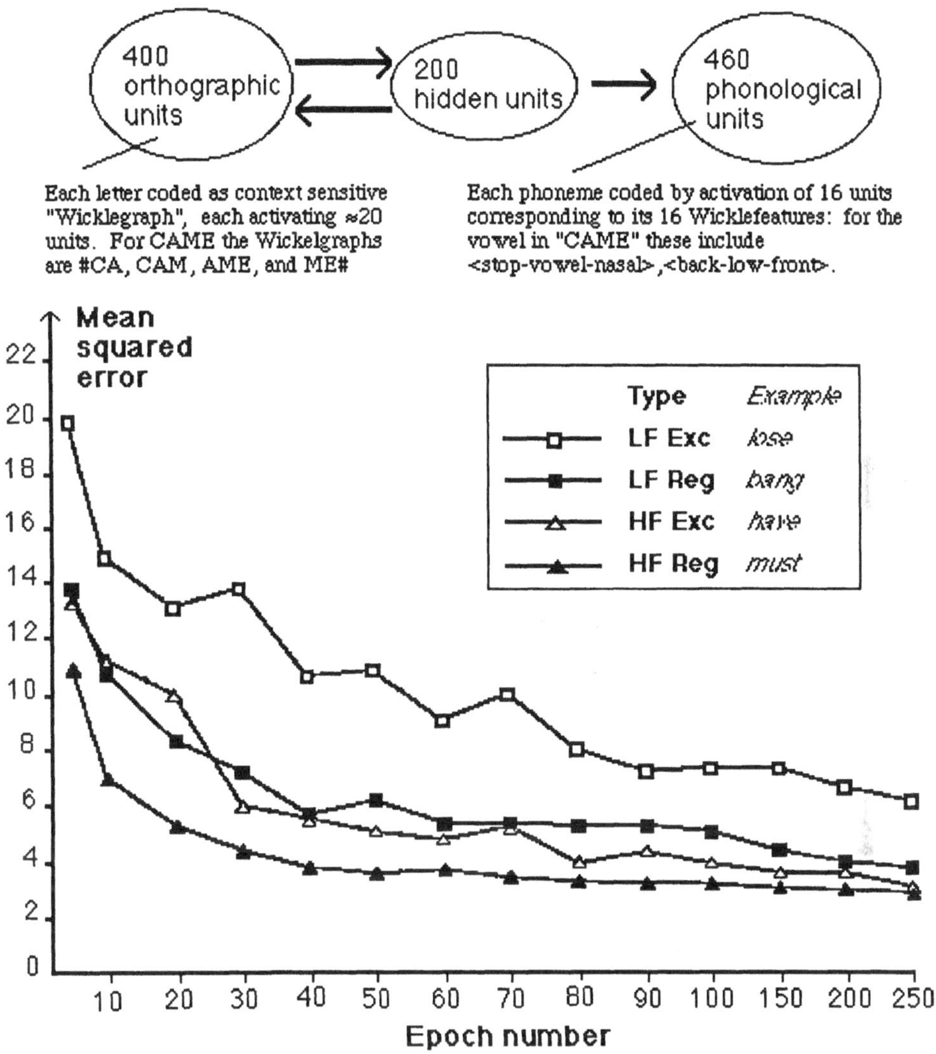

Fig. 3. The basic architecture of Seidenberg and McClelland's (1989) model for transcoding orthography to phonology, and the performance of the model as a function of experience, for the high and low frequency "regular" and "exception" words used by Taraban & McClelland (1987). (Data redrawn from Figure 3 of Seidenberg, M.S. & McClelland J.L., 1989, A distributed, developmental model of word recognition and naming. *Psychological Review.*)

"xxg," do not actually occur in English). The phonological units employ a similarly coarse and distributed coding scheme, the one used in Rumelhart and McClelland's (1986) past-tense model. The orthographic units project to a set of 200 hidden units, which project both to the phonological units, and back to the orthographic units. The model learns by means of the "back-propagation" development of the Delta-rule, which allows the mismatch between actual and target output at the terminal nodes of a multi-layered system to be used to propagate optimal weight changes back through one or more levels of intermediate nodes.

The presence of hidden units allows the system to learn to detect useful input patterns: i.e., the model can make use of the fact that certain elements of words tend to co-occur in combination, and are predictive of the output. This is especially useful for picking up subpatterns that are predictive of pronunciation. Hence, in English, *vowel* followed by *consonant(s)* followed by *e* followed by *space* tends to imply <long vowel>, and it would be to the advantage of the system to develop the ability efficiently to detect this pattern. But because such pattern learning occurs, the model must be sensitive to word frequency. That is, the model is not just developing the ability to map efficiently from orthographic elements to phonological elements, it is detecting and learning frequently occurring patterns over orthographic elements of every scope up to the whole word. Indeed, although Seidenberg and McClelland emphasize with polemical fervour that their network does not, after learning, contain any representations of *words*, this is a touch too strong in that the network must in *some* sense be "identifying" whole words in order to transcode successfully spelling patterns with very exceptional spelling-sound correspondences, such as ONE, YACHT, AISLE, etc. The frequency sensitivity of this network is illustrated in the lower part of Figure 3, which shows performance of Seidenberg and McClelland's simulation after training on most of the monomorphemic monosyllabic English words, during which words were randomly sampled with a probability proportional to the log of their frequency of occurrence (according to Kucera & Francis, 1967). The measure of the model's performance given — "mean squared error" — is the sum of the squared differences between the phonological units' actual and target activation levels. The assumption is that this measure maps monotonically onto naming latency in human performance. In addition to the frequency sensitivity exhibited by this measure, another important result of these simulations is that, after training, the error score simulates the interaction between frequency and spelling-sound regularity observed in many naming latency studies. (See Table 1 and discussion in Section VI).

Seidenberg and McClelland's model also includes connections from hidden units back to the orthographic units. The purpose of these is to provide a basis for simulating performance in lexical decision, a task that does not *require* transcoding to phonology, but does require (in some sense) an estimate of the familiarity to the subjects of the orthographic pattern presented. This is assumed (under most circumstances[6]) to be the error score computed over the orthographic units. Weights on the connections from orthographic to hidden units are thus modified simultaneously on the basis of two measures of "success": success in generating the appropriate phonology and success in reproducing the pattern of input. Both influences result in the learning of input patterns per se. If, after training, we disconnected the hidden from the output units, we could observe "identification without transcoding," as in an auto-associative network, and this process would be sensitive to word frequency, as well as to the frequency of spelling-sound correspondences.

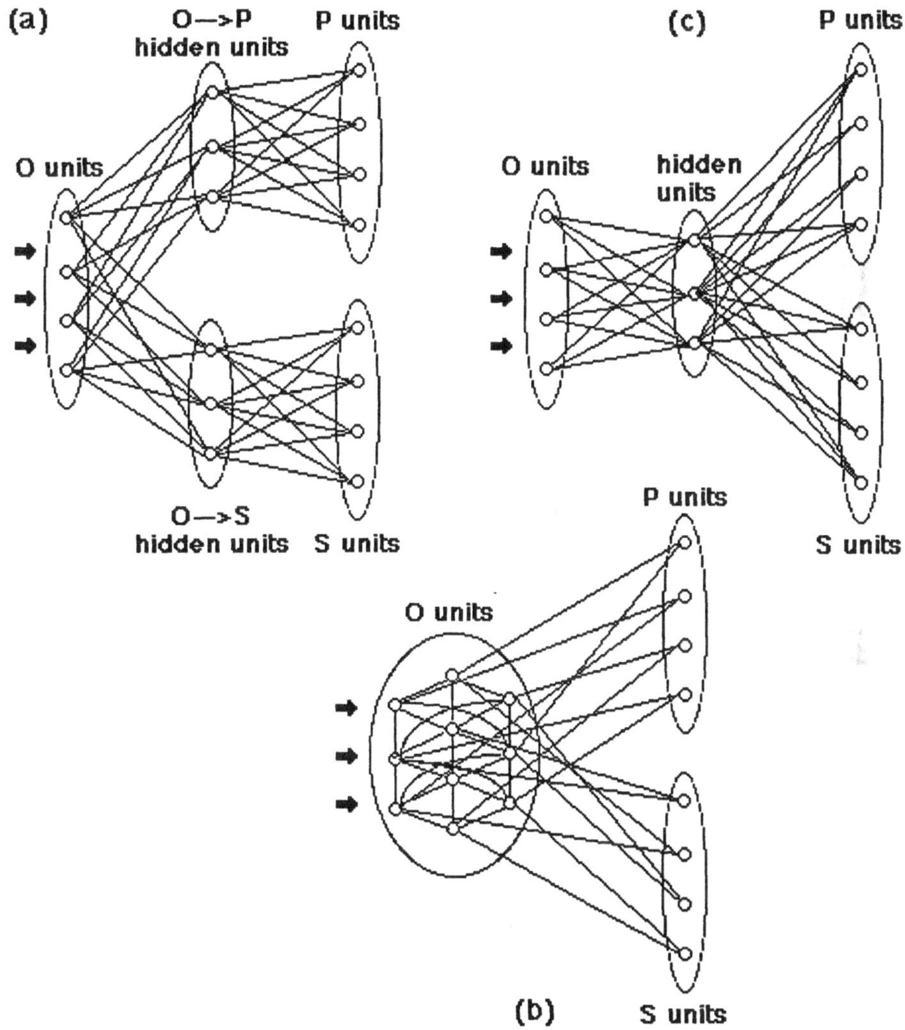

Fig. 4. Possible relationships between networks for transcoding orthography to phonology and orthography to semantics (see text).

So far, I have been concerned to show in simple but (I hope) relatively universal terms how "identification" and "transcoding" may be realized and related in connectionist networks that learn to transcode patterns in an input domain (like orthography) to patterns in an output domain (like phonology, or semantics). The point I have been concerned to establish is that transcoding efficiency and, inasmuch as this is distinct, identification efficiency, *must* be sensitive to frequency in such a network. I will conclude this section by briefly exploring an additional complexity. In the case of reading, we have one input mapped not to one, but to at least two, output domains — phonology and semantics.

Consider some possibilities for realizing the mapping of orthographic (O) to both phonological (P) and semantic (S) units. One extreme possibility (Figure 4a) is that O units would project to S units via one set of hidden units (the OS set), and to the P units via a different set of hidden units (the OP set), with no reciprocal connections. This would allow the system to detect (via the OS units) one set of orthographic subpatterns predictive of meaning and another (via the OP units) predictive of phonology. Inasmuch as these subpatterns are in conflict, this would lead to the hidden units in the two pathways evolving different "receptive fields." In fact, for English, these two sets of subpatterns *are* to some extent in conflict, because written English tends to preserve morphemic form more than spoken English. In such a network the "identification" that results in access to meaning is distinct from the "identification" that results in access to pronunciation. At the other extreme consider a system (Figure 4b) in which auto-association occurs directly among O units, each of which projects (unidirectionally) to separate arrays of P and S units. In this case, the subpatterns learned by the system will reflect the statistics of experienced O input and a *compromise* among those subpatterns' utility for predicting interpretation and pronunciation, inasmuch as these are in conflict. In this case, we would be able to say that the "identification" component of transcoding was identical for semantic and phonological access. Now consider an intermediate possibility (one of many), the system in Figure 4c, with transcoding mediated by a common set of hidden units, projecting to both S and P units. It seems likely (though this needs to be confirmed by simulation) that inasmuch as the orthographic substructures useful for specifying pronunciation and meaning conflict, these initially "promiscuous" hidden units will, to some extent, come to specialize in morphemically or phonologically predictive elements of orthography. Finally, if we add connections from hidden units back to input O units, as do Seidenberg and McClelland, this will tend to encourage the evolution of hidden units toward capturing frequently occurring input patterns and subpatterns irrespective of their transcoding utility. In these last two cases, the "identification" underlying access to meaning and the identification underlying access to pronunciation are no longer quite the same, but nor are they entirely different.

Clearly much work needs to be done to develop connectionist learning models to the point where they are true performance models (i.e.,producing patterns of RTs as output, rather than dot products of activation, or summed squared differences between target and actual activation levels), and to explore the different architectures for mapping one to several (and several to one) domains. It is nevertheless already obvious that they have one major advantage over the conventional models reviewed in the previous section. The same mechanism that enables them to acquire new words in the first place also generates frequency effects. Nothing special has to be done — there is no switch into "learning mode" — to add a new word to "the mental lexicon" ; the first encounter with a word is processed just like the second, third, etc.. As a result, frequency effects are not an optional "add-on": identification and transcoding *must* in such a model be frequency sensitive. (The exact form of frequency effects will depend on more detailed assumptions, though in general, the delta-rule results in most learning when there is maximal discrepancy between the computed and target output, with the consequence that experience with items the network is already transcoding well will produce only minor weight changes, i.e.,little additional learning.) I have also tried to bring out two additional points. The first is that in a connectionist learning network with distributed representation and either auto-association or hidden units, an "identification" process can be logically distinguished as a component part of the overall transcoding process, but it is certainly not to be conceived of as a discrete processing step prior to the activation of phonology or meaning, as in the conventional models reviewed in Section 1. Secondly, connectionist architectures appear to permit a wide gamut of possible relationships between identification-for-access-to-meaning and identification-for-access-to-pronunciation. That being so, while access to meaning and access to pronunciation must both influenced by word frequency, it is not a necessary consequence of this general class of models that such effects be *quantitatively* identical.

IV. LOCALIZATION OF FREQUENCY EFFECTS: RECENT ARGUMENTS

We have seen that each of the three major classes of "conventional" models of visual word recognition (word-detector, serial search, and hybrid) were constructed around the central proposition that the *identification* process is sensitive to frequency. Proponents of these models have paid little attention to the possibility that the subsequent processing step required for transcoding — accessing the meaning or pronunciation associated with the best-matching lexical entry — might also be frequency sensitive. That is, the implicit assumption was that the frequency sensitivity of the identification process was *sufficient* to explain the observed frequency sensitivity of performance in various tasks. One reason may be that the word recognition task favoured by most experimenters using RT measures since the early 1970s — lexical decision — has tended to be seen as a rather direct measure of lexical identification, not requiring access to meaning or pronunciation, but merely (an attempt at) identification of the letter string. More recently, several lines of evidence have shown this picture of lexical decision to be inadequate, and focused attention on the idea that processes subsequent to lexical identification, subsequent even to access to meaning or pronunciation, might be a locus of frequency effects. I shall review four: Balota and Chumbley's (1984) semantic categorization experiment; Balota and Chumbley's (1985) argument from delayed naming; arguments from pseudohomophones due to McCann, Besner and colleagues (McCann & Besner, 1987; McCann, Besner & Davelaar, 1988; Besner & McCann, 1987); other evidence on "post-identification" effects in the lexical decision task.

1. Balota and Chumbley's (1984) Semantic Categorization Experiment

Their first experiment examined the effects of frequency upon RT in a semantic categorization task. On each trial the subject saw a category label (e.g., FRUIT) followed after 800 msec by a word. The subject pressed one key if the word was a member of the category (e.g., APPLE) another if it was not (e.g. CHAIR). The second experiment tested a different group of subjects on lexical decision time for the same words (mixed now, of course, with nonwords), and without the preceding category labels. Balota and Chumbley assumed, reasonably enough, that semantic categorization requires identification no less than does lexical decision. Hence if the effect of frequency on LDT is primarily attributable to its influence on the duration of the identification process, we would expect to observe a strong effect of frequency on semantic categorization time. Their analyses regressed mean RT against (log) frequency and other variables over words. The unique effect of frequency on semantic categorization time (after removing the effects of other factors such as instance dominance and word length) did not reach significance, while for LDT it was highly significant. The correlations between log frequency and RT were significantly greater for LDT than for semantic categorization time. The regression coefficient relating semantic categorization to log frequency was less than a third of the effect for lexical decision. Balota and Chumbley's conclusion was that, since lexical decision and semantic categorization both require identification, most of the effect of frequency on lexical decision must be attributed to the decision stage specific to the lexical decision task. Taken at face value, their result suggests that the whole transcoding between orthography and meaning, not just the identification substage postulated by the conventional models, is at most weakly frequency sensitive. This is a claim at odds with expectations about transcoding performance derived from a generic PDP learning model no less than with the assumptions of conventional models.

2. Balota and Chumbley's (1985) Argument From Delayed Naming

Balota and Chumbley (1984) found, in a third experiment following on from the lexical decision and categorization experiments already mentioned, that the effect of frequency on naming latency for these words was, although significant, smaller than that obtained for lexical decision. This merely replicates the general observation in the literature that frequency effects tend to be smaller for naming latency than for lexical decision time. As already noted, this has not been seen as a problem for the standard account because of the widespread acceptance of a "dual-process" account of naming (Patterson & V. Coltheart, 1987).[7] Inasmuch as naming is driven in part by an assembly process that does not involve identification of the target word we would expect the effect of the frequency of that word to be diluted. However, Balota and Chumbley (1985) obtained a rather more surprising result. They gave subjects a "delayed naming" task, in which the subject saw a word and then, after a delay, pronounced it in response to a "go" signal. They argued that if the "go" signal is presented after a delay of 400 msec or so, subjects should have completed any identification process. Nevertheless, they reported frequency effects at that and at much longer delays. Though the effect of frequency on delayed naming time was not as large as the effect on immediate naming, and tended to diminish with delay, the former was a substantial fraction of the latter, and did not diminish to zero at long delays. Their interpretation was that a significant component of the effect of frequency on naming latency must be localized in "the production stages" (p. 89) of the pronunciation task, i.e.,"processes occurring after lexical access" (p. 105). (By "access" they mean what I am terming "identification"). Given that the effect of frequency on naming latency is modest to begin with, this would appear to leave little of the frequency effect over to attribute to lexical identification. (Of course, this kind of argument assumes that any effects of frequency on successive processes would be approximately additive).

Now, in both their papers, Balota and Chumbley are careful to insist that "we are not arguing that word frequency has *no* impact on lexical access" (Balota & Chumbley, 1984, p. 355, my italics). Nevertheless, the thrust of their argument is unmistakable. If the unique effects of frequency on a task requiring identification and access to meaning are indeed "negligible" (op. cit., same page) and a substantial component of the (usually modest) effect on naming is attributed to post-identification processes, then, at least within the (broadly) additive factors framework Balota and Chumbley espouse (p. 103 of the 1985 paper) that leaves very *little* effect of frequency to be localized in either identification or access to meaning. Their conclusion clearly challenges the traditional localization of frequency effects in an identification stage prior to access to meaning or pronunciation, and has been widely cited as so doing (see, e.g. Brown, 1987; Paap et al., 1987).

3. McCann and Besner's Argument From Pseudohomophones

Pseudohomophones are nonword letter strings like PHOX that, when pronounced according to the normal spelling-sound correspondences of English, yield a pronunciation identical to that of a word (in this case FOX), which I will refer to as the "base" word. McCann and Besner (1987) showed that pseudohomophones were pronounced more rapidly than control nonwords matched for orthographic properties. This effect, they argued, indicated some contact with lexical representations. However, they also found that pseudohomophone latency was uncorrelated with the frequency of the base word in spite of the fact that, when the base words were named, a respectable frequency effect was obtained. McCann, Besner and Davelaar (1988) made use of another pseudohomophone effect: pseudohomophones take longer to reject than control nonwords in the lexical decision task. Again, the performance measured must (sometimes, to some degree) be reflecting contact with lexical representations. Yet, although they obtained such a pseudohomophone effect in their study, it was uninfluenced by the frequency of the base word. Hence, they argue, this lexical contact is not frequency sensitive.

The alert reader will be impatient for the link to the reading of ordinary words. The account offered by McCann and Besner is as follows. For normal reading, an orthographic code is used to access a lexicon of orthographic word forms; the best-matching entry is then mapped to a lexicon of phonological word forms via a direct connection. (This is the nonsemantic "lexical" route of the contemporary three-pathway models, e.g., Coltheart, 1985). Pseudohomophones activate entries in the phonological lexicon (inasmuch as they do) via a different spelling-sound conversion process (the "assembly" process of the three-pathway model). The absence of a frequency effect for pseudohomophones coupled with evidence that they do activate lexical representations (at least to some degree) indicates that mere activation of the phonological lexicon cannot be the locus of the the frequency effect for ordinary naming. Therefore this must be localized in either (activation of) the orthographic lexicon ("identification" in my terminology) or the mapping process ("retrieval"). McCann and Besner (1987, p. 20) argue that the locus of the effect is unlikely to be the former: "considerations of architectural parsimony suggest that the most plausible scenario is one where either both of these lexicons are frequency sensitive, or neither of them is." They therefore conclude that a principal locus of frequency effects is "within the links that join the various components of lexical memory. These links are commonly described as condition-action rules for mapping representations in one domain onto representations in another domain. For word naming, the relevant condition-action rules are those that link lexical entries in the orthographic input lexicon with lexical entries in the phonological output lexicon" (p. 20).[8]

It will be apparent that this argument is both indirect and heavily dependent upon a dubious appeal to parsimony. There may be more specific problems with their data. Inasmuch as they are examining effects of frequency upon access to a phonological lexicon used also for auditory recognition, and inasmuch as the "assembly" process may be assumed to operate on the letter string from left to right, it would be appropriate to control for the effects of a variable well known to have major effects on auditory lexical decision time, namely "recognition point"; that is, that point in the phonological string where it diverges from other words in the lexicon (Marslen-Wilson, 1987). (Marslen-Wilson, 1987 and Taft & Hambly, 1986, have recently demonstrated frequency effects for auditory lexical decision with this variable controlled). Secondly, the effects of lexical status (pseudohomophone versus matched control) obtained in McCann et al.'s studies were small (24 msec in McCann and Besner, 1987, if one partials out a difference obtained in delayed naming of the same words, 20 msec in McCann et al., 1988). The frequency of the base-word could only *modulate* this difference. Modulation of such a small effect cannot be easy to detect reliably. As a benchmark , we may note that in Frederiksen and Kroll's (1976) classic naming latency study (in which the lowest and highest frequency bands were 1 per million or less and greater than 30 per million) the range of the frequency effect in both mixed and blocked conditions was only about half the difference between words and nonwords. Thirdly, Seidenberg and McClelland (1989) have argued that McCann and Besner's (1987) pseudohomophones are more orthographically word-like than their control nonwords in spite of their being roughly equated in terms of summed bigram frequencies.

4. Changing Conceptions of the Lexical Decision Task

Ever since lexical decision studies began to be reported, lexical decision time has been known to be a highly frequency sensitive measure (Rubenstein et al., 1970). This, coupled with the implicit assumption that the task could be performed on the basis of *identification without transcoding*, had perhaps discouraged researchers until recently from considering post-identification loci for the frequency effect. It has nevertheless always been obvious that some decision process must monitor the identification process or inspect its outcome to determine whether a match has been achieved, and that access to meaning or pronunciation might well occur automatically even though only lexical identification is logically required. Two possible post-identification loci for the effect of frequency on lexical decision need now to be considered: the activation of meaning, and the decision process.

There is quite a lot of evidence that lexical decision time is influenced by semantic properties of words. James (1975) obtained a faster average lexical decision time for concrete than for abstract low-frequency words matched for frequency and other properties (at least when they were novel). Jastrzembski and Stanners (1975), Jastrzembski (1981), and Millis and Button (1989) have demonstrated substantial effects on LDT of the number of meanings possessed by a word, although this effect is not uncontroversial (see Gernsbacher, 1984). (Jastrzembski, 1981, also suggests that since words of high frequency tend to possess more meanings, part of the frequency effect observed in a number of studies may be due to confounding with number of meanings.) In Whaley's (1978) multiple regression study of lexical decision, the inclusion of various "richness of meaning" variables (concreteness, meaningfulness, imagery) accounted for significant variance after the effects of word frequency and word length had been removed. Chumbley and Balota (1984) report a correlation between lexical decision time and the ease of generating an associate, after various other variables (including length, frequency, and number of dictionary meanings) had been partialled out. Of course, in this kind of study, the possibility that some property of the word's *form*, not explicitly controlled or allowed for, might have been correlated with the semantic variable must be borne in mind, especially when the effects of the semantic variable are modest. Nevertheless, we must take seriously, it would seem, the idea that the decision process is influenced by not only the output of word detectors (or the activation of distributed orthographic pattern representations), but also the activation of "word senses" (or distributed semantic representations), at least under some conditions (cf. Seidenberg & McClelland, 1989). If this is so, then any frequency sensitivity in the post-identification activation of meaning would contribute to LDT as it must to RT in tasks that explicitly demand access to meaning.

Secondly, the possibility has been widely touted that the decision process involved in lexical decision might be the locus of various effects previously attributed to lexical identification. For example, effects of word (DE Groot, 1984) or sentence (Forster, 1981) context upon LDT have been attributed to the decision process being biased toward "Yes" or "No" by the post-access detection of "congruence" or "incongruence" between the word's sense and that of the context. Feustel, Shiffrin, and Salasoo (1983) suggested that the facilitatory effects of repetition on LDT were due to the decision process being "biased" by the "familiarity" of the letter string, detected on the basis of retrieval of an episodic memory trace of a prior encounter with the letter string. In relation to frequency effects, Balota and Chumbley (1984) and Besner and McCann (1987, following an earlier proposal by Besner, Davelaar, Alcott & Parry, 1984) attribute a major component of the frequency effect in the lexical decision task to a familiarity discrimination process distinct from lexical identification.[9]

There is no denying that lexical decision is a kind of familiarity judgment, but we need to be careful about translating this bland characterization into the radical claim that frequency effects in lexical decision have a "post-lexical" locus. Two possible sources of a "familiarity" estimate must be distinguished.

4.1. Extra-lexical Sources of Familiarity Information

One possibility is that subjects make use of (or their decision stage is involuntarily biased by) information about the familiarity of the letter string derived from some source quite independent of the lexicon. Feustel, Shiffrin, and Salasoo's (1983) suggestion was that episodic memory (i.e.,memory for specific instances of letter strings) is the source. Being independent of the lexicon, this source contributes equally for both words and nonwords. The source of familiarity information proposed by Besner and colleagues (Besner, 1983; Besner & McCann, 1987; Besner et al., 1984) also appears to be extra-lexical: ." . . the process of lexical decision includes an assessment of *visual* familiarity which contributes bias to the decision stage. This visual familiarity assessment process is "wholistic"; it treats printed stimuli as visual patterns rather than individual letters. This mechanism is not involved in the word identification process per se; it merely assesses the visual familiarity of a stimulus." (Besner & McCann, 1987, p. 211).

4.2. Lexical Identification/access As the Basis For Familiarity Estimation

Balota and Chumbley (1984) propose a two-stage process, based on the idea that words and nonwords differ on a "familiarity/meaningfulness" (FM) dimension. "The first stage of the decision process involves a global computation of the FM value of the letter string." (op cit., p. 352). In the second stage, the FM value is compared to high and low criteria. If falls outside the criteria, a positive or negative decision is made immediately; if it falls between them "a more analytic evaluation of the letter string" (op cit., p.352) is made. The source of the initial FM estimate is clearly assumed to be some sort of (partial?) lexical identification or access process: "A particular letter string's value on this FM dimension is based primarily on its *orthographic and phonological similarity to actual words.*" (op cit., p.352, my italics)[10]. In the light of this exegesis, it seems clear that Balota and Chumbley cannot be claiming that the locus of frequency effects is restricted to the decision process, for the driving of the decision process by FM value could not be influenced by frequency unless FM was correlated with frequency. The process from which the FM value is obtained — identification or partial identification — must therefore be sensitive to frequency. Their claim about localization can only be that the *duration* of this predecision process is not sensitive (or is negligibly sensitive) to frequency.

Monsell et al.'s (1989) account of the decision process illustrates even more clearly that to ascribe frequency effects to the duration of a "familiarity"-based decision process is very different from denying localization of frequency effects in an identification process. Our proposal was that subjects globally monitor levels of activation or change of activation during the identification process. [These activation growth functions might be illustrated by those averaged in Figure 2a.] It must be generally true that words result in a higher rate of activation accrual and higher asymptotic level than nonwords. Hence criteria defined upon these parameters or their derivatives can in principle provide a basis for making (or at least being biased toward) a positive or negative decision. This basis is different from (or additional to) the occurrence of unique identification based on *one* word-detector's activation reaching a *high* threshold (whether absolute or differential). Frequency will influence both the average time until unique identification, and the global activation parameters or their derivatives serving as the source of "familiarity/novelty" information. How these two sources of information are combined to drive lexical decisions we do not know; we would assume that the mixture and the criteria can be adjusted depending on the nature of the nonwords expected, the expected range of orthographic weirdness of the words, payoffs for accuracy and speed, etc. However, one feature of such a mechanism is clear. The duration of the decision process is only "sensitive to frequency" as a consequence of the time-course of the identification process being sensitive to frequency.

Irrespective of the details, the conclusion I want to stress is plain enough. If the source of the proposed familiarity estimate in lexical decision is lexical, then it simply makes no sense to say that the locus of frequency is the decision process *rather than* processes of lexical identification or access to meaning or pronunciation. It is only models which include a strictly *extra-lexical* source of familiarity information in lexical decision that supply a genuine alternative to the proposal that frequency effects are attributable to processes of lexical identification and/or access to meaning and pronunciation. As it happens, there are grounds for believing that "extra-lexical" sources of familiarity knowledge actually have little influence on lexical decision. I will review these grounds in Section VIII, when considering the relation between repetition and frequency effects. The task of the three intervening sections will be to examine further the effects of frequency on, respectively: the time required for semantic/syntactic categorization (Section V), naming latencies (Section VI), and more indirect indices of lexical identification/transcoding (Section VII).

V. EFFECTS OF FREQUENCY ON SEMANTIC ACCESS: FURTHER DATA

I first address Balota and Chumbley's (1984) empirical claim, based on one experiment, that RT in tasks requiring access to meaning is relatively insensitive to frequency. As a general principle, this claim appears to be refuted by, among others, a pair of experiments recently conducted in my laboratory. They are described in detail by Monsell et al. (1989), so I sketch only the bare bones here. However, it is worth dwelling briefly on the question of what task it is appropriate to use should one wish to assess the influence of frequency on transcoding from print to meaning.

Matching tasks (e.g., picture-word) are problematic because they involve the simultaneous processing of two stimuli, with all the attendant problems of multiple levels of comparison, comparison strategies, and cross-priming. Tasks involving word responses (e.g. naming a superordinate category, or an antonym) are problematic because of the difficulty of unconfounding frequency of the stimulus, frequency of the response, and the "strength" of the link between them. So, some kind of categorization task seems desirable: one in which the subject can make a simple binary response (in the category versus not in the category) and we can select items such that the correct answer is unambiguous. However, it is clear that the *arbitrariness* of the target category we choose will be a major determinant of our ability to detect effects of frequency. Suppose, for example, we had subjects classify concrete nouns according to the criterion of whether their referent contained carbon or not, or would cost more than $10. We would expect longish RTs and a great deal of variability over subjects and items. Subjects would presumably have to *compute* the answer from knowledge retrieved; for the majority of items these properties would not be prestored. Even if effects on transcoding time and decision time were perfectly additive, any effects of frequency on identification or access to meaning would tend to be swamped by the variability in RT contributed by the decision stage, and a giant experiment would be needed to detect the effects. The effects on transcoding and decision time are at least as likely, a priori, not to be perfectly additive. In that case, it seems at least plausible that the greater the duration and variability of the decision process the greater the likelihood that any effects of frequency on transcoding time would not propagate through to the measured RT.

Thus, to stand a fair chance of picking up an effect of frequency on transcoding per se, the categorization task should involve as simple a decision as possible based on a semantic attribute that is *prestored* and *highly available*. The attribute must also be *consensual* — that is, all subjects must have the same answer prestored, so that we can specify what is a correct answer and what is not. Ideally, possession of the criterial attribute should not be a matter of degree, or we will expect typicality effects to become important (Rips, Shoben & Smith, 1973), and typicality could be confounded with frequency. This consideration steered us away from the Battig-and-Montague type categories used by Balota and Chumbley (1984). To maximize similarity to the lexical decision task, and to minimize repetition and priming effects, we needed a large set of items that could be classified against a single, consistent, criterion, without repetition of items, and without presentation and repetition of category labels. For these reasons our first experiment used concrete nouns and had subjects make one response if the word referred to a Person, another if it referred to an Inanimate Thing. These seem like strong candidates to be semantically or procedurally primitive properties (see Johnson-Laird, 1983, 1987, for a discussion of semantic primitives). For example, possession of Personhood (not the same as Humanness, cf. angels, goblins, and, possibly, robots) specifies that a noun can be used in conjunction with a large range of mental-state and agentive verbs ("think," "believe," "administer"), while possession of Inanimacy specifies that it cannot. (The ambiguous, and culturally dependent status of animals and robots does not belie this basic claim.) This provides an a priori argument that this property must be prestored and readily available, rather than computed by comparison to a prototypical Person or Thing (if the latter can be conceptualised at all).

Our experiment was simple in design. There were 72 Person-nouns and 72 Thing-nouns, divided equally into three (fairly broad) frequency bands. Each subject was presented with half of each band in the semantic categorization task, and half in a lexical decision task, in which the words were mixed randomly with nonwords matched in orthographic properties to the words. Over subjects, assignment of words to tasks and order of tasks were counterbalanced. (See Monsell, Doyle & Haggard, 1989, for further details.) Figure 5 shows mean RTs averaged over subjects for each of the frequency bands. While strong and significant effects of frequency class were obtained for both Person and Thing words, there was no significant interaction between Task and Frequency. The effect of frequency on mean categorization time was nearly as large as the effect on LDT. The effects of frequency on the

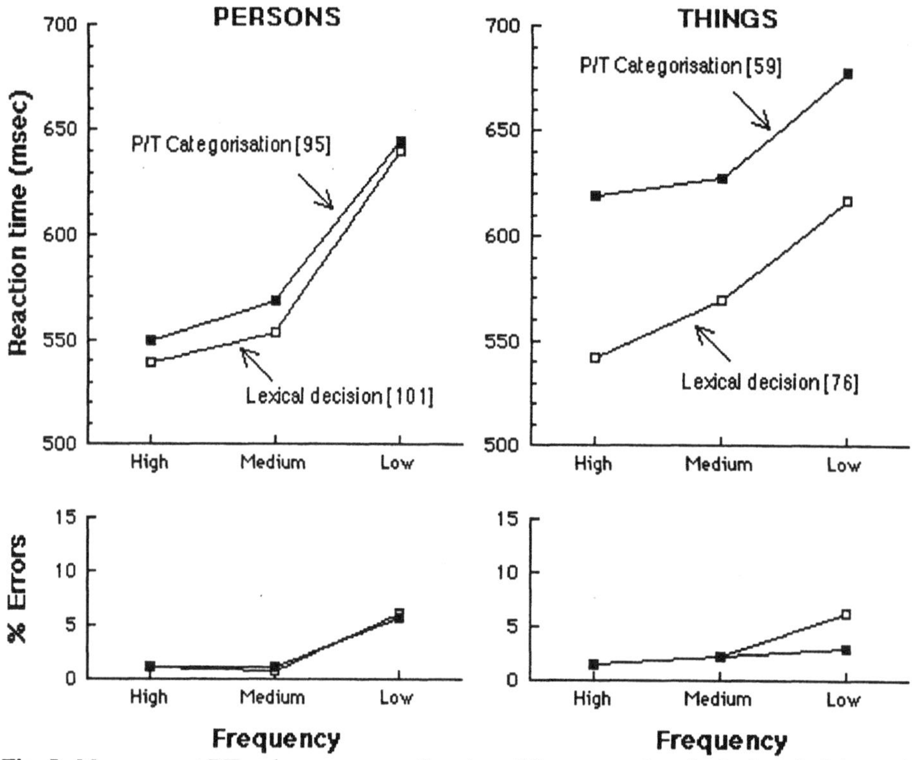

Fig. 5. Mean correct RT and accuracy as a function of frequency class for lexical decision task and person/thing categorization. Numbers in brackets show the difference in msec between mean RTs for high and low frequency words. (Reproduced, with permission, from Monsell S., Doyle, M.C. and Haggard, P.N. (1989) The effects of frequency upon visual word recognition: Where are they? *Journal of Experimental Psychology: General,* **118**, 43-71, © American Psychological Association.)

rest of the RT distribution was also similar in both tasks. A similar story emerged from regression analyses (like those of Balota & Chumbley, 1984) assessing the extent to which log frequency predicted mean RT for individual words in the two tasks. Strong and significant frequency effects were found for both tasks, and although the slope coefficients for the categorization task were not quite as large as those for lexical decision the difference was not significant. In short, by whatever measure, the effects of frequency were clearly very similar across tasks.

This outcome appears to be in conflict with that of Balota and Chumbley (1984). Could the difference be due to a gross confounding of typicality with frequency in our experiment? (Balota and Chumbley partialled out effects of "category dominance" in their regression analyses.) With large amorphous categories such as Persons and Inanimate Things, defined by (it might be supposed) a single feature, the idea of a prototypical member seems less appropriate than for taxonomic categories such as Fruits. Given the words we used, the presence of such a confounding in our experiment seems possible, if at all, only for the category of Persons: the high frequency band did contain some items like "girl," which might be taken as "good" or "central" exemplars of the concept "person" (though perhaps it could equally be argued that they are atypical, since they differentiate a clear partition of the superordinate category) while the low frequency band contained a few "atypical" exemplars like "dwarf" (though it might be perhaps argued that dwarves are atypical of Persons only in a small subset of features — those to do with size). Could such a confounding at least provide an explanation for why the frequency effect was larger for Persons than for Things? Apparently not: this interaction between frequency and class was just as strong for lexical decision as for semantic categorization.

In my view, the conflict of outcomes derives from other differences between the tasks. Monsell et al. (1989) mention some procedural details that might have limited the sensitivity of Balota and Chumbley's semantic categorization task to frequency. More interesting is the possibility that our task and theirs asked the subject to do something different. We were asking the subject to retrieve a *single* semantically primitive feature and respond on the basis of its presence or absence. Figure 5 shows that they were able to press the button to categorize an item as quickly (for Persons) or nearly as quickly (for Things) as they were to indicate it was a word. Balota and Chumbley were, I suggest, asking their subjects to perform a semantic *comparison* task: does the *constellation* of semantic attributes activated by the target word sufficiently match the *constellation* just activated by the category label (perhaps that corresponding to the prototype)? Their subjects performed this task on average about 90 msec slower than the lexical decision task in spite of the fact that (a) each categorization trial was primed in the sense of being immediately preceded by the category name, and (b) the difficulty of their lexical decision task was almost certainly enhanced by the use of nonwords constructed by altering one to three letters of members of primed target categories. Problematic as such cross-experiment comparisons are, the overall RTs are compatible with the idea that the semantic decision they required of their subjects was somewhat more "difficult" than ours.

The idea that the complexity or difficulty of the post-transcoding decision may be an important factor in masking effects of frequency on an earlier process receives some support from our second experiment, in which we used another "primitive" property as a decision criterion: this time whether the word was a noun or an adjective or, as we also put it to subjects, whether the word usually described an *object*, or a *property* of an object. (We avoided ambiguous cases.) The nouns were (with a few changes) those of our first experiment, and the adjectives were matched to them in distribution of length, frequency and orthographic redundancy. This syntactic task also showed a substantial and significant effect of frequency, but the effect on mean RT was now significantly smaller than (about 60-70 % of) the effect on mean lexical decision time for the same nouns. At the same time, syntactic categorization was substantially slower, by about 125 msec (though not more error prone) than lexical decision by the same subjects. Finally, analysis of the distribution of RTs within subjects revealed that the smaller average effect of frequency on syntactic decision time than on lexical decision time could be attributed largely to those items the subject found it most difficult to make decisions about (for whatever reason). In fact, if we used median correct RTs from each subject rather than means as our measure, the effect of frequency now appeared identical in the two tasks!

There is thus a case to be made that the sensitivity of RT to word frequency in tasks requiring access to conceptual or functional attributes of a word is attenuated the greater the difficulty of the post-transcoding decision required.[11] This hypothesis is evidently incompatible with transcoding and decision being discrete processing stages with independent mean durations, and implies some form of cascade architecture.[12] It must be acknowledged that the general class of cascade architectures only permits, and does not require, an *underadditive* interaction between effects of frequency on transcoding, and the difficulty of the decision. However, for the sake of the present argument we need only to consider the implications of the interaction, not its mechanism. Weak frequency effects in any particular instance (e.g., Balota & Chumbley, 1984, Exp. 1) do not permit us to conclude that lexical identification or access to meaning are only weakly frequency sensitive, because the strong frequency effects observed in another instance, (Monsell et al., Exp. 1) then lack an explanation. The parsimonious account is that the propagation of frequency effects localized in "early" processes through to measured RT depends on properties of later processes that we can presently characterize only with the crude label "difficulty."

I have been careful to characterize the frequency effects we observed in these two experiments as effects on transcoding. There is no a priori basis for apportioning these effects between identification per se and post-identification access to meaning. Knowledge of both word-form and the link between word-form and word-sense (not to mention the integrality of a word-sense) are likely to be strengthened by word-specific experience. The generic PDP learning models discussed above illustrate how these two (or three) kinds of strengthening may occur. However, it is noteworthy that, as our data in Figure 5 illustrate, the effects of frequency upon performance in lexical decision and semantic categorization were very similar not only in size, but also in form. Two interpretations are possible, but cannot presently be distinguished. One is that lexical decision is, like categorization, based on access to a word-*sense* representation. The other is that lexical decision and categorization share processes only up to and including identification with respect to lexical *form* and that this is the main locus of the frequency effect.

VI. EFFECTS OF FREQUENCY ON NAMING TASKS: FURTHER DATA

In my introductory remarks, I repeated a common generalization: effects of frequency upon naming latency are weaker than those upon lexical decision time. This generalization rests both upon common experience in the laboratory, and some systematic comparisons of frequency effects in the two tasks using the same words, as in the classic studies of Forster and Chambers (1973) and Frederiksen and Kroll (1976), and more recently, the experiments of Balota and Chumbley (1984). I will now show that this generalization, while capturing the average result, conceals a crucial second order generalization: *the more that naming depends on transcoding at a lexical level, and the less on sublexical transcoding, between spelling and sound, the larger the frequency effect.*

A known word may be pronounced by identifying it as a learned orthographic pattern and retrieving its learned pronunciation; that is, *lexical transcoding.* In addition, for any pronounceable letter string, fragments of the orthography (letters, letter groups like CH- or -GHT, "bodies" like -OOK, patterns like vowel followed by consonant (cluster)- followed by final E) may be assigned a pronunciation, using general knowledge of the sound-spelling correspondences of English, and these pronunciations "assembled" into a pronunciation: *i.e., sublexical transcoding.* There has long been a debate (reviewed by Patterson & V. Coltheart, 1987, among many others, and recently refuelled by Seidenberg and McClelland, 1989), between the hypothesis that these two levels of transcoding are encapsulated in separate processing pathways which can be damaged selectively (e.g., Coltheart, 1985) and perhaps subject to independent strategic control (Monsell, Patterson, Tallon & Hill, 1989), and the hypothesis that both levels are represented undifferentiably within a single transcoding module (as in the model of Shallice & McCarthy, 1985, and the computationally explicit PDP model of Seidenberg & McClelland, 1989). I shall strive to evade this debate in what follows. But I shall need to assume (following the arguments of Seidenberg, Waters, Barnes & Tanenhaus, 1984, Seidenberg, 1985a, 1985b, Waters & Seidenberg, 1985) that, whether lexical and sublexical transcoding processes are in this sense separately encapsulated or not, phonological descriptions generated by them are continuously pooled until a sufficient, unambiguous, description of the pronunciation is available to drive pronunciation.

What are the consequences for frequency effects? First, while sublexical transcoding might well be influenced by the frequency of orthographic *subpatterns*, and the frequency of spelling-sound correspondences associated with word *fragments*, since it does not identify the whole *word* it will not be sensitive to *word* frequency. Both "conventional" and PDP learning models lead us to expect that lexical transcoding to phonology should be sensitive to word frequency. Inasmuch as naming is driven by the pooled output of these levels of transcoding we would expect the effects of word frequency to be weaker than on performance of a task driven by lexical transcoding (or identification) alone — such as lexical decision. And indeed they are — on average. However, there are numerous "exception" words in English, that is, words with irregular spelling-sound correspondence whose pronunciation cannot be correctly computed on the basis only of general knowledge of spelling-sound correspondences in English. (Some of the ways in which a word can be "exceptional" will be illustrated below.) For these words sub-lexical transcoding will tend to assemble a (wrong) pronunciation conflicting with the (correct) pronunciation yielded by lexical transcoding. If such a conflict develops prior to the initiation of articulatory execution, we would expect that time will be required to resolve the conflict in favour of the lexically specified description. In contrast, for a "regular" (nonexception) word the congruence of the output from the two levels of transcoding may permit articulation to be initiated before lexically specified information would alone be sufficient to initiate pronunciation. For either reason, we would expect naming latency to depend more on the duration of lexical transcoding, and hence be more sensitive to word frequency, for exception than for regular words.

Table 1 shows a summary of data from several experiments in which frequency and regularity have been varied orthogonally in the naming task, and, in some cases, for lexical decision with the same words as well. The critical point is captured in the boldface numbers, which show the effect of frequency on RT (i.e.,the difference between average correct RT for high and low frequency words). Several studies have compared monosyllabic regular words and exception words like PINT and HAVE, in which the pronunciation of the vowel differs from that generally found in other words with the same "body" (i.e., -INT, and -AVE). The effect of frequency is significantly stronger for the exception words than for regular words. However, these exception words have only modestly irregular spelling-sound correspondence. For instance, /æ/ is a frequent pronunciation of the vowel A in a monosyllable; it is only the -VE context that makes the word exceptional. Seidenberg et al. (1984) tested another class they called "strange" words. These included words like AISLE, BROOCH and GAUGE, with low bigram frequencies (matched for high and low frequency groups), and relatively few close "neighbors" (i.e., other words with similar spelling patterns). As may be seen, the frequency effect observed for these items is large and nearly as strong as the effect upon lexical decision for the same words. Finally, Monsell et al. (1989, Exp. 3) looked at the naming of disyllabic words. These were chosen so that their orthography does not obviously specify which syllable receives stress. (Consider ENJOY and ENVOY, to get the idea.) Half the words were stress-initial, half stress-final. By far the majority of polysyllabic words in English are pronounced with initial stress, and this is especially true for disyllabic words. Thus, stress-final words are, in an important sense, "exceptional." Inasmuch as the sub-lexical transcoding tended to assign the "default" stress pattern for a disyllabic word, this output would be

Table 1
Interactions of Frequency With Regularity in Naming Tasks.

	Naming			Lexical decision		
	Hi fr	Lo fr	RTΔ	Hi fr	Lo fr	RT Δ
Seidenberg (1985b)						
Experiment 2						
"Exception" monosyllables	541 (1)	583 (5)	**42**			
Regular monosyllables	540 (0)	556 (2)	**16**			
Taraban & McClelland (1987)						
Experiment 1						
"Exception" monosyllables	573 (6)	623 (9)	**50**			
Regular monosyllables	591 (0)	560 (0)	**31**			
Seidenberg , Waters, Barnes & Tanenhaus (1984)						
Experiment 3						
"Exception" monosyllables	590 (1)	639 (10)	**49**	530 (1)	604 (8)	**74**
Regular monsosyllables	588 (1)	610 (1)	**22**	533 (1)	601 (11)	**68**
Experiment 4						
"Strange" monosyllables	590 (1)	680 (28)	**90**	570 (2)	673 (11)	**103**
Regular monosyllables	603 (2)	608 (4)	**5**	601 (0)	633 (2)	**32**
Monsell, Doyle and Haggard (1989)						
Experiment 3						
Stress-final disyllables	448 (0)	522 (4)	**74**	543 (1)	617 (5)	**74**
Stress-initial disyllables	451 (1)	510 (4)	**59**	538 (2)	642 (9)	**104**

Mean correct reaction time in msec (percent error)

inappropriate for the stress-final words. So we expected subjects to be unusually dependent on lexical transcoding in our experiment, and to exhibit an especially large effect of frequency for stress-final words. In conformity with these expectations, the overall frequency effect for naming latency was (as may be seen in Table 1) a substantial fraction of that observed for LDT. For the exceptional stress-final words the effect was not only significantly bigger than for the stress-initial words, but equal to the effect on LDT for the same words.

Hence, there seems to be ample evidence to support the generalization: the more pronunciation depends on *lexical* transcoding, the larger the effect of frequency on naming latency. This being so, current evidence on comparison of frequency effects across the tasks is perfectly compatible with there being an identification process common to lexical decision and naming that is strongly sensitive to frequency. At the same time, these data are equally compatible with the hypothesis that the frequency sensitivity of naming and lexical decision arises in task-specific processes subsequent to identification.

What might these post-identification processes be in the case of naming? In addition to identifying the word (matching it to an orthographic "lexical entry"), one must activate a particular mapping from this representation to a phonological representation, use this to generate a phonological description sufficient to drive articulatory programming and then execute the resulting articulatory program. For reasons already discussed, McCann and Besner (1987, McCann et al., 1988), quite specifically locate the effect in the process of mapping from orthographic to phonological descriptions, not "in" the phonological lexicon per se or subsequently, and, as I have acknowledged, there is no evidence to deny this localization. Balota and Chumbley (1985) attribute (most of) the effect of frequency on naming latency frequency effect somewhat unspecifically within the chain of post-identification processes. However, the delayed naming data they used to support this claim suggests that they have in mind a later locus than McCann and Besner — articulatory programming or execution.

There are problems in interpreting Balota and Chumbley's (1985) delayed-naming result, that is their finding of frequency effects even when the signal to speak followed display of the word by several hundred msec (see Section IV). One is that the RTs they obtained even with relatively long delays were substantially longer than those typically observed in experiments on RT for speaking prepared utterances consisting of a single word (e.g., Monsell, 1986; Sternberg, Monsell, Knoll & Wright, 1978; Sternberg, Wright, Knoll, & Monsell, 1980). This suggests that Balota and Chumbley's subjects were not as prepared to speak as they could be; that is, they were in some state prior to having a fully prepared articulatory "program" ready to execute. Monsell et al. (1989) conducted a delayed naming experiment with the disyllabic words already mentioned.[13] We obtained much shorter latencies, probably because much stronger incentives for full preparation were given. Each word was produced on three trials in a row. On the first trial, there was a marginally significant frequency effect, but tiny: about 10% of the effect on immediate naming. On the second and third productions there was no frequency effect. McRae, Jared and Seidenberg (1990) have also found no effect of frequency on delayed naming with delays individually calibrated to be beyond the range of normal naming latencies. Savage, Bradley and Forster (1989) have similarly failed to obtain an effect of frequency on naming after a delay of about a second. Thus it cannot be in the process of articulation per se that Balota and Chumbley's delayed naming effect arose (unless frequency was confounded with articulatory properties in their study). And, given a state of incomplete preparation, we do not know how far back in the chain of processes Balota and Chumbley's subjects (and perhaps our subjects on a few of the first production trials) "resumed" processing when the signal arrived, especially as Balota and Chumbley left the the display visible until the reaction signal.

In short, there is no evidence for an effect of frequency on articulatory processes, and McCann and Besner's (1987) finding of a lack of any frequency effect on pseudohomophone naming constitutes modest, if not unassailable, evidence against any post-transcoding locus. It might be hoped that the localization of frequency effects in oral reading could be further constrained by consideration of tasks in which a word must be pronounced in response to stimuli other than text, such as in object naming. There is a clear relationship between frequency and performance in object naming (Oldfield & Wingfield, 1965). And it has further been claimed that these effects of frequency are manifest only when the the object must be named, not when it must merely be identified (Wingfield, 1968). However, even were this unambiguously so, it would not discriminate an influence of frequency on transcoding between semantics and phonology from a later locus. The conclusion we are currently left with, then, is that the effect of frequency upon naming is located in either the identification component of lexical transcoding from orthography to phonology, or in the activation of phonology, or both, but not later. And the extent to which this influence will be manifest in naming performance depends on the extent to which the words used force the subjects to rely upon lexical rather than sublexical transcoding.

VII. EFFECTS OF FREQUENCY ON INDIRECT MEASURES OF LEXICAL ACCESS

Besides lexical decision, we have so far looked only at tasks which explicitly require subjects to access pronunciation, or semantic/syntactic attributes. There are many performance measures studied in the laboratory which, although they do not logically require identification of the word, nevertheless exhibit sensitivity to lexical variables, and thus provide another possible index of the locus of frequency effects.

By far the most important measure, because it is a by-product of "normal" reading, is fixation duration during reading. Our reading mechanisms could have been so organized that the eye moved from fixation to fixation without waiting for identification to occur. But they are not. Fixation duration in unconstrained silent reading for comprehension has widely been observed to depend not only on "visual" properties of the word, but also on properties which could only have their effect through contact with lexical knowledge (see Rayner & Duffy, 1986, for summary). In particular, effects of frequency have been widely reported (Just & Carpenter, 1980; Rayner, 1977). However, Kliegl, Olson and Davidson (1982) drew attention to the fact that frequency had been confounded in such studies with formal properties of words such as their length, and found very little effect of frequency with such variables partialled out. In response, Rayner and Duffy (1986) and Inhoff and Rayner (1986) have now reported experiments with word length, orthographic redundancy, and certain semantic/syntactic complexity properties carefully controlled. They report substantial and significant frequency effects (about 40 msec for first fixation duration, 90 msec for gaze duration.) Now it is surely clear that the fixation duration does not include the sort of "familiarity decision" process to whose duration Balota and Chumbley (1984) attribute the bulk of the frequency effect in lexical decision time. Nor is it likely to include the time required for generation of a pronunciation. Thus these effects seem to provide an additional fragment of evidence that the process(es) of lexical identification and/or access to meaning are frequency sensitive. Of course, it may be that additional processing is accomplished before the eyes move, such as partial integration of the word's meaning into that of the sentence. Inasmuch as frequency was confounded with the ease of such integration, effects on fixation duration might overestimate those on transcoding to meaning. But it is at least as likely that there is underestimation, because the eyes may sometimes move before identification is complete: hence, perhaps, some repeated fixations on the same word, and Rayner and Duffy's (1986) additional observation of long gaze durations on the word *following* a low-frequency word.

Another class of measures which appear to index lexical identification even though it is not necessary for the task is the "word-superiority effect" (WSE) observed in a number of tasks requiring report of or decision about individual letters in a displayed string. An accuracy advantage for letters embedded in words over letters embedded in nonwords has been reported when all the letters must be reported in a masked string, when a letter in a particular position in a masked string must be reported, and when a forced choice must be made about the letter in a particular position in a masked string (see Henderson, 1982, for review). Shorter RTs are also reported for "same" judgments to pairs of letter strings when the item is a word than when it is not (see Henderson, 1980, 1982, for review). As in the studies of McCann and Besner (1987) reviewed above, such an effect of lexical status may be interpreted as indicating some contact with lexical representations in the determination of performance, and the question can then be asked: is this effect modulated by frequency? However, few of the large number of studies using these paradigms both include frequency manipulations and meet the following criteria. (a) Are the words and nonwords carefully matched for orthographic redundancy? If not, the so-called "WSE" may, in fact, be attributable to the influence of differences in sub-lexical orthographic structure. (b) Similarly, are the high and low frequency words matched for orthographic redundancy? These properties tend to be correlated in the language (Landauer & Streeter, 1973). (c) Is there a substantial WSE? If not, we will be hard put to detect a modulation of it by frequency. (Recall my comment on McCann and Besner's studies.) (d) In the case of the masking paradigms, can we rule out a "sophisticated," or post-perceptual guessing account? Verbal report of whole words after tachistoscopic exposures has long been known to be sensitive to frequency (Howes & Solomon, 1951), but it has proved hard to distinguish between an account in terms of primary lexical identification, and one that says that in attempting to reconstruct the display from a fragmentary percept, subjects find it easier to generate high than low frequency words matching the fragmentary percept as guesses (see Broadbent, 1967; Johnston, 1978, for discussion). This difficulty is one reason for the decline in popularity of masking paradigms in favour of RT paradigms.

In the case of letter recognition there have been two approaches to controlling for sophisticated guessing. The first is to use Reicher's (1969) forced-choice procedure. Subjects must choose between two letter candidates for a given position, so that no generation of guesses is required. There seems to be a substantial consensus that with forced choice responding, the effect of frequency is at best small and insignificant (Günther,Gfroerer & Weiss, 1984; Manelis, 1977; Paap & Newsome, 1980; Paap et al., 1978). Paap et al. (1982) use this as support for their claim that the initial activation stage in their two-stage activation-verification model is not influenced by frequency. The other approach is to use report accuracy, and check for guessing by testing whether letters that are more predictable from their context are in fact better reported. Johnston (1978) and McClelland and Johnston (1977) looked for and found no such predictability effect. Under the same conditions, McClelland and Johnston observed a substantial WSE and a signifiant word frequency effect for completely accurate reports of the whole letter string.

So, under masking conditions we seem to have a frequency effect for successful report of a whole string even in the absence of evidence for sophisticated guessing, but little sign of a frequency effect for forced choice of a single letter. Are these in conflict? Like McClelland and Johnston (1977), I think not. Even if we attribute the WSE in the forced-choice paradigm to activation of word-detectors (as do McClelland and Rumelhart, 1981, and Johnston, 1978) this activation must on most trials be only fractional, substantially subcriterial, and distributed over many members of an orthographic neighborhood. Hence any contribution from activation of the detector of the word whose frequency is being used as the independent variable will be small. Were this not the case, we would expect more successful complete reports. But most of the relatively few trials when successful complete reports *do* occur are likely to result from criterial activation of the relevant word-detector, which word-detector models expect to be strongly sensitive to frequency.

A similarly inconclusive story appears to apply to the same-different RT paradigm. Effects of word frequency on "same" RTs have been reported in combination with a substantial word-superiority effect, (Bruder, 1978; Chambers & Forster, 1975). Whether the stimuli in these studies were adequately controlled for properties other than frequency may be open to doubt (see Jastrzembski, 1981). Bruder's (1978) frequency effect was substantially attenuated by use of mixed case letter strings. This could be interpreted as due either to the slowing of lexical identification (relative to the parallel form-matching process) by mixed case, or to an influence on form matching of "visual" familiarity instead of an effect of word frequency on lexical identification (as Besner et al., 1984, suggest). We may never know the answer. Research on the WSE in both masking and matching paradigms seems to have petered out in favor of tasks that explicitly require lexical identification or transcoding. This seems like a good thing for several reasons, prominent among them being several generations of students baffled by chapters on "word recognition" that appear to be entirely about tasks that do not require word recognition!

VIII. FREQUENCY, REPETITION, AND "FAMILIARITY"

In Sections IV, V, and VI, I considered effects of frequency on RT in lexical decision, semantic or syntactic categorization, and naming, all tasks that (unlike the measures considered in Section VII) seem necessarily dependent on processes of lexical identification and/or transcoding. In this final section I shall review briefly the effects of "repetition priming" on this same array of RT tasks, and their relation to frequency effects. Repetition of a printed word has been shown to facilitate (among many other measures) lexical decision time (Scarborough, Cortese, & Scarborough, 1977), naming latency (Scarborough et al., 1977), syntactic classification time (Monsell, 1985), and semantic categorization time (Monsell, 1985, 1987b). In each case, the facilitation was observed with long lags between the two occurrences — that is, more than a few trials, and sometimes up to several days.

There are two reasons for considering repetition priming here. The first is that frequency and long-lag repetition priming effects seem likely to have a common cause: a mechanism that mediates persisting effects of experience with words on later reading. When we do frequency experiments, we use tables of frequency norms as a rough estimate of pre-experimental experience with particular words. In the case of repetition priming, we deliberately manipulate recent experience for some of the words, by arranging one or more prior encounters within the experiment. Because the priming episode is thus within the experimental context, the idea of an extra-lexical, *episodic* source of "familiarity" information (Section IV) has become popular in accounting for repetition priming of lexical decision. This supplies a second reason for considering data from repetition priming. Inasmuch as there are data relevant to the role of episodic familiarity, they come from repetition priming experiments (because the relevant "episodes" are under experimental control). I shall argue that, nevertheless, there is scant evidence in support of an episodic source, at least in the RT tasks listed above (in which the subject sees a legible display and is able to perform rapidly and accurately in the absence of any priming), and at long lags. The picture is complicated at short lags by transient influences, including semantic priming (Meyer & Schvaneveldt, 1976), sublexical priming (Evett & Humphreys, 1981), temporary partial activation of lexical representations (Forster & Davies, 1984) and, perhaps, the greater availability of episodic traces (see below). Moreoever, as Scarborough et al. (1977) pointed out, any repetition effect that does not persist over substantial intervals is unlikely to have the same mechanism as the frequency effect.

It is easy to imagine versions of the conventional word-detector model, in which repetition priming is a consequence of the same change that mediates frequency effects. This was essentially the line taken by Morton (1969) in whose model each successful recognition of an item caused a long-lasting, but slowly decaying, reduction in the threshold of the corresponding logogen; variations in this threshold were seen as the source of both repetition priming and frequency effects. In connectionist models, the weight changes wrought by each encounter generally both influence the next encounter and accumulate to generate frequency effects.

Figure 2b shows the effect of "priming" a pattern, with extra presentations, on the time-accuracy curves generated by McClelland and Rumelhart's 24-unit model.

Some authors (Besner & Swan, 1982; Humphreys, Besner & Quinlan, 1988; Scarborough et al., 1977) have considered it congenial to this idea — that frequency and repetition effects have the same mechanism — that repetition priming effects are typically smaller for high than for low frequency words (e.g., Scarborough et al., 1977, Norris, 1984a, for lexical decision time; Jacoby & Dallas, 1981, for tachistoscopic identification). However, while such an interaction of repetition and frequency effects renders it unlikely that the two effects have loci in distinct discrete processing stages as defined by Sternberg (1969), that is a long way short of asserting that the loci - or the mechanisms - are the same. Variables influencing parameters of separate processing levels in cascade may, after all, have interacting effects, though not always, or not necessarily over all of their range (McClelland, 1979). And there exist one or two cases where effects of frequency and repetition on RT have been observed to be additive (Monsell, 1985, Exp. 1 using syntactic categorization time) or a respectable repetition effect has not been modulated by frequency (Scarborough et al., 1977, Exp. 3, on naming latency). Hence, while the typical interaction of repetition and frequency effects encourages belief in a common mechanism, it does not compel it.

Nor is there likely to be a single mechanism for repetition priming. The explanation of repetition effects, like that of frequency effects, has provoked much controversy of late. Not surprisingly, parallel arguments are discernible in the two domains. Particular attention has been attracted by proposals that repetition priming is in general due to "episodic" memory rather than any change in "lexical" representations (Jacoby, 1983; Jacoby & Brooks, 1984), and, in the particular case of lexical decision, due to a bias in a post-lexical decision stage because of "episodic familiarity" (Feustel et al., 1983). My own view is that it is a mistake to dichotomize the theoretical space into mutually exclusive "lexical" and "episodic" theories, and that the term "episodic" is often used in a talismanic, inadequately articulated manner. Repetition over long lags may have several effects, only a subset of which may be manifest, or dominant, under the conditions of a particular experiment. I have discussed these possible effects at length elsewhere (Monsell, 1985, 1987b), and will only summarize some major possibilities here. My purpose is to emphasize that repetition priming may have multiple causes, some of which are irrelevant to frequency effects, and to note some evidence from repetition priming experiments that extra-lexical episodic familiarity is unlikely to be a significant influence on lexical decision time under conditions relevant to frequency effects. Reference to Figure 6, (adapted from Monsell, 1987b) may (or may not) help to clarify three plausible causes of long lag priming:

• *Response or decision learning.* If the repetition trial involves production of the same response, or making the same decision, as was made (explicitly or implicitly) on the priming encounter, then one obvious but neglected possibility is that the subject learned (to some degree) from the priming trial to produce that response or make that decision, and hence does it more efficiently on the subsequent encounter, irrespective of any episodic memory of the learning episode. Associative learning of this kind can explain why repetition effects sometimes exhibit task-specificity in the absence of marked contextual-specificity (Monsell, 1985, Exp. 4), and why nonwords may sometimes exhibit marked facilitation effects (Monsell, 1985, Exp. 2). Certain conditions are likely to favour associative learning of this kind (e.g. expectancy of repetition, adequate time, instructions to remember, multiple

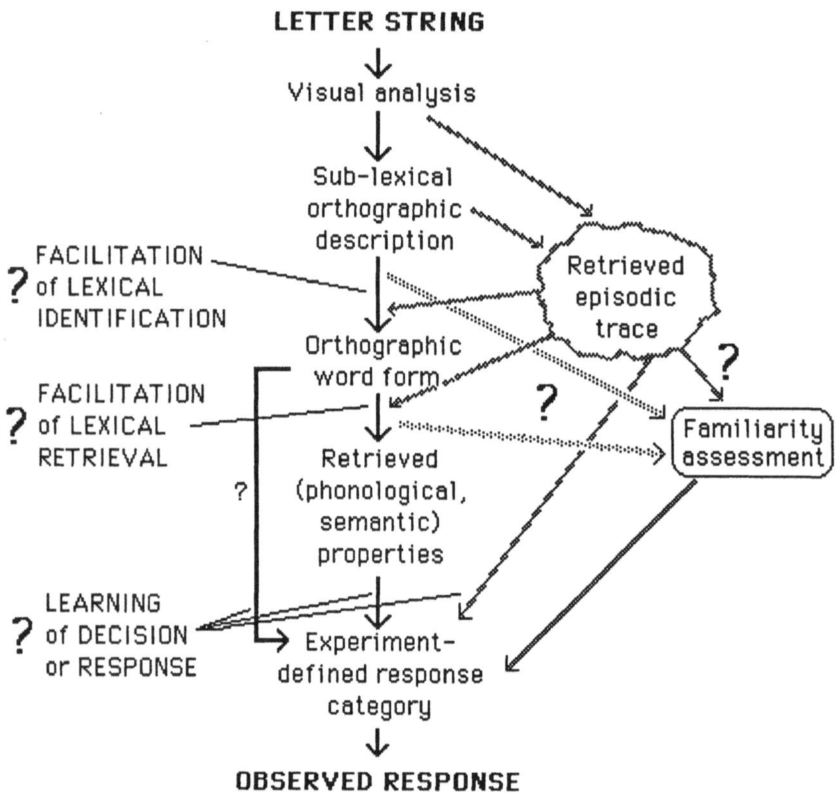

Fig. 6. Possible loci of repetition (and, in some cases, frequency) effects. (Adapted from Monsell, 1987b). See text for explanation.

repetitions) and sufficiently rapid retrieval[14] of associated responses (e.g., relatively few similar associations learned, difficult decisions, short lags). But associative learning certainly cannot be the sole cause of repetition effects, because these are frequently observed to transfer across tasks, sometimes with little or no diminution (see Monsell, 1985, 1987b, for examples). Nor, inasmuch as the effects of frequency on word recognition performance in laboratory tasks stem from everyday reading, can this type of task-specific learning be a significant factor in frequency effects.

• *Facilitation of lexical identification and/or retrieval.* The priming encounter may change the state of the lexical representation, so that it becomes easier to access, or activate to a criterial level,when the word is encountered on a second occasion. In word-detector models, the state changed is usually assumed to be the same detector-specific parameter that is responsible for frequency effects (e.g., the threshold of Morton's, 1969, logogens). In PDP learning models, the state changed is presumably the weights of within or cross-domain connections. Why should one recent experience with a word have so large an effect compared to many earlier encounters — as is indicated by the typical size of repetition priming effect compared to the range of frequency effects? There can be two kinds of reasons why the effect of experience should be dominated by the most recent experiences. One is that, the more time that has elapsed since a prior encounter with the target word (and consequent weight changes in directions optimal for that word), the more experience with other similar words will have shifted the relevant weights back again in the direction of the "average" word. (cf. Rosenberg & Sejnowski,'s 1986, account of the spacing effect as manifest in NETtalk.) Secondly, it is natural for PDP learning models to suppose that there is a slow decay of weight changes. McLaren, Kaye and Mackintosh (1989) provide a slightly more elaborate example of this assumption: in their model, weight changes resulting from a training encounter decay back to an asymptote that is a fixed proportion of the increment to the weight, so that there are both permanent and short-term (but persistent) components to learning. Evidently, the critical test of such powerful assumptions will be their ability to account for a wide range of learning data, not just one or two phenomena.

• *Recovery of an episodic trace.* The proposal of Jacoby (1983) was that the presentation of a particular stimulus pattern would sometimes result in the retrieval of a memory trace for a particular prior episode involving that pattern, typically the most recent one. How might this assist the rapid or accurate production of a suitable response? Several possibilities exist. One is that being reminded what one did on a previous occasion would help one determine what to do this time - i.e.,an episodically mediated variant of response or decision learning. Jacoby (1983), however, appears to suggest that it is perceptual identification that is facilitated: being reminded of a previous occasion on which one has seen a stimulus helps one determine *what it is* — an episodically mediated variant of facilitation of identification. A third possible role of retrieval of (or failure to retrieve) an episodic trace could be to give an estimate of the "familiarity" of the stimulus which would partially or wholly determine the response in a lexical decision task. This is Feustel et al.'s (1983) account, which I characterized in Section IV as proposing an extra-lexical source of familiarity information or bias.

There thus could be several different facilitatory consequences of retrieving an episodic trace, though "familiarity bias" presumably applies only in the case of a task dependent on a familiarity criterion, such as lexical decision. However, several facts suggest that episodic traces cannot be the only source of repetition priming effects, and that they are likely to be an atypical source, at least in RT paradigms with long lags. First, over lags for which robust and persistent repetition priming of RTs typically occurs without rapid decay (see Monsell, 1985), it is quite clear from experiments using the continuous recognition paradigm (e.g., Hintzman, 1969, Okada, 1971, and especially Hockley, 1982) that episodic traces become rapidly harder to retrieve. This is so even at short lags: Monsell (1985, Exp. 2) obtained a direct contrast between repetition priming over lags 2 to 4 (no decay) to episodic recognition performance (substantial decline in RT and accuracy). Ratcliff, Hockley and McKoon (1985) demonstrated a similar contrast over longer lags. Second, an episodic familiarity effect is expected by some (e.g., Feustel et al., 1983) to be manifest in inhibitory repetition priming of nonword decisions in lexical decision. Although this sometimes occurs (see McKoon & Ratcliff, 1979; Monsell, 1987b, for examples), it is noteworthy that there are numerous studies in which stable long-lag repetition priming has been observed for words coupled with either insignificant, or transient facilitatory, effects for nonwords (e.g., Bentin & Moscovitch, 1988; Monsell, 1987a). Third, it has proved very hard to demonstrate robust effects on repetition priming of environmental context (Jacoby & Witherspoon, 1982; Monsell, 1985, Exp. 4). Fourth, major changes in the physical appearance of the orthography across the two encounters have often been found to have no little or no effect on the strength of repetition priming (for typecase see Scarborough et al., 1987; for script, see Feldman & Moskovljevic, 1987; for cursive script versus print, see Manso de Zuniga, Humphreys, & Evett, this volume). Yet changes of context and changes of type case should have a marked effect on the likelihood of retrieving episodic records of *individual visual experiences*. If a memory trace does not encode the context, or perceptual features of the instance encountered, then in what sense is it "episodic"?

My conclusions from this excursion into repetition priming are these. First, there is no reason to deny that repetition priming is in some conditions wholly or partly a manifestation of the same mechanism as explains frequency effects (whether change in a word-detector's parameters, or change in connection weights). The patterns of interaction (or additivity) between repetition and frequency effects observed to date have little to say about this, provided that one avoids making additive factor assumptions a priori. There may be additional causes of repetition priming, such as learning the decision or the response, which are not relevant to frequency effects. Further, while it is undoubtedly *possible* to find circumstances in which the retrieval of episodic traces contributes to repetition priming, via familiarity bias or other means, it is equally possible to find conditions in which recovery of episodic traces is slow, inaccurate, and manifests rapid forgetting, while repetition priming is robust and stable. These conditions (long lags, many intervening items, little opportunity or incentive for memorization, no expectation of repetition, stimuli presented clearly without masking) happen to be those that are relevant to the idea that frequency effects are just cumulative repetition priming.

Hence, an extra-lexical "episodic" familiarity estimate seems implausible as a major source of the effects of frequency upon lexical decision time.

IX. CONCLUSIONS

This chapter has developed two main themes. The first has been that we need an account of frequency effects in which they arise out of a mechanism that is continuously *learning* to identify and transcode words, whether new or previously encountered. Such an account is now available in the general class of PDP learning models for transcoding between lexical domains, but not in the more traditional models, in which provision for frequency effects is essentially ad hoc. The PDP models also offer a useful alternative to the conventional conception of lexical identification as a process separate from and prior to access to meaning or phonology. I have argued in several places that (whether Processing is Distributed or not) the data also discourage us from conceiving of these two logically necessary processing steps as discrete stages.

My second theme has been the endeavor to determine the locus of frequency effects on the basis of comparisons of frequency effects across tasks. I first described some new data indicating that, contrary to recent claims, tasks requiring categorization of a word on the basis of its semantic properties are not inherently insensitive to frequency. Instead, I suggested that the effect of frequency on the efficiency of transcoding from orthography to meaning may sometimes be masked – perhaps when the subsequent decision process is relatively difficult. In the case of reading a word aloud, effects of frequency turn out to be large (i.e.,comparable to effects on lexical decision) when correct pronunciation of the word largely depends on identification of the whole word and retrieval of a learned pronunciation, rather than on sublexical "assembly." There is little evidence that frequency effects are associated with phonological word-forms per se, or their articulatory execution. However, there is no basis (yet) for apportioning the effects of frequency on naming between the process of identifying the orthographic pattern and subsequent retrieval of the phonological pattern (inasmuch as these are distinct).

As another component of the debate about localization, I elaborated upon the idea that lexical decision may be based (at least in part) on a familiarity discrimination process. On the basis of data from repetition priming, I argued that the frequency effect was unlikely to be attributable to a familiarity estimate derived from extra-lexical recovery of an episodic trace. Instead, I suggested that as well as being being driven by successful unique identification (should this occur), the decision process globally monitors parameters of the activation of orthographic pattern detectors, and/or semantic attribute units. (Global measures available in PDP learning models provide concrete illustrations of such parameters.) This is indeed a familiarity discrimination process, but instead of being *subsequent* to lexical identification/transcoding and a *separate* locus of frequency effects, as some have suggested, it is *parasitic* upon lexical identification/transcoding, and would not work unless the time-course of the latter was highly sensitive to frequency

Thus, constrained by new reasons, we can relax into an old conclusion. The effects of frequency typically observed in laboratory measurements of RT for tasks requiring identification or transcoding are not task-specific. They are due to the continuously (if asymptotically) cumulative effect of repeated experience with a word upon the efficiency with which a reader can identify its form and retrieve its associated meaning or pronunciation. This effect may also be seen in fixation durations recorded during "natural" reading of continuous text, and in certain "word superiority effects," though neither type of measure, especially the latter, is transparent. The effect may also be seen, in somewhat different guise, in the phenomenon of repetition priming, though this phenomenon sometimes has additional causes. It must be emphasized that the data still do not permit a clear fractionation of frequency effects between the identification and retrieval phases of the transcoding process (inasmuch as these are distinct). But, by the same token, there is absolutely no reason at present to conclude that either is any less sensitive to frequency than the other.

FOOTNOTES

[1]The term "lexical access" is sometimes used for this identification process. However, others use the term to refer to access from orthography to a particular property of a presented word -- e.g., its phonology , or its meaning, that is, transcoding rather than (just) identification. Given this fundamental ambiguity, it seems best to avoid unqualified use of the term, though I shall occasionally speak (unambiguously, I hope) about "access to meaning" or "access to phonology". Otherwise I shall use the terms "identification" and "transcoding" with the senses defined here.

[2]I mean models which specify the process by which the best match is found and phonological or semantic attributes accessed, as opposed to "functional anatomy" or "pathway" models of word recognition, especially those deployed in contemporary neuropsychology, which merely assume such a process exists.

[3]Actually Morton's logogens had two thresholds: one which had to be exceeded for associated semantic representations in the "cognitive system" to be activated, and a higher threshold which had to be exceeded for a verbal response (i.e., phonology) to be generated in the response buffer.

[4]I assume here that, while "degree of learning" may approach an asymptote, we are not contrasting words at asymptote.

[5]In this discussion, "semantic" should be interpreted extremely loosely, as including not only attributes of meaning but also syntactic and usage properties (e.g., whether the word is taboo in polite society). Elsewhere (Monsell, 1985, 1987a) I have used the cumbersome term "conceptual/functional" properties, but here I shall just be imprecise.

[6]Given observations that semantic (see Section IV) and phonological features of words sometimes influence lexical decision times, Seidenberg and McClelland allow that there are conditions under which the error score over orthographic units alone may be an insufficient basis for lexical decision.

[7]Most "dual process" theorists are now, in fact, three-pathway theorists, in that they believe a lexical transcoding from orthography to phonology to be available via either a direct pathway, or (more slowly and less reliably) via semantics (see Coltheart, 1985, for the largely neuropsychological justification).

[8]McCann and Besner appear to be assuming that there is but one "phonological lexicon" used for both auditory recognition and word production. There are reasons for believing the contrary (Monsell, 1987a), in which case one might suppose that McCann and Besner's (1987) pseudohomophone effect in reading would reflect (occasional, partial) activation of the output lexicon, whaile McCann et al.'s (1988) pseudohomophone effect in lexical decision would reflect (occasional, partial) activation of the input lexicon.

[9]It is to this process that McCann et al. (1988) attribute the effect of frequency they obtain for yet another pseudohomophone measure, namely "phonological lexical decision" (i.e., deciding whether a printed non-word is homophonous with any real word).

[10]Note that the lack of a frequency modulation of pseudohomophone effects in McCann and Besner (1987) and McCann et al. (1988) might suggest deleting the words "and phonological" from this sentence.

[11]An attractive feature of this generalization is that it helps to explain some otherwise puzzling inconsistencies in prior work. For example, Monsell (1985) describes a noun/adjective categorization experiment (Exp 1) which exhibited a significant and sizeable frequency effect. However, a frequency analysis (admittedly post hoc) of a later experiment (Exp 4) using the same task, but different items and a different subject group who clearly found syntactic categorization more difficult, failed to find a significant effect of frequency, even though they did show a significant frequency effect in a parallel (and apparently easier) semantic categorization task.

[12]Successive processes are said to be in cascade when the later process receives and begins to operate upon information from the earlier before the earlier is complete.

[13]The data described here are from the stress-final words. No frequency effects were obtained for stress-initial words either, but the subjects had seen these words in an earlier experiment during the same session.

[14]Bear in mind that subjects can do the probe task completely accurately without benefit of priming; whether a response retrieved from memory determines the response to a primed item, rather than a response computed from scratch, presumably depends on which process wins the race (cf. Logan, 1988).

ACKNOWLEDGMENTS

This work has been supported by a project grant from the Science and Engineering Research Council (UK). I am grateful to the editors and to Saul Sternberg for their comments on the first draft.

REFERENCES

Allport, D.A. (1985). Distributed memory, modular subsystems and dysphasia. In S. Newman & R. Epstein (Eds.), *Current perspectives in dysphasia.* Edinburgh: Churchill Livingstone.

Balota, D.A., & Chumbley, J.I. (1984). Are lexical decisions a good measure of lexical access? The role of word frequency in the neglected decision stage. *Journal of Experimental Psychology: Human Perception & Performance*, **10**, 340-357.

Balota, D.A., & Chumbley, J.I. (1985). The locus of word-frequency effects in the pronunciation task: lexical access and /or production? *Journal of Memory & Language*, **24**, 89-106.

Becker, C.A. (1976). Allocation of attention during visual word recognition. *Journal of Experimental Psychology: Human Perception & Performance*, **2**, 556-566.

Becker, C.A. (1979). Semantic context and word frequency effects in visual word recognition: an analysis of semantic strategies. *Journal of Experimental Psychology: Human Perception & Performance*, **5**, 252-259.

Becker, C.A. (1980). Semantic context effects in visual word recognition. *Memory & Cognition*, **8**, 493-512.

Bentin, S., & Moscovitch, M. (1988). The time course of repetition effects for words and unfamiliar faces. *Journal of Experimental Psychology: General*, **117**, 148-160.

Besner, D. (1983). Basic decoding components in reading: Two dissociable feature extraction processes. *Canadian Journal of Psychology*, **37**, 429-438.

Besner D., & Swan, M. (1982). Models of lexical access in visual word recognition. *Quarterly Journal of Experimental Psychology*, **34A**, 313-325.

Besner, D., Davelaar, E., Alcott, D, & Parry, P. (1984). Basic processes in reading: evidence from the FDM and the FBI. In L. Henderson (Ed.), *Orthographies and reading*, (pp. 121-135). Hillsdale, NJ: Erlbaum.

Besner D., & McCann R.S. (1987). Word frequency and pattern distortion in visual word identification and production: an examination of four classes of models. In M. Coltheart (Ed.), *Attention and performance XII*. Hove, E. Sussex: Lawrence Erlbaum Associates.

Broadbent, D.E. (1967). Word frequency effect and response bias. *Psychological Review*, **74**, 1-15.

Brown, G.D.A. (1987). Resolving inconsistency: A computational model of word naming. *Journal of Memory & Language*, **26**, 1-23.

Bruder, G.A. (1978). Role of visual familiarity in the word-superiority effects obtained with the simultaneous-matching task. *Journal of Experimental Psychology: Human Perception & Performance*, **4**, 88-100.

Chambers, S.M., & Forster, K.I. (1975). Evidence for lexical access in a simultaneous matching task. *Memory & Cognition*, **3**, 549-559.

Chumbley, J.I., & Balota, D. A. (1984). A word's meaning affects the decision in lexical decision. *Memory & Cognition*, **12**, 590-606.

Coltheart, M. (1985). Cognitive neuropsychology and the study of reading. In M.I. Posner & O.S.M. Marin (Eds.), *Attention and performance XI*. Hillsdale, NJ: Erlbaum.

Coltheart, M., Davelaar, E., Jonasson, J.T., & Besner, D. (1977). Access to the internal lexicon. In S. Dornic, (Ed.), *Attention and performance VI*. London: Academic Press..

DE Groot, A.M.B. (1984). Primed lexical decision: combined effects of the proportion of related prime-target pairs and the stimulus-onset asynchrony of prime and target. *Quarterly Journal of Experimental Psychology*, **36A**, 253-280.

Evett, L.J. & Humphreys, G.W. (1981). The use of abstract graphemic information in lexical access. *Quarterly Journal of Experimental Psychology*, **33**, 325-350.

Feldman, J.A. & Ballard D.H. (1982). Connectionist models and their properties. *Cognitive Science*, **6**, 205-254.

Feldman, L. B. & Moskovljevic, J. (1987). Repetition priming is not purely episodic in origin. *Journal of Experimental Psychology: Learning, Memory & Cognition*, **13**, 573-581.

Feustel, T.C., Shiffrin, R.M., & Salasoo, A. (1983). Episodic and lexical contributions to the repetition effect in word identification. *Journal of Experimental Psychology: General*, **112**, 309-346.

Fodor, J.A., & Pylyshyn, Z.A. (1988). Connectionism and cognitive architecture: a critical analysis. *Cognition*, **28**, 3-71.

Forster, K.I. (1976). Accessing the mental lexicon. In R.J. Wales & E. Walker (Eds.), *New approaches to language mechanisms* . Amsterdam: North-Holland.

Forster, K.I. (1981). Priming and the effects of sentence and lexical contexts on naming time: evidence for autonomous lexical processing. *Quarterly Journal of Experimental Psychology*, **33A**, 465-495.

Forster, K.I. (1985). Lexical acquisition and the modular lexicon. *Language and Cognitive Processes*, **1**, 87-108.

Forster, K.I., & Chambers, S.M. (1973). Lexical access and naming time. *Journal of Verbal Learning & Verbal Behavior*, **12**, 627-635.

Forster, K.I., & Davies, C. (1984). Repetition priming and frequency attentuation in lexical access. *Journal of Experimental Psychology: Learning, Memory & Cognition*, **10**, 680-698.

Frederiksen, J.R., & Kroll, J.F. (1976). Spelling and sound: approaches to the internal lexicon. *Journal of Experimental Psychology: Human Perception & Performance*, **2**, 361-379.

Gernsbacher, M.A. (1984). Resolving 20 years of inconsistent interactions between lexical familiarity and orthography, concreteness, and polysemy. *Journal of Experimental Psychology: General*, **113**, 256-281.

Glanzer, M., & Ehrenreich, S.L. (1979). Lexical access and lexical decision: mechanisms of frequency sensitivity. *Journal of Verbal Learning & Verbal Behavior*, **18**, 381-398.

Glucksberg, S., Kreuz, R.J., & Rho, S.H. (1986). Context can constrain lexical access: implications for models of language comprehension. *Journal of Experimental Psychology: Learning, Memory & Cognition*, **12**, 323-335.

Gordon, B. (1983). Lexical access and lexical decision: mechanisms of frequency sensitivity. *Journal of Verbal Learning & Verbal Behavior*, **22**, 24-44.

Günther, H., Gfroerer, S., & Weiss, L. (1984). Inflection, frequency and the word superiority effect. *Psychological Research*, **46**, 261-281.
Henderson, L. (1980). Is there a lexicality component in the word superiority effect? *Perception & Psychophysics*, **28**, 179-184.
Henderson, L. (1982). *Orthography and word recognition in reading*. London: Academic Press.
Hintzman, D.L. (1969). Recognition time: Effects of recency, frequency, and the spacing of repetitions. *Journal of Experimental Psychology*, **79**, 192-194.
Hockley, W.E. (1982). Retrieval processes in continuous recognition. *Journal of Experimental Psychology: Learning Memory & Cognition*, **8**, 497-512.
Howes, D.W., & Solomon, R.L. (1951). Visual duration threshold as a function of word probability. *Journal of Experimental Psychology*, **41**, 401-410.
Humphreys, G.W., Besner, D, & Quinlan, P.T. (1988). Event perception and the word repetition effect. *Journal of Experimental Psychology: General*, **117**, 51-67.
Inhoff, A.W., & Rayner, K. (1986). Parafoveal word processing during eye fixations in reading: effects of word frequency. *Perception & Psychophysics*, **40**, 431-439.
Jacoby, J.L., & Dallas, M. (1981). On the relationship between autobiographical memory and perceptual learning. *Journal of Experimental Psychology: General*, **3**, 306-340.
Jacoby, J.L., & Witherspoon, D. (1982). Remembering without awareness. *Canadian Journal of Psychology*, **36**, 300-324.
Jacoby, J.L. (1983). Perceptual enhancement: persistent effects of an experience. *Journal of Experimenatal Psychology: Learning, Memory & Cognition*, **9**, 21-38.
Jacoby, J.L., & Brooks, L.R. (1984). Nonanalytic cognition: Memory, perception and concept learning. In G. Bower (Ed.), *The psychology of learning and motivation, Vol 18*. New York: Academic Press.
James, C.T. (1975). The role of semantic information in lexical decisions. *Journal of Experimental Psychology: Human Perception & Performance*, **1**, 130-136.
Jastrzembski, J.E. (1981). Multiple meanings, number of related meanings, frequency of occurrence, and the lexicon. *Cognitive Psychology*, **13**, 278-305.
Jastrzembski, J.E. & Stanners, R.F. (1975). Multiple word meanings and lexical search speed. *Journal of Verbal Learning & Verbal Behavior*, **14**, 534-537.
Johnson-Laird, P.N. (1983). *Mental models*. Cambridge, MA: Harvard University Press.
Johnson-Laird, P.N. (1987). The mental representation of the meaning of words. *Cognition*, **25**, 189-211.
Johnston, J.C. (1978). A test of the sophisticated guessing theory of word perception. *Cognitive Psychology*, **10**, 123-153.
Just, M.A., & Carpenter, P.A. (1980). A theory of reading: from eye fixations to comprehension. *Psychological Review*, **87**, 329-354.
Kliegl, R., Olson, R.K., & Davidson, B.J. (1982). Regression analyses as a tool for studying reading processes: Comment on Just and Carpenter's eye fixation theory. *Memory & Cognition*, **10**, 287-296.
Kucera, H., & Francis, W.N. (1967). *Computational analysis of present-day American English*. Providence, R.I.: Brown University Press.
Landauer, T.K., & Streeter, L.A. (1973). Structural differences between common and rare words: Failures of equivalence assumptions for theories of word recognition. *Journal of Verbal Learning & Verbal Behavior*, **12**, 119-131.
Manelis, L. (1977). Frequency and meaningfulness in tachistoscopic word perception. *American Journal of Psychology*, **99**, 269-280.
Marslen-Wilson, W. (1987). Functional parallelism in spoken word-recognition. *Cognition*, **25**, 71-102.
Massaro, D.W. (1988). Some criticisms of connectionist models of human performance. *Journal of Memory and Language*, **27**, 213-234.
McCann, R.S., & Besner, D. (1987). Reading pseudohomophones: Implications for models of pronunciation assembly and the locus of word frequency effects in naming. *Journal of Experimental Psychology: Human Perception & Performance*, **13**, 13-24.

McCann, R.S., Besner, D., & Davelaar, E. (1988). Word recognition and identification: Do frequency effects reflect lexical access? *Journal of Experimental Psychology: Human Perception & Performance*, **14**, 693-706.
McClelland, J.L. (1979). On the time relations of mental processes: an examinaton of systems of processing in cascade. *Psychological Review* , **86**, 287-330.
McClelland, J.L., & Johnston, J.C. (1977). The role of familiar units in perception of words and nonwords. *Perception & Psychophysics,* **22**, 249-261.
McClelland, J.L., & Rumelhart, D.E. (1981). An interactive activation model of context effects in letter perception: Part 1. An account of basic findings. *Psychological Review,* **88**, 375-407.
McClelland, J.L., & Rumelhart, D.E. (1985). Distributed memory and the representation of general and specific information. *Journal of Experimental Psychology: General,* **114**, 159-188.
McClelland, J.L., Rumelhart, D.E., & the PDP Research Group (1986). *Parallel distributed processing. Explorations in the microstructure of cognition: Volume 2: Psychological and biological Models.* Cambridge, Mass: MIT Press.
McKoon, G. & Ratcliff, R. (1979). Priming in episodic and semantic memory. *Journal of Verbal Learning & Verbal Behavior,* **18**, 463-480.
McLaren, I. P.L., Kaye, H., & Mackintosh, N. J. (1989). An associative theory of the representation of stimuli: applications to perceptual learning and latent inhibition. In R.G.M. Morris (Ed.), *Parallel distributed processing: Implications for psychology and neurobiology.* Oxford: Oxford University Press.
McRae, K., Jared, D., & Seidenberg, M.S. (1990). On the roles of frequency and lexical access in word naming. *Journal of Memory & Language,* **2a**, 43-65.
Meyer, D.E., & Schvaneveldt, R.W. (1976). Meaning, memory structure, and mental processes. *Science,* **192**, 27-33.
Millis, M.L. & Button, S.B. (1989). The effect of polysemy on lexical decision time: Now you see it, now you don't. *Memory & Cognition,* **17**, 141-147.
Minsky, M.L. & Papert, S.A. (1988). *Perceptrons: Expanded edition,* Cambridge, MA: MIT Press.
Monsell, S. (1985). Repetition and the lexicon, In A.W. Ellis (Ed.), *Progress in the psychology of language, Vol 2* . London: Lawrence Erlbaum Associates.
Monsell, S. (1986). Programming of complex sequences: evidence from the timing of rapid speech and other productions. In C. Fromm & H. Heuer (Eds.), *Generation and modualtion of action patterns.* Berlin: Springer.
Monsell, S. (1987a). On the relation between lexical input and output pathways for speech. In A. Allport, D. MacKay, W. Prinz, and E. Scheerer (Eds.), *Language perception and production: relationships between listening, speaking, reading and writing.* London: Academic Press.
Monsell, S. (1987b). Non-visual orthographic processing and the orthographic lexicon. In M. Coltheart (Ed.), *Attention and Performance XII* . London: Lawrence Erlbaum.
Monsell, S., Doyle, M.C., & Haggard, P.N. (1989). The effects of frequency upon visual word recognition: Where are they? *Journal of Experimental Psychology: General,* **118**, 43-71.
Monsell, S., Patterson, K., Tallon, J., & Hill, J. (1989, January). *Voluntary surface dyslexia: A new argument for two processes in oral reading.* Paper presented at a meeting of the Experimental Psychology Society, London, England.
Morton, J. (1969). The interaction of information in word recognition. *Psychological Review,* **76**, 340-354.
Norris, D.G. (1984a). The effects of frequency, repetition and stimulus quality in visual word recognition. *Quarterly Journal of Experimental Psychology,* **36A**, 507-518.
Norris, D.G. (1984b). The mispriming effect: Evidence of an orthographic check in the lexical decision task. *Memory & Cognition,* **12**, 470-476.
Norris, D. (1986). Word recognition: context effects without priming. *Cognition,* **22**, 93-136.
Okada, R. (1971). Decision latencies in short-term recognition memory. *Journal of Experimental Psychology,* **90**, 27-32.

Oldfield, R.C., & Wingfield, A. (1965). Response latencies in naming objects. *Quarterly Journal of Experimental Psychology*, **17**, 273-281.

Paap, K.R., McDonald, J.E., Schvaneveldt, R.W. & Noel, R.W. (1987). Frequency and pronounceability in visually presented naming and lexical decision tasks. In M. Coltheart (Ed.), *Attention and performance XII*. Hove, E. Sussex: Lawrence Erlbaum Associates.

Paap, K.R. & Newsome, S.L. (1980). A perceptual-confusion account of the WSE in the target search paradigm. *Perception & Psychophysics*, **27**, 444-456.

Paap, K.R., Newsome, S.L., McDonald, J.E. & Schvaneveldt, R.W. (1982). An activation-verification model for letter and word recognition. *Psychological Review*, **89**, 573-594.

Patterson, K.E. & Coltheart, V. (1987). Phonological processes in reading. In M. Coltheart (Ed.), *Attention and performance XII*. Hove, E. Sussex: Lawrence Erlbaum Associates.

Patterson, K.E., Seidenberg, M.S., & McClelland, J.L. (1989). Connections and disconnections: acquired dyslexia in a computational model of reading processes. In R.G.M. Morris (Ed.), *Parallel distributed processing: Implications for psychology and neurobiology*. Oxford: Oxford University Press.

Pinker, S., & Prince, A. (1988). On language and connectionism: Analysis of a parallel distributed processing model of language acquisition. *Cognition*, **28**, 73-193.

Ratcliff, R., Hockley, W., & McKoon, G. (1985). Components of activation: Repetition and priming effects in lexical decision and recognition. *Journal of Experimental Psychology: General*, **114**, 435-450.

Rayner, K. (1977). Visual attention in reading: Eye movements reflect cognitive processes. *Memory and Cognition*, **4**, 443-448.

Rayner K., & Duffy S.A. (1986). Lexical complexity and fixation times in reading: effects of word frequency, verb complexity, and lexical ambiguity. *Memory & Cognition*, **14**, 191-201.

Reicher, G.M. (1969). Perceptual recognition as a function of meaningfulness of stimulus material. *Journal of Experimental Psychology*, **81**, 274-280.

Rips, L.J., Shoben, E.J., & Smith E.E. (1973). Semantic distance and the verification of semantic relations. *Journal of Verbal Learning & Verbal Behavior*, **12**, 1-20.

Rosenberg, C.R. & Sejnowski, T.J. (1986). The spacing effect on NETTALK, a massively parallel network. Proceedings of the Eighth Annual Conference of the Cognitive Science Society, Amherst, MA, August, 1986.

Rubenstein, H., Garfield, L., & Millikan, J.A. (1970). Homographic entries in the internal lexicon. *Journal of Verbal Learning & Verbal Behavior*, **9**, 487-494.

Rumelhart, D.E. & McClelland, J.L. (1986). On learning the past tense of English verbs. In J. L. McClelland, D. E. Rumelhart, & the PDP Research Group (Eds.), *Parallel distributed processing: Explorations in the microstructure of cognition, Vol 2: Psychological and biological models*. Cambridge, MA: MIT Press.

Savage, G.R., Bradley, D.C., & Forster, K.I. (1989). *Word frequency and the pronunciation task: The contribution of articulatory fluency*. Manuscript submitted for publication.

Scarborough, D. L., Cortese. C, & Scarborough, H. L. (1977). Frequency and repetition effects in lexical memory. *Journal of Experimental Psychology: Human Perception & Performance*, **3**, 1-17.

Schvaneveldt, R.W., & McDonald, J.E. (1981). Semantic context and the encoding of words: evidence for two models of stimulus analysis. *Journal of Experimental Psychology: Human Percpetion and Performance*, **7**, 673-687.

Seidenberg, M.S. (1985a). The time course of information activation and utilization in visual word recognition. In D. Besner, T.G. Waller & G.E. MacKinnon (Eds.), *Reading research: Advances in theory and practice, Vol 5*. Academic Press, Orlando, FL.

Seidenberg, M.S. (1985b). Constraining models of visual word recognition. *Cognition*, **20**, 169-190.

Seidenberg, M.S. (1989). Visual word recognition and pronunciation: a computational model and its implications. In Marslen-Wilson, W. (Ed.), *Lexical representation and process*. Cambridge, MA: MIT Press.

Seidenberg, M.S. & McClelland, J.L. (1989). A distributed, developmental model of word recognition and naming. *Psychological Review*.

Seidenberg, M. S., Waters, G.S., Barnes, M.A., & Tanenhaus, M.K. (1984). When does irregular spelling or pronunciation influence word recognition? *Journal of Verbal Learning & Verbal Behavior*, **23**, 383-404.
Sejnowski, T.J. & Rosenberg, C.R. (1986). *NETtalk; A parallel network that learns to read aloud.* Report #13 of the Cognitive Neuropsychology Laboratory, The Johns Hopkins University. [Reprinted in J.A. Anderson & E. Rosenfield (Eds, 1988), *Neurocomputing* . Cambridge, MA: MIT Press.]
Selfridge, O.G., & Neisser, U. (1960). Pattern recognition by machine. *Scientific American*, **203** (Aug), 60-68.
Shallice, T., & McCarthy, R. (1985). Phonological reading: from patterns of impairment to possible procedures. In K.E. Patterson, J.C. Marshall, & M. Coltheart (Eds.), *Surface dyslexia: Neuropsychological and cognitive studies of phonological reading*. London: Lawrence Erlbaum Associates.
Sternberg, S. (1969). The discovery of processing stages: extensions of Donders' method. In W.G. Koster (Ed.), *Attention and performance II*. Amsterdam: North-Holland.
Sternberg, S., Monsell, S., Knoll, R. L., & Wright, C.E. (1978). The latency and duration of rapid movement sequences: comparisons of speech and typewriting. In G.E. Stelmach (Ed.), *Information processing in motor control and learning*. New York: Academic Press.
Sternberg, S., Wright, C.E., Knoll, R. L., & Monsell, S. (1980). Motor programs in rapid speech: Additional evidence. In R. A. Cole (Ed.), *The perception and production of fluent speech*, (pp. 507-534). Hillsdale, NJ: Lawrence Erlbaum Associates.
Taft, M. (1979). Lexical access via an orthographic code: The Basic Orthographic Syllable Structure. *Journal of Verbal Learning & Verbal Behavior*, **18**, 21-39.
Taraban, R., & McClelland, J.L. (1987). Conspiracy effects in word pronunciation. *Journal of Memory & Language*, **25**, 608-631.
Treisman, A.M. (1964). Monitoring and storage of irrelevant messages in selective attention. *Journal of Verbal Learning & Verbal Behaviour*, **3**, 449-459.
Waters, G.S., & Seidenberg, M.S. (1985). Spelling-sound effects in reading: Time course and decision criteria. *Memory & Cognition*, **13**, 557-572.
Whaley, C.P. (1978). Word-nonword classification time. *Journal of Verbal Learning & Verbal Behavior*, **17**, 143-154.
Wingfield, A. (1968). Effects of frequency on identification and naming of objects. *American Journal of Psychology*, **81** , 226-234.

7

WORD RECOGNITION PROCESSES IN FOVEAL AND PARAFOVEAL VISION: THE RANGE OF INFLUENCE OF LEXICAL VARIABLES

DAVID A. BALOTA

Department of Psychology
Washington University
Missouri, USA

KEITH RAYNER

Department of Psychology
University of Massachusetts
Massachusetts, USA

In this chapter, we will review research addressing the influence of lexical variables in foveal and parafoveal vision. Clearly, this topic has relevance to a number of distinct issues in cognitive psychology. First, some of this research is relevant to the long-standing and controversial debate concerning conscious and unconscious semantic processing (see Holender, 1986, and the accompanying commentaries). Second, this research provides important information about how much (and what type of) information an individual can utilize when fixated at a particular location. Obviously, any model of visual word recognition must cope with the constraints imposed by varying levels of information utilization as a function of retinal eccentricity. Third, and most importantly, the utilization of parafoveal information is highly relevant to models of reading. Consider a reader fixated at a particular location in text. The reader has a clear and sharp visual representation for the foveal information, but how much and what types of information can the reader utilize to the right or left of fixation in parafoveal vision? As we will see, there are considerable differences across the different models of reading regarding this issue.

The organization of this chapter is as follows: First, a simple operationalization of the terms "foveal" and "parafoveal" will be presented. Second a brief description of the methods used to address the influence of parafoveal information will be presented. Third, some current views concerning how parafoveal information is used in reading will be discussed, especially noting the different levels of emphasis on parafoveal vs... foveal information. Fourth, research addressing foveal and parafoveal information processing will be reviewed, especially noting the similarities and differences across foveal and parafoveal effects. Fifth, an interactive threshold model of parafoveal information utilization will be outlined. Finally, implications of the reviewed literature for both models of reading and visual attentional mechanisms will be discussed.

I. FOVEA VS. PARAFOVEA: A DEFINITION

In this review, letter spaces falling within the central two degrees of vision will be considered *foveal* information. Letter spaces beyond the foveal region out to five degrees to the left of fixation will be considered *parafoveal* information. Finally, letter spaces outside five degrees from fixation will be referred to as *peripheral* information. In normal reading situations, three or four letter spaces subtend one degree of visual angle (depending upon the size of the print). For the sake of illustration, consider print in which three letters equal one degree of visual angle. In this case, the fovea would include approximately six letter spaces around fixation, with the parafovea including the next twelve letter spaces both to the left and right of the fovea, and finally, the periphory would include any information beyond fifteen letter spaces from fixation.

It is worth noting here that the discrimination among the fovea, parafovea, and periphery is not simply a convenient labelling system referring to distance from central fixation, but rather, is based on the physiological structure of the retina. The relative density of rods and cones varies across these categories (Rayner & Pollatsek, 1989). As expected, one finds a concomitant decrease in acuity across these different categories. This shift in acuity places limits on the degree of parafoveal information utilization, and could potentially influence the strategies a reader might use in dealing with such parafoveal information. For example, because of these acuity limitations, one might ask how much a reader will rely on degraded parafoveal information? We shall now turn to the methods used to address such questions.

II. METHODS OF ANALYSIS

There have been a number of experimental techniques used to investigate the impact of parafoveal information. One approach is to measure a response to a foveal stimulus when a parafoveal stimulus is simultaneously presented (e.g., Bradshaw; 1974: Stanovich & West, 1983a). In most of these experiments, the stimuli are presented so quickly that there is little opportunity for an eye-movement. Although in most cases it is reasonable to assume that the subject is fixated at the appropriate location, it should be noted that such studies typically do not involve eye-tracking systems to insure the actual location of fixation.

The more recent experiments addressing the utilization of parafoveal information have relied upon rather sophisticated eye movement monitoring equipment and a technique known as the *eye-contingent display change* technique. There are a number of variations of this technique, but the basic principle is that, contingent upon the subject's eye-movements, changes are made in the text as the subject is reading. Because we will rely quite heavily on data from such studies, at various points in this chapter, we will briefly describe two of the major variations of this technique that were developed by McConkie and Rayner (1975) and Rayner (1975).

In the *moving window paradigm*, subjects read text on a cathode ray tube (CRT) while their eyes are monitored. Thus, subjects move their eyes as they normally do in reading, but the amount of information available for processing on each fixation is controlled by the experimenter. Within an experimenter defined "window" region, normal text is available for the reader to process. However, the text outside of the window is distorted in some way. For example, all letters outside the window might be replaced by dissimilar letters or by Xs.

When the reader moves from one position in the text to another, the window of available information moves with the eyes. Figure 1 shows an example of a moving window. The question addressed in such studies is the extent to which reading performance decreases as the window size decreases. Obviously, if subjects do not use parafoveal information then one would expect little breakdown in reading performance when parafoveal information is outside the reading window. However, McConkie and Rayner (1975) found with this technique that parafoveal and peripheral information is acquired out to about 15 character spaces to the right of fixation (also see DenBuurman, Boersma, & Gerrissen, 1981; Rayner & Bertera, 1979, Rayner, Inhoff, Morrison, Slowiaczek, & Bertera, 1981).[1]

A second variation of the eye contingent display change technique is the *boundary technique* (Rayner, 1975). In this situation, readers again read text as their eye movements are monitored. However, rather than a display change occurring with each eye movement, only a single display change occurs in association with a given target word location in the text. Figure 1 shows an example of the boundary technique in which a word (or nonword) initially presented in the text is replaced by a target word when the reader's eyes cross over an invisible boundary location. By examining how long a reader fixates on the target word as a function of the relationship between the initially displayed parafoveal word and the target word, inferences can be made about the type of information acquired different distances from fixation.

III. THE PARAFOVEA IN READING: A RANGE OF VIEWS

There are a wide range of views concerning how parafoveal information is used in reading. These range from views emphasizing rather deep meaning analyses of parafoveal information to views emphasizing that the only useful information obtained from parafoveal vision is primarily word-length information. First, on the deep end, there is the view that parafoveal words are semantically preprocessed and that this level of preprocessing influences where and how long a reader will fixate (Hyona, Niemi, & Underwood, 1989; Underwood, 1980, 1981; Underwood, Bloomfield, & Clews, 1988; Underwood, Clews, & Everett, 1989). We should note here that this view is somewhat consistent with a class of "hypothesis testing" or "guessing game" models that place considerable emphasis on anticipating the parafoveal word on the current fixation (Goodman 1967; Haber, 1978; Hochberg, 1970; Levin & Kaplan, 1970, Smith, 1971). According to these models, the reader makes guesses about the parafoveal word based on both partial parafoveal information and the earlier available context. Based on these sources of information, the reader generates a hypothesis about the to-be-fixated word. The reader then moves his/her eyes to the next location, quickly confirms the hypothesis, and begins the process over again by generating a hypothesis about the new parafoveal information. Thus, these models suggest that the reader at some level attempts to identify the parafoveal word before actually fixating on that word. A second view concerning the use of parafoveal information in reading is that super-letter access processes take place parafoveally. In this view, the first syllable or morpheme can be used to initiate lexical access of parafoveal words (Inhoff, 1987). A third

Normal Text

The fluent processing of words during silent reading

13-Character Window (spaces filled)

xxxxxxxxxxxprocessing ofxxxxxxxxxxxxxxxxxxxxxxxxxxxx
F

xxxxxxxxxxxxxxxxxssing of wordxxxxxxxxxxxxxxxxxxxxxxx
F

13-Character Window (spaces preserved)

xxx xxxxxx processing of xxxxx xxxxxx xxxxxx xxxxxxx
F

xxx xxxxxx xxxxxssing of wordx xxxxxx xxxxxx xxxxxxx
F

Boundary Technique

The fluent processing of green during silent reading
F

The fluent processing of words during silent reading
F

Fig. 1. Examples of eye-contingent display techniques used to study the processing of parafoveal information. The top example displays a normal segment of text. The second and third examples display 2 fixations using the moving window paradigm: In this example the window size is 13 character spaces. The fourth example displays the boundary technique. Here, during the reader's saccade, the target word (words) replaces the initially presented stimulus (green). In each of the examples the dot indicates where the eyes are currently fixated.

view is that primarily letter-level information is obtained parafoveally, and this information influences access processes at an abstract letter-code level (Rayner & Pollatsek, 1989). Finally, there is the view that only identified parafoveal word information actually influences reading processes (McConkie, Zola, Blanchard, & Wolverton, 1982). Thus, parafoveal words, unless identified and in most cases directly fixated, have very little impact on reading performance. According to this latter view, parafoveal word length information is used to determine where to look next, but not to aid word identification.

We shall now turn to the empirical data that hopefully helps discriminate between these different approaches. In this discussion, a comparison between foveal and parafoveal priming effects will be made. In each section, the literature concerning foveal effects will be first reviewed, followed by the literature concerning parafoveal effects. The brief description of foveal influences of lexical variables will provide a frame for discussing the impact of such variables in parafoveal vision.

Most of these studies involve various types of priming tasks. The priming paradigm involves the presentation of two stimuli with the subject's task being to respond to one of the stimuli and the relationship between the two stimuli is manipulated. The notion is that if the codes/representations needed for processing the target stimulus are influenced by the prime stimulus, then this should be reflected in changes in performance on the target.

1. Orthographic Priming

It seems safe to assume that orthographic information is somehow used in visual word recognition. However, it turns out that specifying the manner in which orthographic information plays a role in word recognition is not so simple. Moreover, as noted above, there are varying views concerning the influence of orthographic information in parafoveal vision.

1.1. Foveal Studies

Evett and Humphreys (1981) used a four-field masking procedure to address orthographic foveal priming. On each trial, a pattern mask both preceded and followed the presentation of two briefly presented letter strings. The two letter strings varied in terms of orthographic, phonological, or semantic relatedness. Here, we will emphasize the orthographic manipulations. The subjects' task was to identify any of the words that were presented. There are five aspects of Evett and Humphreys' data that are noteworthy. First, subjects were better at identifying the second letter string when it shared letters with the first letter string. Second, this effect apparently occurred because of letter code information instead of simple energy summation because the effect occurred across letter case. That is, the prime letter strings were presented in lower case and the target letter strings were presented in upper case. Third, the authors provided evidence that the similarity in the visual characteristics of the letters (contour and featural overlap) did not appear to modulate the effect. Fourth, the orthographic priming effect occurred when the prime items were nonwords. Thus, the effect did not require lexical-level information. Fifth, the effect was on early visual analyses, apparently subconscious processes, because subjects were very poor at identifying the prime items. Identification of the primes was less than 1.5% across the experiments. Based on these results, Evett and Humphreys argued that the primes automatically activated orthographic abstract letter codes needed for word identification.

Humphreys, Evett, Quinlan, and Besner (1987) have recently replicated the masked orthographic priming effect and eliminated the possibility that the effect was simply due to an increase in errors in the orthographically unrelated condition. That is, it is possible that in the orthographically unrelated condition, subjects were more likely to transpose letters between words. However, an analysis of the error patterns indicated that simple transposition of letters in the unrelated condition could not account for the masked orthographic priming effect. In addition, Humphreys et al. found qualitative differences between orthographic priming when the primes could be identified and when the primes could not be identified. When the primes could be identified, same identity primes (e.g., *lost-LOST*) facilitated identification, compared to both orthographically related (e.g., *list-LOST*) and unrelated (e.g., *tame-LOST*) primes, with no difference between the latter two conditions. However, when the primes could *not* be identified there was clear priming for both identity and orthographically related primes, compared to the unrelated condition, thereby replicating the Evett and Humphreys' (1981) original finding.

Humphreys et al. suggest that because such effects occurred at threshold levels of prime identification, orthographic priming effects involve the early processing of letter strings. Presumably, the primes initiate the production of an abstract orthographic description of the letter string. Primes that are consistent with the target's orthographic description will reinforce that description, whereas, primes that are unrelated will produce different descriptions. Such different orthographic descriptions could have the effect of competing for an orthographic description of the target, thereby lowering target identification.

Before leaving this area, it is important to note our first, and definitely not our last, caveat in the literature. Forster (1987) and Forster and Davies (1984) have failed to find orthographic priming effects from masked primes in a speeded lexical decision task. Thus, when one switches the task from identification to lexical decision performance, it appears that the orthographic priming effect is lost. In this same light, it should be noted that Manso de Zuniga, Quinlan, and Humphreys (1987), have reported orthographic masked priming effects in a pronunciation task. Our preference is to agree with Humphreys et al. that the failure to find the orthographic priming effect in the lexical decision task may be due to the decision component involved in the lexical decision task (e.g., Balota & Chumbley, 1984; Besner, 1983). Finally, our confidence in orthographic priming effects is increased by similar patterns of data in parafoveal priming studies.

1.2. Parafoveal Orthographic Priming

The studies indicating that there are foveal orthographic priming effects when subjects are apparently unaware of the primes might lead one to speculate that there may also be such effects from the parafovea across saccades. In some ways the situation is similar to the masked foveal priming situation. That is, on fixation *n* the reader has parafoveal information available that will come into the fovea on fixation *n* +1. Thus, subjects are receiving a prime from the parafovea for the next fixated target stimulus. Moreover, the saccade between fixations might produce a masking stimulus just as in foveal masked priming studies, reviewed above.

However, there are obvious differences between foveal and parafoveal orthographic priming situations. The major being the retinal location of the stimuli. Humphreys et al. suggest that their effects are due to the construction of an orthographic representation of the stimulus that holds positional information. It is possible that their effects are intimately tied to the translation of retinal positional information to orthographic positional information. If this were the case, then one might not expect parafoveal orthographic priming because the prime on fixation *n* is at a different retinal location than the target on fixation *n* +1.

It is, of course, possible that a more central buffer could integrate visual information across saccades. If this were the case then the importance of retinal location might be less crucial. In fact, some early research on this topic supported the existence of something akin to a purely visual buffer (Jonides, Irwin, & Yantis, 1982; McConkie & Rayner, 1976; Rayner, 1978;). However, although the notion is tantalizing, the more recent research indicates that there is little evidence for such a buffer (Jonides, Irwin, & Yantis, 1983; Irwin, Yantis, & Jonides, 1983; Rayner, McConkie, & Ehrlich, 1978; Rayner, McConkie, & Zola, 1980; Rayner & Pollatsek, 1983). Thus, any influence of parafoveal orthographic information must not be on processes that are tied to a purely visual integrative buffer nor to processes tied to specific retinal locations. In this way, such parafoveal orthographic priming effects may provide important insight into the mechanism(s) underlying the impact of orthographic information.

McConkie and Zola (1979) provided support for the notion that parafoveal orthographic information has an impact on reading performance. In their study, subjects read passages that alternated case across adjacent letters. Furthermore, across fixations, the cases changed from lower to upper case and vice versa. For example, "The cat chased the dog," might be displayed as "ThE cAt ChAsEd ThE dOg." on fixation *n* and "tHe CaT cHaSeD tHe DoG." on fixation *n* +1, and so on. The interesting result was that subjects read as quickly with the characters alternating across fixations as they read when the characters did not switch across fixations. If subjects were using parafoveal information, as the moving window experiments cited earlier clearly suggest, it appears that switching the case of that parafoveal information does not influence reading performance. Thus, these results suggest that the information used from the parafovea is at the abstract letter level, i.e., the parafoveal information is neither tied to visual form nor case.

Research by Rayner et al.(1980) provides some of the clearest evidence of parafoveal orthographic priming. In this research, a word was presented to the subject's parafovea and during the saccade was replaced by a target word that the subject pronounced aloud. Rayner et al. varied the orthographic relationship between the preview string and the to-be-pronounced target. The results indicated that pronunciation latency to the target decreased with increasing orthographic similarity between the preview item and the target. In particular, if the first two or three letters in the initial parafoveal stimulus and the target word were identical, facilitation occurred. It is noteworthy that there was relatively little facilitation when the last two or three letters of the target occurred in the parafoveal preview. The Rayner et al. study also provided evidence that the parafoveal orthographic priming effect depended upon how far into the parafovea the stimuli occurred, i.e., there was more facilitation at 3 degrees than at 5 degrees. Finally, and most importantly, Rayner et al. found that there was as much parafoveal orthographic priming in conditions where the case changed between the parafoveal preview and the target item, compared to conditions where case did not change. Thus, this is a "true" orthographic priming effect that reflects abstract letter code information instead of visually based information.

More recently, Inhoff (1989a) demonstrated that a parafoveal orthographic priming effect can also be produced by letters at the end of a word that provide a parafoveal preview. In this study, Inhoff found that word-initial and word-final trigrams produced parafoveal facilitation when the remaining letters of the word were replaced by Xs. (It is worth noting that the word final previews did produce smaller parafoveal preview effects than the word initial previews in this condition.) However, when the remaining letters were replaced by dissimilar letters, preview benefits were obtained only from conditions where the beginning letters were available in the parafovea. Thus, it appears that word-final letters can produce a parafoveal preview effect when these letters are made distinct by flanking them to the left with Xs. Interestingly, Inhoff also found that the saccades were longer when the whole word preview was available compared to a no preview control condition. Hence, not only does the parafoveal information influence access processes for a lexical representation, such information also can influence the subsequent saccade. We shall return to the relationship between parafoveal information and saccade length below.

It is important to note that there has been some controversy in the literature regarding the parafoveal orthographic priming effect. For example, McConkie, Zola, Blanchard, and Wolverton (1982) reported results that appeared to question the use of parafoveal orthographic information during reading. In this research, short texts were constructed such that four different words could potentially fit within a sentence context. These words differed in their initial and/or fourth letter positions (e.g., *weedy, weepy, seedy, seepy*). In the visually dissimilar condition, two of the words alternated across successive conditions. For example, *weedy* changed to *seepy* and *seepy* changed to *weedy* on successive fixations. The notion is that if subjects use parafoveal information then this alternating condition should produce longer fixations than a control condition in which there were no display changes. Although the alternating conditions did slow single fixations on the target by 12.5 ms, this difference did not reach significance. In addition, McConkie et al. found that subjects' later recognition memory for the words was uninfluenced by the parafoveal information that they received on subsequent fixations and was primarily dependent upon the words that they had actually fixated. Based on this overall pattern of data, McConkie et al. argued that readers only process (in any meaningful fashion) the words they directly fixate.

We feel that there are a number of problems with McConkie et al.'s (1982) acceptance of the null hypothesis. These are elaborated in Balota, Pollatsek, and Rayner (1985) and so we will simply list these concerns here. First, with respect to the episodic recognition memory results, these data are not conclusive because primes can have an impact on word recognition processes without influencing later episodic memory performance (Balota, 1983). Second, the size of the effect in the McConkie et al. study on the single fixation duration data was comparable to a highly significant effect reported by Balota et al. The major difference across these studies is that in the Balota et al. study there was more than 3 times the number of observations reported by McConkie et al. Third, the target stimuli in the McConkie et al. study were relatively low in frequency of occurrence and were relatively unconstrained by the preceding sentence context. As described below, constraint can influence the degree of parafoveal priming. In fact, when viewed in this light, the small effects reported by McConkie et al. could be viewed as more consistent than inconsistent with the research demonstrating parafoveal orthographic priming effects.

2. Contextual Constraint and Stimulus Degradation

Because of acuity limitations, one might consider parafoveal information as similar to degraded foveal information. If this were the case, then it might be useful to compare the research addressing foveal stimulus degradation and its interaction with other variables to the research addressing parafoveal stimulus presentation and its interactions with the same variables. One such variable that has received a considerable amount of attention in both the foveal and parafoveal literature is contextual constraint. The original research involved foveal priming and addressed whether semantic prime relatedness has additive or interactive effects with stimulus degradation. Through the use of Sternberg's (1969) additive factors logic, it was hoped that this research might provide information regarding the stage(s) that the prime context exerted its influence (see Meyer, Schvaneveldt, & Ruddy, 1975). More recently, as described below, similar questions have been asked regarding the impact of context on the utilization of parafoveal information.

2.1 Foveal Priming

The research on single word foveal priming is quite clear. Across a wide variety of tasks and stimulus degradation manipulations, subjects produce larger priming effects when the stimuli are degraded compared to when they are not degraded (e.g., Becker & Killion, 1977; Massaro, Jones, Lipscomb, & Scholz, 1978; Meyer et al., 1975). Although the early research on sentence context effects and degradation produced some inconsistencies (e.g., compare Schuberth, Spoehr, & Lane, 1981, with Stanovich & West, 1979), the more recent research by Stanovich and West (1983b) suggests that the previous failures to find context by degradation interactions were, in part, due to the lack of a strong degradation manipulation. Stanovich and West consistently produced such an interaction in their experiments, and provided information about the underlying nature of the interaction by teasing apart facilitation and inhibition effects. Moreover, Stanovich and West demonstrated that the pattern of facilitation and inhibition effects can be modulated by the type of degradation manipulation (i.e., degradation via the insertion of asterisks between letters vs. degradation via decreases in clarity of the letters). The important point for the present discussion is that there is strong evidence from the foveal priming studies that there are larger context effects for degraded stimuli than nondegraded stimuli.

2.2. Parafoveal Priming Studies

Interestingly, the research addressing context and parafoveal priming developed out of a concern with the early Rayner et al. studies on the integration of orthographic information across saccades (e.g., Rayner, 1978; Rayner et al., 1978; 1980). Both McClelland and O'Regan (1981) and Paap and Newsome (1981) pointed out that in the earlier Rayner et al. studies, a rather small set of stimuli were used and these stimuli were repeated within a given experimental session. Thus, it was possible that some of the parafoveal orthographic priming effects may have been due to subjects building up an expectancy that certain stimuli would appear in the parafovea, thereby facilitating their use of that parafoveal information. In fact, both McClelland and O'Regan and Paap and Newsome argued that when subjects have no expectancy regarding the parafoveal information, there is no impact of that information.

First, let us address the possibility that there are no parafoveal orthographic priming effects without constraining context. Although detailed reservations about this argument can be found elsewhere in the literature (e.g., Balota & Rayner, 1983; Rayner & Slowiaczek, 1981), it is sufficient here to simply note three points. First, in a control experiment, Paap and Newsome did not find orthographic priming effects with their stimuli in foveal vision. Therefore, it is unlikely that such effects would be found in the parafovea. Interestingly, the Paap and Newsome study involved a lexical decision task, and therefore, is consistent with our earlier arguments concerning Forster's failure to find orthographic priming effects in foveal lexical decision performance. Second, both McClelland and O'Regan and Paap and Newsome's arguments about no parafoveal priming effects rely on the notion of an appropriate neutral prime condition. Clearly, there are concerns in the literature regarding the nature of a true "neutral baseline" (DE Groot, Thomassen, & Hudson, 1982; Jonides & Mack, 1984; Rayner & Slowiaczek, 1981).

Third, and the most serious difficulty with the argument that context totally modulates the use of parafoveal orthographic information, are the results of a study by Balota and Rayner (1983). In this study, the total pool of target words was increased to 512 in an attempt to minimize the likelihood that subjects could generate an expectancy for the parafoveal items. The results from two experiments indicated that even when no context is provided subjects benefitted considerably from orthographically related previews compared to unrelated previews. Thus, although context may indeed influence the utilization of parafoveal information, the results from Balota and Rayner's study clearly indicate that the availability of related context is not a necessary condition for the utilization of parafoveal information.

Balota and Rayner also addressed whether there are interactive effects between parafoveal orthographic information and contextual constraint, as both McClelland and O'Regan and Paap and Newsome suggested. On each, in the Balota and Rayner study, subjects were presented a foveal word (e.g., *reptile*) along with an initial parafoveal preview item (e.g., *snckks*). The subject's task was to pronounce the parafoveal item as quickly as possible. During the eye-movement to the parafoveal item, the parafoveal preview was replaced by a word that was either (a) semantically related to the foveal word and visually related to the parafoveal preview (e.g., *snakes*), (b) semantically unrelated to the foveal word and visually related to the parafoveal preview (e.g., *sneaks*), (c) semantically related to the foveal word and visually unrelated to the parafoveal preview (e.g., *lizard*), or (d) semantically unrelated to the foveal word and visually unrelated to the parafoveal preview (e.g., *limits*). The results indicated that when subjects only had 250 ms to use the semantic context (Experiment 1), there were additive effects of semantic context and parafoveal preview; however, when subjects were given 1250 ms to use the semantic context (Experiment 2), there were interactive effects of semantic context and parafoveal preview. Thus, when subjects are given sufficient time to generate expectancies concerning the parafoveal preview there are interactive effects between context and parafoveal information. We now have three studies yielding interactive effects of contextual constraint and parafoveal visual information (Balota & Rayner, 1983; McClelland & O'Regan, 1981; Paap & Newsome, 1981).

Balota and Chumbley (1985) attempted to extend the earlier Balota and Rayner (1983) study to determine if additive or interactive effects of contextual constraint and parafoveal orthographic information will be found in a more natural reading situation. Subjects were presented sentences such as: "Since the wedding was today, the baker rushed the wedding ____ to the reception." At the critical target location (as indicated by the underlined area), subjects either received a high-predictable word (cake) or a low-predictable word (pies). This manipulation was factorially crossed with the visual similarity of the parafoveal preview that was presented before the subject fixated on the critical area. This was accomplished via the invisible boundary technique described above. In the present example, the eyes had to cross the letter "n" in wedding before the target was displayed, thereby replacing the initially displayed parafoveal word or letter string. The results yielded two patterns that indicated that contextual constraint influenced the use of parafoveal orthographic information. First, subjects were more likely to skip the target area when the parafoveal preview was visually consistent with the high-predictable word compared to when it was consistent with the low-predictable word. Second, there was a significant interaction between parafoveal preview and predictability in the gaze duration data. (Gaze duration refers to the total time spent fixating the target word before making a saccade to another word.) This interaction indicated that there was a larger parafoveal priming effect for the high-predictable words compared to the low-predictable words, precisely as the earlier studies indicated.

The results reviewed in this section appear to be rather straightforward. Both the foveal and the parafoveal priming studies clearly provide evidence that contextual constraint has different effects on degraded and nondegraded stimulus presentation. Although we will return to this pattern later, it is important to note a potential dilemma. It appears that the interactions are of a different nature in foveal and parafoveal priming studies. In the foveal priming studies, context has a greater impact for degraded stimuli than nondegraded stimuli. In the parafoveal priming studies, context has a greater impact when the parafoveal visual information is in some sense not degraded, i.e., when it is visually consistent with the to-be-fixated target.

One major difference in the foveal and parafoveal priming studies that may help to resolve this dilemma is the subject's response requirements. In the foveal priming studies, subjects are forced to make a response to a degraded stimulus. Thus, any contextual constraint might prove especially helpful in identifying the stimulus. However, in the parafoveal studies, the subjects do not make a direct response to the degraded parafoveal item. For example, in the Balota et al. study, the subjects always received a clear and sharp presentation of the target in 200-250 ms, i.e., when they moved their eyes to the target word. Thus, there was no need to rely on context to "force" a response. In this light, the potential dilemma may be resolved by assuming that in the foveal studies, the target is degraded and subjects use context to help identify the stimulus, whereas, in the parafoveal studies, there is no forced reliance on context (i.e., no need to guess based on partial information) because the parafoveal stimulus will soon receive a very sharp and clear fixation.

Of course, the above discussion does not specify the underlying mechanism(s) producing the context by parafoveal information superadditive interaction. We believe this superadditive interaction is due to lexical-level representations that are receiving top-down information from preceding context along with bottom-up parafoveal orthographic information. The superadditive influence of these two variables suggests both the role of (a) interactive thresholds and (b) interlexical inhibitory processes. With respect to the notion of interactive thresholds, we are simply suggesting that when activation reaches a specific level at a logogen (Morton, 1969), there is a qualitatively different impact on performance. For example, one might assume that there is a level of activation that is sufficient to engage attentional resources. This would be quite consistent with the impact of SOA across the two experiments in the Balota and Rayner (1983) study described above.

With respect to the notion of interlexical inhibitory processes, we are simply suggesting that when a given lexical representation begins to accumulate activation, it will also inhibit the activation of related lexical representations within a given domain. For example, if the word "pastry" is presented as semantic context, then all members of that category will become at least partially activated and serve to mutually inhibit each other. Such a mutual inhibition mechanism might produce a situation where there is little net activation for any given member within the general category. Likewise, with respect to parafoveal activation, a subject may pick up "ca" from the parafovea and this might partially activate many different lexical candidates. However, because "ca" activates many candidates, there is considerable mutual inhibition from these partially activated candidates such that there is relatively little facilitation for any single member that is consistent with "ca". These are examples concerning how partial activation of lexical representations might produce little net facilitation. However, in some cases either contextual constraint or parafoveal information may be sufficient to allow one lexical representation to dominate. For example, if the context specifies a relatively unique response such as *cat* to *dog* then the lexical representation for *cat* may dominate the relatively lower levels of interlexical inhibition produced by other possible candidates. This would produce a net facilitation effect for *cat*. Likewise, with respect to parafoveal activation, if *cak* is available from the parafovea, then this may be sufficient for the lexical representation cake to dominate the inhibition from related neighbors, and therefore, produce facilitation. The important point here is that the scope and strength of the activation pattern is crucial in predicting whether one will find any net facilitation.

This framework nicely accounts for the superadditive effects of context and parafoveal information. First, consider the possibility that on some trials contextual constraint (e.g., pastry), by itself, may not be sufficient to surpass the interactive threshold and influence performance. As noted, although contextual constraint may produce some activation, it may activate a number of consistent logogens, and these may mutually inhibit each other such that there is little net impact on performance. Likewise, on some trails, the influence of parafoveal activation (e.g., *ca*), by itself, may not be sufficient to surpass the interactive threshold. Again, parafoveal information may produce some activation for a number of visually consistent logogens, and these may mutually inhibit each other. However, when both sources of information are available, nearly all trials should produce sufficient activation for a single logogen to surpass the interactive threshold (see Grossberg, 1978; McClelland & O'Regan, 1981, for similar accounts). For example, if *ca* is available from the parafovea and *pastry* is available from context, then this should provide sufficient activation for the logogen representing *cake* to surpass the interactive activation threshold and therefore, dominate the inhibition produced by partially activated representations. It is important to note the importance of the inhibitory mechanism. If there was not an inhibitory mechanism, then it is unclear how one could account for the observed superadditivity. Thus, we believe that this pattern provides important support for the notion of interlexical inhibitory mechanisms. McClelland and Rumelhart (1981) describe a similar phenomenon referred to as the "rich get richer" effect. The important point for the present discussion is that this interactive threshold model nicely accounts for the superadditive interactions between context and parafoveal information reported in the literature.

3. Word-frequency Effects

3.1. Foveal Vision

Across a wide variety of foveal word recognition tasks, high-frequency words produce better performance than low-frequency words (e.g., Becker, 1979; Broadbent, 1967; Frederiksen & Kroll, 1976; Rayner & Duffy, 1986; Whaley, 1978). Although there has been considerable discussion about both the underlying theoretical account of the frequency effect (e.g., Becker, 1979; 1980; Morton, 1969; 1982, Forster, 1976, 1979) and the particular loci of the effect across the various tasks (e.g., Balota & Chumbley, 1984, 1985; Catlin, 1969, 1973; Chumbley & Balota, 1984; Kliegl, Olson & Davidson, 1982, 1983; McCann & Besner, 1987; Theios & Muise, 1977), we are unaware of any researcher who has argued that word-frequency has *no* impact on foveal word recognition. Thus, we state with confidence that word-frequency does indeed have some impact on foveal word recognition. The more intriguing question is whether it also has an impact in parafoveal vision.

3.2. Parafoveal Vision

Inhoff and Rayner (1986) reported a study which appears to indicate that frequency can modulate the impact of parafoveal information. This study involved the moving window technique described above. As a reminder, this procedure involves a window of that moves with the reader's eyes to expose new information on each fixation. Inhoff and Rayner manipulated how much information was available to the right of fixation. (Across these conditions, all letters to the left of fixation were always available.) The three different window conditions were: (a) a one-word condition, in which there was no information available to the right of the fixated word; (b) a two-word condition, in which the currently fixated word and the word immediately to its right were available; and (c) a full-line condition, in which all characters on the line were available. In addition to these preview conditions, Inhoff and Rayner manipulated the word frequency of a given word in the sentence frame. These words were equated on length and contextual predictability.

The results of the first fixation duration data on the target word indicated that frequency had no impact in the one-word window condition, but did have a substantial impact in the two-word and the full-line window conditions. This appears to indicate that part of the impact of the parafoveal preview is on early processes that are reflected in the first fixation duration data. Moreover, such early processes are sensitive to word frequency. These results could again be viewed as consistent with the interactive threshold model described above. If high-frequency words have lower thresholds than low-frequency words then the interactive threshold should be more likely to be surpassed with a high-frequency preview than a low-frequency preview[2].

4. Within-Word Lexical Constraints

There have been a number of studies indicating that the letters at the beginning of a word play an especially important role in word recognition. This special status of word initial information is quite consistent with models of lexical access developed by Marslen-Wilson and Welsh (1978), Taft and Forster (1976), and Taft (1979). Although the Marslen-Wilson and Welsh model was developed primarily to account for auditory word recognition, it serves to highlight the potential importance of word initial information. Basically, the suggestion is that in speech perception the initial few phonemes of an input word activate a cohort set in the lexicon. This set contains a representation for all words that begin with the phonemes that are currently available. As more of the stimulus unfolds, the cohort set is reduced until there remains only one candidate in the set. Presumably, for some words, recognition occurs before the full word is presented, i.e., at the point at which there are no longer any potential candidates (Marslen-Wilson & Tyler, 1980; Marslen-Wilson & Welsh, 1978). One might expect similar effects in visual word recognition. That is, the earlier a letter sequence produces a unique candidate, the earlier recognition will occur. Moreover, because, as the above literature indicates, beginning word information appears to be available in the parafovea, one might expect similar effects in parafoveal vision.

4.1. Foveal Information

Experiments by Lima and Pollatsek (1983) and Mewhort and Beal (1977) indicate that word-initial information plays a special role in word recognition. In both studies it was found that delaying presentation of the final segment of a word produced less interference than delaying presentation of the beginning segment of a word.

A study by Lima and Inhoff (1985) provides evidence concerning "how" word-initial information plays a role in word recognition. Within the cohort framework, they suggested that word-initial information may influence word recognition processes via within-word lexical constraints. In order to address this, they presented target words embedded in sentence contexts that varied in the degree of constraint provided by the first three letters of the words. For example, consider the words *dwarf* and *clown*. The word *dwarf* is a high-constraint item because the first three letters *dwa* produce very few alternative strings, whereas *clown* is a low-constraint item because the first three letters *clo* produce many possible candidates, e.g., *clone, close, cloud, clods*. The predictions were quite clear. If constraint influences lexical access in a left-to-right fashion then one would expect fixations on the high-constraint words to be shorter than on the low-constraint words. That is, the recognition point in *dwarf* is earlier than the recognition point in *clown*. The results provided no support for this prediction. In fact, the high-constraint words led to longer fixations than the low-constraint words, precisely opposite to the constraint hypothesis. Thus, the special status of word initial information does not appear to be at the level of lexical constraint, at least in the fovea.

4.2. Lexical Constraint and Parafoveal Information

In addition to addressing the influence of constraint on foveal processing, Lima and Inhoff also looked at the influence of constraint on parafoveal processing. As described earlier, Rayner and his colleagues have demonstrated that subjects are especially sensitive to the beginning letters of parafoveal previews. Thus, it is possible that subjects might use the constraint imposed by these parafoveal letters to influence the speed of access for a parafoveal word when it is eventually fixated. Lima and Inhoff again relied on the moving window technique to test this possibility. Like Inhoff and Rayner (1980), they used the one-word window condition, the two-word window condition, and the full-line condition. The notion is that only in the two-word and full-line condition will parafoveal information be available for the high- and low-constraint words. Thus, one might expect an interaction between constraint and window size with the high-constraint words being especially facilitated by the parafoveal preview. The results yielded additive effects of constraint and window size. Thus, there was no evidence that lexical access was initiated in the parafovea on the basis of the degree of lexical constraint provided by the word-initial sequence. This basic pattern was replicated in a second experiment with a slightly different window size manipulation.

We should reiterate here that within-word constraint did not simply fail to produce an effect in foveal vision, but it actually produced a significant effect that was opposite to the constraint hypothesis. Lima and Inhoff suggested that subjects spent less time on the low-constraint items than on the high-constraint items because the word initial trigrams in the low-constraint items were more "familiar" to the subjects. Thus, the effect of constraint was simply an effect of familiarity. However, this influence of familiarity only occurred when the words were directly fixated and did not occur parafoveally, i.e., there was no evidence of an interaction between constraint and window size. This is an interesting finding when compared with the Inhoff and Rayner results described above. That is, Inhoff and Rayner found that frequency (a strong correlate of familiarity) modulated parafoveal utilization. Possibly, the degree of familiarity produced by the word initial trigrams in the Lima and Inhoff study was not sufficient to influence parafoveal processing. In support of this, it is noteworthy that the main effect of constraint in the Lima and Inhoff study was rather small, 10-16 ms, compared to the rather large main effect of frequency in the Inhoff and Rayner study, 30-40 ms. In fact, according to the interactive threshold model, one might not expect variables that produce small main effects in foveal vision to produce significant interactions when crossed with parafoveal preview.

5. Access Codes and Prefix Stripping

There has been considerable discussion in the literature concerning the access codes in word recognition. For example, Taft and Forster (1975) suggested that subjects use morphological access codes, which necessitates partitioning a word into its corresponding morphemes prior to lexical access. On the other hand, Spoehr and Smith (1973, 1975) argued that syllables may be the major access code. Finally, Taft's (1979) Basic Orthographic Syllabic Structure (BOSS) emphasizes both syllabic and morphemic information in parsing a word into its access code.

The present section addresses foveal and parafoveal access codes. Again, because there is evidence for the use of word initial information in the parafovea, it is possible that subjects may use this word initial information as an access code for word recognition.

5.1. Foveal Vision

There has been considerable evidence supporting the notion of morphemic access codes in foveal word recognition (e.g., Lima, 1987; Lima & Pollatsek, 1983; Snodgrass & Jarvella, 1972; Taft, 1979, 1981; Taft & Forster, 1975). Consider, for example, the Taft (1981) study. Taft reported evidence from both lexical decision and pronunciation tasks that prefixed words (e.g., *remind*) were responded to more quickly than pseudoprefixed words (e.g., *relish*). This finding provides support for the notion of "prefix stripping." That is, in recognizing a word, subjects first attempt to strip any common prefixes from that string to determine the base morpheme used for lexical access. Because subjects should inappropriately strip the prefix from pseudoprefixed words, this should force them to reach a "dead-end" after the prefix is stripped and then go back and use the non-stripped version of the word as the access code. Thus, subjects should be slower for pseudoprefixed words than prefixed words, precisely as Taft reported. Lima (1987) has recently replicated this basic pattern in a more natural reading situation.

5.2. Parafoveal Vision

As suggested above, it is possible that subjects use the beginning letters of parafoveal words to help identify the beginning morpheme of the to-be-fixated word. Lima (1987) conducted a study that addressed this possibility. In Lima's experiment, subjects were presented either pseudoprefixed (e.g., *relish*) or prefixed (e.g., *remind*) words in a critical location within a sentence. Lima used the boundary technique described above. She manipulated the type of parafoveal information that was available to subjects before their eyes crossed a critical boundary prior to the critical word location. For example, the reader might receive the letters common to the two words along with random letters or x's (e.g., *rensbl* or *rexxxx*) before crossing the critical boundary. This condition provides the reader with consistent parafoveal information concerning the prefix. In the control conditions subjects might parafoveally receive random letters or all x's (e.g., *kmnsbl* or *xxxxxx*). When the eyes crossed the critical boundary location, the stimuli changed to either the word *relish* or *remind*. Lima found a main effect of prefixed vs. pseudoprefixed words and a main effect of parafoveal preview on fixation duration. However, there was no evidence of an interaction between these two variables in either of two experiments.

As Lima points out, if the model of prefix stripping is simply that the primary route for lexical access necessitates prefix stripping, then the additive effects of preview and prefixed vs. pseudoprefixed words is not damaging. That is, readers could have begun prefix stripping for both prefixed and pseudoprefixed words in the parafovea. On the other hand, Lima points out that it is possible that words can be accessed through two routes. One route is based on the prefix-stripped morpheme while a second route is based on the whole word. This model would involve a race between these two routes, with lexical access involving the first completed. Lima suggests that this model predicts parafoveal preview will interact with the prefix manipulation. That is, for the pseudoprefixed word, the preview should disrupt performance via the prefix-stripping route, whereas, the preview should facilitate performance via the whole word access route. However for the prefixed word, both access routes should benefit from a parafoveal preview. That is, the preview should benefit access via the prefix stripping route and the whole word access route. Thus, there should be a larger preview effect for prefixed words than pseudoprefixed words. The results provided no evidence for such an interaction. Thus, although Lima's data cannot dismiss a model of parafoveal processing that assumes a primary prefix-stripped access route, her data are difficult to accomodate within a model of parafoveal processing that assumes both a prefix-stripped and a whole word access route. Finally, it should again be noted that the size of the main effect was quite small in this study, and therefore, based on the interactive threshold model, one might not expect an interaction.

6. Semantic Parafoveal Processing

One of the more seductive notions in the literature on parafoveal processing, is that readers can analyze meaning from words available in the parafovea. In fact, as noted in the beginning of this chapter, some models of reading (e.g., Goodman, 1967; Hochberg, 1970; Neisser, 1967; Smith, 1971) suggest that readers combine contextual information with parafoveal information to make guesses about the parafoveal word. Fixations on a given area are primarily for confirming earlier semantic preprocessing. It should be noted that we are using the term semantic preprocessing here to indicate that subjects have not consiously attended to the parafoveal item. If subjects have time to attend or consciously process the parafoveal item, we have no reason to doubt that one will find semantic effects.

There are a number of reasons why one might expect parafoveal semantic preprocessing effects. First, consider how pictures are processed. It appears that when one looks at a picture, the eyes move very quickly to regions that are judged to be informative (e.g., Antes, 1974; Mackworth & Morandi, 1967). This would appear to suggest that parafoveal processes guide the eyes to the most informative region. However, as Rayner and Pollatsek (1989) have argued, this finding in picture processing may not be relevant to reading because pictures provide many more cues than print regarding informative areas. When one considers print, there is very little in the way of informative areas that stand out on a page of normal text.

The research on foveal threshold priming could also be viewed as supporting the possibility of parafoveal semantic preprocessing (Balota, 1983; Evett & Humphreys, 1981; Fowler, Wolford, Slade, & Tassinary, 1981; Marcel, 1983). This research suggests that stimuli presented very briefly and pattern masked (presumably "unconscious") appear to produce meaning-level analyses. If briefly presented degraded stimuli can access meaning-level analyses in the fovea then why couldn't parafoveally presented stimuli access the same meaning-level analyses?

There are clear differences between foveal pattern masked primes and parafoveal word information. In the foveal masking situation, the primes are presented very briefly and followed by patterned masks. In the reading situation the parafoveal primes are available considerably longer and receive lateral masking. Accounts of foveal masking suggest that the pattern mask interrupts the visual codes necessary for conscious awareness of the prime (Marcel, 1983). In fact, if the prime was not pattern masked, subjects could identify the prime items. This contrasts with the parafoveal processing situation. The major limitation of processing parafoveal primes is the visual acuity breakdown in the parafovea, not the mask preventing conscious awareness. Finally, in the typical masked foveal priming paradigm, attention is directed to the same spatial location of the prime, whereas, in the typical parafoveal priming situation, attention is directed away from the spatial location of the parafoveal prime.

6.1. *Foveal Priming Studies*

When both the context and target are consciously available to the subject in the fovea, associative relatedness facilitates word recognition processes. Such effects have been reported in numerous studies involving lexical decision (e.g., Meyer & Schvaneveldt, 1971; Neely, 1977), pronunciation (Balota & Lorch, 1986; Stanovich & West, 1983b), and threshold identification (e.g., Morton, 1964; Tulving & Gold, 1963). In addition, such effects have also been reported in more natural reading situations. That is, gaze duration on a given target word is influenced by the predictability of that target word based on the preceding sentential context (Balota et al., 1985; Carroll & Slowiaczek, 1986; Ehrlich & Rayner, 1981; Schustack, Ehrlich, & Rayner, 1987; Zola, 1984).

Although the results are quite clear when subjects have time to consciously process the prime information, there is some debate concerning such priming effects when the primes are masked below a conscious identification threshold. The impact of such subthreshold stimuli has produced a long-standing debate in psychology. The focus of the debate in the masked-priming literature is whether the prime stimuli are truly presented below the subjects' conscious threshold (see Holender, 1986, and the accompanying commentary on this issue).

As we shall see the issue of objectively defined subthreshold presentation is also critical in our evaluation of the parafoveal priming literature. If true "semantic preprocessing" of parafoveal items occurs then this implies that the subjects were not consciously aware of such items. If subjects were aware of such parafoveal items, then it is not surprising that such items have an impact on performance.

6.2. *Parafoveal Priming*

We will begin our discussion of this literature with an often-cited study by Bradshaw (1974). In this study, subjects were presented three letter strings centered horizontally at fixation. The foveal word was always a homograph (e.g., *bank*). The two parafoveal strings included a disambiguating word (e.g., *river*) and a nonsense string of consonants (e.g., *spcrnf*). Across trials, the two parafoveal items randomly alternated between the left and right adjacent sides of the foveally presented homograph. The three-word displays were presented for 125 ms, after which subjects made a forced-choice decision between two words related to the two different meanings of the homograph. Finally, subjects wrote down all they had seen on a given trial. The results indicated that on trials in which subjects could not identify the parafoveal disambiguating stimulus, it still had an impact on the interpretation of the homograph. (Although this effect was significant, it was quite small, 53% vs. 47%). Thus, the Bradshaw results do support the notion of parafoveal semantic preprocessing.

Inhoff (Inhoff, 1982; Inhoff & Rayner, 1980) has conducted research to further address this effect. First, Inhoff and Rayner attempted to replicate the pattern of data reported by Bradshaw. They monitored eye movements and presented the disambiguating stimulus at six different parafoveal locations (one, three, or five degrees to the left or right of fixation). Inhoff and Rayner found no evidence for semantic preprocessing. That is, the results of the forced-choice test could be completely accounted for by two factors: identification of the parafoveal word and chance guessing of the biased meaning. Inhoff (1982) subsequently reported three experiments that extended and replicated the earlier Inhoff and Rayner results. Again, Inhoff found no influence of a parafoveal word on the interpretation of a foveal word above and beyond the probability of (a) correctly identifying the parafoveal word and (b) guessing the biased meaning.

The above results clearly indicate that the conscious choice of an interpretation of a foveally presented word does not appear to be modulated by parafoveal semantic preprocessing. However, it is still possible that a semantically related parafoveal item could influence the speed of recognizing a foveally presented item. In fact, Balota (1983) demonstrated that in a foveal priming situation, a masked prime could influence the speed of recognizing a target homograph but did not influence the conscious interpretation of that homograph. Thus, although the Inhoff research rather conclusively dispels the impact of parafoveal semantic preprocessing on the conscious interpretation of foveal information, it does not eliminate all possible aspects of parafoveal semantic preprocessing.

In fact, the research of Underwood and his colleagues (Underwood, 1976, 1977, 1980, 1981; Underwood, Rusted, & Thwaites, 1983; Underwood & Thwaites, 1982) appears to indicate that parafoveal information has a semantic influence on "speeded" performance. Underwood's research is intriguing because he has reported parafoveal semantic preprocessing across a wide variety of tasks including lexical decisions, category naming, picture naming, and paired-associate naming. Consider, for example, the results reported by Underwood and Thwaites (1982). In this study, subjects made lexical decisions about a centrally located letter string. On each trial a fixation dot was presented, along with a preexposure masked field in the parafovea; after which the foveal and parafoveal strings were presented simultaneously for 50 ms. Following this presentation, the parafoveal masking stimulus was again presented. The results of this study indicated that response latency to the centrally located target (e.g., *rubbish*) was significantly slower when a semantically related word appeared in the parafovea (e.g., *waste*) compared to when a semantically unrelated word appeared in the parafovea (e.g., *bear*). Moreover, there was also significant inhibition when an unrelated homophone (e.g., *waist*) was presented in the parafovea. This basic pattern was replicated in a second experiment. Thus, Underwood and Thwaites argued that their results support the notion of unattended parafoveal semantic and phonological processing.

Underwood's research is clearly provocative. However, we have a number of concerns that diminish our confidence in accepting it as strong support for semantic parafoveal preprocessing. First, Underwood has reported facilitation in some experiments and inhibition in other experiments (e.g., compare

Underwood, 1980, with Underwood, 1981). This difference in pattern of results may eventually be quite important, but currently, there is some debate regarding the underlying cause of the opposite patterns of effects (see Holender, 1986; Underwood, 1986). Second, in none of the experiments were subject's eyes monitored to determine whether they were truly looking at a fixation stimulus. This is particularly problematic in the Underwood and Thwaites study. In this study, the parafoveal cue was always presented to the right of fixation. It is possible that subjects might look slightly to the right of fixation toward the parafoveal stimulus. Of course, one might ask why would subjects look away from the centrally located lexical decision stimulus? It is possible that the presentation of two stimuli might produce a slight bias in the direction of the middle of the two stimuli. If this were the case then subjects may have processed more of the parafoveal stimulus than expected. Third, in none of the studies, were subject's thresholds individually set. Most typically, subjects were informally asked at the end of the experiment whether they recognized any of the words. Clearly, for a brief period of time it is possible that subjects could identify the parafoveal stimulus but by the end of the session, they may be unwilling to guess about the identity of such stimuli, because they no longer remembered these fleeting perceptual experiences. Fourth, even if one finds clear evidence of parafoveal semantic preprocessing in the type of tasks used by Underwood, it is unclear whether such effects truly reflect semantic *pre*processing. For example, consider the possibility that subjects pick up partial information from the parafoveal stimulus but not sufficient information to analyze it for meaning. However, when the foveal item is presented it provides a context to interpret the partial parafoveal information. In fact, this interpretation of the parafoveal item could account for the inhibition effects found in the lexical decision task. That is, on related trials subjects may have sufficient context and parafoveal information to recognize the parafoveal item, and the recognition of that item may distract the subject from the main task of making a lexical decision. On unrelated trials, the context provided by the foveal stimulus should not allow subjects to recognize the parafoveal stimulus based on partial information, thereby not distracting the subject from the lexical decision task. This, of course, would not be true semantic parafoveal preprocessing because subjects would not be able to extract meaning from the partial parafoveal information without the foveal contextual information.

There are two further issues that should be noted here. First, the notion of parafoveal semantic preprocessing is in conflict with the research indicating that within-word constraints (e.g., orthographic and morphological constraints) do not influence parafoveal access processes. If within-word constraints have no impact on parafoveal access processes, then it is unclear how semantic information would play a role in parafoveal processing. It would seem that such within-word access processes in the parafovea should precede any whole-word semantic preprocessing.[3]

Our major concern about the notion of parafoveal semantic preprocessing is that there have been repeated failures to produce evidence for such preprocessing in speeded performance. Consider the results from four separate sets of studies. First, Paap and Newsome (1981, Experiment 2) found no impact of a semantically related parafoveal stimulus on lexical decisions to a foveally presented word. In their third experiment, subjects were required to attend to the parafoveal item by making a lexical decision to that item before they made a lexical decision to the foveal item. Interestingly, the results of the foveal lexical decision task in this situation yielded significant inhibition from semantically related parafoveal items compared to unrelated parafoveal items. This finding is consistent with Underwood and Thwaites observation of inhibition in lexical decision performance from semantically related parafoveal items, described above. The important point to note here is that Paap and Newsome found evidence for such inhibition only when subjects were forced to attend to the parafoveal item. This supports the contention that the parafoveal inhibition effects reported in the Underwood and Thwaites study may not be due to "unattended" processing of the parafoveal items.

Second, Stanovich and West (1983a) failed to find evidence for parafoveal semantic preprocessing. They reported three experiments in which subjects pronounced a given target word that was preceded either by congruous, incongruous, or neutral sentence contexts. In addition, when the target word was presented, it was accompanied by either a parafoveal related modifier noun that was consistent with the continuation of the sentence context or a parafoveal nonword anagram. The results of the three experiments were quite clear. Subjects were faster to name the target word when it followed a congruous context than when it followed an incongruous context (Experiment 1) or a neutral context (Experiments 2 and 3). More importantly, there was no evidence of an impact of the parafoveally presented stimulus.

Third, in a study by Rayner et al. (1980) subjects were initially presented a stimulus word (e.g., *chair*) in the parafovea. During the eye movement to the word, it was replaced by a semantically related target word (e.g., *table*). Rayner et al. found no facilitation in naming the associatively related target word, compared to a visually matched unrelated parafoveal preview word (e.g., chore).

Finally, Rayner, Balota, and Pollatsek (1986) had subjects read sentences that included a critical target word. The invisible boundary technique described previously was used in this study. These researchers manipulated the parafoveal information available before the subject fixated on the target word. For example, if the target word was *song* then the preview was either (a) the identical word *song*, (b) a related word *tune*, (c) an unrelated word *hall*, or (d) a visually related nonword *sorp*. The results were quite clear. The visually similar preview facilitated processing almost as much as the identical preview. More importantly, there was no difference between the related and unrelated preview conditions. Finally, a control experiment yielded a highly significant effect of semantic relatedness for these very same related stimuli (e.g., *tune-song*) when they were foveally presented in a simple pronunciation task. Thus, although these items produced foveal semantic priming, there was no evidence of parafoveal semantic preprocessing in a relatively natural reading situation.

In sum, we have tried to provide a fair appraisal of the research on semantic *pre*processing in the parafovea. Overall, we believe that the best conclusion at present is that there is very little, if any, semantic parafoveal *pre*processing. When such effects are reported, it is simply unclear whether subjects have identified the parafoveal words. If the parafoveal words were identified, then the results simply indicate that there is an effect of a semantic relationship between two visually presented words.

Before leaving this section, we should note that Underwood and colleagues (Hyona et al., 1989; Underwood, Bloomfield & Clews, 1988; Underwood, Clews, & Everett, 1989) have recently reported some studies which are consistent with a version of semantic preprocessing that differs somewhat from our portrayal of such a view. In this section, we have discussed semantic *pre*processing of parafoveal words according to the view that is such words are *pre*processed, the amount of time necessary to identify them in reading when directly fixated should be reduced (as per our discussion of the Rayner et al., 1986, study.) We also discussed semantic *pre*processing wherein processing of a parafoveal word influences the processing of a foveal word. In both of these situations, we have argued that there is little evidence for semantic *pre*processing. In the recent studies by Underwood, readers' eye movements were found to be influenced by the characteristics of parafoveal words. In the experiments, subjects read sentences containing long target words that were informative either at the beginning or the end of the word. A word such as *relocation* is informative at the beginning and redundant at the ending. In other words, if given *ation* subjects cannot determine the identity of the word, but given *reloc* they can. A word such as *intermarry* is redundant at the beginning and informative at the end. Underwood and colleagues have found that readers' eye movements are pulled further into words when the informative part of the word is at the end.

While this finding is consistent with a semantic *pre*processing view, there are some issues that need to be addressed. First, this finding conflicts with a large body of data (see Rayner & Pollatsek, 1987) which indicates that how far the eyes move is largely determined by word length information from parafoveal vision. Second, as Hyona et al. (1989) acknowledge, the effect is quite small and is within the noise level of their eye-tracking system. Third, and more critically, Underwood and colleagues have not provided an account concerning the mechanism by which such preprocessing would work. Of course, these results may simply indicate that letter string information can produce familiarity values in the parafovea that are available to conscious the processing system that guides the eyes to the next fixation. Thus, until further evidence is available on the issue, we will continue to accept the position that semantic preprocessing does not occur in reading.

IV. GENERAL DISCUSSION

The review of the available literature suggests the following: (a) Orthographic letter code information is utilized both foveally and parafoveally. (b) The utilization of such parafoveal information can be modulated by contextual constraints, but is not totally dependent upon contextual constraints. (c) Word frequency influences both foveal and parafoveal access processes. (d) Within-word orthographic constraints influence foveal access processes, but do not influence parafoveal access processes. (e) Within-word morphological constraints influence foveal access processes, but do not influence parafoveal access processes. (f) If true semantic preprocessing occurs, it appears to be restricted to foveal presentations, and there is little in the way of compelling evidence to suggest that true semantic parafoveal preprocessing occurs; when such effects do emerge, the results may really be due to subjects identifying the parafoveal stimulus. We shall now turn to the implications of these data.

1. Superadditive Interactions

One intriguing finding in this literature is that contextual constraint appears to modulate the use of parafoveal information (Balota & Chumbley, 1985; Balota & Rayner, 1983; McClelland & O'Regan, 1981; Paap & Newsome, 1981). There are greater influences of parafoveal information when context constrains that information. As described earlier, one way of interpreting this pattern of superadditivity is to assume an interactive activation model (Balota & Chumbley, 1985; Balota & Rayner, 1983; McClelland & O'Regan, 1981). Within this framework, we have relied on both the notion of lexical thresholds and within-lexical inhibitory processes. These theoretical mechanisms are especially important when one considers massively parallel processing systems and response latency data. Such systems must deal with multiple sources of activation and continuously varying levels of activation. The notions of interactive thresholds and within-level inhibitory processes provide a useful selection heuristic that minimizes the impact of relatively low-levels of activation on performance (also see Balota, Boland, & Shields, 1989; Reder, 1983).

The notion of interactive thresholds handles other aspects of the data in this area. For example, one might account for the Inhoff and Rayner (1986) results indicating that word frequency modulates the size of the parafoveal preview effect by assuming that high-frequency words have lower thresholds than low-frequency words. Obviously this is not a novel approach to word frequency effects (Morton, 1969). It is also possible that the lack of an effect of within-word constraints on parafoveal information utilization may be due to the fact that such constraints produce relatively small effects even in foveal vision. Thus, it is possible that the utilization of such information in the parafovea is not sufficient to avoid the within-level inhibitory effects.

There are further aspects of eye-movement data that support the notion of interactive thresholds. For example, Balota and Chumbley (1985), Ehrlich and Rayner (1981), and Schustack, Ehrlich, and Rayner (1987) have all reported that subjects are more likely to skip over a highly constrained target word than a less constrained target word. This might suggest that in these situations sufficient parafoveal and foveal information combined to surpass the identification threshold. In addition, Pollatsek, Rayner, and Balota (1986) and Inhoff and Rayner (1986) have provided evidence that parafoveal information can sometimes influence the decision *when* to move the eye but not the decision *where* to move the eye. Interestingly, this latter finding suggests that there may be multiple thresholds in the system that influence different decisions in the eye-movement control system (see Rayner & Balota, 1989; Rayner & Pollatsek, 1987).

It is important to note here that we are unaware of other interactive effects in the word recognition literature that are similar in nature to the context by parafoveal information interaction. That is, most interactions are of the nature that the level of Factor A that produces the *slowest* response latency also produces the *largest* impact of Factor B. For example, this is the case for the interactions between (a) word frequency and context (Becker, 1979), (b) degradation and context (Becker & Killion, 1977), (c) developmental stage and context (Stanovich, West, & Freeman, 1981), (d) context and word difficulty (Stanovich & West, 1983b), (e) context and pronounceability of nonwords (Shulman & Davison, 1977), and (f) repetition and frequency (Scarborough, Cortese, & Scarborough, 1977; Scarborough, Gerard, & Cortese, 1979). Moreover, one also finds a similar type of interaction in experiments addressing task (lexical decision vs. pronunciation) by variable interactions (e.g., Balota & Chumbley, 1984; Chumbley & Balota, 1984; Lorch, Balota, & Stamm, 1986; Seidenberg, Waters, Sanders, & Langer, 1984; West & Stanovich, 1982). It should be noted here that these types of interactions are especially susceptible to scaling problems. A 40 ms effect of a variable is approximately the same percentage effect when the subject's overall response latency is 700 ms as a 28 ms effect when the subject's overall response latency is 500 ms. Thus, the interactive effects of contextual constraint and parafoveal information are quite provocative because (a) they provide relatively novel evidence regarding a type of superadditive interactive effect, and (b) they are less susceptible to scaling problems.

2. The Impact of Attentional Demands on Parafoveal Utilization

The utilization of parafoveal information may not only be limited by the acuity of the visual system but may also be intimately tied to the demands placed on the individual's basic cognitive resources. This would be consistent with Mackworth's (1965) classic notion of tunnel vision. Tunnel vision refers to the phenomenon that the useful visual field shrinks when there is a heavy load placed on the central processing system. For example, Williams (1982) has reported evidence that the detection of a parafoveal stimulus is dependent upon the cognitive demands of a foveal task. When foveal task demands are great the utilization of the parafoveal information decreases in a tunnel-vision type fashion. Thus, parafoveal processing is not a constant but may vary with foveal load.

Henderson and Ferreira (1987) have recently reported a study that provides support for tunnel vision in a more natural reading situation. They manipulated foveal difficulty by either varying a lexical variable (word frequency) or a syntactic variable (forcing syntactic reanalysis). This experiment utilized the boundary technique. On fixation *n* subjects received either visually consistent or inconsistent information with the word they would fixate on fixation *n* +1. The important question was whether the impact of parafoveal information would be modulated by the difficulty the reader was having on the currently fixated word. The results indicated that there was a significant parafoveal preview effect when subjects had a relatively easy time in processing the word on fixation *n* (i.e., high-frequency words or words that did not force syntactic reanalysis of the earlier portions of the sentence); however, when the currently fixated word was relatively difficult (i.e., low-frequency words or words that forced syntactic reanalysis), there was a relatively smaller parafoveal preview effect. This is quite consistent with the notion of tunnel vision. When subjects had difficulty on fixation *n*, the functional visual field in some sense shrank, thereby, decreasing the subjects' utilization of parafoveal information. Rayner (1986) and Inhoff, Pollatsek, Posner, and Rayner (1989) have reported similar effects.

The importance of the work on tunnel-vision type effects is quite important with respect to the present discussion. This work suggests that the notion of a relatively stable parafoveal influence is incorrect. It appears to be the case that the use of parafoveal information is dependent upon the current cognitive load. This is an especially important consideration in discussing parafoveal processes in reading where the cognitive load appears to vary considerably across fixations.

V. CONCLUSIONS

This chapter has focused on the literature addressing the influence of variables in foveal and parafoveal visual word recognition. The review has indicated that although a number of variables influence foveal processing, the safest conclusion regarding parafoveal word processing is that abstract letter code information is utilized. Such a finding is inconsistent with models of reading that place a heavy emphasis on parafoveal lexical and/or semantic preprocessing and is also inconsistent with views that minimize the role of parafoveal processing. It appears that the research in this area supports a view between these two extremes.

We have interpreted these data within an interactive threshold model of parafoveal information utilization, whereby, the influence of variables on performance seems to be limited by the degree of activation at a particular lexical-level presentation. This framework appears to be necessary to account for the consistent superadditive effects of context and parafoveal visual information. Finally, it appears that any model of parafoveal processing must eventually deal with its sensitivity to attentional demands. Very simply, the window of useful parafoveal information is not constant across different levels of demand placed on the processing system.

ACKNOWLEDGMENTS

This work was supported by Grants NIA54126A to D.B. and NSF BNS8609336 and NIHHD12727 to K.R. The authors also express their gratitude to the Netherlands Institute for Advanced Study for their generous support while portions of this chapter were completed.

FOOTNOTES

[1] It appears that the perceptual span is not symmetric around fixation. That is, Rayner, Well, Pollatsek, and Bertera (1982) found that there is relatively little distortion when information to the left of the fixated word is distorted, whereas, as noted above, distortion of information to the right of fixation dramatically influences reading performance. Moreover, this asymmetry appears to be dependent upon the particular orthography. For example, Pollatsek, Bolozky, Well, and Rayner (1981) found that for native Israeli readers that were reading Hebrew, the perceptual span was asymmetric to the left of fixation, whereas, when these same readers were reading English, their perceptual span was asymmetric to the right of fixation. The obvious difference being that English is read from left to right and Hebrew is read from right to left. The Pollatsek et al. results are particularly interesting because they suggest that the asymmetry of the window is not "hardwired" but is dependent upon reading experience and, more importantly, readers can switch from one type of asymmetry to the next dependent upon the demands of the orthography.

[2] It should be noted here, that the pattern is somewhat different when one considers the results from the gaze duration data. Here one finds that frequency has additive effects with window size. That is, when considering the total time looking at a given word, low-frequency words were looked at longer than high-frequency words, and this was independent of window size. The different pattern of results for the first fixation data and the gaze duration data indicate that subjects were much more likely to refixate a word in the one-word preview condition than in the remaining conditions. Thus, although the frequency of the target word did not influence first fixation duration on that word in the one-word window condition, it did have an impact on the probability that the word was refixated. In the one-word window condition, 33% of all refixations were on high-frequency words, whereas, 66% were on low-frequency words. This differential influence of frequency on when to leave the current fixation vs. where to send the eyes has been viewed as implicating different decisions

regarding these two components of the eye-movement system (see Pollatsek, Rayner, & Balota, 1986; Rayner & Balota, 1989).

[3] Inhoff (1987) has reported evidence that there is morphological coding in the parafovea. In this research, Inhoff compared compound words (e.g., cowboy) that were based upon two morphological subcomponents (e.g., cow and boy) and pseudocompound words (e.g., carpet) that could not be decomposed into morphological subcomponents (e.g., car and pet). Using the moving window technique, Inhoff found that there were significant parafoveal preview benefits from the word initial trigram of a compound word, but there was no significant preview effect from the word initial trigram of a pseudocompound word. However, Inhoff (1989b) has recently failed to replicate this general pattern when the compound and psuedocompound words were matched on word frequency. Inhoff did however find that preview benefits were largest for pseudocompound words that involved beginning and ending high-frequency subword units, and smallest for control words that did not contain subword units that involved lexical representations. Inhoff interpreted these results as supporting a framework in which all letters of a parafoveal word contribute to access processes, and that letters that form mutually reinforcing letter coalitions will produce additional activation. This general framework is quite consistent with the interactive threshold model described in the present chapter.

REFERENCES

Antes, J. R. (1974). The time course of picture viewing. *Journal of Experimental Psychology*, **103**, 62-70.

Balota, D.A. (1983). Automatic semantic activation and episodic memory encoding. *Journal of Verbal Learning and Verbal Behavior*, **22**, 88-104.

Balota, D.A., Boland, J.E., & Shields, L.W. (1989). Priming in pronunciation: Beyond pattern recognition and onset latency. *Journal of Memory and Language*, **28**, 14-36.

Balota, D.A. & Chumbley, J.I. (1984). Are lexical decisions a good measure of lexical access? The role of word frequency in the neglected decision stage. *Journal of Experimental Psychology: Human Perception and Performance*, **10**, 340-357.

Balota, D.A. & Chumbley, J.I. (1985). The locus of word-frequency effects in the pronunciation task: Lexical access and/or production? *Journal of Memory and Language*, **24**, 89-106.

Balota, D.A. & Lorch, R.F. (1986). Depth of automatic spreading activation: Mediated priming effects in pronunciation but not in lexical decision. *Journal of Experimental Psychology: Learning, Memory, and Cognition*, **12**, 336-345.

Balota, D.A., Pollatsek, A., & Rayner, K. (1985). The interaction of contextual constraints and parafoveal vision information in reading. *Cognitive Psychology*, **17**, 364-390.

Balota, D.A., & Rayner, K. (1983). Parafoveal visual information and semantic contextual constraints. *Journal of Experimental Psychology: Human Perception and Performance*, **5**, 726-738.

Becker, C.A. (1979). Semantic context and word frequency effects in visual word recognition. *Journal of Experimental Psychology: Human Perception and Performance*, **5**, 252-259.

Becker, C.A. (1980). Semantic context effects in visual word recognition: An analysis of semantic strategies. *Memory & Cognition*, **8**, 493-512.

Becker, C.A. & Killion, T.H. (1977). Interaction of visual and cognitive effects in word recognition. *Journal of Experimental Psychology: Human Perception and Performance*, **3**, 389-401

Besner, D. (1983). Basic decoding components in reading: Two dissociable feature extraction processes. *Canadian Journal of Psychology*, **37**, 429-438.

Bradshaw, J. L. (1974). Peripherally presented and unreported words may bias the meaning of a centrally fixated homograph. *Journal of Experimental Psychology*, **103**, 1200-1202.

Broadbent, D.E. (1967). Word-frequency effect and response bias. *Psychological Review*, **74**, 1-15.

Carroll, P., & Slowiaczek, M.L. (1986). Constraints on semantic priming in reading: A fixation time analysis. *Memory & Cognition*, **14**, 509-522.

Catlin, J. (1969). On the word-frequency effect. *Psychological Review*, **76**, 504-506.

Catlin, J. (1973). In defense of sophisticated-guessing theory. *Psychological Review*, **80**, 412-416.

Chumbley, J.I. & Balota, D.A. (1984). A word's meaning affects the decision in lexical decision. *Memory & Cognition*, **12**, 590-606.

DE Groot, A.M.B., Thomassen, A.J.W.M., & Hudson, P.T.W. (1982). Associative facilitation of word recognition as measured from a neutral prime. *Memory & Cognition*, **10**, 358-370.

DenBuurman, R., Boersma, T., & Gerrisen, J.F. (1981). Eye movements and the perceptual span in reading. *Reading Research Quarterly*, **16**, 227-235.

Ehrlich, S.F., & Rayner, K. (1981). Contextual effects on word perception and eye movements during reading. *Journal of Verbal Learning and Verbal Behavior*, **20**, 641-665.

Evett, L.J., & Humphreys, G. W. (1981). The use of abstract graphemic information in lexical access. *Quarterly Journal of Experimental Psychology*, **33A**, 325-350.

Forster, K.I. (1976). Accessing the mental lexicon In R. J. Wales and E. C. T. Walker (Eds.), *New approaches to language mechanisms*. Amsterdam: North-Holland.

Forster, K.I. (1979). Levels of processing and the structure of the language processor. In W. E. Cooper & E. Walker (Eds.), *Sentence processing: Psycholinguistic studies presented to Merill Garrett*. Hillsdale, N.J.: Lawrence Erlbaum Associates.

Forster, K.I. (1987). Form-priming with masked primes: The best match hypothesis. In M. Coltheart (Ed.), *Attention and Performance XII*. London: Lawrence Erlbaum Associates.

Forster, K.I., & Davies, C. (1984). Repetition priming and frequency attentuation in lexical access. *Journal of Experimental Psychology: Learning, Memory, and Cognition*, 10, 680-698.

Fowler, C., Wolford, G., Slade, R., & Tassinary, L. (1981). Lexical access with and without awareness. *Journal of Experimental Psychology: General*, **110**, 341-362.

Frederiksen, J.R., & Kroll, J.F. (1976). Spelling and sound: Approaches to the internal lexicon. *Journal of Experimental Psychology: Human Perception and Performance*, **2**, 361-379.

Goodman, K. (1967). Reading: A psycholinguistic guessing game. *Journal of the the Reading Specialist*, **6**, 126-135.

Grossberg, S. (1978). A theory of visual coding, memory, and development. In E. L. J. Leeuwenberg, & H. G. J. M. Buffart (Eds.), *Formal theories of visual perception*. New York: Wiley.

Haber, R.N. (1978). Visual perception. *Annual Review of Psychology*, **29**, 31-59.

Henderson, J. M., & Ferreira, F. (1987). *Visual attention and the perceptual span in reading*. Paper presented at the annual Joseph R. Royce Research Conference, University of Alberta.

Hochberg, J. E. (1970). *Perception*. Englewood Cliffs, NJ: Prentice-Hall.

Holender, D. (1986). Semantic activation without conscious identification in dichotic listening, parafoveal vision, and visual masking: A survey and appraisal. *The Behavioral and Brain Sciences*, **9**, 1-66.

Humphreys, G. W., Evett, J. J., Quinlan, P. T., & Besner, D. (1987). Priming from identified and unidentified primes. In M. Coltheart (Ed.), *Attention and performance XII*. Lawrence Erlbaum Associates, London.

Hyona, J., Niemi, P., & Underwood, G. (1989). Reading long words embedded in sentences: Informativeness of word halves affects eye movements. *Journal of Experimental Psychology: Human Perception and Performance*, **15**, 142-152.
Inhoff, A. W. (1982). Parafoveal word perception: A further case against semantic preprocessing. *Journal of Experimental Psychology: Human Perception and Performance*, **8**, 137-145.
Inhoff, A. W. (1987). Lexical access during eye fixations in sentence reading: Effects of word structure. In M. Coltheart (Ed.), *Attention and performance XII*. Lawrence Erlbaum Associates, London.
Inhoff, A. W. (1989a). Parafoveal processing of words and saccade computation during eye fixations in reading. *Journal of Experimental Psychology: Human Perception and Performance*. **15**, 544-555.
Inhoff, A. W. (1989b). Lexical access during eye fixations in sentence reading: Are word access codes used to integrate lexical information across interword fixations? *Journal of Memory and Language*. **28**, 444-461.
Inhoff, A. W., Pollatsek, A., Posner, M.I., & Rayner, K. (1989). Covert attention and eye movements in reading. *Quarterly Journal of Experimental Psychology*, **41A**, 63-89.
Inhoff, A. W., & Rayner, K. (1980). Parafoveal word perception: A case against semantic preprocessing. *Perception & Psychophysics*, **27**, 457-464.
Inhoff, A.W. & Rayner, K. (1986). Parafoveal word processing during eye fixations in reading: Effects of word frequency. *Perception & Psychophysics*, **40**, 431-439.
Irwin, D. E., Yantes, S., & Jonides, J. (1983). Evidence against visual integration across saccadic eye movements. *Perception & Psychophysics*, **34**, 49-57.
Jonides, J., Irwin, D. E., & Yantes, S. (1982). Integrating visual information from successive fixations. *Science*, **215**, 192-194.
Jonides, J., Irwin, D. E., & Yantes, S. (1983). Failure to integrate information from successive fixations. *Science*, **222**, 188.
Jonides, J., & Mack, R. (1984). On the cost and benefit of cost and benefit. *Psychological Bulletin*, **96**, 29-44.
Kliegl, R., Olson, R.K., & Davidson, B.J. (1982). Regression analyses as tool for studying reading processes: Comment on Just and Carpenter's eye fixation theory. *Memory & Cognition*, **10**, 287-296.
Kliegl, R., Olson, R.K., & Davidson, B.J. (1983). On problems of unconfounding perceptual and language processes. In K. Rayner (Ed.), *Eye movements in reading: Perceptual and language processes*. New York: Academic Press.
Levin, H., & Kaplan, E.L. (1970). Grammatical structure and reading. In H. Levin and J.P. Williams (Eds.), *Basic studies on reading*. New York: Basic Books.
Lima, S.D. (1987). Morphological analysis in sentence reading. *Journal of Memory and Language*, **26**, 84-99.
Lima, S.D., & Inhoff, A.W. (1985). Lexical access during eye fixations in reading: Effects of word-initial letter sequence. *Journal of Experimental Psychology: Human Perception and Performance*, **11**, 272-285.
Lima, S.D., & Pollatsek, A. (1983). Lexical access via an orthographic code? The Basic Orthographic Syllable Structure (BOSS) reconsidered. *Journal of Verbal Learning and Verbal Behavior*, **22**, 310-332.
Lorch, R.F., Balota, D.A., & Stamm, E.G. (1986). Locus of inhibition effects in the priming of lexical decisions: pre- or postlexical access? *Memory & Cognition*, **14**, 95-103.
Mackworth, N.H. (1965). Visual noise causes tunnel vision. *Psychonomic Science*, **3**, 67-68.
Mackworth, N.H., & Morandi, A.J. (1967). The gaze selects informative details within pictures. *Perception & Psychophysics*, **2**, 547-552.
Manso de Zuniga, C., Quinlan, P.T., & Humpheys, G.W. (1987). Task effects on priming under masked conditions. Unpublished manuscript.
Marcel, A.J. (1983). Conscious and unconscious perception: An approach to the relations between phenomenal experience and perceptual processes. *Cognitive Psychology*, **15**, 238-300.

Marslen-Wilson, W.D., & Tyler, L.K. (1980). The temporal structure of spoken language understanding. *Cognition*, **8**, 1-71.
Marslen-Wilson, W.D., & Welsh, A. (1978). Processing interactions and lexical access during word recognition in continuous speech. *Cognitive Psychology*, **10**, 29-63.
Massaro, D.W., Jones, R.D., Lipscomb, D., & Scholz, R. (1978). Role of prior knowledge on naming and lexical decision with good and poor stimulus information. *Journal of Experimental Psychology: Human Learning and Memory*, **4**, 498-512.
McCann, R.S., & Besner, D. (1987). Reading pseudohomophones: Implications for models of pronunciation and the locus of word-frequency effects in word naming. *Journal of Experimental Psychology: Human Perception and Performance*, **13**, 14-24.
McClelland, J.L., & O'Regan, J.K. (1981). Expectations increase the benefit derived from parafoveal visual information in reading words aloud. *Journal of Experimental Psychology: Human Perception and Performance*, **7**, 634-644.
McClelland, J.L. & Rumelhart, D.E. (1981). An interactive activation model of context effects in letter perception: Part 1. An account of basic findings. *Psychological Review*, **88**, 375-407.
McConkie, G.W., & Rayner, K. (1975). The span of the effective stimulus during a fixation in reading. *Perception & Psychophysics*, **17**, 578-587.
McConkie, G.W., & Rayner, K. (1976) Identifying the span of the effective stimulus in reading: Literature review and theories of reading. In H. Singer & R.B. Rudell (Eds.), *Theoretical models and processes in reading*. Newark, Delaware: International Reading Association.
McConkie, G.W., & Zola, D. (1979). Is visual information integrated across successive fixations in reading? *Perception & Psychophysics*, **25**, 221-224.
McConkie, G.W., Zola, D., Blanchard, H.E., & Wolverton, G.S. (1982). Perceiving words during reading; Lack of facilitation from prior peripheral exposure. *Perception & Psychophysics*, **32**, 271-281.
Mewhort, D.J.K., & Beal, A.L. (1977). Mechanisms of word identification. *Journal of Experimental Psychology: Human Perception and Performance*, **3**, 629-640.
Meyer, D.E., & Schvaneveldt, R.W. (1971). Facilitation in recognizing of words: Evidence of a dependence between retrieval operations. *Journal of Experimental Psychology*, **90**, 227-234.
Meyer, D.E., Schvaneveldt, R.W., & Ruddy, M.G. (1975). Loci of contextual effects on word recognition. In P.M.A. Rabbitt & S. Dornic (Eds.), *Attention and performance V*. New York: Academic Press.
Morton, J. (1969). Interaction of information in word recognition. *Psychological Review*, **76**, 165-178.
Morton J. (1982). Disintegrating the lexicon: An information processing approach. In J. Mehler, S. Franck, E.C.T. Walker, & M. Garrett (Eds.), *Perspectives on mental representation*. Hillsdale, NJ: Lawrence Erlbaum Associates.
Neely, J.H. (1977). Semantic priming and retrieval from lexical memory: The roles of inhibitionless spreading activation and limited capacity attention. *Journal of Experimental Psychology: General*, **106**, 1-66.
Neisser, U. (1967). *Cognitive Psychology*, New York: Appleton, Century, Crofts.
Paap, K.R., & Newsome, S.L. (1981). Parafoveal information is not sufficient to produce semantic or visual priming. *Perception & Psychophysics*, **29**, 457-466.
Pollatsek, A., Bolozky, S., Well, A.D., & Rayner, K. (1981). Asymmetries in the perceptual span for Israeli readers. *Brain and Language*, **14**, 174-180.
Pollatsek, A., Rayner, K., & Balota, D.A. (1986). Inferences about eye movement central from the perceptual span in reading. *Perception & Psychophysics*, **40**, 123-130.
Rayner, K. (1975). The perceptual span and peripheral cues in reading. *Cognitive Psychology*, **7**, 65-81.
Rayner, K. (1978). Foveal and parafoveal cues in reading. In J. Requin (Ed.), *Attention and performance VII*. Hillsdale, NJ: Lawrence Erlbaum Associates.
Rayner, K. (1986). Eye movements and the perceptual span in beginning and skilled readers. *Journal of Experimental Child Psychology*, **41**, 211-236.

Rayner, K. & Balota, D.A. (1989). Parafoveal preview effects and lexical access during eye fixations in reading. W. Marslen-Wilson (Ed.), *Lexical representation and processes.* Cambridge, Mass.: MIT press.

Rayner, K., Balota, D.A., & Pollatsek, A. (1986). Against parafoveal semantic preprocessing during eye fixations in reading. *Canadian Journal of Psychology*, **40**, 473-483.

Rayner, K., & Bertera, J.H. (1979). Reading without a fovea. *Science*, **206**, 468-469.

Rayner, K., & Duffy, S.A. (1986). Lexical complexity and fixation times in reading: Effects of word frequency verb complexity, and lexical ambiguity. *Memory & Cognition*, **14**, 191-201.

Rayner, K., Inhoff, A.W., Morrison, R., Slowiaczek, M.L., & Bertera, J.H. (1981). Masking of foveal and parafoveal vision during eye fixations in reading. *Journal of Experimental Psychology: Human Perceptions and Performance*, **7**, 167-179.

Rayner, K., McConkie, G.W., & Ehrlich, S.F. (1978). Eye movements and integration across fixations. *Journal of Experimental Psychology: Human Perception and Performance*, **4**, 529-544.

Rayner, K., McConkie, G.W., & Zola, D. (1980). Integrating information across eye movements. *Cognitive Psychology*, **12**, 206-226.

Rayner, K., & Pollatsek, A. (1983). Is visual information integrated across saccades? *Perception & Psychophysics*, **34**, 39-48.

Rayner, K., & Pollatsek, A. (1987). Eye movements in reading: A tutorial review. In M. Coltheart (Ed.), *Attention and performance XII*. London: Erlbaum.

Rayner, K., & Pollatsek, A. (1989). *The psychology of reading*. Englewood Cliffs, N.J.: Prentice Hall.

Rayner, K., & Slowiaczek, M.L. (1981). Expectations and parafoveal information in reading: Comments on McClelland and O'Regan. *Journal of Experimental Psychology: Human Perception and Performance*, **7**, 645-651.

Rayner, K., Well, A.D., Pollatsek, A., & Bertera, J.H. (1982). The availability of useful information to the right of fixation in reading. *Perception & Psychophysics*, **31**, 537-550.

Reder, L.M. (1983). What kind of a pitcher can a catcher fill? Effects of priming in sentence comprehension. *Journal of Verbal Learning and Verbal Behavior*, **22**, 189-202.

Scarborough, D.L., Cortese, C., & Scarborough, H. (1977). Frequency and repetition effects in lexical memory. *Journal of Experimental Psychology: Human Perception and Performance*, **3**, 1-17.

Scarborough, D.L., Gerard, L., & Cortese, C. (1979). Accessing lexical memory: The transfer of word repetition effects across task and modality. *Memory & Cognition*, **7**, 3-12.

Schuberth, R.E., Spoehr, K.T., & Lane, D.M. (1981). Effects of stimulus and contextual information on the lexical decision process. *Memory and Cognition*, **9**, 68-77.

Schustack, M.W., Ehrlich, S.F., & Rayner, K. (1987). The complexity of contextual facilitation in reading: Local and global influences. *Journal of Memory and Language*, **26**, 322-340.

Seidenberg, M.S., Waters, G.S., Sanders, M., & Lange, P. (1984). Pre- and postlexical loci of contextual effects on word recognition. *Memory and Cognition*, **12**, 315-328.

Shulman, H.G., & Davison, T.C.B. (1977). Control properties of semantic coding in a lexical decision task. *Journal of Verbal Learning and Verbal Behavior*, **16**, 91-98.

Smith, F. (1971). *Understanding reading: A psycholinguistic analysis of reading and learning to read.* New York: Holt, Rinehart, and Winston.

Snodgrass, J.G., & Jarvella, R.J. (1972). Some linguistic determinants of word classification time. *Psychonomic Science*, **27**, 220-222.

Spoehr, K.T., & Smith, E.E. (1973). The role of syllables in perceptual processing. *Cognitive Psychology*, **5**, 71-89.

Spoehr, K.T., & Smith, E.E. (1975). The role of orthographic and phonotactic rules in perceiving letter patterns. *Journal of Experimental Psychology: Human Perception and Performance*, **1**, 21-34.

Stanovich, K.E., & West, R.F. (1979). Mechanisms of sentence context effects in reading: Automatic activation and conscious attention, *Memory and Cognition*, **7**, 77-85.

Stanovich, K.E., & West, R.F. (1983a). The generalizability of context effects on word recognition: A reconsideration of the roles of parafoveal priming and sentence context. *Memory and Cognition*, **11**, 49-58.

Stanovich, K.E. & West, R.F. (1983b). On priming by sentence context. *Journal of Experimental Psychology: General*, **112**, 1-36.
Stanovich, K.E., West, R.F., & Freeman, D.J. (1981). A longitudinal study of sentence context effects on second-grade children: Tests of an interactive-compensatory model. *Journal of Experimental Child Psychology*, **32**, 185-199.
Sternberg, S. (1969). The discovery of processing stages: Extensions of Donders' method. In W.G. Koster (Ed.), *Attention and performance II*. Amsterdam: North Holland.
Taft, M. (1979). Lexical access via orthographic code: The Basic Orthographic Syllabic Structure (BOSS). *Journal of Verbal Learning and Verbal Behavior*, **18**, 21-39.
Taft, M. (1981). Prefix stripping revisited. *Journal of Verbal Learning and Verbal Behavior*, **20**, 289-97.
Taft, M., & Forster, K.I. (1975). Lexical storage and retrieval of prefixed words. *Journal of Verbal Learning and Verbal Behavior*, **14**, 638-647.
Taft, M., & Forster, K.I. (1976). Lexical storage and retrieval of polymorphemic and polysyllabic words. *Journal of Verbal Learning and Verbal Behavior*, **15**, 607-620.
Theios, J., & Muise, J.G. (1977). The word identification process in reading. In N.H. Castellan, D.B. Pisoni, & G.R. Potts (Eds.), *Cognitive theory*. Hillsdale,NJ: Lawrence Erlbaum Associates.
Tulving, E., & Gold, C. (1963). Stimulus information and contextual information in tachistoscopic recognition of words. *Journal of Experimental Psychology*, **66**, 319-327.
Underwood, G. (1976). Semantic interference from unattended printed words. *British Journal of Psychology*, **67**, 327-338.
Underwood, G. (1977). Attention, Awareness, and hemispheric differences in word recognition. *Neuropsychologia*, **15**, 61-67.
Underwood, G. (1980). Attention and the non-selective lexical access of ambiguous words. *Canadian Journal of Psychology*, **34**, 72-76.
Underwood, G. (1981). Lexical recognition of embedded unattended words: Some implications for reading processes. *Acta Psychologica*, **47**, 267-283.
Underwood, G. (1986). Facilitation or inhibition from parafoveal words? *The Behavioral and Brain Sciences*, **9**, 48-49.
Underwood, G., Bloomfield, R., & Clews, S. (1988). Information influences the pattern of eye fixations during sentence comprehension. *Perception*, **17**, 267-278.
Underwood, G., Clews, S., & Everett, J. (1989). How do readers know where to look next; Local information distributions influence eye fixation. *Quarterly Journal of Experimental Psychology*.
Underwood, G., Rusted, J., & Thwaites, S. (1983). Parafoveal words are effective in both hemifields: Preattentive processing of semantic and phonological codes. *Perception*, **12**, 213-221.
Underwood, G., & Thwaites, S. (1982). Automatic phonological coding of unattended printed words. *Memory and Cognition*, **10**, 434-442.
West, R.F. & Stanovich, K.E. (1982). Source of inhibition in experiments on the effect of sentence context on word recognition. *Journal of Experimental Psychology: Learning, Memory, and Cognition*, **8**, 385-399.
Whaley, C.P. (1978). Word-nonword classification time. *Journal of Verbal Learning and Verbal Behavior*, **17**, 143-154.
Williams, L.J. (1982). Cognitive load and the functional field of view. *Human Factors*, **24**, 683-692.
Zola, D. (1984). Redundancy and word perception during reading. *Perception & Psychophysics*, **36**, 277-284.

8
A DISTRIBUTED MEMORY MODEL OF CONTEXT EFFECTS IN WORD IDENTIFICATION

MICHAEL E. J. MASSON

Department of Psychlogy
University of Victoria
Victoria, B.C., Canada

Theories of word identification and priming or context effects have been powerfully influenced by two principal assumptions. One is that the representation of word concepts can be modelled in terms of a single representational unit for a single concept. The other assumption is that activation of one concept spreads automatically to other concepts that are directly connected to it. My claim is that although these assumptions have been supported by a number of empirical results, a number of recent findings constitute a serious challenge to the validity of these assumptions.

An additional claim is that an alternative set of representational and processing assumptions provides a more promising basis for modelling word identification and context effects. The critical feature of the alternative view is that representation of word concepts does not maintain a one-to-one correspondence between nodes and concepts. Rather, representation of each concept is distributed across an entire network of nodes. I will show how this alternative approach can be used to construct a rather simple model of word identification that is capable of simulating results that are consistent with classic views of word identification and priming (e.g., Collins & Loftus, 1975) and results that challenge that kind of theory. My argument is that the distributed memory view of word identification provides the basis for an alternative conceptualization of knowledge representation and processing that may reshape our way of thinking about lexical activation and the influence of context.

I. SPREADING ACTIVATION THEORY

The view of lexical activation and priming that has dominated much of the work on word identification is based on the theory of *spreading activation* (e.g., Anderson, 1976; Collins & Loftus, 1975). In this theory it is assumed that a concept is represented by a single node, and that nodes are linked to one another if they are related in some way, such as sharing properties. When nodes have many properties in common they have many links between them. Further, the strength of a link may vary depending on factors such as the frequency with which the concepts are experienced together (Conrad, 1972; Freedman & Loftus, 1971; Perlmutter, Sorce, & Myers, 1976).

In this system the key processing mechanism is *activation*. The level of activation of a node is analogous to the amount of energy or excitation at the node. When the amount of activation at a node exceeds some threshold, information about the node becomes available to the decision making and response generation system. A node may be activated either by presentation to the sensory system of a symbol for the concept (e.g., a printed word) or by activation that has spread from a related concept that already is activated. The increased level of activation of a node that results from spreading activation *primes* the node in the sense that a smaller increase in activation now is necessary for the recognition threshold to be reached.

Other critical aspects of theories of spreading activation are based on the characteristics of the spread of activation among nodes. One of the most important assumptions about the spread of activation is that the process takes measureable amounts of time (Anderson, 1976; Collins & Loftus, 1975). For example, time taken for activation to spread from one concept to another is assumed to be inversely related to the strength of the link between the two concepts. Moreover, activation will spread more slowly between two concepts that are not directly connected but instead share a common intermediary node.

The impression of the representational system that is encouraged by the spreading activation view is one of a great number of simultaneously active nodes and links. Consequently, it usually is assumed that spreading activation is an automatic process in the sense intended by Posner and Snyder (1975). That is, activation of nodes (a) occurs outside conscious awareness (as long as level of activation is below threshold), (b) is initiated without intention, and (c) does not interfere with other ongoing mental activity.

Support for the view of spreading activation as an automatic activity has been provided by many word identification experiments in which a target word is preceded either by a related or an unrelated prime word or by some neutral stimulus. These studies have actually provided evidence for *two* sources of facilitation in word identification. One is the automatic spread of activation from the prime (Forster, 1981; Neely, 1976, 1977) and the other is the generation of expectations about the upcoming target based on the concepts activated by the prime (Becker, 1980; Neely, 1977). Each of these two sources of facilitation are associated with a specific pattern of priming effects. When targets primed with a related word produce facilitation and targets primed with an unrelated word produce inhibition, relative to a condition in which a neutral prime is used, it is assumed that attentional processes were involved. Relatively long stimulus onset asynchronies appear to induce subjects to engage in strategies (e.g., conscious generation of expectations) that lead to inhibition effects (Neely, 1977; Smith, Briand, Klein, & den Heyer, 1987).

The pattern of priming effects attributed to automatic spreading activation is one in which related primes produce significant facilitation, but unrelated primes produce no inhibition (Forster, 1981; Neely, 1977). This source of facilitation is assumed to result from activation that spreads automatically, in the sense intended by Posner and Snyder, among related items in the lexicon (Fischler, 1977a; Forster, 1981; Neely, 1977; Seidenberg, Waters, Sanders, & Langer, 1984). The occurrence of facilitation without inhibition is consistent with the principle of automaticity that holds that an automatic process can be carried out without interfering with other ongoing activity. The fact that a prime has caused other related concepts to be activated should have no influence on the time taken to identify an unrelated target as long as primed concepts have not yet entered conscious awareness (cf. Neely, 1977; Posner & Snyder, 1975).

II. ANOMALOUS RESULTS

The combination of spreading activation theory and the Posner and Snyder (1975) theory of automatic processes has served as the foundation of much of our understanding of word identification, and as the framework within which empirical results on priming usually are interpreted. Although the automatic spreading activation view has been successful in this sense, a number of anomalous results have begun to emerge that question the validity of some of its fundamental assumptions.

1. Relatedness and Stimulus Onset Asynchrony

An important phenomenon for which spreading activation theory can account is the positive relationship between amount of facilitation due to presentation of a related prime and the degree of relatedness between prime and target (Anderson, 1976; Collins & Loftus, 1975; Hayes-Roth, 1977). At issue here is the mechanism proposed by spreading activation models to account for this result. One possibility is that activation takes longer to spread from one node to another if the two nodes are more weakly related. This might be expected if the links between the nodes are few or weak or because the nodes are not directly connected but are linked by one or more intervening nodes in the network. Furthermore, it is assumed that activation weakens as it travels away from the source node, so more distantly related nodes would receive lower levels of activation (e.g., Anderson, 1976; Collins & Loftus, 1975). Consequently, strong associations produce larger facilitation effects because a greater amount of activation is received by the node representing the target concept.

This explanation of the effect of relatedness yields two important predictions regarding the time course of priming effects. First, spreading activation should reach more closely related nodes sooner than more distant nodes, so facilitation effects should begin to appear earlier for closely related targets. Second, because the activation received by closely related nodes is relatively strong, the time taken for the build up of activation to reach asymptote might be expected to be less than for distantly related nodes.

These two predictions have been tested by manipulating the stimulus onset asynchrony (SOA) between a prime and target and the strength of relationship between the prime and target (Lorch, 1982; Ratcliff & McKoon, 1981). The results of these studies have been remarkably consistent. Using categorization, word naming, and recognition memory tasks it was found that the onset of priming effects appeared at the same time for both strongly and weakly related prime-target pairs. Moreover, time taken to reach asymptotic priming was virtually the same for both kinds of pairs. The only influence of degree of relatedness was on the amount of asymptotic priming, with a larger effect observed for more strongly related pairs.

The conclusion required by these data is that the strength of the relationship between a prime and target does not affect the time taken for activation to spread from the prime to the target. This is a serious problem for the spreading activation model because the model relies heavily on the assumption that activation takes time to spread and this is the basis for the model's account of stronger priming effects with stronger semantic relatedness. On the basis of their results Ratcliff and McKoon (1981) and Lorch (1982) have suggested that concepts related to a prime begin to be activated instantly and simultaneously, but that the asymptotic level of activation varies as a function of relatedness. In this view of priming the concept of spreading activation does not play a central role in accounting either for effects of semantic relatedness on amount of priming or for the build up of priming effects over time.

2. Depth of Spreading Activation

In classic models of spreading activation (e.g., Collins & Loftus, 1975; Collins & Quillian, 1969) it is assumed that activation spreads not just from an initially activated node to those directly connected to it, but also to the neighbors of nodes activated by the originally active node, and perhaps even to the neighbors of the neighbors, etc. The assumption of multi-step activation is a fundamental part of the models' account of memory retrieval phenomena.

The validity of this assumption was seriously questioned by the outcome of a series of lexical decision studies by DE Groot (1983). These experiments compared the effectiveness of primes that were assumed to be directly linked to targets (e.g., dog-cat) and of primes that were assumed to be linked to targets via one intervening concept node (e.g., bone-cat, via dog). When primes were masked to reduce the likelihood that subjects would identify them and hence try to find a relationship between prime and target, directly related primes significantly reduced response time but indirectly related, or *mediated*, primes produced response times that were virtually the same as those obtained with unrelated primes. This result was taken as evidence that activation did not automatically spread beyond concepts directly connected to the initially activated node.

More recently, however, Balota and Lorch (1986) argued that the lack of mediated priming effects in the DE Groot (1983) experiments may have been due to a form of post-access search for a relationship between prime and target. This kind of strategic processing could override the effects of automatic spreading activation. They argued that the masking procedure used by DE Groot was not sufficient to ensure that subjects could not identify the primes, a claim supported by subjects' post-experimental reports. In the case of mediated primes the search for a prime-target relationship may either have taken longer than for directly related primes, or it may have failed. This could have increased response times on trials involving mediated primes.

To test this claim, Balota and Lorch first attempted to obtain a mediated priming effect using a lexical decision task with unmasked primes to allow post-access processes to operate. As predicted, they failed to find a reliable mediated priming effect. Next they tested the hypothesis that mediated priming effects could be obtained using a word identification task, word naming, that was less likely to involve post-access processes. In this experiment they obtained mediated priming effects that were somewhat smaller than the effects obtained with directly related primes. Contrary to the conclusions derived from the DE Groot experiments, then, it appears that multi-step automatic activation does occur just as assumed by spreading activation models.

Although the Balota and Lorch results vindicate the assumption of multi-step spreading activation, I have raised this issue because its very existence depends on a central assumption of spreading activation theory. The assumption is that concepts may be represented as individual nodes and that some concepts are directly connected but others are linked only via one or more intervening neighbors. The model that I will develop later is based on an alternative representational scheme in which the concept of multi-step spreading activation is interpreted very differently. Consequently the results of experiments on multi-step priming serve as an important basis for comparison of the two models.

3. Automaticity

The plausibility of simultaneous activation of many nodes in semantic memory depends on the assumption that activation takes place automatically. Within the framework of automatic processes developed by Posner and Snyder (1975) and adopted in many versions of spreading activation theory, an automatic process is one that can carry on without interfering with other processes and, in turn, is not obstructed by concurrent processes. The pattern of facilitation without inhibition observed in word identification experiments (e.g., Forster, 1981; Neely, 1977) is consistent with this attribute of automaticity. Presentation of an unrelated prime activates an irrelevant region of semantic memory but this process is assumed to be automatic and therefore should not interfere with identification of the target, as long as the target appears before attention is directed to the activated but inappropriate concepts.

By this logic it should be possible for a number of regions of semantic memory to be simultaneously activated without mutual interference. Evidence for this phenomenon has been provided by Meyer, Schvaneveldt, and Ruddy (1972) and by Davelaar and Coltheart (1975). They constructed series of lexical decision trials so that two related target words were separated by an unrelated intervening item (e.g., dark-even-light). Other sequences of trials consisted of three consecutive unrelated words. It was found that reaction time to the third item in the former type of sequence was reliably less than for the third item in the latter sequence. Unlike Meyer et al., Davelaar and Coltheart found the same result when the intervening item was a nonword. The conclusion was that the activation produced by the first item in the sequence was unaffected by activation induced by the intervening word.

Gough, Alford, and Holley-Wilcox (1981) have challenged this conclusion and have carried out a lexical decision experiment in which varying numbers of items intervened between targets and "closely related priming" words. They found that only when the prime and target occurred in consecutive positions in the list of items did a priming effect occur. If even one intervening item appeared between two related words, no significant facilitation was observed. This result suggests that activation produced by one word can be eliminated completely by presentation of a single unrelated word. The implication is that one source of spreading activation in some way interferes with unrelated activation spreading in a different part of the network.

It may be possible to reconcile these conflicting results in terms of post-access processes. Forster (1981), Seidenberg et al. (1984), and others have demonstrated that lexical decision response time may be influenced by the outcome of a process in which a candidate interpretation for a letter string is compared to contextual information prior to making a response. A positive outcome permits an immediate response whereas a negative one induces a more careful check of the perceptual information prior to making a response. Given the relatively frequent occurrence of the pattern of two related items separated by an unrelated item in the Meyer et al. (1972) and Davelaar and Coltheart (1975) experiments, it is possible that subjects were engaging in such a process. In fact, subjects may have attempted specifically to check an interpretation of a target against the item that had occurred two positions back. In the Gough et al. study, however, the number of items intervening between two related words varied greatly and no pattern would have been apparent. Subjects may have been less likely to rely on post-access checking, particularly involving items prior to the immediately preceding one, before making a response under these circumstances.

If post-access processes rather than automatic spreading activation were responsible for the persistent influence of a prime, it should be possible for an intervening item to eliminate priming effects in paradigms where post-access processes are unlikely to operate. One means of accomplishing this would be to use very short stimulus onset asynchronies for consecutive items. Ratcliff and McKoon (1988) used a recognition memory task in which the target of a trial was either related or unrelated to the target of the preceding trial. The prime for the current trial served as an intervening item and was either a unrelated word or a neutral stimulus (a row of X's). With a 300-msec SOA the facilitation produced by having a related target on the preceding trial was eliminated when an unrelated rather than a neutral prime was used on the critical trial. This replicates the Gough et al. (1981) result with lexical decision and suggests that when an unrelated word intervenes between two related words spreading activation may be disrupted.

In a number of recent experiments I have used sequences of two primes with short stimulus onset asynchronies in lexical decision and word naming tasks (Masson, 1988). In a lexical decision experiment each prime was visible for 117 msec and appeared sequentially in the same display location. The first prime was either related or unrelated to the target, and the second prime was either unrelated or neutral. The sequence involving two unrelated primes, however, was not tested. A neutral stimulus not containing letters (a random dot pattern covering an area similar to that of a word) was chosen in order to minimize the possibility of activating real words. The target word appeared as soon as the second prime was erased so the SOA between the first prime and the target was 234 msec. These prime sequences did not produce reliable differences in nonword reaction times, indicating that a priming sequence involving two words did not significantly differ from a sequence consisting of a word and a random pattern of dots with respect to preparing the subject to respond to a target.

The mean response times for word targets in this experiment are shown in the first row of Table 1. A significant priming effect was observed when the related-neutral and unrelated-neutral prime sequence conditions were compared. The related-unrelated sequence produced a mean response time that was not reliably different from the mean for the unrelated-neutral condition. This result is consistent with the Ratcliff and McKoon (1988) and the Gough et al. (1981) finding that an unrelated intervening prime can eliminate the facilitation produced by an initial related prime.

Table 1
Mean Response Time (in Msec) as a Function of Priming Sequence

	Priming sequence			
Experiment	Related-neutral	Unrelated-neutral	Related-unrelated	Unrelated unrelated
1 (Lexical decision)	583	610	605	---
2 (Word naming)	518	530	545	548
3 (Word naming)	529	543	528	533

It is conceivable that elimination of priming by an intervening unrelated prime might involve post-access processes rather than interference among sources of activation in the lexicon during lexical access. Therefore, two additional experiments involving a word naming task were carried out. It was expected that priming effects obtained with this task would be more likely to reflect lexical activation and would provide a stronger test of the hypothesis that unrelated sources of activation in the lexicon may interfere with one another. In both experiments critical word naming targets were preceded by a two-prime sequence. The first prime was either related or unrelated to the upcoming target and the second was either a neutral stimulus (a row of x's) or a word unrelated to the target.

One of the word naming experiments followed the same procedure as the lexical decision experiment, except that primes were visible for 200 msec. The mean naming times for each of the four prime sequences are shown in Table 1. When the second prime in the sequence was neutral, naming times were significantly faster when the first prime was related rather than unrelated to the target. When the second prime was unrelated to the target, however, the nature of the first prime did not reliably influence response time. Overall, response times were faster when the second prime was neutral. Thus the presence of an intervening unrelated prime not only eliminated the facilitation produced by the initial related prime, it also generally elevated response times.

In the second naming experiment, trials were arranged so that the first prime in a two-prime sequence for a critical target actually was the target word on the immediately preceding trial (e.g., leash-DOG, xxxx-CAT). On each trial the prime was presented for 300 msec, and there was a delay of only 250 msec between naming a target on one trial and the onset of the prime for the next trial. The mean naming times are shown in Table 1. This experiment produced the same pattern of results as the first, except that response times generally were faster when the prime immediately preceding the target was an unrelated word rather than the neutral prime.

The experiments with recognition memory, lexical decisions, and word naming clearly indicate that presentation of an unrelated word between a related prime-target pair reduces or eliminates what is assumed to be an automatic facilitation effect. The influence of an intervening word prime on potential facilitation effects does not appear to be the result of differential ability of neutral versus word primes to prepare a subject to respond (cf. Jonides & Mack, 1984).

This is because elimination of facilitative priming effects was observed when intervening word primes generally elevated response times and when such primes tended to reduce response times. Instead, interference with priming seems to be a result of the influence of the intervening prime on the activation induced by the initial prime. This type of phenomenon is not consistent with the view that activation can spread automatically from a node in semantic memory without interfering with activation that may be spreading from other, unrelated areas of semantic memory.

III. AN ALTERNATIVE VIEW OF PRIMING AND LEXICAL ACTIVATION

The anomalous results discussed in the previous section provide grounds for consideration of a view of semantic memory representation and processing that is fundamentally different from the view expressed in current models of spreading activation. It is clear that a model is needed in which there is some form of interaction between activated concepts, even when the concepts are unrelated. Moreover, there must be a means by which activation of a concept instantaneously influences the activation of related concepts and drives them simultaneously to asymptotic levels of primed activation regardless of the degree of relatedness.

The word identification model I have been developing is a simple modification of the type of network that Hopfield (1982; Hopfield & Tank, 1986) has proposed. Hopfield networks are intended as models of the computational properties of neural structures. Many of the representational and dynamic aspects of these networks are motivated by neurological constraints (Hopfield, 1982). Although the similarities between biological mechanisms and characteristics of Hopfield networks are interesting in themselves, the relevance of this modelling technique for present purposes lies in its method of representing memories and its procedures for reconstructing learned patterns of activation from partially complete patterns.

Hopfield networks are related to the general approach taken by Rumelhart and McClelland (1986) and their colleagues, in that activation of a concept is assumed to consist of a pattern of activation across an entire collection of nodes. In addition, in both systems information about known concepts is captured in the connections between nodes. But there are two major differences between these classes of models. First, Rumelhart and McClelland use a representational system consisting of layers of nodes that can take on continuous values of activation, including a *hidden* layer that does not directly code input or output patterns. This layer of nodes is essential in capturing complex relationships between sets of learned concepts and allowing such concepts to be represented by a single set of connection strengths. On the other hand, Hopfield nets consist of a single collection of undifferentiated nodes, each of which can be in one of only two possible states. The lack of a hidden layer means that there are restrictions on the sets of memories that can be encoded into and recovered from the system. This issue will be discussed in greater detail below.

The second distinction between the two types of models, however, reflects the advantage gained by using a Hopfield network. When there are no hidden units, a simple learning algorithm can be used for determining the strength of connections between nodes. In this algorithm the strength of connection between two nodes is changed as a simple function of whether, for a given pattern, the two nodes are in the same or different state of activation. In contrast, the back propagation learning algorithm used by Rumelhart and McClelland (1986) for networks containing hidden units is a relatively complicated form of credit assignment that allows for gradual adjustment of connection strengths over many presentations of each stimulus. Similarly, Hinton and Sejnowski (1986; Ackley, Hinton, & Sejnowski, 1985) proposed the Boltzmann machine learning algorithm as a means of incorporating hidden units into Hopfield networks. This algorithm involves potentially hundreds or even thousands of sweeps through a two-phase learning procedure.

The typical objective in simulations involving networks with hidden units is to generate a set of connection weights that is capable of representing the higher order structure underlying an entire collection of patterns. Interest centers on (a) whether the system is able to capture the entire set of associations, (b) the number of learning trials required, and (c) performance of the system at different stages of learning. In the case of the Boltzmann machine, performance of the system on pattern completion problems after learning also is of interest. But in Hopfield networks with no hidden units, learned patterns need be presented to the system only once and the key issue is whether an entire pattern can be reconstructed from a smaller part. In the simulation enterprise reported here, the most important issue was not how learning occurs but how an entire pattern can be accessed by presentation of only a subset of its features. The Hopfield network was chosen as the basis of the simulation model because of its emphasis on this issue and the simplicity with which it accomplishes its goal.

1. Distributed Memory Representation

The priming phenomena reviewed here encourage a view of semantic memory in which representation of concepts is even more interdependent than in the classic network models. I advocate abandoning the fundamental assumption that a semantic memory concept should be represented as a single node in a network. In place of this scheme, the proposed alternative model uses a distributed memory representation system (Eich, 1985; McClelland & Rumelhart, 1985, 1986; Murdock, 1983; Rumelhart & McClelland, 1986). Memory consists of a network of nodes, but rather than assigning each node to a unique concept, a concept is represented as a pattern of activation across the entire network. Different patterns of activation represent different concepts, only one of which may be completely instantiated at a given instant.

A simple example is shown in Figure 1. The sample memory system consists of just 10 nodes, each of which can be in one of two states, on or off. Connections between nodes are assumed to exist and will be discussed in detail later, but for now they have been omitted from the figure. In Figure 1 three different concepts are represented as unique patterns of activation that may occur at different times. The individual nodes are assumed to represent features of the concepts (Eich, 1985; Smith, Shoben, & Rips, 1974; Tversky, 1977). Those concepts with many features in common are represented by similar patterns of activation, and are assumed to be related to one another. By this metric, concepts A and B in Figure 1 are similar or related to one another, but not to concept C.

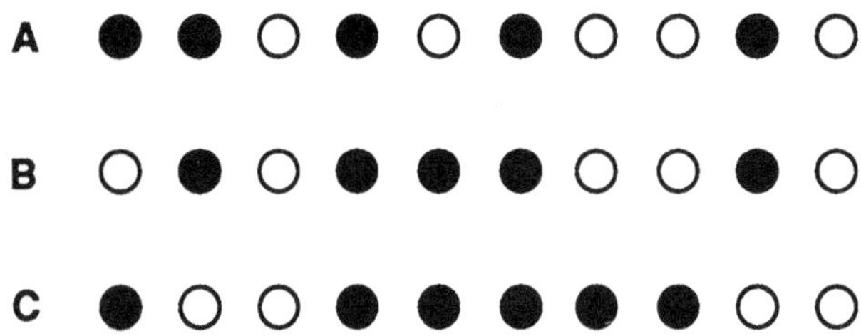

Fig. 1. Three different patterns of activation in a network consisting of 10 nodes. Each pattern, A, B, and C, corresponds to a unique concept and each of the 10 nodes can be in an on (white) or off (black) state.

Only one pattern of activation can be represented in the system at a given instant, and this implies that the system will not allow multiple concepts to be *fully* activated simultaneously. But this restriction does not mean that multiple concepts cannot be *partially* activated simultaneously. Degree of activation of a concept in this system is conceived as the proportion of nodes in the currently activated pattern that match the concept. For example, in the system depicted in Figure 1 suppose that the current pattern of activation is equivalent to that used to represent concept B. That concept is fully activated, but related concept A is partially activated because many of the nodes in the current pattern (8 of 10) are in states that correspond to the pattern used in representing A. On the other hand, concept C is no more active than would be expected if any other randomly chosen unrelated pattern were fully activated. In this sense, concept C is not active at all.

2. Connections Between Nodes

If only one pattern of activation can be represented at a given instant, how can the system have a memory representation of more than one pattern? The answer to this problem lies in the connections between the nodes. In a Hopfield network each node is linked to every other node in the network, but there are no links between a node and itself. Each link has a weight that could be characterized as connection strength and information about patterns that the system has learned is represented in the link weights.

2.1. *Learning*

When the system learns a new concept the link weights are adjusted according to a prescription of the general type proposed by Hebb (1949). The weight of the link connecting any two nodes is altered as a function of the on/off states adopted by the two nodes when representing the concept. Specifically, if both nodes are in the same state (both on or both off) then the link between them is increased in strength, reflecting a positive correlation between the two nodes. On the other hand, if the two nodes are in different states (one on and one off) their link is reduced in weight to reflect the negative association between the two nodes as dictated by that concept.

Once a number of concepts has been learned, correlational patterns among pairs of nodes across the different concepts are reflected in the link weights. For instance, if for most of the learned concepts two nodes are in the same state (e.g., the seventh and eighth nodes in Figure 1), there will be a strong positive weight assigned to the link between them. Conversely, two nodes that typically take on different values when a concept is activated (the third and fourth nodes in Figure 1) will have a strong negative weight on their connecting link.

The equation for computing the change in each link weight when a new concept is learned is

$$\Delta w_{ij} = n_i \, n_j \, , \qquad (1)$$

where w_{ij} represents the weight of the link between nodes i and j, and n_i and n_j represent the states taken on by those nodes when the new concept is activated. A node in the on state takes the value 1 and a node in the off state is assigned the value -1. Consequently, any pair of nodes in the same state produce $\Delta w_{ij} = 1$ and any pair in opposite states yield $\Delta w_{ij} = -1$. For example, suppose that the network depicted in Figure 1 began with all $w_{ij} = 0$, and the three concepts shown were learned. The strength of the connection between the first and second node would change from 0 to 1 as a result of learning concept A, then back to 0 after learning B, then to -1 after learning C. A stronger negative connection (-3) is obtained between the third and fourth nodes because the negative correlation between node states holds across all learned concepts. A strong positive link (3) would develop between the seventh and eighth nodes.

2.2. *Pattern Completion*

A critical computational ability of Hopfield networks involves pattern completion. Once the system has encoded a set of concepts, it can be provided a pattern of activation that partially matches a target concept. The system can then gradually change the pattern of activation until it reconstructs the entire pattern of the target concept. This is accomplished through a process of *asynchronous* updating of each node in the network. Updating consists of randomly selecting a node and computing the total amount of activation directed to it by the other nodes in the system. If the activation exceeds some threshold the node is set to the on state, but if the activation does not exceed threshold the node is set to the off state. No adjustment is made if the node already is in the state dictated by this updating rule. Updating is asynchronous in the sense that at a given instant any node in the system may be selected for updating. This means that some nodes may be updated multiple times before others are selected even once, and reflects delays in neural signal propagation (Hopfield, 1982).

The activation received by a node is a function of the on/off states of the other nodes in the system and the weight of the links between those nodes and the node selected for updating:

$$a_i = \sum_{j \neq i} w_{ij} n_j , \qquad (2)$$

where a_i represents the amount of activation directed to the selected node. Setting a threshold of zero means that if a_i is positive node i will be turned on, otherwise it will be turned off. The activation received by an individual node must be distinguished from the degree of activation of an entire concept, described earlier. I take activation of a concept to be the proportion of nodes in the network that fit the pattern used to represent the concept.

An important property of Hopfield networks is that the asynchronous updating scheme will drive the network toward a pattern of activation that is *stable* in the sense that any further updates will not produce adjustments in the pattern. The updating process can be allowed to run until a stable state is achieved, indicating that the pattern has been recognized. Under the appropriate circumstances, discussed below, those patterns that represent concepts learned by the system will be stable patterns of activation, and therefore can be recognized. Furthermore, the stable pattern that is achieved through the updating scheme likely will be the one that most closely matches the initial pattern (Hopfield, 1982). We can see intuitively how this is accomplished by noticing that, according to Equation 2, a neighbor with a positive link to the node selected for updating will tend to drive the selected node toward the same state as the neighbor. In addition, a neighbor with a negative link to the selected node will tend to push it to the state opposite its own. The updating algorithm tends to make pairs of nodes with positive links take on the same state and those with negative links take on opposite states. This is a valid heuristic because link weights capture the positive and negative correlations between pairs of nodes that hold across the patterns of activation representing known concepts.

Hopfield (1982) has shown that learned concepts are most likely to constitute stable states if their patterns of activation are dissimilar from one another and if they are few in number relative to the number of nodes in the memory system (e.g., no more than 10 concepts per 100 nodes). Encoding too many concepts overloads the capacity of the link weights to maintain distinct represenfions of the concepts. The result is that a number of spurious stable states are produced that do not correspond to any learned concept, and some of the states corresponding to learned concepts are rendered unstable, and therefore unrecognizable. If learned concepts are too similar to one another, the system may establish spurious stable states that are similar to the original concepts, but fail to make the encoded pattern of activation a stable state.

The consequences of loading into a Hopfield network concepts that are too many in number or too great in similarity might provide the basis for a model of memory phenomena such as forgetting or generalization (Hopfield, 1982). The objective of the simulation project described here, however, was to explore the time course of successful pattern completion. For this reason, sets of concepts were constructed to maximize the probability that the network would form stable states identical to the learned concepts.

3. Modelling Word Identification

The model of word identification proposed here is based on a modified Hopfield network. Concepts known to the network constitute words that the system is capable of identifying. Each concept is represented as a unique pattern of activation across the network of nodes. In order to simulate visual word identification, I assume that some of the nodes in the network, the *perceptual* nodes, are responsible for encoding the visual pattern of the word and the remainder, the *conceptual* nodes, represent its semantic features. The semantic features are aspects of the context within which the word has been experienced. Consequently, words that are experienced in similar contexts turn out to have similar patterns across the conceptual nodes (i.e., similar meanings).

In its current form, the model emphasizes the influence of context and perceptual input on pattern completion. It is assumed that visual input is immediately read into the perceptual nodes and is not influenced by the state of the conceptual nodes (i.e., perception is purely data driven). In this sense, the perceptual nodes constitute a modular system (Fodor, 1983) unlike the interactive activation model developed by McClelland and Rumelhart (1981; Rumelhart & McClelland, 1982) in which activation at the word level influences activation at the letter level. I do not deny the potential importance of these interactive connections for perceptual processes. Rather, my current purpose is to use the simplest possible model in accounting for a number of context effects operating within the system of conceptual nodes.

Once a word's visual pattern has been encoded in the perceptual nodes, asynchronous updating is applied to the conceptual nodes which receive input from both perceptual and conceptual nodes. Because no updating of perceptual nodes is carried out, the model contains no connections between pairs of perceptual nodes, and links between perceptual and conceptual nodes transmit activation from perceptual to conceptual nodes only. A simple example of such a network is shown in Figure 2 which presents a system of two perceptual and three conceptual nodes. Arrows indicate permissible flow of activation. Only those nodes with activation directed toward them (the conceptual nodes) are selected for updating.

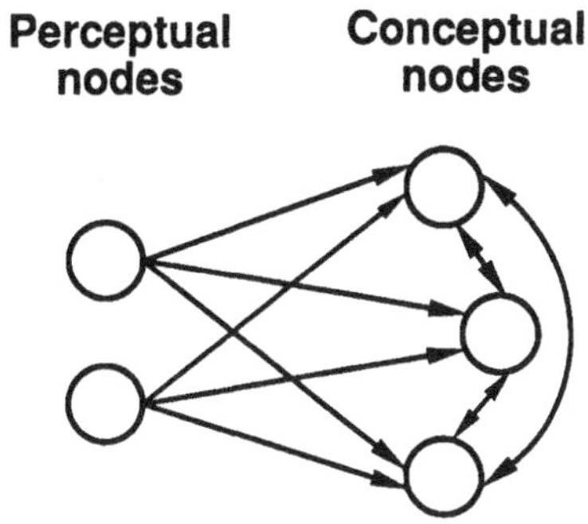

Fig. 2. A simple example of a modified Hopfield network.

To simulate word identification processes, the network first learns a small vocabulary according to the learning rule expressed in Equation 1. Identification of a printed word is simulated by assigning to the network's perceptual nodes the pattern of activation for the target word. The conceptual nodes are assigned a random pattern of activation. Then a series of updating *cycles* is run until the network reaches a stable state. That is, no matter which node is selected for updating, its present state is appropriate given the amount of activation currently directed toward it. Consequently, no further changes to the nodes' states will be made by the updating algorithm. Ordinarily the stable state eventually achieved is the complete pattern for the target word. The updating scheme has moved the pattern of activation among the conceptual nodes from a random one to a stable pattern that represents the conceptual information relevant to the target word designated by the perceptual pattern.

It is assumed that once a stable state is reached and the pattern of activation across the conceptual nodes matches that assigned to the target word, the word is fully activated and lexical access has occurred. The system can then move to the processes involved in generating a word identification response (e.g., word naming, lexical decision). These processes are not simulated by the model so it is not capable of producing effects that are typically attributed to post-access processes such as the influence of proportion of trials involving related primes (e.g., Seidenberg et al., 1984).

3.1. Basic Reaction Time Effects

The number of updating cycles required to move the network to a stable state is taken as a measure of word identification time. Simulations using this metric regularly produce a number of results that closely resemble some of the fundamental patterns of empirical stimulus identification reaction times. One is a positively skewed distribution of response times (e.g., Ratcliff & Murdock, 1976), and another is a negatively accelerated speed-accuracy trade-off curve (e.g., Reed, 1976) which reflects a continuous build up of activation (Yantis & Meyer, 1988). Sample simulation results illustrating these two effects are shown in Figure 3. The simulations are based on a network of 75 perceptual and 50 conceptual nodes with four unrelated concepts encoded into the network. Identification of a word was simulated by loading its perceptual pattern into the perceptual nodes and setting the conceptual nodes to a random starting point. Updating cycles were then initiated and continued until a stable state had been reached. In all cases this was the state representing the target concept. The figure is based on data taken a number of simulations involving different sets of four concepts. In the right panel of Figure 3 *activation* refers to the proportion of conceptual nodes that match the target pattern toward which the network is moving.

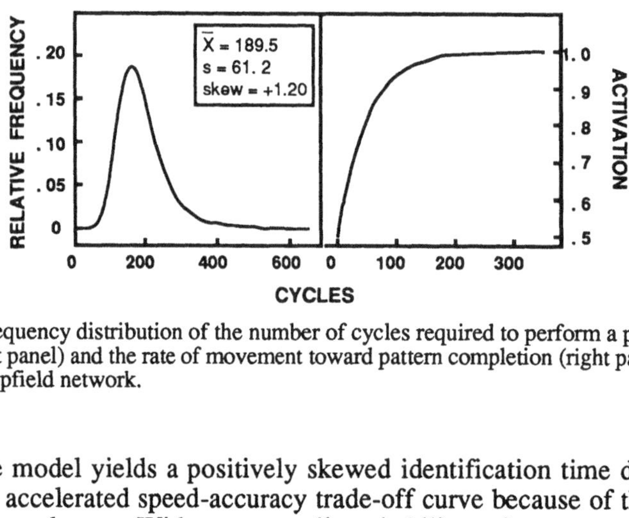

Fig. 3. A frequency distribution of the number of cycles required to perform a pattern completion problem (left panel) and the rate of movement toward pattern completion (right panel) using a modified Hopfield network.

The model yields a positively skewed identification time distribution and a negatively accelerated speed-accuracy trade-off curve because of the asynchrony in its updating scheme. With some small probability a few or even one conceptual node that must be adjusted before the conceptual pattern is complete fails to be selected until many updating cycles have passed. This phenomenon produces the positive skew. For the speed-accuracy trade-off curve, I assume that the accuracy of a response is determined by the degree of activation of the correct target concept. The activation of the target concept rises as a negatively accelerated function of number of update cycles. This is due to the fact that the probability of selecting a node that needs to be adjusted is reduced as more and more update cycles occur. In the early cycles many of the randomly selected conceptual nodes will be adjusted but later only a very small number require adjustment and the probability of selecting one of them is quite small. Therefore, longer and longer sequences of cycles will pass with no change in the degree of activation of the concept.

3.2. Priming Effects

The fact that the modified Hopfield network model produces two well-known features of response time data is encouraging. The major objective for the model, however, was simulation of priming effects. In the model priming effects are determined by the state of the conceptual nodes after one perceptual stimulus (the prime) has been processed and is replaced by a new stimulus (the target). To simplify the model it is assumed that the perceptual system is capable of processing only one visual pattern at a time, so when the target appears its perceptual pattern immediately replaces the prime's pattern in the perceptual nodes. Although the interactive effects of simultaneously available patterns (e.g., Mozer, 1983) are important and interesting, the purpose of the current version of the model is to simulate the processing of a series of discrete events.

When the perceptual pattern of the target replaces the pattern for the prime in the perceptual nodes, the asynchronous updating of conceptual nodes continues as before, but with the new perceptual configuration. In the case of a prime that is related to the target, similar patterns of activation across the conceptual nodes are used to represent the two items. Therefore, processing of the prime moves the activation in the conceptual nodes toward a pattern that is similar to the target's. In a sense, updating cycles devoted to the prime provide a head start for target identification. When the target is presented the pattern of activation in the conceptual nodes already approximates the pattern that is to be achieved. Consequently, relatively few update cycles are required to move the conceptual nodes to the target pattern.

A greater number of update cycles would be required if the prime were not related to the target because processing the prime would move the conceptual nodes to a pattern with only a chance amount of overlap with the target pattern (e.g., patterns B and C in Figure 1). No distinction is made between the influence of an unrelated prime word and a neutral prime; both would produce the same result because neither would move the pattern of activation among the conceptual nodes toward the upcoming target's pattern. The overall pattern of priming effects generated by the model, then, is one of facilitation without inhibition (Forster, 1981; Neely, 1977). Inhibition effects are not a natural part of the model and are assumed to be a product of attentional processes (Neely, 1977; Posner & Snyder, 1975) not simulated in the model.

IV. SIMULATION OF EMPIRICAL RESULTS

The distributed memory model view of priming is analogous to that of classic spreading activation models in that both assume that a prime activates related concepts. There are, however, some fundamental differences as well. These differences are reflected in the ease with which the distributed memory model accounts for the empirical results that are very difficult to handle with models that assume each concept is represented by a single node in memory.

1. Semantic Relatedness and the Time Course of Priming

The Ratcliff and McKoon (1981) and Lorch (1982) results reviewed earlier provided clear evidence of two aspects of priming that cause difficulty for classical spreading activation theories. One is the fact that priming effects have a virtually immediate onset, and the other is that this immediacy holds regardless of the degree of relatedness between prime and target. These findings pose problems for the classical view because its predictions depend on the assumptions that activation takes time to spread among nodes and that time needed for activation to travel between two nodes is inversely related to the strength of relationship between them. Moreover, spreading activation models usually assume that asymptotic activation will be reached sooner in cases of stronger semantic relatedness between prime and target. None of these expectations have been realized in empirical tests.

The effects of semantic relatedness and SOA are perfectly consistent with the distributed memory model. This can be appreciated by examining the dynamics of the activation of the conceptual nodes during processing of the prime. As soon as a prime appears update cycles begin to influence the pattern of activation in the conceptual nodes. The conceptual nodes immediately begin to move toward a pattern that represents the prime concept, continuously raising its level of activation (see the right panel of Figure 3). The pattern of activation across the conceptual nodes also determines the degree of activation of all other concepts known to the system. Consequently, to the extent that the pattern of activation in the conceptual nodes approximates the prime concept, it also approximates (although to a lesser degree) those concepts related to the prime (e.g., in Figure 1 consider pattern A the target and B the prime). Thus, as activation of the prime grows over time, so does activation of its related concepts. This means that as the first few updates move the conceptual nodes toward the prime's pattern, the conceptual nodes also immediately begin to approximate (i.e., activate) related concepts. Furthermore, concepts more strongly related to the prime are more similar to the prime in their patterns of conceptual node activation, so their degree of activation will be higher than that for less strongly related concepts.

On the average, during processing of the prime the highest degree of similarity between the pattern of activation in the conceptual nodes and the patterns for concepts related to the prime will occur when the prime is fully activated. Complete activation of the prime means that the system has settled into a stable state so that any further updating cycles will have no influence on the state of the conceptual nodes. Once full activation of the prime has been achieved, therefore, asymptotic priming effects appear. Further postponement of the target will yield no additional priming effect.

The time required for complete activation of the prime is independent of the nature of the upcoming target, so priming effects will asymptote at the same SOA regardless of strength of relatedness between prime and target. The amount of asymptotic activation of primed targets depends on semantic relatedness between prime and target because relatedness is assumed to be determined by the degree of similarity in the conceptual activation patterns of the prime and target. When the prime is fully activated the pattern of conceptual node activation will be more similar to strongly related target concepts than to weakly related ones, thereby producing a greater asymptotic priming effect for items of the former type.

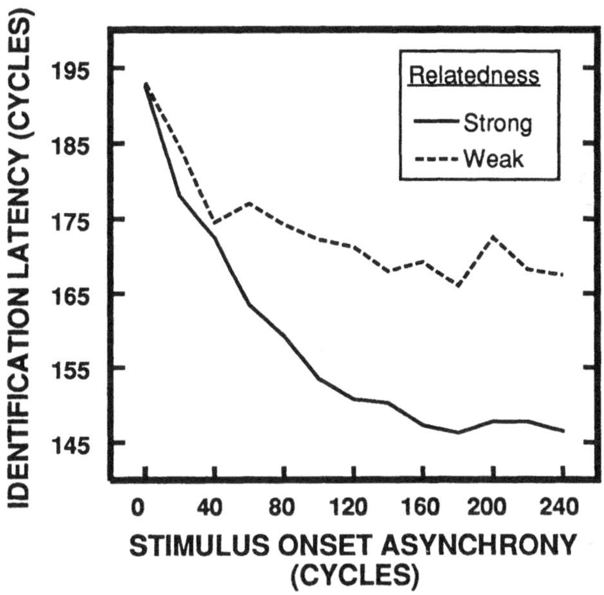

Fig. 4. Simulation of priming effects on identification of a target as a function of stimulus onset asynchrony and semantic relatedness between prime and target.

These effects were simulated using a network consisting of 75 perceptual and 50 conceptual nodes. In all cases, the perceptual part of a concept's pattern was randomly determined. These two aspects of the simulation held for all simulations reported in this article, except where noted. The set of learned concepts included a target and two primes, one more similar to the target than the other. The strongly related prime consisted of a conceptual pattern in which 40 of the 50 nodes matched the target's pattern. The weakly related prime had 35 of its conceptual nodes in common with the target pattern. These values were chosen on the basis of pilot simulations to produce a large effect of relatedness. Theoretically, a priming effect might be obtained using a prime concept with many fewer nodes in common with the target, but the effect would be very small. Using primes with nearly perfect overlap with the target runs the risk of generating spurious stable states and making the states representing the learned patterns unstable.

In addition, a fourth concept was learned. This concept was chosen to have 40 conceptual nodes in common with the weak prime and 35 in common with the strong prime. The reason for adding this "filler" concept was to equate the two prime concepts with respect to amount of similarity to other known concepts. This was important because the number of updating cycles required to move the network to a concept's stable state depends on that concept's degree of similarity to other learned concepts. An explanation of this phenomenon is beyond the scope of this article, but is related to the concept of *energy* of network states which is discussed by Hopfield (1982).

Priming was simulated by assigning the prime's perceptual pattern to the perceptual nodes and starting the conceptual nodes in a random configuration. Updating cycles for the conceptual nodes began and ran for the prescribed SOA, then the perceptual pattern of the target was assigned to the perceptual nodes and updating resumed. Identification latency was measured from the point at which the target's perceptual pattern was presented. The simulation was run on 300 independently constructed sets of concepts. In each set a target pattern was randomly determined, then a strong and a weak associate and a filler pattern were produced. For each set of concepts the network connection strengths were set to zero, the set of concepts learned, and five presentations of prime-target pairs at each level of associative strength were simulated at each of 13 SOA values. The mean number of updating cycles required for the system to reach the target's stable state was computed for each combination of relatedness and SOA. Each mean was based on a maximum of 1500 trials (five trials with each of the 300 sets of concepts), although less than 1% of the trials were discarded because the system failed to reach the target state within 600 update cycles. The results of the simulation are shown in Figure 4. The pattern of results is perfectly consistent with the data obtained by Ratcliff and McKoon (1981) and by Lorch (1982). For both types of prime, facilitation effects have an immediate onset and asymptotic facilitation, defined as the minimum target identification time, is reached at the same SOA value (180 cycles). Unlike classic network models of spreading activation, the distributed memory model readily produces this pattern of results.

2. Mediated Priming Effects

Although DE Groot (1983) obtained results that suggested priming effects were not obtained between two concepts that were not directly linked, Balota and Lorch (1986) have provided convincing evidence to the contrary as discussed earlier. Balota and Lorch concluded that activation could spread between concepts that are not connected directly by first passing through a mutual neighbor. In the classic view of one node for one concept, if one word elicits another in a word association task, it is assumed that the two words are connected directly. If a word does not evoke another, however, the two words are assumed not to be linked directly. The issue of mediated priming, however, is interpreted very differently in the context of the distributed memory model. Rather than treating concepts as single nodes, the model represents concepts as different patterns of activation across a shared system of nodes. In this system, there are two possible analogies to the distinction made in classic network models between directly and indirectly connected nodes.

One possibility is words that do not evoke one another on word association tasks are completely unrelated, having only a chance number of conceptual features in common. In this case, a mediating concept would be one that shared many features with each of two unrelated concepts. According to the classic view of spreading activation, one unrelated concept can prime the other by sending activation to it via the mediating concept. In the distributed memory model there is no means by which the two unrelated concepts can prime one another. Presenting the perceptual pattern of one of the concepts as a prime moves the conceptual nodes toward a pattern of activation consistent with the prime, but this pattern is unrelated to the upcoming target. In this case no priming effect would occur--target identification time would be no different than if an unrelated prime with no mediating concept or no prime at all were presented.

The pattern of results expected by this reasoning was simulated by encoding in a network (a) a target concept, (b) a related concept, (c) a concept unrelated to the first, but related to the second, and (d) a concept unrelated to all of the other concepts. The target and related concepts patterns matched in 38 of the 50 conceptual nodes. Four types of priming trials were simulated, one for each of items (b) through (d) representing related, mediated, and unrelated primes, respectively, and a fourth constituting a neutral prime in which the conceptual nodes were in a randomly determined pattern when the target was presented. The simulation was run 100 times, with each run based on an independently determined set of concepts. In each run five trials were attempted in each of the priming conditions, producing a total of 500 trials per condition. Less than 1% of these trials failed to reach the stable state represented by the target concept. Results are expressed as the mean numbers of cycles required for the system to reach the target's stable state.

The results of this simulation, shown in the first row of Table 2, replicated the DE Groot (1983) findings. If one assumes that the results obtained by Balota and Lorch (1986) using the word naming task are more representative of mediated priming effects, it might appear as though ability to produce the DE Groot results is evidence for a serious problem in the model.

A second interpretation of mediated priming effects, however, appears to be closer to the mark. This view holds that although one word may not elicit another on a word association task, the two words may still be related to one another (i.e., have similar patterns of conceptual features). One might expect that the degree of similarity in such cases would be less than when a prime elicits the target in an association task, but there would be some nontrivial amount of relatedness. In the distributed memory model it is relatedness that determines the effectiveness of a prime rather than ability to elicit the target on an association task. In support of

Table 2
Simulation of Mediated Priming Effects Under Different Assumptions of Relatedness between Target and Mediated Prime.

	Prime			
Relation between target and mediated prime	Related	Mediated	Neutral	Unrelated
Unrelated	170	191	187	192
Related	172	178	183	193

Note. Values represent mean number of update cycles required for the simulation to complete the target pattern.

this view, Fischler (1977b) and Seidenberg et al. (1984) have shown that *semantically* related word pairs produce priming effects in lexical decision and word naming that are about as strong as priming effects produced by *associatively* related word pairs. Moreover, Fischler found that the magnitude of facilitation for associatively related pairs appeared to be more closely related to semantic similarity of the pairs than to degree of associative strength.

A simulation of this scenario was produced by altering the previous simulation to allow the mediated prime to be moderately similar to the target (34 of the 50 conceptual nodes in the mediated prime's pattern matched the target's pattern). The related prime was more strongly related to the target as might be expected of a strong associate. The results of the simulation are shown in the second row of Table 2. This simulation very closely approximated the results obtained by Balota and Lorch (1986) using a word naming task. It is quite plausible that the results obtained by DE Groot (1983) with lexical decision were a product of post-access processes associated with the lexical decision task. In its present form the distributed memory model has no means of capturing such effects and is therefore a better approximation of the word naming task, under the assumption that the naming task is less prone to post-access effects. Consequently, the model's account of mediated priming effects rests on the claim that nonassociatively related pairs nonetheless may be semantically related.

3. Influence of an Intervening Prime

In the automatic spreading activation view presentation of a prime has no influence on the level of activation of unrelated concepts. In the distributed memory system, presentation of any concept influences the activation of all other concepts because activation level of all concepts is determined by the current state of the conceptual nodes. These two views make differential predictions about the influence of placing an unrelated prime between a related prime and target.

Spreading activation models based on Posner and Snyder's (1975) two-process theory would predict that an unrelated intervening prime should not influence the effectiveness of an earlier related prime as long as stimulus onset asynchronies are appropriately short. As discussed above, however, recognition memory, lexical decision, and word naming paradigms (Masson, 1988; Ratcliff & McKoon, 1988) have produced clear evidence that facilitation is reduced or eliminated when an unrelated intervening prime is presented.

In the distributed memory model presentation of a familiar stimulus alters significantly the pattern of activation in the conceptual nodes. This means that an intervening prime will change the pattern constructed by earlier presentation of a related prime. The intervening prime effect was simulated by encoding into a network a target pattern along with one related and two unrelated patterns. The pattern of activation in the target's conceptual nodes matched the activation in the related concept in 38 of 50 nodes. Presentation of a series of two primes consisted of loading the perceptual pattern for the first prime and updating conceptual nodes for 40 cycles. When the second prime was an unrelated concept its perceptual pattern was loaded and updating of conceptual nodes continued for another 40 cycles. When the second prime was a neutral stimulus a random pattern was loaded into the perceptual nodes and the system was allowed to run for 40 cycles.

Four conditions were simulated, representing a factorial combination of initial prime (related or unrelated) and intervening prime (neutral or unrelated). The simulation consisted of 100 runs, each based on an independently determined set of concepts and five trials in each of the four priming conditions. The mean numbers of cycles for the network to reach the target's stable state are shown in Table 3. The network succeeded in reaching the target state on every trial. The model produced a pattern of means that is consistent with the empirical finding that an intervening unrelated prime reduces or eliminates the facilitation that otherwise would have been generated by the initial prime.

4. Lexical Ambiguity

The distributed memory model's success at reproducing a number of empirical results that cause difficulty for spreading activation theories is due to the incorporation of a shared representational system. Full activation of a concept requires that all conceptual nodes in the system fit that concept's pattern of activation. An important implication of this scheme is that unrelated concepts cannot simultaneously reach full or even high levels of activation. If one concept dominates the conceptual nodes, few of the nodes will correspond to the patterns used to represent other unrelated concepts. This characteristic of the model appears to be at odds with some work on lexical ambiguity. A number of studies have produced evidence to suggest that multiple, unrelated interpretations of an ambiguous word may be simultaneously activated (Onifer & Swinney, 1981; Seidenberg, Tanenhaus, Leiman, & Bienkowski, 1982; Swinney, 1979).

Table 3
Simulation of the Influence of an Unrelated Intervening Prime on the Facilitation Produced by a Related Initial Prime.

	Initial prime	
Intervening prime	Related	Unrelated
Neutral	159	187
Unrelated	182	191

Note. Values represent mean number of update cycles required for the simulation to complete the target pattern.

In an attempt to use the model to account for the empirical results that yielded this conclusion, ambiguous words were created by encoding two items into the network with *identical perceptual* patterns but *unrelated conceptual* patterns. It was not immediately obvious how the system would deal with the task of producing a conceptual pattern in response to the ambiguous perceptual pattern. One possibility was that it might attempt some form of compromise, producing moderate activation of both conceptual interpretations and remaining unable to select among them. Another option was that the system would activate only one interpretation and move toward completion of that pattern only. Selection of an interpretation would be determined by the randomly chosen initial pattern for the conceptual nodes. The interpretation most similar to the starting pattern would be the state toward which the network would move.

Simulations showed that one effect of encoding two items with identical perceptual patterns was to produce some spurious stable states that were highly similar but not identical to an encoded state. The result was that when the model was presented the ambiguous perceptual pattern it sometimes moved into one of these spurious stable states rather than into one of the learned states. Despite this phenomenon, it was clear that the model moved toward a stable conceptual configuration that was consistent with only one of the two known interpretations of the pattern. In cases where the stable state achieved was equivalent to an encoded conceptual pattern, the alternative interpretation received almost no activation. The activation that was observed came about only because of coincidental similarity between the conceptual patterns of the two interpretations. That is, a fully activated interpretation sometimes sometimes shared more than half of its conceptual pattern of activation with the alternative interpretation.

Given the model's handling of ambiguous words, it is important to determine whether it is capable of producing empirical results that appear to support the multiple activation hypothesis. The model was tested by attempting a simulation of the results of Experiment 1 reported by Seidenberg et al. (1982). In this study subjects listened to clauses that ended with a prime word and named aloud a visually presented target word. The target appeared immediately after the prime word had been pronounced (interstimulus interval = 0 msec) or 200 msec after pronunciation. Three kinds of primes were used in the clauses: (a) an ambiguous word, one meaning of which was related to the upcoming target (e.g., *Joe buys the straw-HAY*), (b) an unambiguous word related to the target (e.g., *Joe buys the wheat-HAY*), and (c) an unambiguous word unrelated to the target (e.g., *Joe buys the soda-HAY*). The clauses were constructed so as not to bias the interpretation of the ambiguous prime word.

It was found that when the target appeared immediately after the prime the advantage of using a related prime word, relative to the unrelated condition, was not significantly different for the ambiguous and unambiguous cases. This result was taken as evidence for activation of both meanings of the ambiguous prime. Seidenberg et al. reasoned that had only one meaning of the ambiguous prime been active, priming would have been found on only half the trials and the overall priming effect for the ambiguous prime would be less than for the unambiguous related prime. When a delay of 200 msec was used, however, facilitation *was* greater for the unambiguous prime, indicating that during the delay one meaning of the ambiguous prime had been selected arbitrarily.

This pattern of results was simulated by constructing concepts with two types of perceptual nodes, visual and auditory. An ambiguous word was created by constructing two concepts that had identical patterns of activation in their perceptual nodes but unrelated patterns in their conceptual nodes. In addition to the two concepts representing an ambiguous word, two pairs of concepts constituting unambiguous words also were encoded. One pair consisted of words related to one of the ambiguous word's meanings and the other pair was related to the other meaning. These items were used to simulate the three priming conditions tested by Seidenberg et al. (1982, Experiment 1). An unambiguous word was the target and its prime could be the related ambiguous word, the related unambiguous word, or an unrelated unambiguous word.

The network used in the simulation consisted of 85 perceptual nodes, 35 devoted to the visual pattern and 50 to the auditory pattern, and 40 conceptual nodes. Related concepts shared patterns of activation in 28 of the 40 conceptual nodes. At the start of a trial the conceptual nodes were set at a random pattern under the assumption that the previously presented word was not semantically related to the prime. Seidenberg et al. specifically avoided use of semantically related words in the sentence materials for Experiment 1. For the 0-msec interstimulus interval (ISI) condition the auditory pattern of the prime and the visual pattern of the target were loaded simultaneously into the network. Both parts of the perceptual pattern were loaded at the same time under the assumption that processing of the auditory prime would not begin until the entire stimulus had been pronounced, and by that time the visual target had appeared.[1] A series of 75 updating cycles were run, representing simultaneous processing of the auditory and visual stimuli. Then the auditory pattern was set to zero to reflect termination of auditory processing and concentration on the visual target. Updating continued until the target was identified. For the 200-msec ISI condition processing of the auditory prime was allowed to continue for 75 cycles, then the auditory perceptual pattern as set to zero, the visual perceptual pattern corresponding to the target was loaded, and updating continued. This arrangement reflects the assumption that after 200 msec processing of the auditory signal is terminated by appearance of a visual target.

The simulation was run on 100 independently selected sets of concepts. For each set 10 trials involving each priming condition were tested. Even with the high degree of similarity among the conceptual nodes of the related concepts, only 10.6% of the trials failed to reach the stable state representing the target concept. The mean number of cycles required to identify the target as a function of type of prime and ISI is shown in Table 4.

Table 4
Simulation of Identification of a Visual Target Following an Auditory Prime.

	Prime		
Interstimulus interval	Related ambiguous	Related unambiguous	Unrelated unambiguous
0 msec	194	196	230
200 msec	152	138	179

Note. Values represent mean number of update cycles required for the simulation to complete the target pattern.

The simulation results very closely approximated the data obtained in Experiment 1 of Seidenberg et al. (1982). With immediate presentation of the target the ambiguous and unambiguous related primes produced nearly equal facilitation. The model's account of this result, however, is *not* that both interpretations of the ambiguous prime are equally activated. Nor does the model engage in what Glucksberg, Kreuz, and Rho (1986) described as *backward priming*, whereby activation of the target concept spreads to the appropriate interpretation of the ambiguous prime and the resulting activation of that concept spreads back to the target, enhancing its identification.

A more accurate characterization of the model's behavior would be *simultaneous priming*. It is assumed that there is a period during which both the visual target and the auditory prime influence the conceptual nodes. The early onset of the visual pattern for the target moves the conceptual nodes toward a pattern of activation that is consistent with only one interpretation of the ambiguous auditory prime--the one that is consistent with the target. When the visual target is delayed there is no such influence and the auditory prime is equally likely to receive the appropriate or inappropriate interpretation, so on about half the trials the auditory prime is of no benefit.

The model yields an overall reduction in identification time in the delayed condition whereas Seidenberg et al. (1982) obtained an increase. In later experiments Seidenberg et al. found a reduction in response time with delay so it is unclear which effect is valid. One problem is that the experiments manipulated delay between subjects. A within-subject manipulation would be needed to obtain a more accurate picture of the global influence of delay. The model produces faster identification in the delay condition because in that case the target's visual pattern operates entirely on its own without simultaneous influence from an auditory pattern that tries to drive the conceptual nodes toward a configuration that differs from the target pattern.

The model has not yet been applied to an experiment in which evidence was obtained for selective activation of one interpretation of an ambiguous prime using a 0-msec ISI (Seidenberg et al., 1982, Experiment 2). In this study a word strongly related to one interpretation of the ambiguous prime was included in the clause that carried the prime (e.g., *Although the farmer bought the straw-HAY*). This effect could be simulated by assuming that the related word leaves the conceptual nodes in a state of activation that is very similar to only one of the interpretations of the ambiguous word, and so that interpretation is taken as soon as the ambiguous word occurs. The explanation of selective activation offered by Seidenberg et al. (1982) is consistent with this characterization.

V. CONCLUSION

The distributed memory model described here is based on a representational scheme that is consistent with a current trend toward neurally inspired connectionist models (e.g., McClelland & Rumelhart, 1986; Rumelhart & McClelland, 1986). I have attempted to use the model to highlight one important aspect of this approach to the construction of cognitive theories. The fundamental contribution of the model is the use of a distributed representation for concepts in semantic memory. This view is a significant departure from what appears to be the prevalent interpretation of semantic memory structure (a one-to-one correspondence between nodes and concepts).

It is appropriate to consider the distributed memory model and models that allocate a single node to each memory concept as competitors, rather than different levels of description (cf. Broadbent, 1985). Both are intended as explanations of psychological processes at the level of representation and algorithm and there are circumstances under which they make differential predictions. Using very simple learning and pattern completion algorithms based on a distributed memory representation, a number of important results concerning context effects on word identification were simulated. Success was achieved even for effects that cause serious difficulties for classic semantic network models.

The distributed memory model provides rather useful intuitions about why context effects emerge in the way they do. A prime serves to move the pattern of activation among conceptual nodes toward its representation, causing partial activation of all concepts related to it. The activation level of unrelated concepts remains virtually unchanged because as updating of the conceptual nodes continues, the overall similarity between the current pattern and the patterns representing unrelated concepts remain at approximately the chance level of 50% overlap. With a neutral prime the pattern of activation among conceptual nodes moves about randomly, failing to activate any known concepts. This situation yields the classic combination of facilitation without inhibition.

The model also was able to make a contribution to the controversial area of lexical ambiguity. Although the model's account of lexical access of ambiguous words clearly rules out multiple access (at least under the conditions of the experimental paradigm modelled here), it does not go to the extreme of assuming that contextual information outside the lexicon determines which interpretation will be accessed. An alternative view is offered in which modular assumptions about lexical processing can be preserved. The model makes no inherent commitment to the existence or exclusion of contextual influence from sources outside the lexicon. In its current form, however, the model is aligned with modular views of the lexicon (e.g., Fodor, 1983; Forster, 1979; Seidenberg & Tanenhaus, 1986) in its assumption that lexical activation is affected only by perceptual input and intralexical patterns of activation.

The most important virtue of the model described here is its simplicity. The simulation results it produced were obtained with very few and well motivated assumptions. The strategy I have followed is to test the model in its simplest form in an effort to discover the kinds of results that would cause it great difficulty. The model's degree of success has been greater than expected and even surprising in some cases. The next stage of development, however, will consist of extending the model to handle aspects of word identification that involve the influence of a variety of learning episodes such as word frequency and repetition effects. It is expected that although simulation of these effects may require changes in the learning algorithm used in the current model, the foundation of the model will remain committed to a distributed memory representation.

FOOTNOTE

[1]This assumption is not critical. Results very similar to those reported were obtained when the auditory pattern was allowed to influence the conceptual nodes for a short time prior to loading the visual pattern.

ACKNOWLEDGMENTS

The research reported here was supported by a grant from the Natural Sciences and Engineering Research Council of Canada. Computer resources were provided by the University of Victoria and by Microelectronics and Computer Technology Corporation (MCC) in Austin, Texas, where early work on the model was conducted during a sabbatical leave. I am grateful to my colleagues at MCC who provided valuable suggestions and encouragement, particularly Gale Martin and Carsten Peterson.

REFERENCES

Ackley, D. H., Hinton, G. E., & Sejnowski, T. J. (1985). A learning algorithm for Boltzmann machines. *Cognitive Science,* **9,** 147-169.

Anderson, J. R. (1976). *Language memory and thought.* Hillsdale, NJ: Lawrence Erlbaum Associates.

Balota, D. A., & Lorch, R. F., Jr. (1986). Depth of automatic spreading activation: Mediated priming effects in pronunciation but not in lexical decision. *Journal of Experimental Psychology: Learning, Memory, and Cognition,* **12,** 336-345.

Becker, C. A. (1980). Semantic context effects in visual word recognition: An analysis of semantic strategies. *Memory & Cognition,* **8,** 493-512.

Broadbent, D. (1985). A question of levels: Comment on McClelland and Rumelhart. *Journal of Experimental Psychology: General,* **114,** 189-192.

Collins, A. M., & Loftus, E. F. (1975). A spreading activation theory of semantic processing. *Psychological Review,* **82,** 407-428.

Collins, A. M., & Qullian, M. R. (1969). Retrieval time from semantic memory. *Journal of Verbal Learning and Verbal Behavior,* **8,** 240-248.

Conrad, C. (1972). Cognitive economy in semantic memory. *Journal of Experimental Psychology,* **92,** 149-154.

Davelaar, E., & Coltheart, M. (1975). Effects of interpolated items on the association effect in lexical decision tasks. *Bulletin of the Psychonomic Society,* **6,** 269-272.

Eich, J. M. (1985). Levels of processing, encoding specificity, elaboration, and CHARM. *Psychological Review,* **92,** 1-38.

DE Groot, A. M. B. (1983). The range of automatic spreading activation in word priming. *Journal of Verbal Learning and Verbal Behavior,* **22,** 417-436.

Fischler, I. (1977a). Associative facilitation without expectancy in a lexical decision task. *Journal of Experimental Psychology: Human Perception and Performance,* **3,** 18-26.

Fischler, I. (1977b). Semantic facilitation without association in a lexical decision task. *Memory & Cognition,* **5,** 335-339.

Fodor, J. A. (1983). *The modularity of mind.* Cambridge, MA: MIT Press.

Forster, K. I. (1979). Levels of processing and the structure of the language processor. In W. E. Cooper & E. C. T. Walker (Eds.), *Sentence processing: Psycholinguistic studies presented to Merrill Garrett* (pp. 27-85). Cambridge, MA: MIT Press.

Forster, K. I. (1981). Priming and the effects of sentence and lexical contexts on naming time: Evidence for autonomous lexical processing. *Quarterly Journal of Experimental Psychology,* **33A,** 465-495.

Freedman, J. L., & Loftus, E. F. (1971). Retrieval of words from long-term memory. *Journal of Verbal Learning and Verbal Behavior,* **10,** 107-115.

Glucksberg, S., Kreuz, R. J., & Rho, S. H. (1986). Context can constrain lexical access: Implications for models of language comprehension. *Journal of Experimental Psychology: Learning, Memory, and Cognition,* **12,** 323-335.

Gough, P. B., Alford, J. A., Jr., & Holley-Wilcox, P. (1981). Words and contexts. In O. J. L. Tzeng & H. Singer (Eds.), *Perception of print: Reading research in experimental psychology* (pp. 85-102). Hillsdale, NJ: Lawrence Erlbaum Associates.

Hayes-Roth, B. (1977). Evolution of cognitive structures and processes. *Psychological Review* , **84,** 260-278.

Hebb, D. O. (1949). *The organization of behavior.* New York: Wiley.

Hinton, G. E., & Sejnowski, T. J. (1986). Learning and relearning in Boltzmann machines. In D. E. Rumelhart & J. L. McClelland (Eds.), *Parallel distributed processing* (Vol. 1). Cambridge, MA: MIT Press.

Hopfield, J. J. (1982). Neural networks and physical systems with emergent collective computational abilities. *Proceedings of the National Academy of Science,* **79,** 2554-2558.

Hopfield, J. J., & Tank, D. W. (1986). Computing with neural circuits: A model. *Science,* **233,** 625-633.

Jonides, J., & Mack, R. (1984). On the cost and benefit of cost and benefit. *Psychological Bulletin,* **96**, 29-44.
Lorch, R. F., Jr. (1982). Priming and search processes in semantic memory: A test of three models of spreading activation. *Journal of Verbal Learning and Verbal Behavior,* **21**, 468-492.
Masson, M. E. J. (1988). *Interference among unrelated sources of automatic spreading activation.* Manuscript in preparation.
McClelland, J. L., & Rumelhart, D. E. (1981). An interactive acitvation model of context effects in letter perception: Part 1. An account of basic findings. *Psychological Review,* **88**, 375-407.
McClelland, J. L., & Rumelhart, D. E. (1985). Distributed memory and the representation of general and specific information. *Journal of Experimental Psychology: General,* **114**, 159-188.
McClelland, J. L., & Rumelhart, D. E. (Eds.). (1986). *Parallel distributed processing* (Vol. 2). Cambridge, MA: MIT Press.
Meyer, D. E., Schvaneveldt, R. W., & Ruddy, M. G. (November 1972). *Activation of lexical memory.* Paper presented at the meeting of the Psychonomic Society, St. Louis, MO.
Mozer, M. C. (1983). Letter migration in word perception. *Journal of Experimental Psychology: Human perception and performance,* **9**, 531-546.
Murdock, B. B., Jr. (1983). A distributed memory model for serial-order information. *Psychological Review,* **90**, 316-338.
Neely, J. H. (1976). Semantic priming and retrieval from lexical memory: Evidence for facilitatory and inhibitory processes. *Memory & Cognition* , **4**, 648-654.
Neely, J. H. (1977). Semantic priming and retrieval from lexical memory: Roles of inhibitionless spreading activation and limited-capacity attention. *Journal of Experimental Psychology: General,* **106**, 226-254.
Onifer, W., & Swinney, D. A. (1981). Accessing lexical ambiguities during sentence comprehension: Effects of frequency of meaning and contextual bias. *Memory & Cognition,* **9**, 225-236.
Perlmutter, J., Sorce, P., & Myers, J. L. (1976). Retrieval processes in recall. *Cognitive Psychology,* **8**, 32-63.
Posner, M. I., & Snyder, C. R. R. (1975). Attention and cognitive control. In R. L. Solso (Ed.), *Information processing and cognition: The Loyola Symposium* (pp. 55-85). Hillsdale, NJ: Erlbaum.
Ratcliff, R., & McKoon, G. (1981). Does activation really spread? *Psychological Review,* **88**, 454-462.
Ratcliff, R., & McKoon, G. (1988). A retrieval theory of priming in memory. *Psychological Review,* **95**, 385-408.
Ratcliff, R., & Murdock, B. B., Jr. (1976). Retrieval processes in recognition memory. *Psychological Review,* **83**, 190-214.
Reed, A. V. (1976). List length and the time course of recognition in immediate memory. *Memory & Cognition,* **4**, 16-30.
Rumelhart, D. E., & McClelland, J. L. (1982). An interactive acitvation model of context effects in letter perception: Part 2. The contextual enhancement effect and some tests and extensions of the model. *Psychological Review,* **89**, 60-94.
Rumelhart, D. E., & McClelland, J. L. (Eds.). (1986). *Parallel distributed processing* (Vol. 1). Cambridge, MA: MIT Press.
Seidenberg, M. S., & Tanenhaus, M. K. (1986). Modularity and lexical access. In I. Gopnik & M. Gopnik (Eds.), *From models to modules* (pp. 135-157). Norwood, NJ: Ablex.
Seidenberg, M. S., Tanenhaus, M. K., Leiman, J. M., & Bienkowski, M. (1982). Automatic access of the meanings of ambiguous words in context: Some limitations of knowledge toward processing. *Cognitive Psychology,* **14**, 489-537.
Seidenberg, M. S., Waters, G. S., Sanders, M., & Langer, P. (1984). Pre- and postlexical loci of contextual effects on word recognition. *Memory & Cognition,* **12**, 315-328.
Smith, E. E., Shoben, E. J., & Rips, L. J. (1974). Structure and process in semantic memory: A feature model for semantic decisions. *Psychological Review,* **81**, 214-241.

Smith, L. C., Briand, K., Klein, R. M., & den Heyer, K. (1987). On the generality of Becker's verification model. *Canadian Journal of Psychology*, **41**, 379-386.
Swinney, D. A. (1979). Lexical access during sentence comprehension: (Re)consideration of context effects. *Journal of Verbal Learning and Verbal Behavior*, **18**, 645-659.
Tversky, A. (1977). Features of similarity. *Psychological Review*, **84**, 327-352.
Yantis, S., & Meyer, D. E. (1988). Dynamics of activation in semantic and episodic memory. *Journal of Experimental Psychology: General*, **117**, 130-147.

9

SEMANTIC PRIMING EFFECTS IN VISUAL WORD RECOGNITION: A SELECTIVE REVIEW OF CURRENT FINDINGS AND THEORIES

JAMES H. NEELY

Department of Psychology
State University of New York at Albany
USA

Nearly two decades have elapsed since Meyer and Schvaneveldt (1971) reported their seminal experiment on semantic priming. In their experiment, subjects were either to press one key if both of two simultaneously presented visual letter strings were English words or to press another key otherwise. Unsurprisingly, subjects were faster and more accurate in responding to displays containing two semantically/associatively related words (e.g., *bread* and *butter*) than to displays with two unrelated words (e.g., *doctor* and *butter*). Despite its intuitive simplicity, Meyer and Schvaneveldt's semantic priming effect spawned an exponential growth in the number of published papers that examined the general issue of how word recognition is influenced by semantic context. Given the extensive research literature that now exists on this topic, it seems reasonable eighteen years later to pause and review the empirical and theoretical products that literature has yielded. My contribution to this volume attempts to provide such a review.

Because so many publications are potentially relevant to the general issue of how semantic context affects word recognition, I must be somewhat selective in choosing which findings and theories to discuss. To this end, I focus primarily on data collected in what I call the single-word semantic priming paradigm. As I define this paradigm, a trial consists of two events: First, a semantic context is provided by the presentation of a single word (called the *prime*), to which no overt response is required (though I sometimes discuss data from experiments in which a response is required to the prime). Second, this prime is followed by the presentation of a single letter string (called the *target*). In nearly all experiments that have used this paradigm, subjects have been required either to make a word/nonword decision to the target (the lexical decision task, LDT) or to say the target aloud (the pronunciation task). When the target is a word, it is either related or unrelated to its prime. The effect of the related priming context is typically assessed by subtracting reaction times (RTs) or percentage errors for word targets that follow related primes from RTs or percentage errors for word targets that follow either unrelated primes or neutral primes. When performance for targets that follow unrelated primes serves as the baseline, I call the resulting difference an *overall* priming effect. When performance for targets that follow neutral primes serves as the baseline, I call the resulting difference *facilitation* when it is positive and *inhibition* when it is negative.

This single-word semantic priming paradigm has two potential advantages over the earliest procedures used to study semantic priming. First, compared to Meyer and Schvaneveldt's (1971) original procedures, the subject's task is simpler in that she or he must respond on the basis of the lexicality of a single letter string rather than two letter strings. Presumably, this also simplifies our theoretical analysis. Second, with procedures in which subjects first respond to the prime and then some time elapses before the target is presented (e.g., Meyer, Schvaneveldt, & Ruddy, 1975), one cannot examine semantic priming at prime-target stimulus onset asynchronies (SOAs) that are shorter than the subjects' RTs to the prime. When no response is required to the prime, one can examine semantic priming at these shorter prime-target SOAs.

In addition to simplifying my task by focusing on data from this single-word priming paradigm, I will also explicitly ignore the rather large literature on repetition priming (e.g., Besner & Swan, 1982; Humphreys, Besner, & Quinlan, 1988; Forster & Davis, 1984; Kanwisher, 1987; Monsell, 1985; Norris, 1984; Scarborough, Cortese, & Scarborough, 1977). In repetition priming, the prime and target represent the same word and are often separated by several other intervening items. Though the prime and target clearly are semantically related in the repetition priming paradigm, any semantic priming that occurs could be contaminated by other types of priming produced by the shared graphemic and phonemic properties of the prime and target (e.g., Humphreys, Evett, & Taylor, 1982; Jordan, 1986; Meyer, Schvaneveldt, & Ruddy, 1974; Tanenhaus, Flanagan, & Seidenberg, 1980). A discussion of how the effects of these latter types of priming might interact with semantic priming effects lies beyond the scope of this paper. (See den Heyer, Goring, & Dannenbring; 1985, Durgunoglu, 1988; and Wilding, 1986, for evidence that the effects of spaced repetition of the targets and semantic priming effects for those targets are often additive. On the other hand, Snow and Neely, 1987, showed that semantic priming is nearly eliminated when a very high proportion of the trials contain primes and targets that are the same word.) By excluding data from experiments in which the primes and/or targets are repeated, I also eliminate from consideration so-called episodic priming effects, which are based on an association between the prime and target that was learned earlier in the experimental session (e.g., Carroll & Kirsner, 1982; Dosher, 1984; Dosher & Rosedale, 1989; Durgunoglu & Neely, 1987; McKoon & Ratcliff, 1979, 1986; Neely & Durgunoglu, 1985).

Although the foregoing selection criteria help focus my attention on a manageable number of empirical phenonemona relevant to how semantic context influences visual word recognition, I do not slavishly adhere to these criteria. Occasionally I will describe data from other priming paradigms when they are particularly germane to evaluating the validity of current theoretical accounts of the phenomena obtained in the single-word semantic priming paradigm. Finally, after summarizing the data and theories relevant to the single-word semantic priming paradigm, I will close by briefly considering the relevance of these data and theories for promoting our understanding of how semantic context influences visual word recognition in more interesting and ecologically valid situations such as the reading of coherent text. But first, I consider the phenomena from the single-word semantic priming paradigm for which theoretical accounts must be developed.

I. CENTRAL PHENOMENA FROM THE SINGLE-WORD SEMANTIC PRIMING PARADIGM

In this section, I review what I consider to be the core phenomena that must be accounted for by any theory with pretensions to providing an adequate explanation of how semantic context influences word recognition. In so doing, I first consider data from the LDT and then discuss whether the same phenonemon has been examined in the pronunciation task and, if so, whether or not it occurs in that task as well. As we shall see, a major challenge for theory is to explain why some semantic priming effects occur in both of these tasks whereas others do not. Table 1 provides a summary of the phenomena I discuss in this section. Because the error data almost always yield either no effects or the same priming effects as the RT data, I will focus on the RT data.

Table 1.
Priming Phenomena in the LDT and in Pronunciation

Phenomenon (and relevant section and tables)	LDT	Pronunciation
1. Nonassociative semantic priming (Sec. 1; Table 2)	yes	yes
2. Category-name priming of high- and low-dominance exemplars (Sec. 1; Table 3)	for both dominance levels	only for high-dominance exemplars
3. Mediated priming (Sec. 1)	not with standard procedures	yes
4. Backward priming (Sec. 1)	yes	no[a]
5. Related category-name facilitation for exemplar targets (Sec. 2; Tables 4-6)	yes, for both short & long SOAs	yes, for long SOAs; not well-studied for short SOAs
6. Unrelated category-name inhibition for exemplar targets (Sec. 2; Tables 4-6)	yes, but only for long SOAs	no
7. Associatively related prime facilitation (Sec. 2; Table 6)	yes, for both short & long SOAs	yes, for both short & long SOAs
8. Associatively unrelated prime inhibition (Sec. 2; Table 6)	very small effects, if any, at both short & long SOAs	no, for long SOAs; not well-studied for short SOAs
9. Nonword facilitation (Sec. 2 & 5)	yes, but larger at long SOAs; affected by nonword ratio but not by relatedness proportion	rarely examined
10. Target degradation (Sec. 3; Table 7)	increases priming	increases priming
11. Target word frequency (Sec.4)	priming larger for low-frequency targets	priming larger for low-frequency targets
12. Instruction-induced priming from unrelated primes (Sec. 5)	yes, but only for long SOAs	yes, at long SOAs; not well-studied for short SOAs
13. Relatedness proportion effect (Sec. 5; Table 8)	for long SOAs only; affects priming for both high- and low-dominance exemplars[b]	yes, at long SOAs; not well-studied for short SOAs; affects priming for high- but not low-dominance exemplars

14. Nonword ratio effect (Sec. 5)	examined for long SOAs only; affects priming for both high- and low-dominance exemplars	not examined
15. Increasing proportion of strong associate prime-target pairs (Sec. 5)	increases facilitation from related primes; decreases inhibition from unrelated primes; increases priming for high-dominance exemplars relative to low-dominance exemplars	not examined
16. Interposing an unrelated word between a related prime and target (Sec. 6)	reduces/eliminates priming	reduces/eliminates priming
17. "Subliminal" priming (Sec. 7)	yes, for long but not short SOAs	yes, for long SOAs; short SOAs not examined
18. "Shallow" conscious processing of the prime (Sec. 7)	reduces/eliminates priming	not examined

[a]See text for details.

[b]This is so, when the relatedness proportion effect is confounded with the nonword ratio. When it is not so confounded, relatedness proportion has an effect on priming for only high-dominance exemplars.

1. Overall Priming From Different Types of Prime-Target Relations

Associative vs. semantic priming. In most "semantic" priming experiments, the prime and target are either both associatively related items from the same semantic category (e.g., *doctor, nurse*) or are merely associatively related items from different semantic categories (e.g., *rake, leaf*). Clearly, an issue of interest is whether a prime and target that are semantically related but not associatively related will yield a facilitatory priming effect. Although Fischler (1977a) was the first to demonstrate a pure semantic priming effect in the LDT using the Meyer and Schvaneveldt (1971) procedures, here I focus on three published experiments that have examined this issue using both the LDT and the pronunciation task in the single-word semantic priming paradigm.

LDT. Lupker (1984, Experiment 5), Schreuder, Flores d'Arcais, and Glazenborg (1984, Experiment 1), and Seidenberg, Waters, Sanders, and Langer (1984, Experiment 4) examined "pure" semantic priming effects at single prime-target SOAs that varied from 400 ms (Schreuder et al.) to 800 ms (Lupker). Although Lupker and Seidenberg et al. used items such as *glove-hat* and *prince-boy* to instantiate the pure semantic priming condition, Schreuder et al. (1984) used words with perceptually similar referents (e.g., *carrot-paintbrush* and *pencil-nail*). Because this perceptual similarity is in the words' referents (meanings) and not in the words themselves, any priming obtained with these items can be considered to be due to a "semantic" relation, though it must be acknowledged that this kind of semantic/perceptual relation may be different from that instantiated in the Lupker (1984) and Seidenberg et al. (1984) studies. All three studies (Lupker, in Experiment 6; Seidenberg et al., in Experiment 4; Schreuder et al., in Experiment 1) also included associatively related primes and targets for purposes of comparison. (In Schreuder et al.'s Experiment 1 the words in this condition had referents that were both conceptually and perceptually similar, e.g., *banjo-guitar, pencil-pen*). As can be seen in the top half of Table 2, in the LDT, all three studies yielded an overall "pure semantic" priming effect as well as an overall associative priming effect, relative to the unrelated priming condition. However, the "pure semantic" priming effect was not statistically significant in the Schreuder et al. (1984) experiment.

Pronunciation. Lupker (1984) claimed that a "pure semantic" priming effect does not occur in pronunciation. He based this claim on the 7 ms priming effect in his Experiment 2 being small and not statistically significant when items were treated as a random factor in his analysis of variance. However, other data (likely unavailable to him at the time he wrote his paper) challenge this claim. These other data appear in the bottom half of Table 2. The semantic priming data come from Lupker's Experiment 2, and the associative priming data from his Experiment 4, whereas both types of priming data come from Schreuder et al.'s (1984) Experiment 2, and Seidenberg et al.'s (1984) Experiment 4. Averaged across the three studies in Table 2, the 15 ms "pure semantic"priming effect in pronunciation was nearly as large as the 19 ms associative priming effect. Moreover, Chiarello, Burgess, Gage, and Pollock (1989) and Hines, Czerwinski, Sawyer, and Dwyer (1986) have also obtained "pure semantic" priming effects in pronunciation.

A final interesting aspect of the data presented in Table 2 is that with the exception of Schreuder et al.'s (1984) "pure semantic" priming data, the priming effects in the LDT were larger than those in pronunciation. Specifically, averaged across both types of priming, the overall priming effects were 32 ms for the LDT and 17 ms for pronunciation. This is a very common finding in the literature. (See also Table 3 and the overall priming effects in Table 5.)

Priming for high- vs. low-dominance category exemplars. Several studies have used category-names (e.g., *BIRD*) as primes and their high-dominance exemplars (e.g., *robin*) and low-dominance exemplars (e.g., *goose*) as targets. In this section, I confine my attention to those two studies that have used exactly the same category-name primes and exemplar word targets in their LDT and pronunciation tasks. Specifically, I consider the LDT and pronunciation data from Lorch, Balota and Stamm (1986, Experiment 2) and the LDT data from Neely, Keefe, and Ross (1989, Experiment 1) and the pronunciation data from Keefe and Neely (1990, Experiment 1). (In the two Neely experiments, the data come from the group in which the proportion of word-prime/word-target trials

Table 2
Overall "Pure Semantic" vs. Associative Priming Effects (in ms) in the LDT and Pronunciation

Task & Study	Type of priming	
LDT	"Pure Semantic"	Associative
Lupker (1984)	26*	46*
Schreuder et al. (1984)	13	40*
Seidenberg et al. (1984)	31*	32*
Mean	24	39
Pronunciation		
Lupker (1984)	7*	19*
Schreuder et al. (1984)	28*	29*
Seidenberg et al. (1984)	9*	11*
Mean	15	19

Note. An * indicates an individual effect was significant at the .05 level of significance in an analysis of variance with subjects as a random factor.

that were related was .875.). In Lorch et al. (1986), the nonword-target trials that appeared in the LDT test list were removed from the pronunciation test list; in Keefe and Neely (1990), they were not removed. Table 3 presents the relevant data.

LDT. As shown in the top half of Table 3, the overall priming effects were substantial and nearly equivalent for the high- and low-dominance exemplars. This finding is very typical in that Becker (1980, Experiments 2 and 4), den Heyer, Briand, and Smith (1985) and Neely (1977) have also reported statistically equivalent overall priming effects for high- and low-dominance exemplars in the LDT. The one exception to this comes from Schwanenflugel and Rey (1986). Relative to a neutral priming condition, in their LDT they found a related category-name prime produced larger facilitation effects for high- than for low-dominance exemplars. However, Schwanenflugel and Rey's (1986) experiments differed from the other experiments in that they used only short SOAs of 100 and 300 ms, did not include an unrelated priming condition, and tested bilingual subjects.

Pronunciation. As shown in the bottom half of Table 3, a sizeable overall priming effect (at least for pronunciation) occurs for the high-dominance exemplars whereas the low-dominance exemplars yield virtually no priming at all.[1] This contrasts with the LDT data in which large priming effects occur for both high- and low-dominance exemplars.

Table 3.
Overall Priming Effects (in ms) For High- vs. Low-Dominance Category Exemplars From Category-Name Primes in the LDT and Pronunciation

Task & Study	Category Dominance	
LDT	High	Low
Lorch et al. (1986)	62*	46*
Neely et al. (1989)	67*	52*
Mean	65	49
Pronunciation		
Lorch et al. (1986)	22*	2
Keefe & Neely (1990)	32*	6
Mean	27	4

Note. An * indicates an individual effect was significant at the .05 level.

Priming via a mediated association. Mediated priming involves using primes and targets that are not directly associated or semantically related but are related to one another via both being associated with some other word that mediates a link between them. An example would be to use *lion* as the prime and stripes as the target, with *tiger* serving as the mediating link.

LDT. Balota and Lorch (1986), DE Groot (1983), and den Heyer, Sullivan, and McPherson (1987) have all failed to find a mediated priming effect in the LDT using the single-word semantic priming paradigm I defined earlier. However, it is interesting that mediated priming occurs in the LDT under other conditions. For example, den Heyer, Sullivan, and McPherson (1987) found a mediated priming effect in the LDT with exactly the same stimulus lists that failed to yield mediated priming with the standard procedures. The only procedural change they made was to have subjects respond to word targets and withhold responses to nonword targets.

McNamara and Altaribba (1988) have also been able to obtain mediated priming effects in other variants of the LDT. For example, using Meyer and Schvaneveldt's (1971) double-word LDT, in their Experiment 1 they found a mediated priming effect when all of the word-word pairs in the test list were either unrelated or mediationally related but not when some of the word-word pairs in the test list were associatively related. However, in their Experiment 2, in which subjects made a lexical decision to each of the sequentially presented "prime" and target letter strings, they found a mediated priming effect whether or not associatively related primes and targets also appeared in the test list. As we shall see in Section II, Part 2, an explanation exists as to why these apparently chaotic differences in mediated priming effects occur in these various versions of the LDT.

Pronunciation. Using exactly the same set of word-prime/word-target trials for which they had failed to find a mediated priming effect in the LDT, Balota and Lorch (1986) found a statistically significant 17 ms mediated priming effect in pronunciation. Thus, mediated priming occurs in the pronunciation task under exactly the same conditions for which it does not occur in the LDT.

Priming via a backward association. In the backward-association priming paradigm, the prime and target are related only through a backward association (from the target to the prime) and not through a forward association (from the prime to the target). For example, in backward associative priming one tests for priming with the prime *pan* and the target *bed*. Although the prime *pan* is not associated with target *bed* in the forward direction, the target *bed* is associated with the prime *pan* in the backward direction.

The backward-associative priming paradigm should be distinguished from the temporally backward priming paradigm (e.g., Kiger & Glass, 1983). In the latter paradigm, the presentation of the "prime" *bed*, which has a forward association with the target *pan*, actually follows the presentation of the target *pan* by a small amount of time. (See also Dark, 1988, and Briand, den Heyer, and Dannenbring, 1988, for an interesting variation on this theme.) To the degree that the prime *bed* is partially processed before the subject has completed his or her response to the target *pan*, any priming that occurs can be construed as merely another example of forward associative priming from the *prime (bed)* to the *target (pan)*. However, this simple forward-association interpretation of temporally backward priming does not work for a backward-association priming effect. That is, in order for the presence of the prime *pan* to influence the processing of the target *bed*, the backward priming from the *target (bed)* to the *prime (pan)* must somehow feedback to affect processing of the target.

LDT. Koriat (1981, Experiment 3) was the first to report a backward associative priming effect in the LDT. Although counter-intuitive, this effect has been replicated by Seidenberg et al. (1984, Experiment 3).

Pronunciation. Unlike mediated priming, which occurs in pronunciation but not in the LDT, backward associative priming occurs in the LDT but not in pronunciation. Using the same primes and targets that yielded a backward associative priming effect in their LDT, Seidenberg et al. (1984, Experiment 3) failed to find a backward associative priming effect in pronunciation. Indeed, subjects were slightly slower, not faster, to begin pronouncing targets in the backward priming condition, relative to the unrelated priming condition. Quite recently, Peterson and Simpson (1990) have obtained backward priming in pronunciation, but only with auditory primes at very short prime-target SOAs. Thus, the important point is that with visual primes with moderately long (>450 ms SOAs), backward priming has thus far not been obtained in pronunciation though it has been obtained in the LDT.

2. Facilitation vs. Inhibition and Their Time Course

Posner and Snyder (1975a) used a neutral warning signal as a baseline for examining the degree to which priming in a letter-matching task was due to facilitation from the prime being a letter in the target letter display and/or to inhibition from the prime being a letter not in the target letter display. Similar procedures have been used in the semantic priming paradigm so as to examine the time course of facilitation from a related prime and inhibition from an unrelated prime in both the LDT and the pronunciation task. In the LDT, the neutral condition also has been used to assess how a word prime affects the processing of a nonword target.

Category-name primes/exemplar targets

LDT. Neely (1977) used a string of XXXs as a neutral warning signal to determine whether priming in the LDT is due to facilitation from the related prime and/or to inhibition from the unrelated prime. He used category names as primes and category exemplars as targets, with some of the targets being associatively as well as semantically related to the prime. With prime-target SOAs of 500 ms or more, he and many others since (e.g., Becker, 1980; den Heyer et al., 1985; Favreau & Segalowitz, 1983; Lorch et al., 1986; Smith, Briand, Klein, & den Heyer, 1987) have found that semantic priming with these types of materials is due to both facilitation and inhibition. However, when the prime-target SOA is shortened to 250 ms or less, the typical finding is that while facilitation in the related priming condition increases or remains the same, inhibition in the unrelated priming condition is greatly diminished or eliminated. (However, as I discuss below, these general conclusions are qualified by results obtained when the primes and targets are strongly associatively related.)

Table 4 presents data from four experiments that show these time course effects. In Neely (1977), the short 250 ms and the long 2000 ms SOA were randomly intermixed; in Favreau and Segalowitz (1983), the short 200 ms and long 1150 ms SOAs were blocked; in den Heyer et al. (1985) and Smith et al. (1987), the short 200 ms and long 1000 ms SOAs were given to different groups of subjects. In Neely (1977) and Favreau and Segalowitz (1983), the data are taken from the conditions in which subjects expected the category-name prime to be followed by an exemplar of that category. For Favreau and Segalowitz (1983), the data are for the subjects' first language and are averaged across the two groups that differed in their ability to read their second language. That these effects have been obtained in four different laboratories, with different semantic categories and with variations in the manner in which SOA was manipulated attests to their generality.

Table 4
Time Course of Facilitation/Inhibition (in ms) For Category-Exemplar Targets From Related and Unrelated Category-Name Primes in the LDT

	Short SOA		Long SOA	
Study	Related	Unrelated	Related	Unrelated
Neely (1977)	+33*	+3	+14	-70*
Favreau & Segalowitz (1983)	+75*	-11	+93*	-166*
den Heyer et al. (1985)	+28*	-4	+12	-53*
Smith et al. (1987)	+28*	-3	+40*	-82*
Mean	+41	-4	+40	-93

Note. Positive values indicate faster RTs after word primes than after neutral primes (facilitation), whereas negative values indicate slower RTs after word primes than after neutral primes (inhibition). An * indicates the individual priming effect was significant at the .05 level. Smith et al.'s short SOA data, which were not presented in their Table 1, were estimated from their Figure 1.

Pronunciation. Unlike in the LDT, the time course of facilitation and inhibition with category/exemplar materials has not been thoroughly examined in pronunciation. However, at a long SOA, the pronunciation task yields a pattern of facilitation and inhibition that is different from that observed in the LDT. Specifically, although facilitation from related primes is robust in pronunciation as in the LDT, the inhibition from unrelated primes observed in the LDT is either nonexistent or weak in pronunciation.

Because the amounts of facilitation and inhibition one obtains in the LDT depends on the nature of the prime-target relation being examined (see below), the conclusion that the LDT and the pronunciation task yield different patterns of facilitation and inhibition must be based on comparisons in which exactly the same materials are used in the two tasks. Such a comparison can be made with the Neely et al. (1989), Keefe and Neely (1990) and Lorch et al. (1986) data which are summarized in Table 3. Here I report data from only the high-dominance exemplars, since the low-dominance exemplars did not yield a significant overall priming effect in pronunciation. (See Table 3.) The relevant data are displayed in Table 5. As can be seen, averaged across the two studies, comparable facilitation effects of 35 ms and 24 ms were obtained in the related priming condition in the LDT and pronunciation task. However, the 29 ms inhibition effect obtained in the unrelated priming condition in the LDT was much greater than the nearly nonexistent 3 ms inhibition effect obtained in pronunciation.[2]

Table 5
Facilitation/Inhibition (in ms) For High-Dominance Category-Exemplar Targets From Related and Unrelated Category-Name Primes at a Long SOA in the LDT and Pronunciation

	Type of Prime		
Task & Study	Related	Unrelated	Overall Priming
LDT			
Neely et al. (1989)	+51*	-16[a]	+67*
Lorch et al. (1986)	+20[b]	-42[b]	+62*
Mean	+35	-29	+64
Pronunciation			
Keefe & Neely (1990)	+35*	+3	+32*
Lorch et al. (1986)	+13[b]	-9[b]	+22*
Mean	+24	-3	+27

Note. Positive values indicate faster RTs after word primes than after neutral primes (facilitation), whereas negative values indicate slower RTs after word primes than after neutral primes (inhibition). An * indicates the individual priming effect was significant at the .05 level.

[a] $p < .07$, two-tailed
[b] The statistical significance of an individual facilitation/inhibition effect in Lorch et al.'s study is not available.

Associatively related primes and targets

LDT. The time course of facilitation and inhibition with associatively related primes and targets was examined in some detail by Neely (1976) and DE Groot, Thomassen, and Hudson (1986). They used SOAs that ranged from 100 ms to 2000 ms, with the different SOAs being blocked in Neely's (1976) study and manipulated between subjects in DE Groot et al.'s (1986) study. The general pattern in their data was that as the SOA increased, facilitation increased in the related priming condition whereas inhibition did not.[3]

Becker (1980) was the first to note that lists containing primes and targets with a very strong associative relation produce a pattern of facilitation and inhibition effects in the LDT that differs from that observed for lists containing category-name primes and category-exemplar targets. Table 6 summarizes a comparison in three different studies of the facilitation and inhibition effects that are obtained with associatively related and categorically related primes and targets in the LDT. (The category and associative data are taken from Becker's, 1980, Experiments 2 and 1, respectively.) As can be seen in the lower right quadrant of Table 6, at the long SOA with associatively related primes and targets, the facilitation produced by related primes is much larger in magnitude than the inhibition produced by unrelated primes--a pattern of data Becker (1980) refers to as facilitation dominance. On the other hand, with categorically related primes and targets (see the upper right quadrant of Table 6), the facilitation produced by related primes is much smaller in magnitude than the inhibition produced by unrelated primes--what Becker (1980) calls inhibition dominance.

Table 6
Facilitation/Inhibition (in ms) From Related and Unrelated Primes in the LDT as a Function of Type of Prime-Target Relation

Type of Relation & Study	SOA and Type of Prime: 200 ms Rel	200 ms UnRel	1000 ms Rel	1000 ms UnRel
Category				
Becker (1980)	----	----	+10	-64*
den Heyer et al. (1985)	+28*	-4	+12	-53*
Smith et al. (1987)	+28*	-3	+40*	-82*
mean	+28	-3	+31	-66
Associative				
Becker (1980)	----	----	+52*	-4
den Heyer et al. (1985)	+28*	-4	+30*	-2
Smith et al. (1987)	+15	-14	+44*	-15
mean	+22	-9	+42	-7

Note. Positive values indicate faster RTs after word primes than after neutral primes (facilitation), whereas negative values indicate slower RTs after word primes than after neutral primes (inhibition). An * indicates the individual priming effect was significant at the .05 level. Smith et al.'s short SOA data, which were not presented in their Table 1, were estimated from their Figure 1.

Although the data in Table 6 show facilitation dominance for both types of materials at the short SOA, when one also includes the data from Neely's (1976) and DE Groot et al.'s shortest SOAs (i.e., 360 and 100 ms, respectively), facilitation dominance for the associatively related materials is reduced, since these latter two studies obtained comparable magnitudes of facilitation and inhibition at their short SOAs. Furthermore, at a 200 ms SOA, Antos (1979) found inhibition dominance using associatively related materials, i.e., a high-dominance category exemplar prime followed by its category name. However, because the category-name targets were repeated several times such that it was easy for subjects to predict a *particular* target from the prime (i.e., to predict that *FRUIT*, which had been presented several times previously, would be the target that would likely follow the prime *pear*), this result may not generalize to the situation in which related word targets are not repeated and are not *uniquely* specified by the prime. Nevertheless, taken together, the data seem to indicate that facilitation dominance at short SOAs is the rule for category materials but not for associatively related materials, which show more equivalent facilitation and inhibition effects at short SOAs.

Pronunciation. Data on the time course of facilitation and inhibition with associatively related materials are scarce for pronunciation. DE Groot (1985) found that as SOA increased from 240 to 1040 ms, facilitation from an associatively related prime increased from 15 ms to 66 ms. However, because only related and neutral primes were used, the time course of inhibition from an unrelated prime could not be assessed. However, considering only SOAs of 1000 ms or greater, the standard finding has been one of facilitation dominance with associatively related materials (e.g., Lorch et al., 1986; Balota & Lorch, 1986). (But see footnote 2.)

Nonword facilitation effects

LDT. Responses are typically faster and/or more accurate to a nonword target when it follows a word prime that is unrelated to the word from which that nonword target was derived by changing one letter, relative to when that nonword target follows a neutral prime.[4] This nonword facilitation effect occurs when the nonword targets are embedded in lists of either category-name primes and exemplar targets (e.g., Favreau & Segalowitz, 1983; Neely, 1977; Neely et al., 1989) or associatively related primes and targets (e.g., Antos, 1979; Balota, 1983; DE Groot et al. 1986; den Heyer, 1985; Neely, 1976). With both types of materials, this nonword facilitation effect increases as SOA increases (Antos, 1979; DE Groot et al., 1986; Favreau & Segalowitz, 1983; Neely, 1976, 1977; see also Schwanenflugel & Rey, 1986, who failed to find nonword facilitation at their short 100 and 300 ms SOAs). This facilitation effect for nonword targets that are unrelated to their word primes contrasts with the inhibition effect that occurs in the processing of word targets that are unrelated to their word primes.

Pronunciation. Most experimenters exclude nonwords from pronunciation tasks when examining priming effects because they fear that the inclusion of nonwords might encourage subjects to use nonlexical processes to pronounce both words and nonwords. If so, subjects would not be accessing the lexical/semantic structures that are presumably mediating semantic priming effects, with the result that priming might not be observed. Consequently, few data exist relevant to whether or not the nonword facilitation effect occurs in pronunciation.

Are facilitation/inhibition effects artifacts of an inappropriate neutral priming condition? To assess facilitation or inhibition, one must have a neutral priming condition. In the single-word semantic priming paradigm, the neutral priming condition has typically consisted of either a string of XXXXs, the word *ready*, the word *blank* or the word *neutral*. Clearly, the choice of an appropriate neutral priming condition cannot be made in a theoretical vacuum. For example, when I chose a string of XXXXs as a neutral priming condition in my early work (e.g., Neely, 1976, 1977), I was operating within the framework of the Posner-Snyder (1975b) theory. My intent was to have the neutral prime (a) be equated with the related and unrelated word primes in terms of its warning-signal value as a cue that a target was soon going to appear, (b) be unrelated to the target so that it would be a "neutral" (i.e., "zero") baseline with respect to assessing the effects of spreading activation between related memory representations, and (c) not provide any information as to the semantic nature of any word target that would follow, so as to provide a "neutral" (i.e., "zero") baseline for assessing the effects of an expectancy for a word target related to the word prime.

Not surprisingly, challenges have been made as to whether these neutral primes are a proper baseline for assessing facilitation or inhibition (e.g., Antos, 1979; Becker, 1985; DE Groot, Thomassen, & Hudson, 1982; Jonides & Mack, 1984). For example, one obvious criticism of the choice of XXXXXs as a neutral prime is that, unlike a word prime, it is a "nonlinguistic" event (e.g., Antos, 1979). On the other hand, a linguistic prime such as *neutral, ready,* or *blank* may not be entirely semantically neutral.

A more serious problem is that a particular neutral prime may not have warning signal properties equivalent to those of word primes. Because the alerting properties of a warning signal change with SOA (e.g., Posner & Boies, 1971), this becomes particularly problematic when one examines the time course of facilitation and inhibition (see Jonides & Mack, 1984). To understand the problem, consider first a short SOA. A neutral prime likely consumes less processing capacity than a word prime, either because it has been seen more often in the experiment or is perceptually less complex (as in the case of XXXX as a neutral prime). If encoding of the prime causes a psychological refractory period (cf. Kantowitz, 1974), at short SOAs target processing will be hurt more by difficult-to-process word primes than by easy-to-process neutral primes. This would result in inhibition being overestimated and facilitation being underestimated. Obviously, this alone would be working against producing the facilitation dominance that is observed with category materials at short SOAs. On the other hand, because the neutral prime is presented more often than a particular word prime, it will not be as effective in its alerting properties as a word prime is (e.g., Kraut & Smothergill, 1978; Kraut, Smothergill, & Farkas, 1981). This would lead to artifactually slow RTs following the neutral prime, thereby resulting in an overestimation of facilitation and an underestimation of inhibition, which would undermine the validity of facilitation dominance at a short SOA. Clearly, then, the relative contributions that the differential refractory and alerting effects make at the short SOA will be a crucial determinant of whether the observed facilitation dominance should be attributed to an artifact of the "nonneutrality" of the neutral prime.

At long SOAs, the greater psychological refractory effects of word primes relative to nonword primes should have dissipated. Thus, one must focus on the effectiveness of neutral vs. word primes as (a) warning-signals indicating when the target will likely appear and (b) general arousers. Consider first their effectiveness as warning signals. When equiprobable SOAs are manipulated within subjects, temporal uncertainty for target occurrence at the longest SOA is reduced, because if the target has not appeared by the time the next-to-longest SOA has elapsed, it must appear at the longest SOA. However, when SOA is manipulated between subjects, the temporal uncertainty of the target's occurrence is great at long SOAs, presumably because there would be more error variance in predicting exactly when 1200 ms has elapsed than in predicting exactly when 200 ms has elapsed. Thus, it is a complicated problem to determine what the effects of the differential alerting properties of neutral and word primes will be at the long SOA. On the other hand, the overall arousal should be greater following a word prime than a neutral prime at the long SOA. This is so because the word prime has not been habituated as much and because subjects may be using it to generate an expectancy thereby keeping their overall arousal higher. My best guess is that at the longer SOAs all of these factors conspire to make RTs to targets that follow the habituated neutral prime longer than they should be. This would mean that facilitation effects would be overestimated at the long SOAs.

Because of these problems, Jonides and Mack (1984) have gone so far as to suggest that neutral priming conditions not be used. To me that would be throwing out the baby with the bathwater. Typically, we are interested in the relative magnitudes of facilitation and inhibition across various experimental conditions; we are not that interested in the exact magnitude of a facilitation or inhibition effect under a single experimental condition. Thus, the "nonneutrality" of a particular neutral prime is a problem only if the effects of that "nonneutrality" on the processing of targets is different for the different conditions across which the relative magnitudes of facilitation or inhibition are being compared.

Because the effects of warning signals likely interact with the effects of the SOA between the warning-signal and target, the "nonneutrality" of the neutral prime does indeed pose problems for interpreting the time course of facilitation and inhibition. However, there is a potential solution. Consider a variation on a procedure Jonides and Mack (1984) suggested for assessing differences in the neutral primes and word primes in terms of the general attentional resources they usurp and their warning-signal and general arousal properties. Before beginning the LDT, subjects could be trained to press one key to a high tone and one key to a low tone. The LDT would then require that responses be made on these same keys. On a few trials in the LDT, one of the tones could be presented instead of a letter-string target at the various SOAs. Any differences observed for tone RTs following neutral and word primes at a particular SOA could then be used to correct for differences in their warning-signal properties, etc. For example, consider an SOA for which facilitation from a related prime was 32 ms. If tone RTs were 16 ms slower following a word prime than following a neutral prime, this would indicate that RTs to neutral primes were "artificially" short, and that facilitation from a related word prime was being underestimated. Thus, the corrected facilitation effect would be 48 ms. If, on the other hand, tone RTs were 16 ms faster following a word prime than following a neutral prime, this would indicate that RTs to neutral primes were "artificially" long, and that facilitation from a related word prime was being overestimated. Thus, the corrected facilitation effect would be 16 ms. Similar corrections could be made for inhibition effects.

Although many may be wary of the accuracy of the foregoing correction procedure, such corrections often will not be needed. For example, for long SOAs consider the observation of inhibition dominance for category materials and facilitation dominance for associatively related materials. (See right half of Table 6.) Of course, there may have been a bias for finding facilitation or inhibition due to the "nonneutrality" of the neutral priming condition in these experiments. However, the "nonneutrality" doomsayers must explain why this bias should (a) be different when a neutral prime is embedded in a list of category materials vs. when exactly the same neutral prime is embedded in a list of associatively related materials and (b) be different in just the way necessary to have produced the obtained result. (Such an explanation must also accommodate the fact that RTs following neutral primes were nearly identical for Becker's, 1980, categorically related and associatively related lists.) Until such an explanation is provided, my predilection is to accept as genuine the observed difference in the patterns of facilitation vs. inhibition dominance obtained with the two types of materials.

A similar argument applies to the nonword facilitation effect, which many wish to discount as an artifact of an inappropriate neutral baseline. If the nonword facilitation effect is due to an artificial speeding of RTs following word primes due to the "nonneutrality" of the neutral prime being used, then the nonword facilitation effect should be accompanied by facilitation in the processing of word targets that follow unrelated word primes. But a typical finding is that nonword facilitation is accompanied by inhibition in the unrelated priming condition for word targets (e.g., DE Groot et al., 1986; Favreau & Segalowitz, 1983; Neely, 1976, 1977; Neely et al., 1989). Furthermore, as discussed in Section 5 below, studies that have manipulated the probability that a target is a nonword given that it is unrelated to its word prime show that these nonword facilitation effects are lawfully related to other variables. The issue thus becomes whether an explanation based on the putative "nonneutrality" of the neutral primes provides a coherent account of these lawful relationships?

A more general point is that if theories make differential predictions concerning whether a particular priming effect is likely due to facilitation from a related prime and/or inhibition from an unrelated prime, it would be foolish not to look for these facilitation or inhibition effects just because our measurement techniques can be questioned on various grounds. A theory's unified account of the facilitation and inhibition effects that are obtained across a broad range of experimental conditions will always be preferred over a piecemeal account that appeals to different "nonneutrality" biases in different conditions that just happen to yield the complex overall patterns of facilitation and inhibition effects that were observed.[5]

3. Priming For "Degraded" vs. Nondegraded Targets

Considerable research has examined how semantic priming effects and the effects of "visual degradation" of the target combine to influence RTs to that target. In this research the prime is always presented in a nondegraded format and the target is presented in either its nondegraded or degraded format. The general theoretical basis for this research comes from Sternberg's (1969) additive factor method. According to this method, if variables selectively influence one stage in a serially ordered sequence of processing stages, their combined effects on RT will be additive if they affect different processing stages but will be interactive if they influence the same stage. When one manipulates a variable that plausibly would affect the encoding of the target, e.g., target visibility, the following question is raised. Does semantic priming also influence target encoding (if so, its effects will interact with the effects of target visibility) or does it affect some other processing stage (if so, its effects will be additive with the effects of target visibility)? Of course, it may be that the LDT and pronunciation tasks do not involve a sequentially ordered processing system to which the additive factor method applies. They may instead involve concurrent processing stages (e.g., Schweickert, 1978; 1983), cascaded processes in which partial information from an early stage is fed to a later processing stage before the earlier stage has been completed (e.g., McClelland, 1979), or worse yet, be completely interactive processing stages in which "later" stages feedback information to earlier stages (e.g., McClelland & Rumelhart, 1981). But despite these complications, it remains of empirical interest whether the combined effects of semantic priming and target degradation on RTs are interactive or additive. I now turn to the data relevant to this issue and focus on those studies that have examined it in the LDT and pronunciation tasks using the same materials and procedures (i.e., Becker & Killion, 1977; Massaro, Jones, Lipscomb, & Scholz, 1978; and Meyer et al., 1975).

LDT

Overall priming. Becker and Killion (1977) and Meyer et al. (1975) used associatively related materials to examine the combined effects of stimulus degradation and semantic priming. Becker and Killion (1977) used the single-word semantic priming paradigm as I have defined it here with an SOA of 750 ms and manipulated the stimulus intensity of the target. (The intensity of the prime, which was also manipulated, had no effect on RTs to the target nor did its effects interact with any of the effects I discuss here.) In the Meyer et al. (1975) study, subjects made lexical decisions to both the prime and the target, with the target being presented either in visual noise or "in the clear" 250 ms after the response had been made to the prime. The results of their LDT experiments are shown in the top half of Table 7.

Table 7
Priming Effects (in ms) For Nondegraded vs. Degraded Targets in the LDT and Pronunciation

Task & Study	Target Presentation	
LDT	Nondegraded	Degraded
Becker & Killion (1977)	30*	70*
Meyer et al. (1975)	37*	66*
Massaro et al. (1978)		
High-dominance exemplars	6	113*
Low-dominance exemplars	22	73*
Mean	24	81
Pronunciation		
Becker & Killion (1977)	19*	43*
Meyer et al. (1975)	29*	58*
Massaro et al. (1978)		
High-dominance exemplars	11	162*
Low-dominance exemplars	4	80*
Mean	16	86

Note. An * indicates an individual effect was significant at the .05 level. The Becker & Killion and Meyer et al. priming effects are relative to the unrelated priming condition; the Massaro et al. priming effects are relative to the neutral priming condition and for the LDT were estimated from their Figure 2.

As shown in Table 7, the effects of semantic priming and stimulus degradation interacted in the LDT such that priming effects were considerably larger when the target was degraded. This occurred because stimulus degradation slowed RTs more for targets in the unrelated priming condition than in the related priming condition. This type of interaction has also been observed with sentential priming contexts (e.g., Stanovich & West, 1979, 1983, Experiment 6; it was also observed by Schuberth, Spoehr, & Lane, 1981, Experiment 2, though it was not statistically significant using the conservative min F' procedure).

Facilitation vs. inhibition. As far as I know, no one using the single-word semantic priming paradigm has included both a neutral priming and unrelated priming condition when examining the interactive effects of semantic priming and stimulus degradation in the LDT. However, Massaro, Jones, Lipscomb, and Scholtz, (1978) included a neutral priming condition (the word *blank*) as a baseline for assessing facilitation in the processing of high- and low-dominance exemplar targets produced by a related category-name prime. Their degradation manipulation involved presenting the target in its normal orientation or rotated by 180 degrees. The SOA was 1500 ms. As seen in Table 7, they too found priming to be greater for "degraded" than for nondegraded targets and for both high- and low-dominance exemplars. Although Massaro et al.'s (1978) results show that facilitation from related primes is greater for degraded than nondegraded targets, they leave unanswered the question of whether inhibition from unrelated primes in the LDT has an additive or interactive effect with target degradation. (But see below for the pronunciation data relevant to this issue.)

Pronunciation

Overall priming. As shown in the bottom half of Table 7, using the materials and procedures they used in the LDT, Becker and Killion (1977) and Meyer et al. obtained pronunciation data that were strikingly similar to their lexical decision data. That is, they once again found priming to be greater for degraded than nondegraded targets. (In the Meyer et al. study, subjects made lexical decisions to the primes but pronounced the targets.) This degradation x priming interaction is quite typical in pronunciation (e.g., Durgunoglu, 1988; Sanford, Garrod, & Boyle, 1977, but see footnote 1; Sperber, McCauley, Ragain, & Weil, 1979). Furthermore, Besner and Beneschan (1989) have recently shown that it is the same magnitude at a short 200 ms SOA as it is at the more typically used longer SOA, which in their experiment was 1250 ms. (However, with sentential contexts as primes which subjects read aloud, Stanovich & West, 1979, Experiment 2, have obtained a stronger Degradation x Priming interaction when the target appeared 750 ms rather than 150 ms after the last context word was read.)

Facilitation vs. inhibition. Massaro et al. (1978) found that, as was so in their LDT, facilitation from a related category-name prime was larger for degraded than for nondegraded targets for both high- and low-dominance exemplar targets. Durgunoglu (1988, Experiment 4) has examined both facilitation and inhibition with degraded and nondegraded targets in pronunciation in the single-word priming paradigm using associatively related materials. When she degraded the target by briefly presenting it and following it by a mask, she found that degradation enhanced inhibition from unrelated primes but left facilitation from related primes unaffected. However, when she "degraded" the target by inserting asterisks between its letters, she found that facilitation increased and inhibition was unaffected. (The finding that a masking/contrast-reduction type of degradation increases inhibition, whereas asterisk-insertion does not, has also been observed by Stanovich and West, 1983, Experiments 6 vs. 8, using sentential priming contexts in the LDT.) That asterisk insertion does not enhance inhibition is important because it suggests that the slowing of target processing via some sort of degradation manipulation is not sufficient for increasing inhibition from unrelated primes. Apparently the degradation manipulation must degrade the individual letters within a word in order to enhance inhibition from unrelated primes.

4. Priming For High- vs. Low-Frequency Words

Of the many experiments that have examined differences in semantic priming for high- vs. low-frequency words, almost all have used sentential priming contexts (e.g., Schuberth & Eimas, 1977; Schuberth et al., 1981; Stanovich & West, 1981, 1983; Stanovich, West, & Feeman, 1981; West & Stanovich, 1982). In all but the Schuberth and Eimas (1977) and Schuberth et al. (1981) studies, the result has been that priming effects are considerably larger for low-frequency words than for high-frequency words in both the LDT and pronunciation. (Though not statistically significant by the conservative min F' procedure, this pattern also occurred in Schuberth et al.'s, 1981, Experiment 2.) This effect occurs despite the fact that the low-frequency target words are often less predictable from their sentential priming contexts than are the high-frequency words.

As far as I know, the only published study that examines the priming x word-frequency interaction in the single-word semantic priming paradigm has been reported by Becker (1979), using the LDT. One nice feature of his experiment is that he systematically varied and equated the high- and low-frequency targets in terms of how strongly related they were to their related primes. For all strengths of prime-target relatedness, overall priming effects were 36-46 ms larger for the low-frequency words than for the high-frequency words. This was due to the word-frequency effect (slower RTs to the low-frequency words) being reduced by 36-46 ms in the related priming condition relative to the unrelated priming condition.

5. List Context/"Expectancy" Effects

In this section, I discuss experiments that show that the magnitude or nature of the priming that occurs for a particular related prime-target pair depends on (a) the instructions subjects were given as to how the prime might be used to facilitate their processing of targets and/or (b) the kinds of prime-target relations that are instantiated on other trials in the test list.

Instructional manipulations

LDT. In Neely (1977) and Favreau and Segalowitz (1983), subjects were correctly informed that the word targets following certain nonshift category-name primes (e.g., *BIRD*) were likely to be exemplars of that category (e.g., *robin*) whereas the word targets following certain other category-shift category-name primes (e.g., *BODY*) were likely to be exemplars of some other pre-specified category (e.g., were likely to represent parts of a *BUILDING*, such as *door*). In Neely's (1977) experiment, in the latter category-shift condition, when *BODY* was the prime and subjects should have been expecting "building parts" as targets, on a small proportion of the trials the targets were exemplars of an "unexpected" category and were either related (e.g., *arm*) or unrelated (e.g., *robin*) to the prime; in Favreau and Segalowitz's (1983) experiment, the targets from the "unexpected" category were always related to the prime. Across all trials, exemplar targets were equally often chosen from the various categories. Thus, information as to which category a word target was likely to be chosen from on a particular trial was provided solely by the word prime for that trial.

In both the Neely (1977) and Favreau and Segalowitz (1983) studies, very different patterns of priming were observed at the short and long SOAs. At the short SOA, independently of whether the category-name prime was in the shift or nonshift condition, facilitation occurred for targets related to the prime, whereas neither facilitation nor inhibition occurred for targets unrelated to the prime. At the long SOA, on the other hand, facilitation occurred for targets selected from the expected category and inhibition occurred for targets selected from the unexpected category, regardless of whether or not the targets were related to the prime.

Pronunciation. Variations on the Neely (1977) and Favreau and Segalowitz (1983) designs have been used with a pronunciation task. Durgunoglu (1986, Experiment 5) and Pring and Snowling (1986, Experiment 1) used only a long SOA. However, Durgunoglu (1986) did not include "unexpected" targets that were unrelated to the prime and Pring and Snowling (1986) did not include a condition in which related targets followed a category-shift category-name prime. Balota (1988) tested all of the conditions of Neely (1977) and Favreau and Segalowitz (1983) and used both short and long SOAs. However, in his experiment word targets were not equally often selected from all categories. Thus, information as to which category a word target was likely to be chosen from on a particular trial did not reside solely in the word prime for that trial. Durgunoglu (1986) tested college students, Pring and Snowling (1986) tested 7 to 11-year-olds, and Balota (1988) tested college students and 60 to 75-year-olds. Finally, Durgunoglu (1986) also included targets degraded by masking and asterisk insertion (cf. Section 3). However, because she obtained different results for these two types of masking and these effects have not been studied in other experiments using these category-shift procedures, I will discuss only the data from her nondegraded targets.

The results of these pronunciation experiments were generally similar to those obtained for the same conditions in the LDT. Specifically at the long SOA, facilitation occurred for targets that came from the "expected" category.[6] Durgunoglu (1986), who was the only one to report her data separately for high- and low-dominance exemplars, found that the priming for "expected" targets occurred for high-dominance exemplars but not for low-dominance exemplars.

Proportion of related prime-target pairs in the test list.

I define the relatedness proportion effect as the increase in the magnitude of the overall semantic priming effect that occurs as one increases the proportion of related word-prime/word-target trials. This relatedness proportion effect has two variations, one of which involves the procedures discussed in the last section and one of which does not. The relatedness proportion effect has been found in both the LDT and pronunciation.

LDT. One version of the relatedness proportion effect was discussed in the immediately preceding section. To understand this, consider Neely's (1977) procedures. Following nonshift primes, the word targets were related to the prime on .67 of the trials and unrelated to the prime on .33 of the trials. Following category-shift primes, the targets were related to the prime on .17 of the trials and unrelated to the prime on .83 of the trials (coming from the "expected" category on .66 of the trials and from the "unexpected" category on .17 of the trials). Relative to "unexpected," unrelated targets, at the 2000 ms SOA, the related targets in Neely's experiment yielded 84 ms of overall priming following nonshift primes for which the relatedness proportion was .67 and 14 ms of overall priming following category-shift primes for which the relatedness proportion was .17. At the 250 ms SOA, the corresponding overall priming effects were 30 and 36 ms, respectively. Thus, at the long SOA, the relatedness proportion effect was a substantial 70 ms effect (84 minus 14 ms) whereas at the short SOA it was a nonsignificant -6 ms effect (30 minus 36 ms). Favreau and Segalowitz (1983) obtained similar results.

Relatedness proportion effects are also obtained in the more standard LDT semantic priming paradigm in which there is no category-shifting for any of the primes. Specifically, substantial relatedness proportion effects have been obtained at prime-target SOAs longer than 500 ms both for associatively related primes and targets (DE Groot, 1984; den Heyer, 1985; den Heyer et al., 1983; Seidenberg et al., 1984; Tweedy, Lapinski, & Schvaneveldt, 1977) and for category-name primes and exemplar targets (Neely et al., 1989). However, it is also important to note that at SOAs greater than 500 ms the best fitting linear regression equation for predicting overall associative priming from relatedness proportion typically yields a non-zero y-intercept which ranges from 12-26 ms (den Heyer, 1985; den Heyer, Briand, & Dannenbring, 1983; Tweedy, Lapinski, & Schvaneveldt, 1977). Furthermore, Fischler (1977b) obtained a significant priming effect for the eighteenth prime-target pair when the first seventeen prime-target pairs were unrelated. These data suggest that an expectancy for related-prime target pairs is not a necessary condition for obtaining priming. Also, as in the category-shifting paradigm, a relatedness proportion effect for associatively related primes and targets does not occur at prime-target SOAs of 250 ms or less (DE Groot, 1984; den Heyer et al., 1983).

Pronunciation. In the pronunciation task, evidence concerning the relatedness proportion effect is sparse. In the pronunciation analogues of the category-shifting procedure, the conditions necessary for examining a relatedness proportion effect were not all included in Durgunoglu's (1986) and Pring and Snowling's (1986) experiments (see above), and Balota's (1988) unequal probabilities for targets from different semantic categories make his results difficult to interpret (see footnote 6). Thus, data relevant to whether relatedness proportion effects occur in pronunciation with the category-shifting procedure need to be collected.

However, two experiments have examined relatedness proportion effects in pronunciation using procedures in which category shifting was not involved. Seidenberg et al. (1984) failed to find a relatedness proportion effect with the same associatively related materials for which they had found a relatedness proportion effect in the LDT. However, because they replaced their nonword target trials from the LDT with unrelated word target trials in their pronunciation task, the .50 and .29 relatedness proportions they used in their LDT became .33 and .20 in their pronunciation task. Thus, their failure to find a relatedness proportion effect in their pronunciation task could have been due to their weak manipulation.

To further examine this issue Keefe and Neely (1990) manipulated relatedness proportion from .33 to .875, using exactly the same category materials and nonword targets that Neely et al. (1989) used in their LDT experiments. Table 8 gives the overall priming effects they obtained in both their lexical decision and pronunciation tasks for these two relatedness proportions. As can be seen, in the LDT relatedness proportion effects around 30 ms in magnitude were obtained for both high- and low-dominance targets, whereas in pronunciation a significant (19 ms) relatedness proportion effect occurred only for high-dominance targets. That the relatedness proportion effect for low-dominance targets was different for the LDT and pronunciation is of some interest.

Proportion of words vs. nonwords that are unrelated to their primes in the LDT. Neely et al. (1989) have noted that prior experiments on the relatedness proportion effect in the LDT have confounded the effects of relatedness proportion with the effects of the ratio of trials on which a target is a nonword given that the target is unrelated to its word prime. To understand why this is so, consider how relatedness proportion is manipulated in the standard lexical decision experiment. The overall probabilities of word and nonword targets are typically the same for the different relatedness proportion groups and each nonword target is chosen such that it does not resemble a word that is related to the word prime that precedes it (i.e., the nonword target *roben*, which resembles *robin*, would not follow the prime *BIRD*). Thus, for a relatedness proportion of .875, for every 8 word targets, each of 7 word targets would be

Table 8
Overall Priming Effects (in ms) For High- vs. Low-Category Exemplars in the LDT and Pronunciation as a Function of Relatedness Proportion

Task & Relatedness Proportion	Category Dominance	
LDT	High	Low
RP.875	67*	52*
RP.333	37*	23*
RPE	30*	29*
Pronunciation		
RP.875	32*	6
RP.333	13*	5
RPE	19*	1

Note. The LDT and pronunciation data are from Neely et al. (1989, Experiment 1) and Keefe and Neely (1990), respectively. RPE = relatedness proportion effect. An * indicates an individual effect was significant at the .05 level.

related to its word prime and 1 word target would be unrelated to its word prime. Because the probabilities of a word and nonword target are usually equal, for each group of 8 word-prime/word-target trials there would be 8 "unrelated" word-prime/nonword target trials. Thus, given that a target is unrelated to its word prime, the probability that it is a nonword is 8/9 or .889. Neely et al. (1989) have called this latter probability the *nonword ratio*. Now consider a relatedness proportion of .125. For every 8 word targets, 1 word target would be related to its word prime and each of 7 word targets would be unrelated to its word prime, and there would be a corresponding 8 "unrelated" word-prime/nonword target trials. Thus, given that a target is unrelated to its word prime, the probability that it is a nonword is 8/15, yielding a nonword ratio of .533. Thus, the increase in relatedness proportion from .125 to .875 is accompanied by an increase in the nonword ratio from .533 to .889.

This confounding of relatedness proportion and nonword ratio effects necessarily occurs as long as the overall ratio of word/nonword targets is the same for the different relatedness proportion groups. To avoid this confounding, Neely et al. (1989) used category materials, a long prime-target SOA, and manipulated the overall nonword-target probability. For example, to produce a high (.80) relatedness proportion and a low (.25) nonword ratio, for every 16 word-prime trials they had 12 related word-prime/word-target trials, 3 unrelated word-prime/word-target trials and 1 "unrelated" word-prime/nonword-target trial; to produce a low (.22) relatedness proportion and a high (.75) nonword ratio, for every 30 word-prime trials they had 2 related word-prime/word-target trials, 7 unrelated word-prime/word-target trials and 21 "unrelated" word-prime/nonword-target trials. Across 12 different groups of subjects, they were thus able to manipulate orthogonally the relatedness proportion from .20-.89 and the nonword ratio from .08-.91. Multiple linear regression analyses were used to determine how overall priming for high- vs. low-dominance exemplars and nonword facilitation effects were influenced by the separable effects of relatedness proportion and nonword ratio. The results were that increases in relatedness proportion led to an increase in overall priming for high-dominance exemplars but had no significant effect on either the overall priming for low-dominance exemplars or the nonword facilitation effect, whereas increases in the nonword ratio led to significant increases in overall priming for both high and low-dominance exemplars and in the nonword facilitation effect. Additional analyses showed that the increases in the overall priming effects and the nonword facilitation effects that occurred as the nonword ratio increased could not be easily attributed to variations in the overall RTs associated with the variations in the overall probability of a nonword.

Proportion of associatively related vs. categorically related prime-target pairs in the test list in the LDT. Using the LDT and a long prime-target SOA, Becker (1980) examined how priming for high- vs. low-dominance category exemplars varied as a function of the type of prime-target relationship that was instantiated in a preponderance of the related priming trials in which these categorically related primes and targets were embedded. Specifically, he embedded prime-target pairs such as *BIRD-robin* (high dominance) and *BIRD-crow* (low dominance) in test lists in which a large proportion of the related prime-target pairs either were category-names and their related high- and low-dominance exemplars (the categorically related list) or were strongly associatively related primes and targets (e.g., *hot cold*, the associatively related list). The results were quite striking. When embedded in the categorically related list, the categorically related primes and targets yielded the typical pattern of inhibition dominance (see the upper right quadrant of Table 6), with overall priming being comparable for the high- and low-dominance exemplars (see the upper half of Table 3). However, when embedded in the associatively related list, these very same primes and targets yielded facilitation dominance, which is typical of associatively related materials (see the lower right quadrant of Table 6). Furthermore, overall priming was now greater for high- than for low-dominance exemplars due to the greater facilitation effect observed for the former. Thus, these data show that it is not the prime-target relation per se that determines facilitation vs. inhibition dominance, but rather the type of prime-target relation the subject expects to receive that is important.

6. Effects of Interposing an Unrelated Word Between the Prime and Target

Another piece of the empirical puzzle concerns the issue of whether semantic priming between a related prime and target (e.g., *nurse-doctor*) is reduced or eliminated when a word unrelated to either of them is interposed between their presentations (e.g., *nurse-paper-doctor*). Hereafter, I refer to this as the interposition condition. Because Masson (this volume) has provided a very nice review of the data relevant to this issue, I give only a brief summary here.

The interposition condition has been studied with two different paradigms. One is a variation on the original Meyer and Schvaneveldt (1971) procedure in which subjects make one response if all of three simultaneously presented letter strings are words and another response if they are not. With this procedure, priming still occurs in the interposition condition even when there is evidence that subjects are sequentially processing the three simultaneously presented items (e.g., Schvaneveldt & Meyer, 1973). The second procedure that has been used to study priming in the interposition condition involves sequential presentation of the prime, the interposed unrelated item and the target. Although some LDT experiments have found priming in the interposition condition with these procedures (e.g., Davelaar & Coltheart, 1975; Meyer, Schvaneveldt, & Ruddy, 1972), others have not (Dannenbring & Briand, 1982; Gough, Alford, & Holley-Wilcox, 1981; Masson, this volume; see also Foss, 1982). Also, Masson (this volume) has failed to find priming in the interposition condition in pronunciation as well. Furthermore, it is important to note that in Masson's experiments priming still occurred in another condition in which a neutral prime replaced the interposed word. Thus, the absence of priming in his interposition condition cannot easily be attributed to a time-based decay of priming. (An interposition effect also occurs when the prime and target are episodically related by virtue of having been recently studied together and subjects make either an episodic recognition judgment or lexical decision about the target--Ratcliff, Hockley, & McKoon, 1985 and Ratcliff & McKoon, 1988).

Masson (this volume) has argued that in those cases in which priming was not eliminated in the interposition condition, there were many cases in which the unrelated word separated related primes and targets. Thus, it is possible that subjects could have continued rehearsing a priming item through the presentation of the unrelated interposed item so as to have it available to produce priming when a related target appeared after the interposed item.

Other data relevant to the existence of an interposition-like effect come from Neely's (1977) experiment, in which the item "interposed" between the related prime and target was internally generated. That is, when given the prime *BODY*, subjects were to try to think of (interpose) "building parts" before the target appeared. That subjects were accomplishing this is attested to by the fact that the processing of word targets representing building parts (e.g., *door*) was facilitated by the prime *BODY*, relative to a neutral prime, when the prime-target SOA was 700 ms or 2000 ms. However, at these same SOAs, the prime

BODY also produced faster RTs to its related exemplars (e.g., *arm*) than to unrelated exemplars from a different category (e.g., *robin* from the *BIRD* category). This latter priming effect in Neely's internal interposition condition occurred at the 2000 ms SOA in all four groups in which it was measured and at the 700 ms SOA in the one group in which it was measured. Across these five occasions, this priming for related targets ranged from 13-47 ms, for an overall effect of 23 ms. (However, error rates were an average of 1.6% greater for the related targets, raising the possibility of a speed-accuracy trade-off problem.) The important point vis-a-vis Masson's (this volume) rehearsal argument is that priming in Neely's internal interposition condition was observed even though the prime and target were related on only .166 of the word-target trials and on only .083 of the total trials. In short, although it is clear that priming can be eliminated by the interposition of an unrelated word between a related prime and target under certain conditions, it is not yet clear what these conditions are.

7. Effects of Type of Processing on the Prime

Conscious vs. unconscious processing of the prime. Several investigators (see Holender, 1986, for a comprehensive review) have reported that semantic priming effects occur under conditions in which the prime is briefly presented and visually masked such that either its presence vs. absence cannot be discriminated or its identity cannot be reported. These "subliminal" priming effects have been reported for both the LDT (e.g., Balota, 1983; Fischler & Goodman, 1978; Fowler, Wolford, Slade, & Tassinary, 1981; Marcel, 1983) and pronunciation (e.g., Carr, McCauley, Sperber, & Parmelee, 1982; Hines, Czerwinski, Sawyer, & Dwyer, 1986). They seem to occur for long but not short SOAs in the LDT (Balota, 1983; Fowler et al., 1981); in pronunciation the SOA variable has not been systematically examined. Although it is controversial whether the masking conditions in these experiments resulted in the primes being truly undetectable or unidentifiable (e.g., see Cheesman & Merikle, 1984; Holender, 1986; Merikle, 1982), the fact remains that priming occurred under conditions in which subjects could not verbally report the prime.[7]

Deep vs. shallow conscious processing of the prime. There is evidence that the magnitude of semantic priming effects depends on how subjects process the primes. Specifically, when subjects make a lexical decision to the target, Smith, Theodor and Franklin (1983) found that overall semantic priming was eliminated when subjects responded whether or not a prime word had an asterisk beside it. Furthermore, Smith et al. (1983) and Henik, Friedrich, and Kellog (1983) showed that overall priming was eliminated when subjects responded whether or not a prime contained a particular letter. In these experiments, the letter being searched for was duplicated above every letter in the word prime. On the other hand, when Kaye and Brown (1985) presented the to-be-searched-for letter once above the prime, semantic priming occurred in unattenuated form. However, Kaye and Brown did find that semantic priming was eliminated when subjects responded whether the prime was in upper or lower case letters. When subjects' responses to the prime were based on "deeper" semantic or lexical judgments, the normal overall priming effect occurred with these same materials. Thus, the overall pattern is one of semantic priming being eliminated when subjects process the prime to a very shallow level.

II. THEORETICAL ANALYSES OF SEMANTIC PRIMING

The foregoing review of the literature reveals a relatively complex mosaic of several phenomena that occur in the single-word semantic priming paradigm. Clearly, these diverse phenomena (and particularly those that differ for the LDT and pronunciation) provide a daunting challenge for a thorough yet comprehensive theoretical analysis of semantic priming effects. To avoid getting bogged down in the details of several specific theories, in this section I discuss theoretical issues at a rather general level. After first discussing a general metatheoretical issue, I move on to examine three general processing mechanisms that have been instantiated in various theoretical accounts of semantic priming: automatic spreading activation, expectancy, and a post-lexical mechanism that combines information provided by the existence of a semantic relation between the target and the prime. In this examination, I discuss how each mechanism provides a facile account for certain phenomena and fails to account for others. I close by arguing that in order to accommodate all of the data, a theory of semantic priming must in some way embody the operation of all three of these general mechanisms.

1. A Metatheoretical Issue: Word Nodes vs. Distributed Lexical Representations

In most of their instantiations, the three general theoretical mechanisms I discuss below share the assumption that each word an individual knows is represented in lexical memory as a separate unitized node. Presumably, a visually presented word activates lower-order nodes that represent its individual letters and these letter nodes in turn activate that word's lexical node as well as the nodes of other words that share letters in common with the visually presented word (cf., Morton, 1969; McClelland & Rumelhart, 1981).[8] This results in a "recognition" threshold being exceeded by the activation level in the presented word's node (and, by some accounts, in the nodes of words visually similar to the presented word, e.g., Becker, 1980). It is often further assumed that attentional resources must be deployed to select (verify) the particular node, activated above the recognition threshold, that represents the word that is being presented and that this selection process enters the identity of the word into consciousness (e.g., Becker, 1980; Neely, 1977).

A quite different view of the representational format of "lexical" memory has recently materialized in connectionistic parallel distributed processing (PDP) models (see McClelland, Rumelhart, & the PDP Research Group 1986; Rumelhart, McClelland, & the PDP Research Group, 1986). Specifically, PDP models dispense with the concept of word nodes (e.g., Masson, this volume; Seidenberg & McClelland, 1989). According to these models, a word activates a set of distributed features (mini-nodes, if you will) that are shared by many words. These features may represent orthographic, phonological or semantic information and the features representing these different kinds of information are connected via other layers of hidden units. The important aspect of these models is that word recognition is *not* based on the activation of a *single node* that corresponds to the presented word. Rather word recognition depends on the *settling of the activation pattern in several units into the pattern that uniquely specifies the presented word.*

Although PDP models that do not include word nodes provide an exciting and interesting new approach to modelling human cognition and have achieved considerable success in modelling word recognition in isolation (e.g., Seidenberg & McClelland, 1989), there are three reasons I believe it is much too early to abandon the concept of word nodes. First, even for the case of pronouncing an isolated letter string, it is unclear whether a PDP model without word nodes can provide a *complete* account of certain types of phonological effects in the naming of nonword letter strings--i.e., why nonwords that are pronounced like words are pronounced more rapidly than nonwords that are not pronounced like words when orthography is presumably equated for the two types of nonwords (see Besner, 1990, Besner & McCann, 1988, and Besner, Twilley, McCaan, & Seergobin, 1990 vs. Seidenberg, Jared, & McCrae, 1988, and Seidenberg & McClelland, 1990). Second, the effects of semantic priming have not been well explored within the framework of PDP models. Indeed, the mere existence of an overall semantic priming effect has not yet been demonstrated with Seidenberg and McClelland's (1989) model, which is currently the most fully developed distributed PDP model for word recognition, at least in terms of the size of its lexicon. Although other PDP models have recently been applied to semantic priming phenomena (e.g., Hirshman & Gomez, 1988; Masson, this volume; see also Grossberg & Stone, 1986), at present these models are relatively limited in scope in that they have very small lexicons. More importantly for present purposes, they yield only certain main effects of various kinds of priming and provide only a very general picture of the time course of priming. Thus, it is much too early to determine if these models can or cannot account for the diverse range of priming effects reviewed in the first section of this chapter, particularly since it is difficult to know what these models predict without running simulations (Hirshman, 1989, personal commmunication).

The third, and perhaps most important, reason for not using PDP models as a basis for abandoning the concept of word nodes is that even if PDP models are fundamentally correct, one could still have the distributed features that uniquely specify a word all feed into a single word node (cf. Broadbent, 1985, and Fodor & Pylyshyn, 1988). Although this might be viewed as unparsimonious, such system redundancy might be biologically useful. Furthermore, the postulation of word nodes in connectionistic models has proven useful in accounting for phenonmena such as the word-superiority effect (McClelland & Rumelhart, 1981). (It is interesting that Seidenberg & McClelland, 1989, do not demonstrate that their "word-nodeless" model can handle a word-superiority effect.) Finally, in the recent PDP model used by Hirshman and Gomez (1989) to simulate several priming phenomena, each word has a single graphemic-to-semantic mapping node that corresponds to it. To me, that seems like a word node. In short, when I assume the existence of separate word nodes in all of my subsequent theoretical discussions concerning "molar" processing mechanisms, I am not precluding a PDP architecture as a "molecular" account of priming phenomena.

2. Three Theoretical Mechanisms for Semantic Priming

In this section I discuss how automatic spreading activation, expectancy and three different post-lexical priming mechanisms have been used to provide general accounts of semantic priming effects. I then discuss how each of these various mechanisms can or cannot account for the results summarized in Table 1. Table 9 gives an overview of where I am going. In Table 9, the symbol + indicates that the theoretical mechanism heading that column can account for the corresponding effect described in Table 1, the symbol - indicates it cannot (without embellishment) and 0 indicates that relevant data are not available.

In discussing Table 9, I will refer to each phenomenon by its number and also indicate the task of interest. For example, nonassociative priming in pronunciation will be referred to as P1-PRON (for phenomenon 1 in pronunciation).

2.1. Automatic spreading activation (ASA)

The concept of spreading activation has been widely used in cognitive psychology (e.g., Anderson, 1976, 1983; Collins & Quillian, 1969; Collins & Loftus, 1975; Neely, 1977; Posner & Snyder, 1975b). Based on the assumption that semantically/associatively related nodes are "stored close together" (or linked via strong links), activation in the priming word's node spreads to the nodes of semantically related targets, thereby reducing the time required for the activation levels in those related nodes to exceed their recognition threshold. The result is that a prime facilitates the processing of targets that are related to it, with this facilitation being smaller the less strongly related the target and prime are. Since lexical access presumably occurs in both the LDT and the pronunciation task, spreading activation should produce similar priming effects in these two tasks.[9]

Table 9
Successes and Failures of Various Theoretical Accounts of Priming

	Theoretical Mechanism				
Phenomenon	ASA	EXPECT	PC	CC	SM
1. Nonassociative priming					
LDT	+	+	+	-	+
Pronunciation	+	+	+	-	-
2. Category exemplar priming					
LDT	-[a]	+	-[a]	-[a]	+
Pronunciation	+	-	+	-	-
3. Mediated priming					
LDT	-	+	+	+	+
Pronunciation	+	-	-	-	-
4. Backward priming					
LDT	-	-	+	+	+
Pronunciation	+	+	-	+	+
5. Category-name facilitation for related exemplar targets					
LDT	+	+[b]	+[b]	+	+[b]
Pronunciation	+	+[b]	+[b]	-	-
6. Category-name inhibition for unrelated exemplar targets					
LDT	-	+[b]	+[b]	+[c]	+[b]
Pronunciation	+	-[b]	-[b]	+	+
7. Associative facilitation					
LDT	+	+	+	+	+
Pronunciation	+	+	+	-	-
8. Associative inhibition					
LDT	+	+	-	+	-
Pronunciation	+	+	-	+	+
9. Nonword facilitation					
LDT	-	-[d]	-[d]	-[d,e]	+
Pronunciation	0	0	0	0	0
10. Target degradation					
LDT	+	+	+	-	-
Pronunciation	+	+	+	-	-
11. Target word frequency					
LDT	+	+	+	+	-[d]
Pronunciation	+	+	+	-	-
12. Instruction-induced priming					
LDT	-	+[f]	+	+	+[g]
Pronunciation	-	+[f]	+	-	-

13. Relatedness proportion effect[h]					
LDT	-	+[i]	+	-	-[j]
Pronunciation	-	+	+	-	-
14. Nonword ratio effect[k]					
LDT	-	-[l]	-	-	+
Pronunciation	0	0	0	0	0
15. Proportion of associatively related primes					
LDT	-	+	-	+	-
Pronunciation	0	0	0	0	0
16. Interposition effect					
LDT	-	+	+	+	+
Pronunciation	-	+	+	+	+
17. "Subliminal" priming					
LDT	+	-	-	+	-
Pronunciation	+	-	-	-	-
18. "Shallow" prime processing					
LDT	-	+	+	+	+
Pronunciation	0	0	0	0	0

Note. ASA is automatic spreading activation as discussed in Posner and Snyder (1975b); EXPECT is a hybrid expectancy mechanism based on Becker's (1980) and Posner and Snyder's (1975b) theories; PC is Norris' (1986) plausibility checking mechanism; CC is Ratcliff and McKoon's (1988) cue-combination theory; SM is the semantic-matching mechanism of Neely and Keefe (1989). The symbol + indicates the mechanism can account for the corresponding effect described in Table 1; the symbol -, that it cannot. An entry of 0 indicates that data are unavailable.

[a]Cannot account for equivalent high-dominance and low-dominance priming.

[b]Cannot account for facilitation not being accompanied by inhibition at the short SOA in the LDT or at either short or long SOAs in pronunciation.

[c]Cannot account for inhibition being greater at long SOAs.

[d]Although not discussed by the authors of the original version of the theory, the effect can be handled by an elaborated version of the theory. See text.

[e]The theory's elaborated version can explain nonword facilitation but not why it increases with longer SOAs and with higher nonword ratios.

[f]Cannot explain the priming that occurs at the short SOA.

[g]Cannot explain why priming at the short SOA is not accompanied by nonword facilitation.

[h] A "pure" relatedness proportion effect, with nonword ratio effects partialled out.

[i]Cannot account for its absence at short SOAs which do yield priming.

[j]Cannot account for why relatedness proportion effects are different from nonword ratio effects.

[k]A "pure" nonword ratio effect, with relatedness proportion effects partialled out.

[l]Can be elaborated to account for the effect that nonword ratio has on nonword facilitation but not on facilitation from related primes.

In some theories, the spread of activation is assumed to be limited in capacity (e.g., Anderson, 1976, 1983); in other theories, it is not (e.g., Posner & Snyder, 1975b). Here I focus on Posner and Snyder's (1975b) analysis which assumes unlimited capacity. In those cases in which an assumption of limited capacity leads to an accommodation of otherwise embarrassing data, I will follow Posner and Snyder's (1975b) lead and appeal to the operation of a limited-capacity expectancy mechanism that is under strategic control (see next section) rather than assuming that the spread of activation is limited in its capacity. I believe this approach is preferred because a limited-capacity expectancy mechanism provides a much more facile account of list context effects (see Section I, Part 5) than does a limited-capacity spreading activation mechanism.

According to Posner and Snyder (1975b), spreading activation emanating from the priming word's node (a) can occur without a person's intention or awareness, (b) is fast acting, (c) facilitates the processing of semantically related targets (as described above), but (d) does not inhibit the processing of unrelated targets. Because spreading activation is not under a person's conscious control, Posner and Snyder have labelled it an automatic process (but see Logan, 1985, 1988, for a more comprehensive definition of automaticity). The first column of Table 9 provides information pertinent to whether or not ASA can account for the various priming phenomena reviewed in Section I.

Supportive data. If nodes for both semantically and associatively related words are "stored close together," it is clear that for both tasks ASA can account for nonassociative priming (P1, i.e., phenomenon #1, in Tables 1 and 9) as well as for facilitation from both category-name and associatively related primes (P5 and P7). Because ASA does not produce inhibition it also correctly predicts the absence of associative inhibition (P8) in both tasks.

ASA can also accommodate the findings that priming effects are greater for degraded than nondegraded targets (P10) in both tasks and are greater for low-frequency than for high-frequency words (P11) in both tasks. It can do this by making two assumptions: (a) The rate at which the visual features activate their corresponding letter and word nodes is slowed by manipulations that degrade the word's individual letters. (b) The nodal activation levels for related targets and for high-frequency targets are closer to the recognition threshold than they are for unrelated and low-frequency targets, respectively. The manner in which these two assumptions predict the Target Degradation x Priming and Target Word Frequency x Priming interactions can be illuminated by a horse race analogy. (However, this analogy does not account for why inserting asterisks between a word's letters fails to increase priming.) If a fast (nondegraded) horse races a slow (degraded) horse, the difference in their finishing times (RTs) will be greater the further away is the finishing line (the distance of the starting activation level from the threshold activation level).[10]

One of the strongest pieces of evidence supporting an ASA account of priming is the subliminal priming effect. This is so because ASA can account for subliminal priming whereas the other two theoretical mechanisms cannot (see below). That "subliminal" priming is larger at long than short SOAs can be accommodated by the reasonable assumption that "subliminal" activation takes longer to spread than does suprathreshold activation.

Additional evidence that strongly supports the concept of ASA comes from certain aspects of Favreau and Segalowitz's (1983) and Neely's (1977) results and the relatedness proportion effect (see Section I, Part 5). These results show that at short SOAs for which ASA effects should be maximal, a prime facilitates the processing of a related target to the same degree regardless of whether subjects have been instructed to expect unrelated or related targets to follow that prime and independent of the probability that the target following a prime will be related to it. This confirms that activation spreads between related nodes independent of any strategies subjects may be using.

Problematic data. Because ASA is assumed not to produce inhibition, it cannot predict the category-name inhibition that occurs for exemplar targets (P6) in the LDT at long SOAs. Furthermore, because ASA is not under strategic control it cannot predict instruction-induced priming (P12) in either task nor can it predict for either task list-context effects such as those obtained in P13, P14-LDT, and P15-LDT. (However, as noted above, it nicely handles the absence of a relatedness proportion effect, P15, at short SOAs.) Although ASA can predict nonword facilitation for a nonword target visually similar to a word that is related to that nonword target's prime (see Anderson, 1983, pp. 102-103 for the theoretical analysis and footnote 4 for the relevant data), it cannot predict nonword facilitation for a nonword target that is not visually similar to that nonword target's prime (P9-LDT).

ASA cannot predict the interposition effect (P16), which is the finding that interposing an unrelated word between a related prime and target reduces priming relative to the condition in which a neutral prime is interposed between a related prime and target (see Masson, this volume). Since activation from the prime's node should have decayed to the same degree whether an unrelated word or neutral prime was interposed between it and its target, without additional assumptions ASA predicts equivalent priming effects in these two conditions for both tasks. That the interposition effect occurs in both tasks, is thus problematic for ASA. (However, see Section I, Part 6, for some qualifications concerning the generality of the interposition effect).

Another challenge to the concept of ASA is posed by the finding that "shallow" prime processing reduces or eliminates priming in the LDT (in which this effect has been studied, P18). Since the spread of activation between related nodes is presumably automatic, it should occur regardless of the type of processing that is done on the prime.

Perhaps the most severe problems for ASA are posed by priming phenomena (P2, P3, and P4) that differ for the LDT and pronunciation. Because ASA is presumably not under strategic control, its effects should not modulated by differing task demands. Consider first the data relevant to whether priming effects have different magnitudes for high- and low-dominance exemplars when their category names are used as primes (P2). Because the strength of spreading activation is assumed to dissipate the further it spreads from the priming word's node, under the eminently reasonable assumption that high-dominance exemplars are more strongly related to their category names than are low-dominance exemplars, ASA predicts that overall priming should be greater for high- than for low-dominance exemplars. Although this prediction is confirmed in pronunication (P2-PRON), it is disconfirmed in the LDT (P2-LDT).

Of greater interest are the findings that mediated priming occurs in pronunciation but not in the LDT (P3) whereas the opposite is so for backward priming (P4), at least with visual primes and long SOAs. With some elaborations, ASA could account for backward priming in the LDT. That is, one could argue that activation in the node for the target *bed* spreads to the node for the prime *pan* and that this activation somehow feeds back to add to the activation in the "bed" node. The problem with such an analysis is that incorrectly predicts backward priming should also be observed in pronunciation under the same conditions. Of course, an ASA proponent might then argue that the LDT provides a more sensitive measure of ASA effects than does pronunciation. However, this ploy is rebutted by the finding that the pronunciation task yields mediated priming effects whereas the LDT does not. Indeed, DE Groot (1983) has argued that the absence of a mediated priming effect in the LDT is very problematic for the concept of ASA, since activation should spread from the "lion" node to the "tiger" node and then on to the "stripes" node to yield mediated priming. But her argument is undermined by the mediated priming effect that occurs in pronunciation. In short, then, the concept of ASA cannot account the complete pattern of backward and mediated priming effects that occurs in the LDT and pronunciation.

2.2. Expectancy-based priming

Expectancy is a second general mechanism used to account for semantic priming effects. In some cases, expectancy has been used to supplement accounts based on ASA (e.g., Anderson, 1983; Posner & Snyder, 1975b); in other cases expectancy alone has been used to account for priming (e.g., Becker, 1980, 1985). Expectancy theories account for the standard priming effect by assuming that subjects use the prime to generate an expectancy set that consists of potential targets that are related to that prime. Targets that are included in this expectancy set are recognized more quickly than those that are not. In this section, I describe an expectancy mechanism that is a hybrid of the expectancy mechanisms proposed by Posner and Snyder (1975b) and Becker (1980, 1985).

In the Posner-Snyder (1975b) theory, unlike ASA, expectancy (a) is under a person's strategic control and cannot occur without a person's intention or awareness, (b) is relatively slow acting in that it takes time to generate the expectancy set from the prime, (c) facilitates the processing of *expected* targets, whether they be related or unrelated to the prime, and (d) inhibits the recognition of unexpected targets, whether they be related or unrelated to the prime. A major problem for Posner and Snyder's expectancy mechanism is that it cannot readily account for why associative prime-target relationships yield a pattern of facilitation dominance whereas category-name primes and high- and low-dominance exemplar targets yield a pattern of inhibition dominance (see Section I, Part 2 and Table 6). Because of this deficiency, I elaborate on Posner and Snyder's analysis by drawing heavily from Becker's (1980, 1985) more detailed analysis concerning exactly how an expectancy can produce facilitation and/or inhibition for a target that is expected or unexpected, respectively, based on its prime.

According to the clever and innovative analysis of priming proposed by Becker (1980, 1985), when a target word is visually presented in the absence of a semantic context (i.e., following a neutral prime), the visual features corresponding to its letters are extracted. These letter features activate above their recognition threshold a set of word nodes that are visually similar to that target. Attention is then allocated to a "search" of the word nodes in this set, called the visually defined set. This serial self-terminating search is strictly frequency ordered, with nodes corresponding to high frequency words being searched before the nodes corresponding to low frequency words. This search of the visually defined set basically involves a spelling-check process that determines if the presented word's letters completely match the letters of the word corresponding to each node in the visually defined set. If a complete match occurs, the word is recognized and a "word" response is made in the LDT and the pronunciation of the word is retrieved and executed in the pronunciation task. If a complete match doesn't occur, the search of the visually defined set continues through the rest of the nodes until one does occur. If an exhaustive search of the visually defined set fails to find a complete match, a "nonword" response is made. (Because he was primarily interested in the LDT, Becker did not specify how nonwords are pronounced.)

When a word prime precedes a target word, an expectancy set is generated from that word prime. In the typical priming experiment, this expectancy set contains nodes corresponding to words related to the prime. When the target is presented, two things happen. One is that the visually defined set is being activated as previously described. While this is proceeding, attention is serially allocated to matching a visual representation of each word node in the expectancy set with the raw visual image of the presented word in iconic memory. This matching process involves a serial self-terminating search that is randomly ordered rather than being ordered according to word frequency. If a match is found in the expectancy set, the word is recognized and the response appropriate to the LDT and pronunciation task is executed. If an exhaustive search of the expectancy set fails to find a match, attention is re-allocated to a search of the visually defined set once it has been activated. This search through the visually defined set proceeds exactly as described earlier for the case in which the target is presented in the absence of a semantic context. The important feature of Becker's (1980, 1985) analysis is that when a priming word precedes a target, the search through the visually defined must await the completion of an exhaustive search of the expectancy set which failed to find a match. In a neutral priming context, however, the search through the visually defined set begins as soon as the visually defined set is activated.

Supportive data. If the expectancy set can contain words that are semantically but not associatively related to the prime, expectancy could produce nonassociative semantic priming (P1) in both tasks and facilitation from both category-name and associatively related primes (P5 and P7) in both tasks, at least for SOAs that are long enough to permit subjects enough time to generate an expectancy set before the target appears.

Becker (1980, 1985) has also discussed how his expectancy model can account for both the Target Word Frequency x Priming and Target Degradation x Priming interactions (P11, P10) in both tasks. Consider first the finding that priming effects are smaller for high- than low-frequency words. On those related priming trials in which the targets are found in the randomly searched expectancy set, RTs would be the same for high- and low-frequency targets, on the average. On unrelated priming trials (or on related priming trials in which the target was too weakly related to the prime to be included in the expectancy set), the targets would be recognized from the frequency-ordered search of the visually defined set such that RTs would be considerably longer for low- than for high-frequency words. Thus, the speed up in RTs caused by finding a match in the expectancy set (i.e., priming) would be considerably greater for the low-frequency words, which in the unrelated priming condition are found so late in the search of the visually defined set.

Becker's (1980, 1985) model can also account for the Target Degradation x Priming interaction, which is the finding that priming effects are larger for degraded than nondegraded targets (P10). It does so by assuming that the effect of target degradation on how long it takes for the visual representation of the word to be set up in iconic memory is considerably smaller than its effect on how long it takes for the visual feature extraction process to set up the visually defined set. Because degradation has a smaller effect on how long it takes to match the target with an item in the expectancy set than on how long it takes the visually defined set to become available for search, the analysis of the Target Degradation x Priming interaction proceeds analogously to that for the Target Word Frequency x Priming interaction. (Recall that word frequency has no effect on how long it takes for an item to be matched in the expectancy set but has a large effect on how long it takes for an item to be matched in the visually defined set.) That is, on those related priming trials in which targets are found in the expectancy set, RTs will not greatly differ for degraded and nondegraded targets. This is so because degradation has a relatively small effect on the time it takes to form the iconic representation of the target, against which items in the expectancy set are being matched. However, on unrelated priming trials (or on related priming trials in which a target was too weakly related to the prime to be included in the expectancy set), the targets would be recognized from the search of the visually defined set, which could get started much earlier for nondegraded targets than for degraded targets. Thus, the speed up in RTs caused by finding a match in the expectancy set (i.e., priming) would be considerably greater for degraded targets.

Clearly, the prediction of the Target Degradation x Priming interaction holds only if the visually defined set for degraded targets does not get activated until after the expectancy set has been exhaustively searched. (I return to this point after I have discussed variables that influence the size of the expectancy set.) If the visually defined sets for both degraded and nondegraded targets had time to become activated before the search of the expectancy set was completed, the effects of degradation would be over with before the search of the visually defined set could begin in the unrelated priming condition. The result would be that degradation would have little effect on RTs for targets that followed either related or unrelated primes, though it would still have an effect on RTs to targets in the neutral priming condition.[11]

A very attractive feature of Becker's analysis is that it can, as indeed it was designed to do, account for the differing patterns of facilitation and inhibition observed for associatively and categorically related primes and targets in the LDT (P5, P6-LDT, P7, P8). It does so by assuming that subjects generate a smaller expectancy set when strongly associatively related primes and targets are used than when category-name primes and exemplar-targets are used.[12] That is, for associatively related materials, subjects use the prime to generate a small expectancy set containing only a few words with a strong associative relation to the prime. Assuming that this small expectancy set includes the target, the target will be found very quickly in it and the result will be a large facilitation effect in the related priming condition. On the other hand, in the unrelated priming condition the inhibition effect will be small. This is so, because the person will have wasted very little time in exhaustively searching the very small expectancy set before he or she begins the search of the visually defined set, in which the unrelated target resides. For category materials, subjects use the category-name prime to generate a large expectancy set that contains all of that category's exemplars. Because the subject must, on average, search through a large number of category exemplars to find a target related to the prime in the expectancy set, the facilitation effect in the related priming condition will be relatively small. However, inhibition in the unrelated priming condition will be relatively large, because a lot of time will have been wasted exhautively searching this large expectancy set before the search of the visually defined set is initiated. Of course, this analysis cannot explain why inhibition effects for category materials are small in pronunciation (P6-PRON).

There are two heretofore ignored aspects of Becker's (1980) analysis that relate to the size of the semantically defined set. One is that the Target Degradation x Priming interaction should be greater for small rather than large semantically defined sets. This is so, because, as was noted earlier, a necessary condition for obtaining a Target Degradation x Priming interaction is that the degradation manipulation delays the activation of the visually defined sets for degraded targets beyond the time required for an exhaustive search of the expectancy set. Clearly, this necessary condition is more likely to be met the smaller is the semantically defined set. Another unexplored implication of Becker's theory is that the exact magnitudes of the facilitation and inhibition effects depend on the relative sizes of the prime's expectancy set and the target's visually defined set. That is, facilitation will be smaller and inhibition larger when the visually defined set, which serves as the basis for responses in the neutral priming condition, is very small relative to the expectancy set. Indeed, if the visually defined set were very small (such that a match would be found very quickly in the neutral priming condition) and the expectancy set very large (such that a match would be found fairly slowly in the semantically defined set), one could find *inhibition* in the semantically related priming condition! In any case, Becker's analysis could be further tested by experiments that orthogonally manipulated the sizes of the expectancy set and the visually defined set as well as target degradation.[13]

Becker's (1980, 1985) analysis also easily handles most of the list-context effects. For example, it was specifically designed to account for why intermixing a large proportion of trials that contain strongly associatively related primes and targets with a small proportion of trials containing category-name primes and exemplar targets changes the pattern of priming effects typically observed for the categorically related primes and targets (P15-LDT). When most related priming trials contain highly associatively related primes and targets, subjects presumably use a prime to generate a small expectancy set containing items with a strong associative relation to that prime. As described earlier, a small expectancy set yields facilitation dominance such that the category materials also now yield facilitation dominance rather than their typical pattern of inhibition dominance. Also, since low-dominance exemplars are less likely to be in this small expectancy set, they will now yield smaller priming effects than the high-dominance exemplars, which is the obtained finding (P15-LDT).

Becker's (1980) expectancy-set analysis accounts for the relatedness proportion effect (P13) by assuming that the probability that subjects will use the prime to generate an expectancy set increases as the relatedness proportion increases and this increases overall priming by increasing both facilitation in the related priming condition and inhibition in the unrelated priming condition. (However, as discussed later it has trouble accounting for why a relatedness proportion effect occurs only for high-dominance exemplars.) Becker's analysis can also easily explain Neely's (1977) and Favreau and Segalowitz's (1983) instruction-induced priming from unrelated primes (P12) by assuming that the expectancy set contains exemplars from the category specified by the instructions rather than by the prime itself. That a shallow level of prime processing reduces priming (P18-LDT) can be accommodated by assuming that shallow nonsemantic processing of the prime interferes more with generating a semantically based expectancy set than does a deeper semantic processing of the prime. The interposition effect (P16) is also easily explained by assuming that an interposed unrelated word is used to generate an expectancy set that replaces the expectancy set generated from the prime that is related to the target whereas an interposed neutral prime does not lead to the generation of such a replacement expectancy set. (A probabilistic replacement would handle the fact that interposition of an unrelated word does not always entirely eliminate priming.)

Problematic data. One problem encountered by an expectancy-set theory is the different patterns of category-dominance effects that are observed under various conditions. As noted in the preceding section, the theory accommodates the finding that having a high proportion of strongly associatively related primes and targets reduces low-dominance priming relative to high-dominance priming by inducing subjects to use a smaller expectancy set which does not include low-dominance exemplars. However, when categorically related primes and targets predominate, two problems arise. First, priming effects are equivalent for high- and low-dominance targets in the LDT (P2-LDT) but are greater for high- than for low-dominance targets in pronunciation (P2-PRON). The equivalent overall priming effects for high- and low-dominance exemplars can be accommodated by the assumption that the *randomly* searched expectancy set is large enough to include both types of exemplars (see Becker, 1980). The larger priming effect for high- than for low-dominance exemplars could be explained by assuming that not all of the low-dominance exemplars are included in the expectancy set. But since exactly the same materials were used in both tasks, one must face the challenge of coming up with a plausible reason for why expectancy sets are larger for the lexical decision task than for pronunciation.

The second problem posed by category-dominance effects obtained in lists in which categorically related primes and targets predominate is why increases in the relatedness proportion affects priming for high-dominance exemplars but not for low-dominance exemplars. Since increases in the relatedness proportion increased the proportion of related priming trials for both high- and low-dominance exemplars, subjects should have become more and more likely to use the prime to generate a large expectancy set which should have increased overall priming for both high- and low-dominance exemplars.

Two other phenomena that Becker's expectancy-set model has trouble handling are nonword facilitation (P9-LDT) and certain aspects of the nonword ratio effect (P14-LDT). However, these two phenomena can be dealt with by adding an embellishment to the model. The embellishment is that if subjects fail to find the target in the expectancy set they bias a "nonword" response, thereby producing facilitation relative to the neutral priming condition in which no such bias exists.[14] If one further assumes that subjects are sensitive to the probability that a target is a nonword given that it was not matched in the search of the expectancy set (which would be related to the nonword ratio), the analysis also predicts that nonword facilitation should increase as the nonword ratio increases. This could also account for the fact that overall priming for both high- and low-dominance exemplars should increase as the nonword ratio increases. However, this would come about solely because inhibition for unrelated words would increase with increases in the nonword ratio due to the greater "nonword" bias for them when they had not been matched with an item in the expectancy set; facilitation for related items should be unaffected by increases in the nonword ratio. However, this is not what Neely et al. (1989) obtained (see Neely & Keefe,

1990, pp. 238-240, for a discussion of the somewhat complicated pattern of data that was actually obtained.) In short, though the addition of a "nonword" response biasing mechanism to Becker's model permits it to account for nonword facilitation effects, it at the same time leads to problems concerning the model's predictions about inhibition for word targets in the unrelated priming conditions. (As another example of a problem, the "nonword" response biasing mechanism would yield inhibition for unrelated word targets even when the expectancy set is small.)

In addition to these problems, there are two other general classes of effects embodied in the phenomena reviewed in Section I that challenge an expectancy-based explanation of priming. One concerns the effects of SOA and in particular what happens at the shorter SOAs (as Eisenberg & Becker, 1982, p.752 acknowledge). To account for changes in facilitation and inhibition with changes in SOA, the expectancy-set theory could postulate SOA-related changes in the size of expectancy-set and/or in the probability of the formation an expectancy set of the size appropriate to the type of materials being used. However, this leaves unexplained why the priming that occurs at short SOAs (which according to the theory is due to some sort of expectancy set having been formed) is not affected by the relatedness proportion whereas priming at long SOAs is so affected (P13-LDT). Nor can it be explained why in Neely's (1977) experiment at a short SOA, BODY facilitated the processing of a related exemplar such as arm which came from a category that was unlikely to be used for selecting the target whereas at a long SOA it facilitated the processing of an unrelated exemplar such as door which came from a category that was likely to be used for selecting the target. As noted in the previous section, such data provide relatively strong support for the concept of ASA.

The final general problem, which plagues ASA as well, is that priming effects are often different in the LDT and pronunciation. That category-dominance has different effects on priming was discussed in the first paragraph of this section. Another task difference is that inhibition effects in the unrelated priming condition for categorically related materials are large in the LDT and nonexistent in pronunciation (P6). This could be handled by an appeal to large and small expectancy sets being used in the LDT and pronunciation task, respectively. However, this once again invites the question of why exactly the same materials should lead to expectancy sets of different sizes in the two tasks. Worse yet are problems posed by mediated priming (P3) and backward priming (P4). A proponent of an expectancy-set theory of priming can easily explain the absence of mediated priming in the LDT, since the target *stripes* would not be included in the expectancy set of related items generated from the prime *lion*, to which *stripes* is unrelated. However, this analysis cannot explain why mediated priming occurs in pronunciation. Furthermore, although the absence of backward priming in pronunciation provides comfort to the expectancy-set theorist, its presence in the LDT is antithetical to the basic tenets of an expectancy-based theory of priming. This is so because subjects should not be able to use the prime *pan*, which would yield *bed* as an associate with a near zero probability, to generate an expectancy set that includes *bed*.

Finally, subliminal priming (P17) almost rivals backward priming in terms of the severity of the challenge it poses for an expectancy-based theory of priming. Specifially, how can people use a prime to generate an expectancy set of related items when they claim not even to see that prime? This implies an "unconscious" expectancy, which seems to contradict most of the defining features of what an expectancy is.

2.3. "Post-lexical" Priming Mechanisms

As discussed in parts 2.1 and 2.2 in this section, ASA and an expectancy set both yield priming by *speeding access to the target's lexical node*. Because of this, their locus of operation has been called *pre-lexical*. I now discuss a third possible mechanism for priming which has only very recently been taken the least bit seriously. Unlike ASA and expectancy, this mechanism does not produce priming by somehow speeding up access to the target's lexical node. Rather it produces priming via processes that either (a) affect the selection of the target's node *after* it has already been entered into what corresponds to Becker's (1980) visually defined set (e.g., Norris, 1986), (b) use a compound cue consisting of both the prime and target to access memory rather than using only the target itself to access memory (e.g., Ratcliff & McKoon, 1988), or (c) affect decisional and/or response processes that occur after lexical access for the target has occurred (e.g., Balota & Lorch, 1986; Chiarello, Senehi, & Nuding, 1987; DE Groot, 1984; Forster, 1979, 1981; Neely, 1976, 1977; Neely & Keefe, 1989). For want of a better term, I refer to these processes as *post-lexical* priming mechanisms. (However, based on Ratcliff & McKoon's, 1988, discussion of pre- vs. post-lexical priming mechanisms on pp. 392-393, they probably prefer that their compound cue theory be called an *a-lexical* theory of priming.) I now turn to a discussion of the main features of each of these three general "post-lexical" approaches to accounting for priming.

Norris' (1986) plausibility-checking theory. Norris' (1986) model describes how *word* recognition proceeds in both the LDT and the pronunciation task. In Norris' (1986) theory, as soon as a target is presented it begins to activate its visually defined set. At first this set contains a large number of items that share as few as one or two letters in commmon with the target. However, as time passes, this set is reduced to only a few items that share several letters in common with the target. Even though only one item (i.e., the target) may eventually remain in the visually defined set, "conscious" recognition does not occur until the evidence supporting that word's presentation has exceeded its own particular recognition threshold. Three sources of information dynamically control the winnowing of the visually defined candidate set until it contains only one item: (a) Perceptual evidence for each item in the candidate set accumulates in direct proportion to its visual similarity to the target. (b) The perceptual evidence for each candidate word is weighted according to its frequency of occurrence in the language. (Exactly how this frequency weighting combines with the perceptual evidence, e.g., additively or multiplicatively, is not explicitly specified, though additivity is strongly implied.) (c) After the candidate set has been reduced to a manageable number of words based on the first two sources of evidence, each remaining member of the candidate set is accessed and checked to determine its plausibility given the priming context. However, as this plausibility check is occurring, the output from the perceptual analysis is continually updating the set of items on which the plausibility check is being made. If an item in the candidate set is related to the context (i.e., contextually plausible), its recognition threshold will be lowered (producing a facilitation effect); if it is unrelated to the context (i.e., contextually implausible), its recognition threshold will be raised (producing an inhibition effect). Thus, in Norris' (1986) model, context exerts its influence on a process that occurs between lexical access and conscious recognition.

Supportive data. Norris' (1986) model can account for many of the phenomena summarized in Table 1. Clearly, it can account for both facilitation from a related context and inhibition from an unrelated context (P5, P7 and P6-LDT) and can account for nonassociative semantic priming (P1). It can also easily handle Neely's (1977) and Favreau and Segalowitz's (1983) finding that facilitation based on expectancy-shifting priming for words semantically unrelated to the prime requires longer SOAs to develop (P12). It does so by assuming that it takes time for the subject to use the prime *BODY* to create the context *BUILDING* that is used in the plausibility check. The relatedness proportion effect (P13) is easily accommodated by assuming that subjects are more likely to utilize the plausibility checking mechanism as the relatedness proportion increases and the interposition effect (P16) by assuming that the word interposed between the related prime and target probabilistically replaces the prime as the context used for the plausibility check. Because Norris' model assumes that any variable that slows word recognition will give the plausibility checking mechanism more time to exert its influence, it correctly predicts that priming effects for a target will be greater the lower is its frequency of occurrence in the language (P11) and the more visually degraded it is (P10). (However, it incorrectly predicts that inhibition effects should increase whether target recognition is slowed by inserting asterisks between the target's letters or by visually degrading its individual letters.) That shallow processing of the prime reduces or eliminates priming (P18) can be handled by the reasonable but ad hoc assumption that shallow processing of the prime interferes with subjects' extracting semantic information from that prime for use in the plausibility check.

Problematic data. Norris' (1986) model is also embarassed by several of the phenomena summarized in Table 1. For example, how can subjects use a prime they claim not even being able to see to create a context against which they can check the target's plausibility (P17)? Also, because facilitation and inhibition are two sides of the same coin, the model has trouble accounting for variables' differentially affecting facilitation and inhibition. Although Norris (1986, pp. 116-117) discusses the general issue of asymmetries in facilitation and inhibition with sentence contexts, it is not clear whether that discussion can provide adequate answers to the following questions. If facilitation and inhibition both increase with increasing SOAs because it takes time to extract the semantic information necessary for the plausibility check to be made, why should facilitation occur at shorter SOAs than inhibition (P5 vs. P6)? Also, why should facilitation and inhibition in the LDT be differentially affected by the type of prime-target relationship that is instantiated in the preponderance of related prime-target pairs in the test list (P5, P6, P7, P8, P15)? One could explain why overall priming for low-dominance exemplars decreases with an increase in the probability that the related prime-target pairs have a strong associative relationship. This would occur because the plausibility check would be more likely to be based on the presence of a strong associative relationship between the prime and target and this relationship would be absent for a low-dominance exemplar whether or not it was related to its category-name prime. However, why would this decrease inhibition for unrelated high-dominance exemplars and at the same time increase facilitation for related high-dominance exemplars? Finally, why in pronunciation doesn't inhibition in unrelated priming conditions (P6-PRON, P8-PRON) accompany facilitation in related priming conditions (P5-PRON, P7-PRON)? The same question applies to associative priming in the LDT (P8-LDT and P7-LDT).

Because Norris' (1986) theory localizes priming effects between lexical access and conscious recognition, even more problematic are those priming effects that differ for the LDT and pronunciation task. That is, there is no reason for both high- and low-dominance exemplars to yield priming in pronunciation (P2). Furthermore, the theory can explain neither mediated nor backward priming effects (the latter point being explicitly acknowledged by Norris, 1986, p. 134) much less the facts that mediated priming occurs in pronunciation but not in the LDT (P3) whereas the opposite is so for backward priming (P4).

It is also not entirely clear how Norris' (1986) model can deal with nonword facilitation and the nonword ratio effect. Norris (see pp. 129-131) claims that a "nonword" response is made in the lexical decision task as soon as no items remain in the visually defined candidate set. Because it will take longer to remove all candidates from the visually defined set the more words a nonword looks like, this analysis correctly predicts that the more a nonword target looks like a word or words, the longer the reaction time it will yield (e.g., Coltheart et al., 1977; but see footnote 13 for some problematic word data). However, the predictions Norris' model makes concerning nonword facilitation effects (P9) are much less clear. (Indeed, Norris never addresses this issue.) One might argue that when a nonword target looks like a word (or words) unrelated to the prime, the implausibility of these unrelated words will lead to their more quickly being eliminated from the visually defined set. This would produce facilitation relative to a neutral priming condition. On the other hand, early on, before the perceptual analysis has had time to winnow down the visually defined set to include only those items that look very much like the presented nonword target, some of the items will be contextually plausible making it likely they will remain in the visually defined set longer. This would delay the "nonword" response. But even if one goes with the former analysis so as to handle nonword facilitation, it is not clear why increasing the nonword ratio (P14) would affect the plausibility check or, even if it did, how it would affect it differently from increasing the relatedness proportion. (Recall that increases in the relatedness proportion result in increases in priming only for high-dominance exemplars whereas increases in the nonword ratio result in increases in priming for both high- and low-dominance exemplars as well as increases in nonword facilitation).

Ratcliff and McKoon's (1988) cue-combination theory. Ratcliff and McKoon (1988) have developed an ingenious theory of priming that builds on Gillund and Shiffrin's (1984) model of episodic recognition memory. In accounting for priming, Ratcliff and McKoon assume that subjects use a compound cue consisting of both the prime and target to access memory (but with greater weighting given to the target) and then use that compound cue's familiarity value as a basis for making their lexical decisions to the target. The computed familiarity value of the compound cue is then used as the drift rate in a random-walk diffusion process (e.g., Ratcliff, 1978). The claim that subjects use familiarity to make lexical decisions has been made by others (e.g., Balota & Chumbley, 1984). The general idea is that because words are more familiar than nonwords, if a target (compound cue) is highly familiar, a quick "word" response can be made. If a target (compound cue) is highly unfamiliar, a quick "nonword" response can be made. If a target (compound cue) has moderate familiarity, additional processing must occur. This additional processing is modelled by the random-walk diffusion process in Ratcliff and McKoon's (1988) model (and by lexical access processes in Balota & Chumbley's, 1984 model). Priming occurs because related prime-target compound cues are more familiar than unrelated prime-target compound cues.

One important feature of Ratcliff and McKoon's (1988) theory is that it focuses on how familiarity is utilized in binary-response paradigms such as lexical decision or episodic recognition tasks. Indeed, in discussing the relationship between the LDT and the pronunciation task, Ratcliff and McKoon (1988, p. 393) explicitly state that "we believe that although the two tasks could be affected by some variables in similar ways, their processes are fundamentally different. In lexical decision, subjects can provide a response based on some notion of familiarity ... and the response is a binary decision. In contrast, the naming task requires the subject to retrieve one of tens of thousands of names from the mental lexicon. Although both these tasks require some kind of access to the mental lexicon, we believe the processes underlying these tasks probably differ in significant ways...."

A second interesting aspect of Ratcliff and McKoon's analysis is how they treat the neutral priming condition. They argue that on neutral priming trials, the target from the previous trial forms a compound cue with the target from the current trial. Thus, neutral priming trials are really a mixture of related priming trials (when the target from the previous trial is unrelated to the current target) and unrelated priming trials (when the target from the previous trial is related to the current target). As I discuss shortly, this has interesting implications for how their theory accounts for inhibition effects.

Supportive data. Because Ratcliff and McKoon's (1988) theory was primarily intended to deal with priming effects in binary decision tasks such as the LDT, all supportive evidence necessarily comes from that task. Clearly, the theory can handle facilitation from related primes (P5 and P7). Moreover, because there is no direct association between the prime and target on mediated priming trials and because the compound cue used to search memory on trials in which an unrelated word is interposed between a related "prime" and target will consist of the unrelated interposed word and target, the theory also correctly predicts the absence of a mediated priming effect (P3-LDT) as well as the interposition effect (P16).

If one assumes that subjects can form a compound cue from an internally generated "prime" and a target and that the act of internal generation consumes time, the theory easily anticipates Neely's (1977) and Favreau and Segalowitz's (1983) finding that facilitation based on expectancy-shifting priming for words semantically unrelated to the prime occurs only at longer SOAs (P12). With the further assumption that if subjects have not had enough time to generate the internal "prime" from the actually presented prime, then the presented prime enters into the compound cue with the target. The theory also accounts for why at short SOAs facilitation occurs for "unexpected" related targets rather than for "expected" unrelated targets.

Ratcliff and McKoon's (1988) compound-cue theory can also provide admittedly post hoc accounts of subliminal priming (P17) and of why shallow processing of the prime reduces priming (P18). Specifically, if an "unseen" prime can still enter into a compound cue with the target, subliminal priming would occur and if shallow processing of a prime reduces the likelihood of its being combined with the target to form a compound cue for searching memory, priming would be reduced.

Although Ratcliff and McKoon did not discuss the issue, their theory can also nicely explain why inhibition effects are larger for category-name/exemplar materials than for associatively related materials (P6 vs. P8). According to their theory, "inhibition" occurs in the unrelated priming condition only when the neutral priming condition contains a target that is related to the target that appeared on the immediately preceding trial. This is so because these consecutive related targets will be combined to form the compound cue on neutral priming trials, thereby speeding up RTs in the neutral priming condition relative to the unrelated priming condition in which the compound cue always consists of unrelated words. (However, as discussed below, the time course of inhibition is problematic for the theory.) Because targets on consecutive trials are more likely to be related with category materials (by virtue of belonging to the same category) than with associatively related materials (for which any association between consecutive targets would merely be coincidental), Ratcliff and McKoon's analysis correctly predicts that "inhibition" will be greater for the former materials! However, when these same category materials are embedded in a list of mostly associatively related materials, there will be a reduction in the probability that a category exemplar target in the neutral priming condition will have been immediately preceded by a category exemplar target from the same semantic category, thereby leading to a reduction in inhibition (P15). Furthermore, their model also makes the as yet untested prediction that even category materials will fail to yield inhibition if only those neutral priming trials for which the target was unrelated to the immediately preceding target are used as the baseline.

Although Ratcliff and McKoon did not discuss the nonword facilitation effect, it too can be derived from their theory. The derivation proceeds along the same lines as an account of why "inhibition" occurs in the unrelated priming condition. When a word prime precedes a nonword target that was constructed from a word unrelated to that prime, the overall familiarity of the compound cue will always be very low. However, on those neutral priming trials in which the nonword target coincidentally happens to be constructed from a word related to a word target on the immediately preceding trial, there would be a higher familiarity value for the compound cue formed between the previous word target and the "related" current nonword target. This higher familiarity value would lead to slower "nonword" responses in the neutral priming condition than in the word-prime condition, thereby producing the nonword "facilitation" effect (P9). (However, as discussed below, the theory has trouble with the fact that the nonword facilitation effect is greater at the longer SOAs.)

Ratcliff and McKoon's (1988) theory can also easily accommodate the finding (P11) that priming effects are larger for low- than for high-frequency words in the LDT (although once again they did not address this issue). Recall that if the compound cue exceeds some upper familiarity criterion, subjects make a fast "word" response. For unrelated prime-target pairs, these fast "word" responses should occur much less often when the target is an unfamiliar low-frequency word relative to when it is a highly familiar high-frequency word. Because there is a larger proportion of low-frequency targets that remain to be raised above the upper familiarity criterion by the increment in familiarity produced by a related prime, the facilitation produced by a related prime should be greater for low- than for high-frequency targets (cf., Balota & Chumbley's, 1984, account of how the familiarity increment produced by repetition facilitates lexical decisions more for low- than for high-frequency words).[15]

The greatest triumph for Ratcliff and McKoon's (1988) theory is that it predicts backward priming in the LDT (P4)--an effect that totally contradicts the previously discussed mechanisms for priming. Backward priming is predicted because related prime-target compound cues will be more familiar than unrelated prime-target compound cues whether the prime and target are related via a forward or backward association.

Problematic data. Because the familiarity of the compound cue formed by the prime and target is a direct function of their associative strength, Ratcliff and McKoon's theory has trouble dealing with nonassociative semantic priming (P1). In a similar vein, because a category name has stronger associations to its high-dominance exemplars than to its low-dominance exemplars, the theory has trouble explaining that priming effects are nearly equivalent for high- and low-dominance exemplars in the LDT (P2). Furthermore, because Ratcliff and McKoon have never discussed exactly how target degradation would have its effects, the theory has not yet been developed enough to make predictions concerning whether or not priming should interact with target degradation, although one presumes that it would not be that difficult to embellish the theory so that it could "predict" the observed Priming x Target Degradation interaction (P10).

Although the compound cue theory can predict inhibition for the unrelated priming condition, it cannot account for why it increases with increasing SOAs (P6). Recall that "inhibition" in the unrelated priming condition is due to the current target in the neutral priming condition being combined with a related word target from the immediately preceding trial. One would presume that the current target and the target from the immediately preceding trial will be more likely to be combined the more temporally contiguous they are. Since the time between the presentations of the target on trial n and the prime on trial n+1 is typically held constant, two consecutive targets will be temporally more contiguous the shorter the prime-target SOA is for trial n+1. Thus, one would expect larger inhibition effects at the shorter SOAs, which is exactly opposite of what is observed (P6). By similar reasoning, one would expect nonword facilitation effects to be larger at shorter SOAs. This too is contravened by the data (P9).

The compound cue theory also has trouble explaining why increases in the relatedness proportion (P13) and the nonword ratio (P14) should have an effect on overall priming and why the nonword ratio should influence nonword facilitation (P9). One general approach would be to have the relatedness proportion and the nonword ratio affect the placements of the upper and/or lower familiarity criteria for making fast "word" and "nonword" responses, respectively. However, as noted in footnote 15, the predictions one makes from such an analysis will depend on where exactly these criteria fall within the familiarity distributions for the nonword targets and for the word targets on related vs. unrelated vs. neutral priming trials. Another general approach would be to invoke the operation of some sort of strategic mechanism. Although Ratcliff and McKoon (1988, p. 392) seem predisposed to the latter approach, they do not spell out how this mechanism works to produce various strategic priming effects.

The final and major problem with the compound-cue theory is that it does not explain how priming can occur at all in the pronunciation task, in which responses cannot be based on familiarity. In this regard, Ratcliff and McKoon's compound-cue analysis is similar to Neely and Keefe's (1989) retrospective semantic-matching analysis (described next), but is unlike Norris' (1986) theory, which was intended to account for priming in both the LDT and pronunciation using the same general mechanisms[16].

Neely and Keefe's (1989) retrospective semantic-matching model. According to Neely and Keefe (1989), after lexical access for the target has occurred, but before subjects have had time to make their "word"/"nonword" decision and/or execute the corresponding response, subjects can utilize information concerning whether the target semantically matches (is related to) the word prime that preceded it so as to shorten their RTs to both word and nonword targets. The chain of reasoning underlying this claim is as follows. Based on results reported by Rosson (1983), Neely and Keefe assume that a nonword target activates nodes corresponding to words to which that nonword target is visually similar (e.g., *bink* might activate the nodes for "pink", "bank", "fink", "link", etc.). Thus, in the typical LDT in which each nonword target is constructed such that it never looks like a word related to its preceding word prime, a nonword target such as *bink* would activate word nodes all of which would represent words unrelated to the word prime that preceded it, e.g., *tree*. Because of this, subjects can use information about the presence or absence of a semantic/associative relation between the target and prime to bias their "word" vs. "nonword" responses, respectively. Specifically, if the target and prime are related, the correct response must be "word." Moreover, when the nonword ratio is high (see Section I, Part 5), if the target and prime are unrelated, the correct response is very likely to be "nonword." Presumably, subjects use this information to speed up their "word" responses in the related priming condition and to facilitate their "nonword" responses when a nonword target follows a word prime, relative to the neutral priming condition in which the semantic matching process does not operate because of its inutility.

Although knowledge that the target is or is not related to its word prime can in and of itself provide reasonably valid information concerning the correct binary target response in the standard LDT, there is very low validity in the information it provides concerning which particular phoneme sequence should be articulated in pronouncing a target. (If you know that the target is related or unrelated to the prime *concrete*, what target response should you make?) Thus, as was so with Ratcliff and McKoon's (1988) compound-cue theory of priming, Neely and Keefe's (1989) semantic-matching analysis cannot by itself account for priming in pronunciation. However, Neely and Keefe's analysis does specify more clearly than does Ratcliff and McKoon's theory the conditions under which the semantic-matching (cue-combination) strategy will be employed, i.e., when the nonword ratio is high.

Supporting data. If subjects can check for either an associative relation or a nonassociative semantic relation between the target and prime, Neely and Keefe's semantic-matching analysis predicts both nonassociative semantic priming (P1) and equivalent priming for high- and low-dominance exemplars produced by category-name primes (P2). As just outlined, their analysis can also predict facilitation from related primes (P5 and P7) and the nonword facilitation effect (P9). It also accounts for inhibition for word targets in the unrelated priming condition (P6), because of the "nonword" bias that must be overcome before the correct "word" response can be made when the word target is unrelated to its word prime. Furthermore, if shallow processing of the prime makes its meaning less accessible to the semantic-matching mechanism, the theory accounts for why shallow processing of the prime leads to a reduction in priming (P18).

Neely and Keefe's semantic-matching analysis can also account for Neely's (1977) and Favreau and Segalowitz's instruction-induced priming effects in the LDT (P12). Basically, it does so in a fashion quite similar to that described earlier for Ratcliff and McKoon's (1988) cue-compound theory. At long SOAs, the subject checks if the target is related to the internally generated "prime"; at short SOAs, before the internal "prime" has been generated, the subject checks for a relation between the target and the externally presented prime. (However, if such a check is indeed occurring at the short SOA, it is problematic that nonword facilitation did not occur at the short SOA, a point to which I return when I discuss problems for the theory.)

A strong case for the validity of Neely and Keefe's semantic-matching analysis can be made on the basis of its providing a unified account for backward priming, mediated priming, and the interposition effect. Since semantic-matching is occurring from the target back to the prime in the LDT, backward priming in the LDT flows nicely from the theory. Also, since semantic-matching is not useful in pronunciation, the theory correctly predicts an absence of backward priming in pronunciation (P4). The theory also ties together the absence of mediated priming in the LDT (P3) and the interposition effect in the LDT (P16). In both cases, because the target is unrelated to the prime that immediately precedes it for both the "related" and unrelated priming conditions, the semantic-matching process will fail to find a target-prime relation in both the "related" (e.g., *lion-stripes* and *cat-bench-dog*) and unrelated (e.g., *tree-stripes* and *tree-bench-dog*) priming conditions. This will result in an equivalent "nonword" bias in the "related" and unrelated priming conditions, with the result that priming will not be observed.

The greatest triumph for Neely and Keefe's (1989) semantic-matching analysis comes from the principled manner by which it accounts for how increases in the nonword ratio leads to an increase in overall priming (P14) and nonword facilitation (P9). Indeed, prior to Neely and Keefe's theory, there was no reason to believe that the nonword ratio was in any way modulating priming. However, as was outlined earlier, as the nonword ratio increases, there is an increase in the utility of using information that the target is not related to its word prime to bias a "nonword" response. For the higher nonword ratios, this greater "nonword" bias when the target and prime are unrelated will lead to larger nonword facilitation effects and to more inhibition in the unrelated priming condition, which would lead to the increase in overall priming observed for both the high- and low-dominance exemplars. (Although increases in the nonword ratio produced statistically significant increases in overall priming in Neely et al.'s, 1989, experiments, they did not produce statistically significant increases in either facilitation or inhibition, when considered alone. This was likely due to facilitation and inhibition effects being more unreliable, i.e., more inconsistent, than overall priming effects.)

Problematic data. Several of the phenomena outlined in Table 1 pose problems for Neely and Keefe's (1989) semantic-matching analysis. One problem is that inhibition does not occur in test lists in which the related primes and targets are associatively related (P8), even though nonword facilitation has been observed in such lists (e.g., Neely, 1976). These data are problematic because the semantic-matching process that presumably produces nonword facilitation should also yield inhibition for word targets in the unrelated priming condition tested under similar circumstances. A similar problem is posed by the finding with category materials that facilitation in the related priming condition occurs at short SOAs (P5) whereas inhibition in the unrelated priming condition (P6) and nonword facilitation (P9) do not occur at these same short SOAs. To account for the absence of inhibition and nonword facilitation effects at short SOAs, Neely and Keefe (1989) argue that the semantic matching process does not operate at short SOAs because subjects do not have time to access the prime's meaning before the target appears. However, this leaves the facilitation that is observed in the related priming condition unexplained.

Neely and Keefe's semantic-matching hypothesis also encounters problems in explaining the Target Degradation x Priming and the Target Word Frequency x Priming interactions (P10, P11). That is, if one makes the seemingly reasonable assumptions that (a) the effects of target degradation and word-frequency are localized in processes that precede lexical access for a word target, (b) lexical access for a word target precedes semantic access for that target, and (c) the semantic matching process does not begin until semantic access for the target has occurred, then the semantic-matching theory predicts additive effects of degradation and priming and of word-frequency and priming. This is so by Sternberg's (1969) additive-factor analysis, because semantic matching would be affecting post-lexical decisional/response processes that would be occurring *after the completion* of the pre-lexical processing stages that are being affected by target word frequency and target degradation. Of course, Neely and Keefe could avoid these incorrect predictions by changing one or more of the foregoing three assumptions. For example, to account for the Target Word Frequency x Priming interaction, Assumption 1 might be changed based on data reported by Balota and Chumbley (1984, 1985), Chumbley and Balota (1984), and McCann, Besner and Davelaar (1988). Their data suggest that word-frequency exerts an influence on decisional and/or motor programming processes that follow lexical access. Since word frequency and the semantic matching process would both be exerting an influence on post-lexical decisional and/or response processes, their effects would no longer be additive. Furthermore, since the completion of the decisional/response processing stages would take longer for low- than for high-frequency words, the post-lexical semantic-matching process would have more time to be completed and thereby produce more priming for low- than for high-frequency words, as is observed.

To handle the Target Degradation x Priming interaction, Neely and Keefe could challenge Assumption 2 above. Specifically, they could argue that the target pink activates the lexical nodes for "pink", "pint", "mink", "wink", etc., and that these lexical nodes activate their corresponding semantic representations above their semantic threshold values even before their own lexical threshold values are exceeded (cf. Morton, 1969). By this analysis, target degradation would be influencing two *concurrent* processes, semantic access and lexical access. (I know of no data that provide a compelling refutation of the idea that a word activates lexical and semantic representations in parallel.) If it were further assumed that target degradation slows lexical access more than semantic access, semantic matching would have more of an opportunity to be completed before lexical processing was completed for degraded targets relative to nondegraded targets. This leads to the prediction that priming effects should be larger for degraded than for nondegraded targets, as is indeed the case. Although such an analysis works, it seems highly similar to Becker's (1980) analysis of the Target Degradation x Priming interaction (see Section II, Part 2.2), with semantic access replacing the semantically defined set (which is now being defined by the target rather than the prime) and lexical access replacing the visually defined set.[17] Indeed, since this face-saving analysis assumes that semantic access and lexical access proceed in parallel rather than that lexical access precedes semantic access, semantic-matching would no longer clearly have a post-lexical locus of operation. Because this analysis too strongly violates the post-lexical spirit of Neely and Keefe's theory, it cannot be used to account for the embarassing Target Degradation x Priming interaction, if the integrity of their theory is to be maintained.

The Neely-Keefe analysis also has problems explaining why the priming observed for category-name primes and exemplar targets changes when these prime-target pairs are embedded in a test in which most of the related prime/target pairs consist of strong associates (P15). To account for why priming is reduced for low-dominance exemplars but not for high-dominance exemplars when they are embedded in such lists, one could argue that the semantic-matching process checks for an associative, rather than a semantic, relation when a preponderance of the related prime/target pairs consist of strong associates. Since low-dominance exemplars by definition are not strongly associatively related to their category-name primes whereas high-dominance exemplars are, the subject would find an *associative* relation between the high-dominance target and its related prime, which would result in a "word" bias that would produce priming, but would not find an *associative* relation between the low-dominance target and its related prime. This would result in a "nonword" bias comparable to that produced in the unrelated priming condition, with the net effect being no priming.

Unfortunately, the foregoing account has two problems. First, although *BIRD* may not have a strong forward associative relation with a low-dominance exemplar such as *vulture, vulture* does have a fairly strong "backward" associative relation to *BIRD*. Since the semantic-matching process works with this backward association (as it must to account for backward priming), if category-names are often fairly strong associates of their low-dominance exemplars (as intuition tells me will be the case), the semantic-matching process should produce priming even for the low-dominance targets. A second problem is that regardless of whether the semantic-matching process is checking for an associative or a semantic relation between the target and its prime, it should still produce inhibition in the unrelated priming condition. However, inhibition does not occur for unrelated category-name prime/exemplar target trials when they are embedded in a list in which the related prime/target pairs consist mostly of strong associates.

Perhaps the two biggest embarassments for Neely and Keefe's semantic-matching analysis are subliminal priming and the relatedness proportion effect. Since the semantic-matching process is under strategic control, in that subjects are more likely to use it when increases in the nonword ratio increase its utility, the theory needs to explain why a subject would try to adopt a strategy of finding a semantic relation between the target and an event, i.e., the masked prime, which the subject claims doesn't even exist. An appeal to a *veiled* strategy that is unavailable to consciousness but which can be consciously controlled would be a possible solution. However, the hand waving that would be required to make sense of such an appeal would be exhausting.

The problem Neely and Keefe's (1989) semantic-matching analysis encounters in the relatedness proportion effect is not its mere existence. That is, it could be argued that as the relatedness proportion increases, subjects become more likely to adopt the increasingly useful strategy of using a semantic-match between the target and prime to bias "word" responses in the related priming condition, thereby increasing priming. The problem is that increases in the relatedness proportion produce different effects on priming and nonword facilitation than do increases in the nonword ratio. If increases in the relatedness proportion induce subjects' greater reliance on semantic matching, as do increases in the nonword ratio, then why doesn't priming for low-dominance exemplars increase as the relatedness proportion increases, just as it does when the nonword ratio increases? The same question can be asked about nonword facilitation. Of course, analogous reasoning undermines the use of an expectancy mechanism (or any other single mechanism) as a unified account of relatedness proportion and nonword ratio effects.

2.4. Neely and Keefe's (1989) Hybrid Three-Process Theory: Spreading Activation, Expectancy, and Semantic-Matching

Although each of the foregoing general theoretical mechanisms can account for data not easily explained by the other approaches, it is clear that no single one of them provides a complete explanation for the complex array of priming phenomena summarized in Table 1. Furthermore, it seems highly unlikely that one could postulate some new single mechanism that could encompass all of the existing data. For example, the complicated pattern of data reported by Favreau and Segalowitz (1983) and Neely (1977) would seem to provide an insurmountable obstacle for a single-process theory. Furthermore, if increases in the relatedness proportion and the nonword ratio are both assumed to enhance the operation of a single mechanism, it becomes very difficult to explain how the enhanced operation of that single mechanism could yield the *dissociative* effects on priming that increases in the relatedness proportion and nonword ratio produce for low-dominance category exemplars and for nonword facilitation. Finally, it would be difficult for a single-process theory to account for the dissociative priming effects that occur in the LDT and the pronunciation task.

The foregoing makes it clear that to have much of a chance of successfully accounting for all of the extant priming data, a theory must postulate multiple mechanisms for priming. Indeed, Neely and Keefe (1989) reached this same conclusion even though they considered a smaller data base than that reviewed here. However, rather than concocting mechanisms *de novo*, Neely and Keefe constructed a three-process theory that added their retrospective semantic-matching mechanism to the spreading activation and expectancy mechanisms, which had already been shown to provide useful explanations for several priming phenomena, including the complex pattern of priming effects reported by Favreau and Segalowitz (1983) and Neely (1977). Although Neely and Keefe's (1989) three-process theory can account for nearly all of the priming phenomena reviewed here, in discussing their theory I will focus on those phenomena that cannot be easily accommodated by the automatic spreading activation and expectancy mechanisms.

One major strength of Neely and Keefe's (1989) three-process theory is that it accommodates the dissociated priming effects that occur when the same variables are manipulated in the LDT vs. the pronunciation task. Basically, their general approach to accounting for task differences is to assume that whereas the semantic matching process produces priming in only the LDT, spreading activation and expectancy produce similar priming effects in both tasks. The reason for assuming that semantic-matching operates in only the LDT has already been given. That is, knowledge that a target is related or unrelated to its prime provides fairly valid information concerning whether the correct response to a target in the LDT is "word" or "nonword", at least when the nonword ratio is high. However, such knowledge is not very useful for predicting the correct sequence of phonemes that should be given as a response to the target in the pronunciation task.

According to Neely and Keefe (1989), backward priming occurs in the LDT but not in pronunciation (P4) because the retrospective semantic matching process that operates in the LDT finds the backward association from the target to the prime and this biases the correct "word" response, thereby producing a facilitation effect in the backward priming condition. In pronunciation, priming for high-dominance exemplars is greater than that for low-dominance exemplars because the spread of activation is stronger between the nodes for the category-name prime and the nodes for the more closely related high-dominance exemplars and because high-dominance exemplars are more likely to be included in the expectancy set than are low-dominance exemplars. In the LDT, the same is true, but priming is increased for low-dominance exemplars because the backward semantic-matching process finds a relation between the low-dominance exemplar target and its category-name prime. (Stated another way, given the target *vulture*, it is easier to think of the prime *BIRD*, which has been repeated several times in the experiment, than it is to think of the target *vulture*, which has not been seen before in the experiment, given the prime *BIRD*.) Also, since semantic matching can contribute to inhibition in the unrelated priming condition in the LDT, in which it operates, but not in pronunciation, in which it does not operate, Neely and Keefe's analysis correctly predicts that inhibition effects will be larger in the LDT than in pronunciation (cf., Lorch et al., 1986; Stanovich & West, 1983; West & Stanovich, 1982).

Mediated priming occurs in pronunciation because of activation spreading from the "lion" node to the "tiger" node to the "stripes" node. Although the same spread of activation occurs in the LDT, the facilitation it produces is offset by the "nonword" bias that is produced when the semantic-matching process fails to find an association between the target stripes and the prime lion. Although this "cancelling-out" analysis seems too ad hoc, it leads to the interesting prediction that mediated priming could also be observed in the LDT if the operation of the semantic-matching process were somehow curtailed. This curtailment would occur if the nonword ratio were reduced, if the primes and targets were responded to sequentially (making it less likely they would be treated as a pair of items for which a backward relatedness check would be made), and/or if there were no overt "nonword" response required. (In the latter case, since there would be no overt "nonword" response to be facilitated when the semantic-matching process failed to find a target-prime relation, there would be less reason for the subject to use a semantic-matching strategy.) Interestingly, a mediated priming effect does indeed occur in the LDT under these predicted circumstances (den Heyer et al., 1987; McNamara & Altarriba, 1988).

A second major strength of Neely and Keefe's (1989) three-process theory is that it can explain the dissociated priming effects that occur when the nonword ratio and relatedness proportion are orthogonally manipulated within the LDT. Because the semantic-matching process, which produces nonword facilitation and priming for both high- and low-dominance exemplars, is more likely to become operative as the nonword ratio increases, the three-process theory predicts the nonword ratio effect that occurs for nonword facilitation and for priming for high- and low-dominance exemplars. On the other hand, higher relatedness proportions make it more likely that the expectancy mechanism will become operative. This expectancy mechanism should be more likely to produce priming for high-dominance exemplars, which are very likely to be in the expectancy set generated from a category-name prime, than for low-dominance exemplars, which are less likely to be in that expectancy set. Thus, their analysis correctly predicts that the relatedness proportion effect, unconfounded with the nonword ratio effect, should be greater for high- than for low-dominance exemplars (Neely et al., 1989).

The Neely-Keefe three-process theory also provides a very nice explanation of why the typical manipulation of relatedness proportion (which is confounded with the nonword ratio) affects priming for both high- and low-dominance exemplars in the LDT but only affects priming for high-dominance exemplars in pronunciation (see Table 8). The "relatedness proportion" effect that occurs for low-dominance exemplars in the LDT is really due to the confounded increases in the nonword ratio, which in the LDT induce a greater reliance on the semantic-matching process. This enhances priming for low-dominance exemplars. However, since the semantic-matching process does not operate in pronunciation, relatedness proportion effects should be confined to their influence on the operation of the expectancy mechanism, which has a larger effect on priming for high- than for low-dominance exemplars.

According to Neely and Keefe's analysis, then, "pure" changes in the relatedness proportion (with the contaminated effects of the nonword ratio partialled out) modulate only expectancy, which is the only mechanism that produces the relatedness proportion effect in pronunciation. This leads to the prediction that the relatedness proportion effect that occurs for high-dominance exemplars in *pronunciation* should be accurately predicted by the slope of the best-fitting function relating changes in priming for high-dominance exemplars to *"pure"* relatedness proportion effects in the LDT. This prediction received striking confirmation in that the obtained 19 ms relatedness proportion effect that occurred for high-dominance exemplars in Keefe and Neely's (1989) pronunciation task was very close to the 22 ms effect predicted from the "pure" relatedness proportion effect in their LDT data!

Despite its providing a coherent account of almost all of the priming phenomena reviewed here, the Neely-Keefe (1989) three-process theory does have problems with three effects. First, it cannot explain why target degradation produced by inserting asterisks between the target's letters interacts with priming in a way different from that produced by intensity reduction or masking (Durgunoglu, 1988; Stanovich & West, 1983; see Section I, Part 3.) However, notwithstanding Stanovich and West's (1983) preliminary explanation of this effect when sentence fragments are used as priming contexts, I do not believe that anyone has yet devised a closely reasoned principled account of this effect.

A second problem for the Neely-Keefe three-process theory is that while it can easily account for the interposition effect (P16) in the LDT, it cannot account for it in pronunciation. Recall that the interposition effect is the finding that interposing an unrelated word between a related prime and target reduces priming relative to the condition in which a neutral prime is interposed between a related prime and target. As described earlier, in the LDT the facilitation from the residual spreading activation from the related prime would be offset by the inhibition produced by the "nonword" bias that would be created when the semantic-matching process failed to find a relation between the target and the interposed unrelated word. This inhibition would not occur when a neutral prime was interposed, since semantic-matching does not occur for neutral primes. However, since semantic-matching does not occur in pronunciation, one should still see a facilitation effect in the condition in which an unrelated prime was interposed between a related prime and target, relative to the condition in which a neutral prime serves as the interposed item, since activation from the related prime should have decayed by equivalent amounts for these two types of interposed items. However, Masson (this volume) also observed an interposition effect in pronunciation. One potential way for the three-process theory to handle the interposition effect in pronunciation would be to claim that subjects use the interposed unrelated prime to generate an expectancy set that does not include the target. However, since the interposed item was apparently never related to the target that followed it, there would have been no reason for subjects to adopt this strategy. Thus, this finding remains problematic for the Neely-Keefe analysis.

A third problem for the Neely-Keefe three-process theory is that it cannot easily account for why shallow prime processing eliminates priming (P18). Although shallow prime processing might reduce priming by curtailing the use of the expectancy and semantic matching mechanisms, automatic activation should still operate to produce priming. However, one could accommodate the elimination of priming by arguing either that spreading activation has decayed while subjects were making their letter-search task response to the priming and/or that lexical access for the prime does not occur when subjects focus their attention on its individual letters (but see Besner, Smith, & MacLeod, in press).

Notwithstanding its failed encounter with these latter three findings, it seems that of all of the currently available theories, the Neely-Keefe three-process theory provides the most coherent account of the several priming phenomena reviewed here. Of course, one could consider creating other hybrid theories by combining one of the other two post-lexical priming mechanisms with one or both of the pre-lexical mechanisms, spreading activation and expectancy. However, since Norris (1986) intended that his plausibility-checking mechanism could be used to supplant both spreading activation and expectancy accounts of priming, it would violate the spirit of his theory to combine his plausibility checking mechanism with either the spreading activation or expectancy mechanisms. In this same vein, because Ratcliff and McKoon (1988) have claimed that their compound-cue mechanism can supplant spreading activation as a priming mechanism, it would violate the spirit of their analysis to combine spreading activation with their compound-cue mechanism.[18] On the other hand, because Ratcliff and McKoon (1988, see p.392) do not claim that their compound-cue mechanism eliminates the need for postulating an expectancy mechanism, they could construct a hybrid theory which assumes that expectancy produces priming in both the LDT and pronunciation (thereby permitting them to explain some of the pronunciation priming phenomena) whereas the compound-cue mechanism produces priming only in the LDT. An examination of the EXPECT and CC columns in Table 9 shows that this brand of hybrid theory would leave four effects unexplained (i.e., P2-PRON, P3-PRON, P14-LDT, and P17-PRON), as well the ever intractable problem of why target degradation produced by asterisk insertion vs. intensity reduction or masking yields different interactive effects with priming (Durgunoglu, 1988; Stanovich & West, 1983; see Section I, Part 3.) Thus, this hybrid theory does not fare quite as well as Neely and Keefe's hybrid theory. (Of course, this isn't all that surprising since Neely and Keefe's theory postulates three rather than two mechanisms.)

Although Neely and Keefe's three-process theory may seem overly complicated and too redundant in that many priming effects are predicted by at least two of its processes (but such redundancy might be biologically useful), it is specific enough concerning the variables that control each of its mechanisms that it has good heuristic value in terms of its generating several somewhat novel predictions that can be submitted to experimental test. Here I will discuss just three specific examples. First, consider what the Neely-Keefe three-process theory predicts in the standard binary LDT with long SOAs when one increases the nonword ratio for experimental lists that contain mediated and backward priming trials and nonword targets preceded by word primes and neutral primes. The prediction is that one should observe increases in the nonword facilitation and backward priming effects, which are produced by the semantic matching process, accompanied by reductions in mediated priming, which is offset by the "nonword" bias that the semantic matching process would produce.

A second prediction concerns a go/no go task in which subjects make overt responses to word targets but withold responses to nonword targets. Because there would be no overt "nonword" response to facilitate by using the semantic-matching process, subjects should no longer utilize a semantic-matching strategy. Thus, the nonword ratio should no longer have an effect on forward priming, and backward priming should be eliminated for even the high nonword ratios. The third and final prediction involves testing whether the use of nonword targets that looked like words related to their word primes would reduce the subject's reliance on the semantic-matching process in the LDT, thereby decreasing backward priming effects and nonword facilitation effects and increasing mediated priming.

Neely and Keefe's (1989) three-process theory can also be used to generate an even more general program of research designed to create converging operations (Garner, Hake, & Eriksen, 1956) that will isolate the contributions each of the three processes contributes to a particular priming effect. That is, to isolate the effects of automatic spreading activation from expectancy and semantic matching, one could use short SOAs or masked primes in both the LDT and pronunciation task. To isolate the effects of the expectancy mechanism from those produced by the semantic-matching process, one could use a long SOA and manipulate relatedness proportion in a pronunciation task or a go/no go LDT or in the standard binary LDT with a very low nonword ratio. To isolate the effects of semantic matching from those of the expectancy mechanism, one could use a long SOA, a low relatedness proportion, and manipulate nonword ratio in the standard binary LDT.

III. SUMMARY AND GENERAL IMPLICATIONS FOR NORMAL READING

It is quite clear that even when one selectively attends to only those priming phenomena that come from LDTs and pronunciation tasks that have employed the single-word semantic priming paradigm, one encounters a richly complex mosaic of phenomena. (See Table 1). This is both discouraging and encouraging. That is, that these seemingly simple experimental paradigms yield such complex effects dampens one's optimism for developing an understanding of the much more complex situation the reader encounters in trying to comprehend textual materials. Indeed, many may see the dissociated priming effects that have occurred in the superficially similar LDT and the pronunciation task as requiring us to become mired down in seemingly endless analyses of the minute details of how these two tasks are performed. These people will argue that these task analyses divert us from achieving our goal of discovering the *general, fundamental* processes that underly lexical access and reading.

Such arguments notwithstanding, I tend to be more optimistic concerning the ultimate utility of performing detailed analyses of somewhat contrived tasks that permit us to exert very fine control over the variables that we believe are likely to influence word recognition (see also Banaji & Crowder, 1989, and Neely, in press). Although we have learned that the LDT and the pronunciation task are not nearly as simple as was originally thought, we have also learned a considerable amount about the different processing mechanisms they invoke. This latter knowledge affords us the opportunity to choose that task which is most appropriate for providing information concerning the theoretical question of interest. For example, if we are interested in how some variable affects lexical access during reading rather than in how it might affect a post-lexical meaning integration process, we should probably study its effects in pronunciation or in a LDT with a low nonword ratio or with go/no go response requirements. On the other hand, if meaning integration is what we're after, we would be better advised to use a binary LDT with a high nonword ratio. Although it is not likely that the semantic-matching process that is utilized to optimize performance in a binary LDT with a high nonword ratio will be identical to the meaning integration process that occurs in the reading of textual material, it is likely to share some of its characteristics.

In short, I would argue that the task analyses we have performed on the LDT and the pronunciation task (see also Balota & Chumbley, 1985; Balota, Boland, & Shields, 1989) have increased our understanding of these tasks to the point that we can now much more effectively use them as tools to be used in tightly controlled experiments in which we can isolate the effects of the multiple, complicated processes that conjointly operate in the normal reading situation. Indeed, there is already good evidence that the concepts of spreading activation, expectancy, and some sort of post-lexical semantic-matching strategy can be used to good advantage in furthering our understanding of the word recognition processes that occur in single sentential contexts (e.g., Stanovich & West, 1983) and that a person's skill in reading textual material is correlated with whether that person generates a large or small semantically defined set in the single-word priming paradigm in the LDT (Eisenberg & Becker, 1982; see also Becker, 1985).

In closing, I want to share two of my hopes concerning how the material covered in this review may turn out to be useful. My modest hope is that it helps bring the reader up-to-date and to clarify the current state of affairs concerning what we do and do not know about semantic priming effects in the single-word semantic priming paradigm. I believe that the literature I have reviewed here clearly demonstrates that during the nearly two decades of research that has been conducted since Meyer and Schvaneveldt's (1971) seminal research on semantic priming first appeared, we have come a very long way in furthering our understanding of how semantic context affects word "recognition."

Although it is clear we have come a long way, it is just as clear that there are many more roads to travel. Nevertheless, I remain sanguine about the journey ahead. Indeed, my more pretentious hope is that the data and the theoretical analyses provided in this chapter can serve as useful signposts for guiding us along the proper paths to our hoped-for ultimate destination of having a complete understanding of the cognitive processes people utilize in reading textual materials. In covering how far we have come, I have along the way provided some detailed suggestions for future experimentation that could yield results that would help fill in some of the currently existing gaps in our knowledge. I hope that these suggestions have convinced the reader that research on semantic priming should continue to flourish.

FOOTNOTES

[1]Sanford, Garrod and Boyle (1977, Experiment 1) also manipulated the category dominance of the target in a pronunciation task as well as manipulating whether the target was presented "in the clear" or embedded in visual noise. However, the same high- and low-dominance exemplars did not appear in both their related and unrelated priming conditions. Specifically, for their related priming condition they used prime-target pairs such as FRUIT-apple and FRUIT-grape in their high- vs. low-dominance conditions, whereas in their unrelated priming condition, rather than using prime-target pairs such as SPORT-apple and SPORT-grape, they used items such as FRUIT-major, for which the category dominance of the target was not specifically manipulated. Because of this, their design does not permit a clean comparison of overall priming effects for high- vs. low-dominance exemplars. Nevertheless, using their single unrelated priming condition as a common baseline for assessing priming for the high- and low-dominance exemplars, for clearly presented targets there was a small facilitatory priming effect for high-dominance exemplars and no priming effect at all for low-dominance exemplars; for targets presented in visual noise, there was a substantial facilitatory priming effect for high-dominance exemplars and an

actual inhibitory priming effect for low-dominance exemplars. Thus, Sanford et al.'s (1977) data also conform to the general conclusion that in pronunciation facilitatory priming effects occur for high-dominance exemplars but not for low-dominance exemplars.

[2]The conclusion that inhibition from unrelated primes does not occur in pronunciation holds for situations in which adult readers are presented with clearly visible targets. However, in other situations, inhibition from unrelated primes can be obtained in pronunciation. For example, the single-word semantic priming paradigm can yield inhibition from unrelated primes in pronunciation when the targets are degraded through masking (e.g., Durgunoglu, 1988) or when young readers are used as subjects (e.g., Pring & Snowling, 1986). Furthermore, although unrelated sentence priming contexts typically do not produce inhibition in pronunciation for adult readers presented with clearly visible targets, they do produce inhibition under one or more of the following conditions (a) the targets are visually degraded, (b) the subjects are beginning readers, (c) the targets are low-frequency words (e.g., Stanovich & West, 1979, 1981, 1983; Stanovich, West, & Feeman, 1981; West & Stanovich, 1982) or (d) the targets in the related priming condition are acceptable but unlikely completions of the sentential priming context (Becker, 1985, Experiment 1).

[3]Fischler and Goodman (1978) also examined associative priming with SOAs varying from 40-540 ms. However, their procedures were quite different from those used in the Neely and DE Groot et al. studies in that a neutral priming condition was not included and subjects had to report the prime after they responded to the target. Thus, their results will not be discussed here.

[4]When a nonword target is derived from a word that is related to that nonword target's prime (e.g., tigar as a nonword target that follows the prime lion), the results are very mixed both with respect to whether priming occurs relative to a neutral priming condition or an unrelated priming condition (e.g., in which tigar is primed by bench). I refer the interested reader to Antos (1979), Favreau and Segalowitz (1983), Lupker (1984), O'Connor and Forster (1981), and Schvaneveldt and McDonald (1981) for a sampling of these results.

[5]It is interesting that the issue of what constitutes an appropriate baseline for assessing excitation and inhibition has also arisen in the Pavlovian conditioning literature (e.g., Rescorla, 1967). Although this measurement problem has not been completely solved (e.g., Keller, Ayres, & Mahoney, 1977; Kremer, 1974), its existence has not caused theorists to abandon the concepts of conditioned excitation and inhibition because these concepts are so fundamentally basic. I believe we should adopt the same stance in the priming literature.

[6]Balota's (1988) data are somewhat difficult to interpret because targets were not equally often sampled from all categories. Thus, the effects of expectancies based on which targets were overall more likely were overlaid on any effects specific to the word prime given on that trial. This helps to explain why at his short SOA he obtained an effect of expectancy (actually an overall list-wide expectancy effect) but little effect of relatedness, a finding that contrasts with those obtained by Neely (1977) and Favreau and Segalowitz (1983).

[7]Very recently, Dagenbach, Carr & Wilhelmson (1989) have shown that one can obtain either facilitatory or inhibitory "subliminal" priming, depending on the types of judgments (presence/absence vs. meaning) subjects had been asked to make about masked, "subliminal" primes in a prior block. Though I believe this effect is genuine, because it is so new and has not been thoroughly studied, I will not discuss it further here.

[8]Whether these activated letter nodes directly activate the lexical nodes or sometimes activate phonological representations which in turn activate the lexical nodes is a controversial issue (e.g., see Besner & Hildebrandt, 1987, Carr & Pollatsek, 1985, van Orden, this volume, and Van Orden, Johnston, & Hale, 1988, for excellent recent discussions). However, because I believe that the validity of the priming mechanisms I discuss is orthogonal to this issue, I ignore it in subsequent discussions.

[9]Semantically related word nodes probably are neither stored close together nor directly linked to one another in lexical memory (although strongly associatively related nodes may be). Rather, it is their links to similar semantic structures that permits ASA to produce priming. That is, the presentation of cat as a prime causes activation to spread from the "cat" node in lexical memory to its associated semantic structures. This activation then spreads to the related semantic structures for the concept dog and then continues to spread back to the lexical "dog" node, thereby producing priming (see Collins & Loftus, 1975). However, because I believe that this complete machinery for ASA does not, for the phenonomena I discuss here, yield predictions different from those made under the assumption that activation is spreading within lexical memory, I will employ the latter terminology as a convenient shorthand device.

[10]Some (e.g., Besner & Swan, 1982, and Besner & Beneschan, 1989) have argued that this analysis is wrong because it incorrectly predicts that the effects of target degradation and target word-frequency should also interact. (To correct this, Besner and Beneschan, 1989, make the innovative and interesting argument that priming affects activation within the target word's node whereas word frequency affects the strengths of the target word node's connections with its phonological and semantic representations.) While it is true that some experiments have demonstrated that target word-frequency and target

degradation have additive effects (e.g., Becker & Killion, 1977; Stanners, Jastrzembski, & Westbrook, 1975; Wilding, 1988, Experiment 1), other experiments have reported interactive effects (Norris, 1984; Wilding, 1988, Experiment 2). Because the nature of the Target Word-Frequency x Target Degradation interaction can depend on the intertrial interval between targets (Wilding, 1988) and likely depends on the magnitude of the degradation effect, a mega-experiment needs to be done in which target word frequency, target degradation and priming are all manipulated within subjects at a short SOA (see Besner & Beneschan, 1989). Then, the nature of the Target Word-Frequency x Target Degradation interaction could be examined in a neutral priming condition administered under exactly the same conditions used to examine the Priming x Target Word-Frequency and Priming x Target Degradation interactions. The results of such an experiment would strongly undermine the ASA account if the Priming x Target Word-Frequency and Priming x Target Degradation interactions were statistically significant, whereas the Target Word-Frequency x Target Degradation interaction was not significant in the neutral priming condition (assuming that the statistical power associated with detecting the latter interaction was relatively high). Until the results of such an experiment are reported, I believe one must defer a decision as to whether or not ASA is able to accommodate P10 and P11.

[11]Becker's analysis also predicts that degradation and word-frequency should have additive effects. This is so because degradation delays the time it takes for the visually defined set to be activated and available for search but does not affect the search of the visually defined set once it has begun. Thus, degradation lengthens RTs for high- and low-frequency words by the same amount, i.e., by the delay it causes in when the search of the visually defined set can begin. That additive effects of word-frequency and degradation have been (see footnote 10) taken as very strong support for Becker's model. However, this additivity sometimes breaks down (see footnote 10). Thus, until additional data become available, I will provisionally accept Becker's analysis as an adequate account of how target word-frequency, target degradation and semantic priming influence word recognition. (But see Besner and Swan, 1982, for a different view, based in part on problems posed by repetition priming data not reviewed here.)

[12]Becker (1985) actually assumes that the size of the expectancy set is either dichotomously small or large and not a continuous variable. However, because this is of no consequence for the phenomena I discuss here, for ease of exposition I will act as though the size of the expectancy set can be treated as a continuous variable.

[13]Quite recently Andrews (1989) and Grainger, O'Regan, Jacobs, and Segui (1989) have reported results on the effects of manipulating the size of the visually defined set. Both studies manipulated Coltheart, Davelaar, Jonasson, and

Besner's (1977) N, which is the number of other words (called neighbors) that differ from the target word by only one letter. Andrews used both the LDT and pronunciation task whereas Grainger et al. used only the LDT (and in a second study measured gaze durations during normal reading). If we reasonably construe N as a measure of the size of the visually defined set, Becker's (1980) analysis predicts that the slowing of RTs through increasing N should be greater for low- than for high-frequency words. This is predicted because the time to find a match for a low-frequency word, which would occur near the end of the search of the visually defined set, would be delayed more by a near exhaustive search of a large visually defined set than would the time to find a match for a high-frequency word, which would occur near the very beginning of the search of the visually defined set. Stated another way, Becker's analysis predicts that RTs to a target of a given frequency should be slower the greater the number of higher frequency neighbors it has. Unfortunately, the Andrews (1989) and Grainger et al. (1989) studies yielded seemingly conflicting results. Although Andrews found that N had a larger effect on RTs to low-frequency words than on RTs to high-frequency words for both tasks, supporting Becker's analysis, she also found that RTs were faster (not slower) for targets with larger N values, a result that is anathema to Becker's theory. On the other hand, Grainger et al. found that RTs to a target of a given frequency were indeed slower if that target had one or more higher frequency neighbors than if it did not, although there was not a significant increase in RTs as the number of higher frequency neighbors increased from a mean of 2.6-7.9. (Luce, 1986, also found that the identification of an auditorally presented target word embedded in noise worsened as the number of other words that shared phonemes with that target word increased.) Clearly, more research is needed to determine the procedural differences that led to these conflicting results.

[14]This analysis makes the interesting prediction that nonword facilitation effects should be larger, the smaller is the expectancy set. That is, even though the bias to respond "nonword" should be the same following the unsuccessful exhaustive search of either a small or large expectancy set, the initiation of the exhaustive search of the visually defined set would be delayed longer the larger is the expectancy set. Unfortunately, data directly relevant to this issue are unavailable because Becker, (1980), den Heyer et al. (1985) and Lorch et al. (1986) who directly compared the effects of small and large expectancy sets did not report their nonword target data.

[15]Actually this prediction is not as straightforward as it seems. It depends on (a) how much priming increments familiarity for the low- and high-frequency words and (b) exactly where in the familiarity distributions for unrelated priming trials the upper familiarity criterion for fast "word" responses falls for low- vs. high frequency targets in the unrelated priming condition. For example, if the highest familiarity values for unrelated priming trials for low-frequency targets were far below the upper familiarity criterion, the increment in familiarity

produced by priming might not push these values above that criterion, with the result being no priming whatsoever.

[16]Of course, Ratcliff and McKoon's (1988) theory was not intended to account for data from the pronunciation task, but rather to account for data from speeded binary decision tasks such as lexical decision and episodic recognition memory. Thus, their theory explains numerous episodic recognition memory phenomena that other theories discussed in this chapter cannot explain without their being embellished.

[17]This analysis differs from Becker's analysis, however, in that it predicts that nonword facilitation effects should be larger for degraded than for nondegraded targets. The reasoning behind this prediction is perfectly analogous to that used to explain why priming is greater for degraded than for nondegraded word targets. The slower is the lexical access to the nodes that correspond to words that are visually similar to the nonword target, the more time the semantic matching process will have to be completed and to bias the "nonword" response. Becker's model, on the other hand, predicts additive effects of nonword facilitation and target degradation. That is, nonword facilitation is produced by a "nonword" bias that occurs as soon as the semantically defined set has been exhaustively searched without a match having been found. Since the search of the semantically defined set is little affected by target degradation and is completed before the initiation of the search of the visually defined set, the availability of which is being delayed by target degradation, the "nonword" bias that produces nonword facilitation has been completed before the effects of target degradation take hold. Thus, additivity is predicted.

[18]It is interesting to compare the ASA and CC columns in Table 9 for the LDT, which is the task to which Ratcliff and McKoon intended their theory to apply. This comparison shows that the cue-compound theory can be used to explain several effects that automatic spreading activation cannot easily explain (P3, P4, P6, P9, P11, P15, P16, P18) whereas automatic spreading activation can account for only two effects (P1, P10) for which the cue-compound theory has no readily available account.

REFERENCES

Anderson, J. R. (1976). *Language, memory, and thought.* Hillsdale, N.J.: Lawrence Erlbaum Associates.

Anderson, J. R. (1983). *The architecture of cognition.* Cambridge, MA: Harvard University Press.

Andrews, S. (1989). Frequency and neighbourhood effects on lexical access: Activation or search? *Journal of Experimental Psychology: Learning, Memory, and Cognition*, **15**, 802-814.

Antos, S. J. (1979). Processing facilitation in a lexical decision task. *Journal of Experimental Psychology: Human Perception and Performance*, **5**, 527-545.

Balota, D. A. (1983). Automatic semantic activation and episodic memory encoding. *Journal of Verbal Learning and Verbal Behavior*, **22**, 88-104.
Balota, D.A. (1988). The temporal influence of semantic relatedness, expectancy, and age in a semantic priming pronunciation task. Unpublished manuscript.
Balota, D.A., Boland, J., & Shields, L. (1989). Priming in pronunciation: Beyond pattern recognition and onset latency. *Journal of Memory and Language*, **28**, 14-36.
Balota, D.A., & Chumbley, J. I. (1984). Are lexical decisions a good measure of lexical access: The role of word frequency in the neglected decision stage? *Journal of Experimental Psychology: Human Perception and Performance*, **10**, 340-357.
Balota, D. A., & Chumbley, J. I. (1985). The locus of word-frequency effects in the pronunciation task: Lexical access and/or production frequency? *Journal of Memory and Language*, **24**, 89-106.
Balota, D.A., & Lorch, R. (1986). Depth of automatic spreading activation: Mediated priming effects in pronunciation but not in lexical decision. *Journal of Experimental Psychology: Learning, Memory, and Cognition*, **12**, 336-345.
Banaji, M.R., & Crowder, R.G. (1989). The bankruptcy of everyday memory. *American Psychologist*, **44**, 1185-1193.
Becker, C.A. (1979). Semantic context and word frequency effects in visual word recognition. *Journal of Experimental Psychology: Human Perception and Performance*, **5**, 252-259.
Becker, C.A. (1980). Semantic context effects in visual word recognition: An analysis of semantic strategies. *Memory & Cognition*, **8**, 493-512.
Becker, C.A. (1985). What do we really know about semantic context effects during reading? In D. Besner, T.G. Waller, & E.M. MacKinnon (Eds.), *Reading research: Advances in theory and practice, Vol. 5* (pp. 125-166). Toronto: Academic Press.
Becker, C.A., & Killion, T.H. (1977). Interaction of visual and cognitive effects in word recognition. *Journal of Experimental Psychology: Human Perception and Performance*, **3**, 389-401.
Besner, D. (1990). Does the reading system need a lexicon? In D.A. Balota, G.B. Flores D'Arcais, & K. Rayner (Eds.), *Reading comprehension processes* (pp. 73-99). Hillsdale, N.J.: Lawrence Erlbaum Associates.
Besner, D., & Beneschan, S. (1989). *Relatedness and word frequency effects in visual identification: A link-node distinction.* Unpublished manuscript, University of Waterloo.
Besner, D., & Hildebrandt, N. (1987). Orthographic and phonological codes in the oral reading of Japanese Kana. *Journal of Experimental Psychology: Learning, Memory, and Cognition*, **13**, 335-343.
Besner, D., & McCann, R.S. (1988, November). *Connecting data and connectionism: A few words may be necessary.* Paper presented at the meeting of the Psychonomic Society, Chicago, IL.
Besner, D., Smith, M. C., & MacLeod, C.M. (in press). Visual word recognition: A dissociation of lexical and semantic processing. *Journal of Experimental Psychology: Learning, Memory, and Cognition.*
Besner, D., & Swan, M. (1982). Models of lexical access in visual word recognition. *Quarterly Journal of Experimental Psychology*, **34A**, 313-325.
Besner, D., Twilley, L., McCann, R.S., & Seergobin, K. (1990). On the association between connectionism and data: Are a few words necessary? *Psychological Review*, **97**, 432-446.
Briand, K., den Heyer, K., & Dannenbring, G.L. (1988). Retroactive semantic priming in a lexical decision task. *Quarterly Journal of Experimental Psychology*, **40A**, 341-359.
Broadbent, D. (1985). A question of levels: Comment on McClelland and Rumelhart. *Journal of Experimental Psychology: General*, 114, 189-192.
Carr, T.H., McCauley, C., Sperber, R.D., & Parmelee, C.M. (1982). Words, pictures, and priming: On semantic activation, conscious identification, and the automaticity of information processing. *Journal of Experimental Psychology: Human Perception and Performance*, **8**, 757-777.
Carr, T.H., & Pollatsek, A. (1985). Recognizing printed words: A look at current models. In D. Besner, T. G. Waller, & E.M. MacKinnon (Eds.), *Reading research: Advances in theory and practice*, Vol. 5 (pp. 1-81). Toronto: Academic Press.

Carroll, M., & Kirsner, K. (1982). Context and repetition effects in lexical decision and recognition memory. *Journal of Verbal Learning and Verbal Behavior*, **21**, 55-69.
Cheesman, J., & Merikle, P.M. (1984). Priming with and without awareness. *Perception & Psychophysics*, **36**, 387-395.
Chiarello, C., Burgess, C., Gage, L., & Pollock, A. (1990). Semantic and associative priming in the cerebral hemispheres: Some words do, some words don't...sometimes, some places. *Brain and Language*, **38**, 75-104.
Chiarello, C., Senehi, J., & Nuding, S. (1987). Semantic priming with abstract and concrete words: Differential asymmetry may be post- lexical. *Brain and Language*, **31**, 43-60.
Chumbley, J.I., & Balota, D.A. (1984). A word's meaning affects the decision in lexical decision. *Memory & Cognition*, **12**, 590-606.
Collins, A.M., & Loftus, E.F. (1975). A spreading-activation theory of semantic processing. *Psychological Review*, **82**, 407-428.
Collins, A.M., & Quillian, M.R. (1969). Retrieval time from semantic memory. *Journal of Verbal Learning and Verbal Behavior*, **8**, 240-247.
Coltheart, M., Davelaar, E., Jonasson, J., & Besner, D. (1977). Access to the internal lexicon. In S. Dornic (Ed.), *Attention and performance VI* (pp. 535-555). Hillsdale, NJ : Lawrence Erlbaum Associates.
Dagenbach, D., Carr, T.H., & Wilhelmson, A. (1989). Task-induced strategies and near-threshold priming: Conscious influences on unconscious perception. *Journal of Memory and Language*, in press.
Dannenbring, G. L., & Briand, K. (1982). Semantic priming and the word repetition effect in a lexical decision task. *Canadian Journal of Psychology*, **36**, 435-444.
Dark, V. J. (1988). Semantic priming, prime reportability, and retroactive priming are interdependent. *Memory & Cognition*, **16**, 299-308.
Davelaar, E., & Coltheart, M. (1975). Effects of interpolated items on the association effect in lexical decision tasks. *Bulletin of the Psychonomic Society*, **6**, 269-272.
DE Groot, A.M.B. (1983). The range of automatic spreading activation in word priming. *Journal of Verbal Learning and Verbal Behavior*, **22**, 417-436.
DE Groot, A.M.B. (1984). Primed lexical decision: Combined effects of the proportion of related prime-target pairs and the stimulus-onset asynchrony of prime and target. *Quarterly Journal of Experimental Psychology*, **36A**, 253-280.
DE Groot, A.M.B. (1985). Word-context effects in word naming and lexical decision. *Quarterly Journal of Experimental Psychology*, **37A**, 281-297.
DE Groot, A.M.B., Thomassen, A., & Hudson, P. (1982). Associative facilitation of word recognition as measured from a neutral prime. *Memory & Cognition*, **10**, 358-370.
DE Groot, A.M.B., Thomassen, A., & Hudson, P. (1986). Primed lexical decision: The effect of varying the stimulus-onset asynchrony of prime and target. *Acta Psychologica*, **61**, 17-36.
Den Heyer, K. (1985). On the nature of the proportion effect in semantic priming. *Acta Psychologica*, **60**, 25-38.
Den Heyer, K., Briand, K., & Dannenbring, G. (1983). Strategic factors in a lexical decision task: Evidence for automatic and attention-driven processes. *Memory & Cognition*, **11**, 374-381.
Den Heyer, K., Briand, K., & Smith, L. (1985). Automatic and strategic factors in semantic priming: An examination of Becker's model. *Memory & Cognition*, **13**, 228-232.
Den Heyer, K., Goring, A., & Dannenbring, G. L. (1985). Semantic priming and word repetition: The two effects are additive. *Journal of Memory and Language*, **24**, 699-716.
Den Heyer, K., Sullivan, A., & McPherson, C. (1987). *Mediated priming in a single-response lexical decision task*. Unpublished manuscript.
Dosher, B. A. (1984). Discriminating preexperimental (semantic) from learned (episodic) associations: A speed-accuracy study. *Cognitive Psychology*, **16**, 519-555.
Dosher, B. A., & Rosedale, G. (1989). Integrated retrieval cues as a mechanism for priming in retrieval from memory. *Journal of Experimental Psychology: General*, **118**, 191-211.
Durgunoglu, A.Y. (1986). *A comparison of the two versions of the interactive-compensatory model of reading*. Doctoral dissertation, Purdue University.

Durgunoglu, A. Y. (1988). Repetition, semantic priming, and stimulus quality: Implications for the interactive-compensatory reading model. *Journal of Experimental Psychology: Learning, Memory, and Cognition*, **14**, 590-603.

Durgunoglu, A. Y., & Neely, J. H. (1987). On obtaining episodic priming in a lexical decision task following paired-associate learning. *Journal of Experimental Psychology*, **13**, 206-222.

Eisenberg, P., & Becker, C. A. (1982). Semantic context effects in visual word recognition, sentence processing, and reading: Evidence for semantic strategies. *Journal of Experimental Psychology: Human Perception and Performance*, **8**, 739-756.

Favreau, M. & Segalowitz, N.S. (1983). Automatic and controlled processes in the first- and second-language reading of fluent bilinguals. *Memory & Cognition*, **11**, 565-574.

Fischler, I. (1977a). Semantic facilitation without association in a lexical decision task. *Memory & Cognition*, **5**, 335-339.

Fischler, I. (1977b). Associative facilitation without expectancy in a lexical decision task. *Journal of Experimental Psychology: Human Perception and Performance*, **3**, 18-26.

Fischler, I., & Goodman, G.O. (1978). Latency of associative activation in memory. *Journal of Experimental Psychology: Human Perception and Performance*, **4**, 455-470.

Fodor, J.A., & Pylyshyn, Z.W. (1988). Connectionism and cognitive architecture: A critical analysis. *Cognition*, **28**, 3-71.

Forster, K.I. (1979). Levels of processing and the structure of the language processor. In W. E. Cooper & E. C.T. Walker (Eds.), *Sentence processing: Psycholinguistic studies presented to Merrill Garrett.* Cambridge, MA: MIT press.

Forster, K.I. (1981). Priming and the effects of sentence and lexical contexts on naming time: Evidence for autonomous lexical processing. *Quarterly Journal of Experimental Psychology*, **33A**, 465-495.

Forster, K.I., & Davis, C. (1984). Repetition priming and frequency attenuation in lexical access. *Journal of Experimental Psychology: Learning, Memory, and Cognition*, **10**, 680-698.

Foss, D. J. (1982). A discourse on semantic priming. *Cognitive Psychology*, **14**, 590-607.

Fowler, C. A., Wolford, G., Slade, R., & Tassinary, L. (1981). Lexical access with and without awareness. *Journal of Experimental Psychology: General*, **110**, 341-362.

Garner, W.R., Hake, H.W., & Eriksen, C. W. (1956). Operationism and the concept of perception. *Psychological Review*, **63**, 149-159.

Gillund, G., & Shiffrin, R. M. (1984). A retrieval model for both recognition and recall. *Psychological Review*, **91**, 1-67.

Gough, P. B., Alford, J. A., & Holley-Wilcox, P. (1981). Words and contexts. In O. L. Tzeng & H. Singer (Eds.), *Perception of print: Reading research in experimental psychology* (pp. 85-102). Hillsdale, NJ: Lawrence Erlbaum Associates.

Grainger, J., O'Regan, J. K., Jacobs, A. M., & Segui, J. (1989). On the role of competing word units in visual word recognition: The neighborhood frequency effect. *Perception & Psychophysics*, **45**, 189-195.

Grossberg, S., & Stone, G. (1986). Neural dynamics of word recognition and recall: Attentional priming, learning, and resonance. *Psychological Review*, **93**, 46-74.

Henik, A., Freidrich, F. J., & Kellogg, W. A. (1983). The dependence of semantic relatedness effects upon prime processing. *Memory & Cognition*, **11**, 366-373.

Hines, D., Czerwinski, M., Sawyer, P. K., & Dwyer, M. (1986). Automatic semantic priming: Effect of category exemplar level and word association level. *Journal of Experimental Psychology: Human Perception and Performance*, **12**, 370-379.

Hirshman, E., & Gomez, H. (1988). *A model of word recognition.* Unpublished manuscript, New York University.

Holender, D. (1986). Semantic activation without conscious identification in dichotic listening, parafoveal vision, and visual masking: A survey and appraisal. *The Brain and Behaviorial Sciences*, **9**, 1-23.

Humphreys, G. W., Besner, D., & Quinlan, P. (1988). Event perception and the word repetition effect. *Journal of Experimental Psychology: General*, **117**, 51-67.

Humphreys, G. W.,& Evett,.L. J. (1985). Are there independent lexical and nonlexical routes in word processing? An evaluation of the dual route theory of reading. *The Brain and Behavioral Sciences*, **8**, 689-740.
Humphreys, G. W., Evett, L. J., & Taylor, D. E. (1982). Automatic phonological priming in visual word recognition. *Memory & Cognition*, **10**, 576-590.
Huttenlocher, J., & Kubicek, L. (1983). The source of relatedness effects on naming latency. *Journal of Experimental Psychology: Learning, Memory, and Cognition*, **9**, 486-496.
Jonides, J., & Mack, R. (1984). On the cost and benefit of cost and benefit. *Psychological Bulletin*, **96**, 29-44.
Jordan, T. R. (1986). Testing the BOSS hypothesis: Evidence for position-insensitive orthographic priming in the lexical decision task. *Memory & Cognition*, **14**, 523-532.
Kantowitz, B. H. (1974). Double stimulation. In B. H. Kantowitz (Ed.),*Human information processing--Tutorials in performance and cognition* (pp. 83-132). Hillsdale, NJ: Lawrence Erlbaum Associates.
Kanwisher, N. G. (1987). Repetition blindness: Token recognition without token individuation. *Cognition*, **27**, 117-143.
Kaye, D. B., & Brown, S. W. (1985). Levels and speed of processing effects on word analysis. *Memory & Cognition*, **13**, 425-434.
Keefe, D. E., & Neely, J. H. (1990). Semantic priming in the pronunciation task: The role of prospective prime-generated expectancies. *Memory & Cognition*, **18**, 289-298.
Keller, R. J., Ayres, J. J. B, & Mahoney, W. J. (1977). Brief vs. extended exposure to truly random control procedures. *Journal of Experimental Psychology: Animal Behavior Processes*, **3**, 53-65.
Kiger, J. I. & Glass, A. (1983). The facilitation of lexical decisions by a prime occurring after the target. *Memory & Cognition*, **11**, 356-365.
Koriat, A. (1981). Semantic facilitation in lexical decision as a function of prime-target association. *Memory & Cognition*, **9**, 587-598.
Kraut, A. G. & Smothergill, D. W. (1978). A two-factor theory of stimulus-repetition effects. *Journal of Experimental Psychology: Human Perception and Performance*, **4**, 191-197.
Kraut, A. G., Smothergill, D. W., & Farkas, M. S. (1981). Stimulus repetition effects in attention to words and colors. *Journal of Experimental Psychology: Human Perception and Performance*, **7**, 1303-1311.
Kremer, E. F. (1974). The truly random control procedure: Conditioning to the static cues. *Journal of Comparative and Physiological Psychology*, **86**, 700-707.
Logan, G. D. (1985). Skill and automaticity: Relations, implications, and future directions. *Canadian Journal of Psychology*, **39**, 367-386.
Logan, G. (1988). Toward an instance theory of automatization. *Psychological Review*, **95**, 492-527.
Lorch, R. F., Balota, D., & Stamm, E. (1986). Locus of inhibition effects in the priming of lexical decisions: Pre- or post-lexical access? *Memory & Cognition*, **14**, 95-103.
Luce, P. A. (1986). *Structural distinctions between high and low frequency words in auditory word recognition.* Unpublished doctoral dissertation, Indiana University.
Lupker, S. J. (1984). Semantic priming without association: A second look. *Journal of Verbal Learning and Verbal Behavior*, **23**, 709-733.
Marcel, A. J. (1983). Conscious and unconscious perception: Experiments on visual masking and word recognition. *Cognitive Psychology*, **15**, 197-237.
Massaro, D. W., Jones, R. D., Lipscomb, D., & Scholz, R. (1978). Role or prior knowledge on naming and lexical decisions with good and poor stimulus information. *Journal of Experimental Psychology: Human Learning and Memory*, **4**, 498-512.
McCann, R. S., Besner, D., & Davelaar, E. (1988). Word recognition and identification: Do word-frequency effects reflect lexical access? *Journal of Experimental Psychology: Learning, Memory, and Cognition*, **14**, 693-706.
McClelland, J. L. (1979). On the time relations of mental processes: An examination of systems of processes in cascade. *Psychological Review*, **86**, 287-330.
McClelland, J.L., & Rumelhart, D.E. (1981). An interactive model of context effects in letter perception: Part 1. An account of basic findings. *Psychological Review*, **88**, 375-405.

McClelland, J. L., Rumelhart, D. E., & the PDP Research Group (1986). *Parallel distributed processing: Explorations in the microstructure of cognition, Vol. 2: Psychological and biological models*. Cambridge, MA: MIT Press.

McKoon, G., & Ratcliff, R. (1979). Priming in episodic and semantic memory. *Journal of Verbal Learning and Verbal Behavior*, **18**, 463-480.

McKoon, G., & Ratcliff, R. (1986). The automatic activation of episodic information in a semantic memory task. *Journal of Experimental Psychology: Learning, Memory, & Cognition*, **12**, 108-115.

McNamara, T.P., & Altarriba, J. (1988). Depth of spreading activation revisited: Semantic mediated priming occurs in lexical decisions. *Journal of Memory and Language*, **27**, 545-559.

Merikle, P. M. (1982). Unconscious perception revisited. *Perception & Performance*, **31**, 298-301.

Meyer, D. E., & Schvaneveldt, R. W. (1971). Facilitation in recognizing pairs of words: Evidence of a dependence between retrieval operations. *Journal of Experimental Psychology*, **90**, 227-234.

Meyer, D. E., Schvaneveldt, R.W., & Ruddy, M. G. (1972, November). *Activation of lexical memory*. Paper presented at the meeting of the Psychonomic Society, St. Louis, MO.

Meyer, D. E., Schvaneveldt, R. W., & Ruddy, M. G. (1974). Functions of graphemic and phonemic codes in visual word recognition. *Memory & Cognition*, **2**, 309-321.

Meyer, D. E., Schvaneveldt, R. W., & Ruddy, M. G. (1975). Loci of contextual effects on visual word recognition. In P. M. A. Rabbitt & S. Dornic (Eds.), *Attention and performance V*, New York: Academic Press.

Monsell, S. (1985). Repetition and the lexicon. In A. W. Ellis (Ed)., *Progress in the psychology of language* (pp. 147-195). London: Lawrence Erlbaum Associates.

Morton, J. A. (1969). Interaction of information in word recognition. *Psychological Review*, **76**, 165-178.

Neely, J. H. (1976). Semantic priming and retrieval from lexical memory: Evidence for facilitatory and inhibitory processes. *Memory & Cognition*, **4**, 648-654.

Neely, J. H. (1977). Semantic priming and retrieval from lexical memory: Roles of inhibitionless spreading activation and limited-capacity attention. *Journal of Experimental Psychology: General*, **106**, 226-254.

Neely, J. H. (in press). On the influence of response uncertainty and task structure on retrieval from lexical memory. In G. Lockhead & J.R. Pomerantz (Eds.), *The perception of structure* . Washington, D. C.: American Psychological Association.

Neely, J.H., & Durgunoglu, A.Y. (1985). Dissociative episodic and semantic priming effects in episodic recognition and lexical decision tasks. *Journal of Memory and Language*, **24**, 466-489.

Neely, J. H., & Keefe, D. E. (1989). Semantic context effects on visual word processing: A hybrid prospective/retrospective processing theory. In G. H. Bower, (Ed.), *The psychology of learning and motivation: Advances in research and theory*, Vol. 24 (pp. 207-248). New York: Academic Press.

Neely, J.H., Keefe, D.E., & Ross, K. (1989). Semantic priming in the lexical decision task: Roles of prospective prime-generated expectancies and retrospective semantic matching. *Journal of Experimental Psychology: Learning, Memory, & Cognition*, **15**, 1003-1019.

Norris, D. (1984). The effects of frequency, repetition and stimulus quality in visual word recognition. *Quarterly Journal of Experimental Psychology*, **36A**, 507-518.

Norris, D. (1986). Word recognition: Context effects without priming. *Cognition*, **22**, 93-136.

O'Connor, R. E., & Forster, K. I. (1981). Criterion bias and search sequence bias in word recognition. *Memory & Cognition*, **9**, 78-92.

Peterson, R. R., & Simpson, G. B. (1989). The effect of backward priming on word recognition in single-word and sentence contexts. *Journal of Experimental Psychology: Learning, Memory, and Cognition*, **15**, 1020-1032.

Posner, M. I., & Boies, S. W. (1971). Components of attention. *Psychological Review*, **78**, 391-408.

Posner, M. I., & Snyder, C. R. R. (1975a). Facilitation and inhibition in the processing of signals. In P. M. A. Rabbitt & S. Dornic (Eds.), *Attention and performance V*, New York: Academic Press.
Posner, M. I., & Snyder, C. R. R. (1975b). Attention and cognitive control. In R. L. Solso (Ed.), *Information processing and cognition: The Loyola symposium*. Hillsdale, NJ: Lawrence Erlbaum.Associates.
Pring, L., & Snowling, M. (1986). Developmental changes in word recognition: An information processing account. *Quarterly Journal of Experimental Psychology*, **38A**, 395-418.
Ratcliff, R. (1978). A theory of memory retrieval. *Psychological Review*, **85**, 59-108.
Ratcliff, R., Hockley, W., & McKoon, G. (1985). Components of activation: Repetition and priming effects in lexical decision and recognition. *Journal of Experimental Psychology: General*, **114**, 435-450.
Ratcliff, R., & McKoon, G. (1988). A retrieval theory of priming in memory. *Psychological Review*, **95**, 385-408.
Rescorla, R. A. (1967). Pavlovian conditioning and its proper control procedures. *Psychological Review*, **74**, 71-80.
Rosson, M.B. (1983). From SOFA to LOUCH: Lexical contributions to pseudoword pronunciation. *Memory & Cognition*, **11**, 152-160.
Rumelhart, D. E., & McClelland, J. L. (1985). Levels indeed! A response to Broadbent. *Journal of Experimental Psychology: General*, **114**, 193-197.
Rumelhart, D. E., McClelland, J. L., & the PDP Research Group (1986). *Parallel distributed processing: Explorations in the microstructure of cognition, Vol. 1: Foundations*. Cambridge, MA: MIT Press.
Sanford, A. J., Garrod, S., & Boyle, J. M. (1977). An independence of mechanism in the origins of reading and classification-related semanticdistance effects. *Memory & Cognition*, **5**, 214-220.
Scarborough, D. L., Cortese, C., & Scarborough, H. S. (1977). Frequency and repetition effects in lexical memory. *Journal of Experimental Psychology: Human Perception and Performance*, **3**, 1-17.
Schreuder, R., Flores d'Arcais, G. B., & Glazenborg, G. (1984). Effects of perceptual and conceptual similarity in semantic priming. *Psychological Research*, **45**, 339-354.
Schuberth, R.E., & Eimas, P. (1977). Effects of context on the classification of words and non-words. *Journal of Experimental Psychology: Human Perception and Performance*, **3**, 27-36.
Schuberth, R. E., Spoehr, K. T., & Lane, D. M. (1981). Effects of stimulus and contextual information on the lexical decision process. *Memory & Cognition*, **9**, 68-77.
Schvaneveldt, R. W. & McDonald, J. E. (1981). Semantic context and the encoding of words: Evidence for two modes of stimulus analysis. *Journal of Experimental Psychology: Human Perception and Performance*, **7**, 673-687.
Schvaneveldt, R. W. & Meyer, D. E. (1973). Retrieval and comparison processes in semantic memory. In S. Kornblum (Ed.), *Attention and performance IV* (pp. 395-409). New York: Academic Press.
Schwanenflugel, P. J., & Rey, M. (1986). Interlingual semantic facilitation: Evidence for a common representational system in the bilingual lexicon. *Journal of Memory and Language*, **25**, 605-618.
Schweickert, R. (1978). A critical path generalization of the additive factor method: Analysis of a Stroop task. *Journal of Mathematical Psychology*, **18**, 105-139.
Schweickert, R. (1983). Latent network theory: Scheduling of processes in sentence verification and the Stroop effect. *Journal of Experimental Psychology: Learning, Memory, and Cognition*, **9**, 353-383.
Seidenberg, M. S., Jared, D., & McCrae, K. (1988, November). *Frequency and consistency of spelling-sound correspondences in naming*. Paper presented at the meeting of the Psychonomic Society, Chicago, IL.
Seidenberg, M.S., & McClelland, J. L. (1989). A distributed, developmental model of word recognition and naming. *Psychological Review*, 96, in press.
Seidenberg, M.S., Waters, G., Sanders, M., & Langer, P. (1984). Pre- and post-lexical loci of contextual effects on word recognition. *Memory & Cognition*, **12**, 315-328.

Seidenberg, M. S., & McClelland, J. L. (1990). More words but still no lexicon: Reply to Besner et al. (1990). *Psychological Review*, **97**, 447-452.

Smith, L.C., Briand, K., Klein, R.M., & den Heyer, K. (1987). On the generality of Becker's Verification Model. *Canadian Journal of Psychology*, **41**, 379-386.

Smith, M. C., Theodor, L., & Franklin, P. E. (1983). On the relationship between contextual facilitation and depth of processing. *Journal of Experimental Psychology: Learning, Memory, and Cognition*, **9**, 697-712.

Snow, N., & Neely, J. H. (1987, November). *Reduction of semantic priming from inclusion of physically or nominally related prime-target pairs*. Paper presented at the meeting of the Psychonomics Society, Seattle, WA.

Sperber, R. D., McCauley, C., Ragain, R. D., & Weil, C. M. (1979). Semantic priming effects on picture and word processing. *Memory & Cognition*, **7**, 339-345.

Stanners, R. F., Jastrzembski, J. E., & Westbrook, A. (1975). Frequency and visual quality in a word-nonword classification task. *Journal of Verbal Learning and Verbal Behavior*, **14**, 259-264.

Stanovich, K. E., & West, R. F. (1979). Mechanisms of sentence context effects in reading: Automatic activation and conscious attention. *Memory & Cognition*, **7**, 77-85.

Stanovich, K.E., & West, R.F. (1981). The effect of sentence context on ongoing word recognition: Tests of a two-process theory. *Journal of Experimental Psychology: Human Perception and Performance*, **7**, 658-672.

Stanovich, K. E., & West, R. F. (1983). On priming by a sentence context. *Journal of Experimental Psychology: General*, **112**, 1-36.

Stanovich, K. E., West, R. F., & Feeman, D. (1981). A longitudinal study of sentence context effects in second-grade children: Tests of an interactive-compensatory model. *Journal of Experimental Child Psychology*, **32**, 185-199.

Sternberg, S. (1969). The discovery of processing stages: Extensions of Donder's method. *Acta Psychologica*, **30**, 276-315.

Tanenhaus, M. K., Flanagan, H. P., & Seidenberg, M. S. (1980). Orthographic and phonological activation in auditory and visual word recognition. *Memory & Cognition*, **8**, 513-520.

Tweedy, J. R., Lapinski, R. H., & Schvaneveldt, R. W. (1977). Semantic-context effects on word recognition: Influence of varying the proportion of items presented in an appropriate context. *Memory & Cognition*, **5**, 84-99.

Van Orden, G. C., Johnston, J. C., & Hale, B. L. (1988). Word identification in reading proceeds from spelling to sound to meaning. *Journal of Experimental Psychology: Learning, Memory, and Cognition*, **14**, 371-386.

West, R. F., & Stanovich, K. F. (1982). Source of inhibition in experiments on the effect of sentence context on word recognition. *Journal of Experimental Psychology: Learning, Memory and Cognition*, **8**, 385-399.

Wilding, J. M. (1986). Joint effects of semantic priming and repetition in a lexical decision task: Implications for a model of lexical access. *Quarterly Journal of Experimental Psychology*, **38A**, 213-228.

Wilding, J. M. (1988). The interaction of word-frequency and stimulus quality in the lexical decision task--Now you see it, now you don't. *Quarterly Journal of Experimental Psychology*, **40A**, 757-770.

Author Index

Subject Index